The Colombian Novel, 1844–1987

The Texas Pan American Series

The Colombian Novel, 1844–1987

by Raymond Leslie Williams

 University of Texas Press, Austin

First Edition, 1991

Requests for permission to reproduce material from this work
should be sent to Permissions, University of Texas Press, Box 7819,
Austin, Texas 78713-7819.

∞ The paper used in this publication meets the minimum
requirements of American National Standard for Information
Sciences—Permanence of Paper for Printed Library Materials,
ANSI Z39.48-1984.

The Texas Pan American Series is published with the assistance of
a revolving publication fund established by the Pan American
Sulphur Company.

Library of Congress Cataloging-in-Publication Data

Williams, Raymond L.
    The Colombian novel, 1844–1987 / by Raymond Leslie
Williams.—1st ed.
        p.   cm.—(The Texas Pan American series)
    Includes bibliographical references and index.
    ISBN 0-292-75542-2
    1. Colombian fiction—19th century—History and criticism.
2. Colombian fiction—20th century—History and criticism.
I. Title. II. Series.
PQ8172.W47   1991
863—dc20   90-44902
                                       CIP

For Professor John S. Brushwood

Contents

Preface

The present study offers readings of Colombian novels published from 1844 to 1987. It represents the development, over a period of several years, of certain theoretical and empirical assumptions and is based on three fundamental premises. The first of these premises concerns the extraordinary regionalism that has existed historically in the territory we call Colombia. In chapter 1, I discuss briefly how Colombia in fact developed into the four semi-autonomous regions that comprised it for slightly more than a century (the 1830s to the 1950s). The second premise is that many, if not most, Colombian novels have functioned as objects of an ideological dialogue, an issue that is addressed in chapter 2 and referred to throughout the study. Writing has always occupied an absolutely central role in Colombia and has been intimately associated with politics. Publishing books has been a political act, often subversive in nature. The third premise is that Colombian culture and the respective regional cultures of these four semi-autonomous regions of the past have been affected in varying degrees by what Walter Ong, in his study *Orality and Literacy* (1982), has identified as the noetics of orality and writing.[1] More specifically, I analyze how oral noetics have been present in the Colombian novel and affected it over the past century and a half. In chapters 3 through 6 I discuss specific Colombian novels using Ong's study and his related work as one of the most important theoretical bases, even though *Orality and Literacy* in itself is not a theory of the novel (nor, in fact, "theory" of anything). Generally speaking, I am concerned with what Ong calls the technology of writing. Whereas the subject of Ong's work is the differences between orality and literacy, I analyze how these two different modes of expression have affected literary works. Even though I find Ong's conceptual framework useful in discussing the orality of regional traditions, my adherence to some of his work should not be construed as an endorsement of all the propositions presented in *Orality and Literacy*.

This project has other theoretical bases beyond those suggested in the three premises set forth above. In a study that considers more than one hundred novels, I use as a constant point of departure certain principles and concepts of narratology developed by Gérard Genette and Shlomith Rimmon-Kenan.[2] Whatever the relationship these novels might have with ideological context and orality, they have in common the fact that they are all narratives. Consequently, narratological issues are essential for this study. In the case of all novels, but particularly those analyzed in detail in chapters 3 through 6, fundamental narratological questions posed consistently are, How do these texts function as narrative? and, How do they create an experience for the reader? In addition, readers acquainted with the work of Terry Eagleton will note his direct and indirect influence.[3] An underlying supposition present throughout the book is that the Colombian novel in one way or another expresses certain relationships to oral culture and/or writing culture. The latter is explored in the standard relationship one novel may have to another; this relationship, of course, is fundamentally a study of intertextuality. (Intertextuality as a theoretical issue is approached most directly in chapter 6.)

I intend to offer both a broad overview of novelistic production in Colombia from 1844 to 1987 and readings of selected individual texts. Part One, "Colombia in Its Novel," consists of two chapters that introduce Colombia and its novel within a broad historical and ideological context. Chapter 1 presents a brief history of Colombia and its regions. The division of Colombia's nineteenth- and twentieth-century political history into six periods provides the historical background and ideological context for the discussion of novels in chapter 2. The emphasis is not on the "classic" texts of traditional Colombian literary history but rather on a broad range of novels seen as the product of historical contingencies. Following the lead of Jane Tompkins, I see classic texts not as the ineffable products of genius but as bearers of a set of regional, national, social, economic, institutional, and professional interests.[4]

In Part Two, "The Novel in Its Region," the study moves into the novels of the four regions in four consecutive chapters.[5] Chapter 3 deals with the Interior Highland Tradition centered in Bogotá (called in Spanish the *altiplano cundi-boyacense*), which includes Tolima, Huila, and Santander. After a brief introduction to this Interior Highland Tradition (often referred to in the text simply as Highland tradition), the main focus of chapter 3 is the analysis of the novels *Manuela* (1858) by Eugenio Díaz, *Diana cazadora* (1915) by Clímaco Soto Borda, *La vorágine* (1924) by José Eustasio Rivera, and *El buen salvaje* (1966) by Eduardo Caballero Calderón. The novelistic tradition of the Costa is the focus of chapter 4, which includes analyses of *Ingermina* (1844) by Juan José Nieto, *Cosme* (1927) by José Félix Fuenmayor, *La casa grande* (1962) by Alvaro Cepeda Samudio, *Respirando el verano* (1962) by Héctor Rojas Herazo, and *Cien años de soledad* (1967) by Gabriel García Márquez. Chapter 5, defining the Antioquian Tradition, deals with *Frutos de mi tierra* (1896) by Tomás Carrasquilla, *Toá* (1933) by César Uribe Piedrahita, *Risaralda* (1935) by Bernardo Arias Trujillo, and *El día señalado* (1964) by Manuel Mejía Vallejo. In chapter 6, on the novelistic tradition of the Greater Cauca (Gran Cauca), I analyze *María* (1867) by Jorge Isaacs, *El alférez real* (1886) by Eustaquio Palacios, *Las estrellas son negras* (1949) by Arnoldo Palacios, and *El bazar de los idiotas* (1974) by Gustavo Alvarez Gardeazábal.

I submit a double response to the inevitable question of the criteria for selecting these particular seventeen novels. On the one hand, I believe most of them represent a general consensus among readers and critics of the Colombian novel as "major" works.[6] On the other hand, in those regions or periods where there has been a paucity of criticism, I have chosen works I consider "representative" of the region and the period. This is the case for relatively ignored novels such as *Las estrellas son negras* by the Afro-Colombian writer Arnoldo Palacios. The broad vision of the Colombian novel I have produced, combining chapter 2 with the remaining chapters, recognizes Jane Tompkins's proposition (with respect to the American novel) that "major" novelists did not develop in response to a sudden perception of the greatness of a few literary geniuses; they emerged from a series of interconnected ideological circumstances that moved the publication, criticism, and, finally, institutionalization of the novel (Colombian, in this instance) in a certain direction.[7]

Part Three, "After Regionalism," contains two chapters that discuss the contemporary Colombian novel and propose conclusions. While one of the premises of this project is that Colombia consisted of four semi-autonomous regions for over a century, it is equally important to emphasize that radical modernization and changes in communication have resulted in a nation as unified as most over the past three decades. Consequently, chapter 7 treats the postregionalist novel published from the mid-1960s to the mid-1980s. (For certain practical reasons that will become evident in the reading of the first six chapters, the exact years covered are 1965 to 1987. I have arbitrarily chosen 1987 as the cutoff date for this study.) With modernization, primary oral cultures have also vanished. Consequently, in this chapter I attempt to establish the main trends of the Colombian novel over the past two decades under the general categories of the "modern" and "postmodern" novel. Chapter 8 consists of brief conclusions.

In almost all cases I have eschewed providing plot synopses of the novels discussed or mentioned. In many of the analyses I have used Gérard Genette's proposed formulation of a nuclear verb or essential sentence which synthesizes a novel's action. For example, Genette essentializes the action of *The Odyssey* as "Ulysses returns to Ithaca" and of *A la recherche du temps perdu* as "Marcel becomes a writer." These synthetic formulations will provide some idea of plot. Readers in need of detailed plot information should consult Antonio Curcio Altamar's history of the Colombian novel, Donald McGrady's overview of the Colombian historical novel, and Kessel Schwartz's *New History of Spanish-American Fiction.*

I have attempted to avoid excessive specialized terminology. Nevertheless, a brief introduction to concepts and terminology of Ong and Genette may be useful. Ong makes important distinctions between "primary oral cultures" of persons with no knowledge of writing and "writing cultures" and demonstrates how the noetics of individuals from these two cultures are radically different. He points out that we (as readers) are so literate that it is difficult for us to conceive of an oral universe of communication or thought except as a variant of a literate universe. He demonstrates that writing is not just a kind of complement to oral speech but a transformer of verbalization. In chapter 3 of *Orality and Literacy,* titled "Some Psychodynamics of Orality," Ong outlines in detail the characteristics of primary oral cultures. Besides the mnemonic formula character of verbal expression, primary oral cultures include nine further basic characteristics. They are (1) additive rather than subordinative, (2) aggregative rather than analytic, (3) redundant or "copious," (4) conservative or traditionalist, (5) close to the human lifeworld, (6) agonistically toned, (7) empathetic and participatory rather than objectively distanced, (8) homeostatic, and (9) situational rather than abstract. Following Ong's procedure, I use the terms *primary oral culture* and simply *oral culture* interchangeably throughout this text. Colombia has only one region—the Costa—with both a strong oral culture in the twentieth century and a novel that assimilates it, *Cien años de soledad.* Consequently, important factors in this study will be issues such as the distinction between merely oral effects (conversational elements in literary style, approximations of informal speech patterns, the use of colloquial language in dialogue or the narration) and oral residue (habits of thought and expression tracing back to preliterate situations or practice or deriving from the dominance of the oral as a medium in a given culture). As I will demonstrate, factors of orality are significant even in the novel of the Highland area, the strongest writing culture of the four regions and the least affected by orality.

I use terminology from Gérard Genette with some regularity, particularly to identify with precision the nature of narrators. For example, describing a narrator as extradiegetic-heterodiegetic unequivocally identifies a narrator with a precision impossible if one were limited to concepts such as third-person omniscient, a patently ambiguous description of a narrator.[8]

By ideology I mean the ways in which what we say and believe connect with the power structure and power relations of the society in which we live, and I refer the reader to Terry Eagleton's *Theory of Literature*, which has informed my understanding of ideology.[9] Accepting Eagleton's proposition on literature and ideology in general, I will argue in chapter 2 that literature *is* ideology in Colombia, particularly at the crucial turn-of-the-century juncture when the practices of literature and politics were so inextricably bound.

Some clarification may be in order concerning place-names. The Republic of Colombia has undergone several name changes over the centuries. During the Colonial period it was known as the Nuevo Reino de Granada, and in the republican period it was called Colombia (including Venezuela and Ecuador, 1819–1830), Nueva Granada (1832–1857), the Confederación Granadina (1857–1863), Estados Unidos de Colombia (1863–1886), and República de Colombia (1886–present). For the sake of simplicity, I will refer to this territory as the Nuevo Reino de Granada during the Colonial period and Colombia after 1810. The division of the country into departments has also evolved over the decades. I have chosen to identify regions in a fashion quite similar (but not exactly so) to the traditional regional divisions of the nineteenth century (see chapter 1). The *altiplano cundi-boyacense* and surrounding departments are identified in English as the Interior Highland Region. I have chosen to use the Spanish Costa for the Caribbean Coastal Region, since Coastal Region in English could give the false impression that it included only the coastal area itself, when in fact the departments of the Costa are numerous and cover much territory inland from Barranquilla and Cartagena. For example, Gabriel García Márquez is considered a *costeño* in Colombia, but his native Aracataca is inland. Greater Antioquia refers not only to the present-day state of Antioquia but also to the nineteenth-century unit, which included present-day Caldas, Risaralda and Quindío. Greater Cauca (referred to in Spanish as El Gran Cauca) includes several departments in the area. It is important to understand that these four regions, whether the English denominations I have chosen to use for them are ideal or not, represent cultural units that have historical ties in various facets of life, from political and economic to cultural and literary (again, see chapter 1 for further explanation).

Regional context is a fundamental factor in my reading of the seventeen novels analyzed in chapters 3 through 6. It should be noted from the outset, nevertheless, that three Colombian novels—*María*, *La vorágine*, and *Cien años de soledad*—are "national" works in the sense that they have successfully reached the nation's readers and writers beyond a primarily regional context. Consequently, a novel such as *La vorágine* (indeed, Colombia's first "best seller") resulted in the publication of similar books in regions other than the Interior Highland. For this reason, I include the three novels in the chronologies of each region which appear in the appendix.

Of the extant critical studies on the Colombian novel, Antonio Curcio Altamar's *Evolución de la novela en Colombia* (1957) and Seymour Menton's *La novela colombiana: planetas y satélites* (1978) are the most significant predecessors of the present project. Curcio Altamar offers brief commentary, frequently of an impressionistic nature, on the nineteenth- and twentieth-century novel, mentioning over five hundred Colombian novels. Mention sets forth close readings of ten novels from Eugenio Díaz's *Manuela* (1858) to Gustavo Alvarez Gardeazábal's *El titiritero* (1977). Another seminal volume is Ernesto Porras Collantes's *Bibliografía de la novela en Colombia* (1976). I refer to these valuable books frequently, and without them the present study would have been virtually impossible. Other recent books, not as all-encompassing as these three, are Fernando Ayala Poveda's *Novelistas colombianos contemporáneos* (1983), Marvin Lewis's *Treading the Ebony Path: Ideology and Violence in Contemporary Afro-Colombian Prose Fiction* (1987), Román López Tamés's *La narrativa actual de Colombia y su contexto social* (1975), and Bogdan Piotrowski's *La realidad nacional colombiana y su narrativa contemporánea* (1988).

The titles of the novels under discussion appear in the original Spanish. Unless otherwise indicated, the translations of passages from novels are mine. In special cases, such as passages with subtle word play in the original Spanish text (such as that found in Moreno-Durán), I include both the original Spanish and my translation.

Several of these readings have been published in altered forms, usually with a slightly different emphasis: "The Problem of Unity in Fiction: Narrator and Self in *María*," *MLN* 101, no. 2 (March 1986): 342–353; "La figura del autor y del escritor en *La vorágine*," *Discurso literario* 4, no. 2 (1987): 535–551; "Structure and Transformation of Reality in Alvarez Gardeazábal: *El bazar de los idiotas*," *Kentucky Romance Quarterly* 27, no. 2 (1980): 245–261.

This project was supported by grants from the Fulbright Commission of Colombia, the Joint Center for Latin-American Studies of the University of Chicago–University of Illinois-Urbana, the Graduate School of Washington University in St. Louis, and the Office of the Vice Chancellor for Academic Affairs of the University of Colorado at Boulder. In Colombia the Biblioteca Luis Angel Arango, Instituto Caro y Cuervo, Banco de la República, Biblioteca Piloto de Medellín, Centro de Historia de Buga, Biblioteca del Atlántico, FAES in Medellín, and Biblioteca Nacional, and their respective directors, provided kind and impressively efficient support. Numerous individuals in Colombia also extended enormous good will: I particularly thank Belisario Betancur, Ignacio Chaves, Darío Jaramillo Agudelo, Otto Morales Benítez, and Germán Vargas. I have had the privilege of interviewing most living Colombian novelists over the past fifteen years, and I thank them as a group, from the young Héctor Sánchez, who encouraged my first efforts as a dissertation writer in his faithful correspondence from Barcelona in the mid-1970s, to the present-day celebrity Gabriel García Márquez, who has patiently fielded my questions on more than one occasion in recent years.

My special thanks go to the numerous colleagues and students— they know who they are—who have contributed to my understanding of the Colombian novel and the preparation of the manuscript. I appreciated the conscientious work of Jana DeJong, research assistant. I am particularly indebted to the graduate students in my Colombian novel seminars offered in 1983 and 1986 at Washington University in St. Louis and to the eighteen graduate students in a similar seminar offered in 1988 at the University of Colorado at Boulder.

Part One

Colombia in Its Novel

One

Colombia, Its History and Its Regions

El descubrimiento de la imprenta es, sin duda alguna, una gran conquista hecha por el genio del hombre, en favor de la humanidad.
[The discovery of printing is, without a doubt, the great conquest of man's genius in favor of humanity.]
—El Alacrán *(Bogotá, 1849)*

In the early sixteenth century when the Spanish conquistador Gonzalo Jiménez de Quesada explored and conquered the region we now call Colombia, he was motivated by a fiction: the legend of El Dorado. Venturing up the Magdalena River with his soldiers, he found neither gold mines nor the fountain of eternal youth but a mine of emeralds, a mountain full of salt, and butterflies with blue wings.[1] When he returned to Spain he filled the ears of the Spanish Crown with more fictions and was sent back to the New World to pursue his chimera. The experience of Jiménez de Quesada—and the Spanish Crown—was but an early example of the complex, often confounding interaction between a literary and an empirical understanding of Colombia over the centuries. As one contemporary social scientist has recently affirmed, perhaps more than any other country in Latin America, Colombia has frustrated outsiders who try to understand and explain it.[2] In some ways, he notes, Colombia does not exist except in popular myth, academic reification, and the assemblies of international organizations.[3]

The present study does not aim primarily at understanding Colombia. An analysis of ideology and orality in its novel, however, assumes the existence of this "nation" as a political, social, economic, and cultural entity. Because of Colombia's pronounced regionalism, the idea of a nation was quite questionable until modern times. Consequently, the shape of Colombia's history and regional confines must be considered for the purposes of this study.

Jiménez de Quesada's quest in the New World points to other issues that are essential to an understanding of a cultural phenomenon such as the production of novels. Jiménez de Quesada was the quintessential man of letters: a polyglot, author of several tomes on historical, political, and literary topics. His *Antijovio*, written in approximately 1567 and published in the twentieth century, is the earliest literary or historical text to which the contemporary reader has access; it demonstrates the central connection between writing and political power from the very origins of Spanish-American writing. Just as Jiménez de Quesada had defended Spain's world position with his sword in the conquest of New Granada, he proposed to defend Spain's image in *Antijovio*, a rewriting of history in response to the Italian Paulo Jovio's *Historiarum sui temporis libri XLV* (1550–1552). *Antijovio* aims at redressing "errors" committed in previous historical writing about Spain. His failure to discover the legendary city of gold was the only blemish in his otherwise brilliant career.

Angel Rama has convincingly articulated the historical roots of writing and power in Spanish America, describing the Colonial *ciudad letrada*, such as Bogotá, as a ring of power and its administrator surrounded by the executors of his orders: a plethora of ecclesiastics, educators, professionals, and intellectuals, all of whom wielded both the pen and power in the bureaucracy.[4] The ruling aristocracy and *letrados* were thus linked as a powerful elite in colonies in which the vast majority of the population was illiterate; herein lie the historical roots of the connection between writing and power in Spanish America in general and Colombia in particular. Popayán, Cartagena, and Tunja functioned as smaller *ciudades letradas* in Colombia during the Colonial period. From the Colonial period to the twentieth century the *hombres de letras* not only were active in politics but more often than not used literary production as part of their ideological struggles. Although a larger portion of the population is literate in Colombia in the twentieth century than during the Colonial period, literature is still associated with the elite, and in the mid-1980s the illiteracy rate was approximately 22 percent.

In short, Colombia's political and cultural history, from Jiménez de Quesada to García Márquez, exemplifies Foucault's insistence on the direct relationship between power and writing.[5] Nineteenth-century Colombia determined status primarily according to the acquisition or possession of wealth and by political or cultural distinction. A scholar of Colombian history has assessed the *letrado*'s prominent role in Colombian society: "Public service as an ideal could in fact be appropriated by one innoble section of Spanish society, the university-educated *letrados*, who emerged to staff the Spanish royal (and later imperial) bureaucracy. . . . The near nobility of the *letrado* was recognized by special privileges and honors conceded in the *Siete Partidas* and afterward."[6]

The transition from colony to independent state did not signify a change in class structure or the relationship between class and power. When Colombia declared its independence in 1810, the relative geographic isolation of its distinct regions had left a well-defined regional mark on the colony's identity. Once nationhood was proclaimed, however, the political history of these regions unfolded in six basic periods. A brief political and cultural history can be synthesized for the sake of simplicity; in reality, given the conflict of competing socioeconomic and regional interests, Colombian history cannot be explained by a single scheme.[7] Political, socioeconomic, and cultural interests in Colombia have been complex since its birth.

Historical Overview (1500–1987)

The Spanish conquistador Rodrigo de Bastidas explored the Caribbean coast from Cape Vela to Nombre de Dios in 1500–1501, and the following year Columbus sailed along the coast of Colombia. Soon the Spanish Colonial empire was established in the Vice-Royalty of New Granada, with administrative centers in several of present-day Colombia's *ciudades letradas*—Popayán, Tunja, Cartagena, and Bogotá. During this period a Hispanic upper class controlled a subservient labor population, resulting in a virtual upper-class monopoly of all economic resources. The corresponding literary production, of course, remained exclusively elitist and with rare exceptions of little interest in the context of the novel. The first signs of a counter-discourse to the Spanish Colonial model did not appear until the mid-eighteenth century with the entrance of scientific ideas in the person of Spanish scientist José Celestino Mutis, who arrived in Bogotá in 1761.

The Hellenic/Catholic Arcadia:
From Colony to Republic (1810–1862)

The period from 1810 to 1862 comprised the formative years for the new nation and was characterized by conflict and crisis.[8] Colom-

bia proclaimed independence in 1810; within two years occurred the
first of innumerable civil wars between centralists and federalists, a
point of contention in almost all the nineteenth-century civil wars.
Compared to the relatively wealthy vice-royalties of Peru and Mexico, the Nuevo Reino de Granada was not wealthy, facing economic
crises from the outset: "Though the upper class was highly acquisi-
tive, most of its members in the first half of the nineteenth century
were not very rich by the standards of European or North American
bourgeoisie."[9] Many characteristics of the ancien régime remained
unaltered as elites remained in power. For example, there was very
little difference in tariff levels in the Colonial and early independence periods.[10]

The ideological underpinnings of the period derive from early experiments with liberalism under Francisco Paula de Santander and
from the formation of the two traditional parties, Liberal and Conservative. Often seen as a key year, 1826 marks the division between
followers of the liberal Santander and the authoritarian Bolívar. For
most of the period from 1832 to 1858, a centralist political system
dominated, but the 1850s witnessed an intensification of ideological
conflict. The intellectual counterparts of the centralists (called conservatives by mid-century) often viewed the Colonial period with
nostalgia, and their literary writings frequently expressed a desire
for a state that could be called a Hellenic/Catholic Arcadia. The
Conservative party was born in 1849 with a declaration of principles
written by Mariano Ospina Rodríguez and José Eusebio Caro; that
same year Rafael Núñez organized a local Democratic Society in
Cartagena and founded a newspaper of liberal ideas, *La Democracia*.
At mid-century, too, business and artisan interests arose as a political pressure group for the first time.[11] Colombian Liberals held as
their models European Liberals, particularly such figures as Victor
Hugo, Alexandre Dumas, Alphonse de Lamartine, and Eugene Sue.
The paramount Conservative, gentleman/scholar José Eusebio Caro,
followed the British model of the man of letters also knowledgeable
about capitalist economic principles.

The interest groups at mid-century were basically four: the elites,
urban middle groups, rural peasantry, communal Indians. The elites
and urban middle groups, of course, headed the political and literary
expressions of ideological conflict. During the 1850s conflict among
Liberals became particularly acute between *gólgotas* (radical Liberals) and *draconianos* (more moderate Liberals), a situation novelized
by Eugenio Díaz in *Manuela* (1858). The situation of the rural peasantry was typical of oral cultures: The conservative tendencies of

small subsistence farmers were manifested in their regard of primary instruction as an "irrelevant, if not dangerous system constructed by urban elites."[12] The indigenous population was largely ignored and disdained.[13]

The Liberal Utopia (1863–1885)

For Gabriel García Márquez, the second half of nineteenth-century Colombia—when "liberals were real liberals"—figures as one of the most fascinating periods of its history.[14] The Constitution of 1863, comprehending and adding to a series of liberal reforms enacted since 1849, was one of the most liberal documents in the West at the time, assuring absolute freedom, humanitarian justice, the separation of church and state, the secularization of public education, free trade, abolition of slavery, freedom of expression and the press, and a federalist system of independent states. By adopting this constitution, liberals wished to transform Colombia into a liberal utopia. Such a utopia appealed to the likes of José María Samper, Felipe Pérez, and Salvador Camacho Roldán in the nineteenth century as it does to García Márquez today.

Interpretations of Colombian history during this period have followed two basic lines of argument. The more positive one maintains that the liberal program transformed a backward nation into a modern one; an alternative, skeptical view points to economic stagnation and the sometimes disastrous consequences of government policies on the working masses.[15] Neither argument convinces completely, but there is no question that the Liberal Utopia was not attained. Ideological debates, civil wars, and almost all intellectual discourse of the era focused on four basic issues: policy on commerce; federation versus centralization in public administration; public land policy; and the role of the Church.[16] The debate was conducted basically within the educated upper class, and economic power remained firmly centralized: "In the closed, stratified Colombian society of the last century, economic resources were monopolized by a small upper class interested in preserving its position and generally unable to generate new wealth."[17]

Political measures took almost exclusively liberal directions. The Constitution of 1863 ratified Tomás Cipriano de Mosquera's anti-Church measures, which resulted in two civil wars during the period. Liberals Mosquera, Manuel Murillo Toro, and Santiago Pérez held the presidency. The radicals (radical Liberals) carried out an educational reform in 1870 and stimulated the establishment of railroads, telegraph communication, commercial banks, and other technological and industrial change. Tobacco and quinine boomed. The overlapping of political, economic, and cultural activity among the liberals of the era finds representation in individuals such as the political figures/essayists/novelists José María Samper—described by Jaramillo Uribe as a radical romantic and a utopian—Felipe Pérez, and Camacho Roldán.[18]

The Athens of South America: The Regeneration (1886–1909)

In the political sphere, the conservative reaction was dominated by a figure of a very different stamp, former Liberal Rafael Núñez. Among the novelists, José Manuel Marroquín, poet, linguist, president of Colombia, and, above all, conservative Hispanic Highland gentleman-scholar, best embodies the spirit of the Regeneration. A seminal figure of the Regeneration, Conservative politician and intellectual Miguel Antonio Caro was one of the writers of the new Constitution of 1886. Still in use today, this constitution marked "the end of a quarter century of Liberal party leadership and opened the era of the nation state whose shaping would be primarily the work of the Conservative party until 1930."[19] President Rafael Núñez's 1886 administration signaled the beginning of conservative power, adherence to a more Hispanic tradition, and the principle of political centralization and administrative decentralization. The new constitution also reestablished strong relations between the Catholic Church and the state. Under the Regeneration, Marroquín and Caro, in addition to intellectuals such as Rufino José Cuervo, had the support from the power structure to undertake once again the creation of the Hellenic/Catholic Arcadia previously yearned for by José Eusebio Caro and Sergio Arboleda. The Athens of South America was propagated from the center of Bogotá to Europe. The idea has been so pervasive that in the 1980s the concept of Bogotá as the Athens of South America has remained sufficiently entrenched for a young writer such as R. H. Moreno-Durán to satirize it.

During the 1880s, Colombian science teachers and engineers began to create the scientific institutions needed to sustain a technical community.[20] By that time a number of upper-class Colombians were well abreast of Western engineering, and a few even undertook minor innovations in mathematics and engineering. In 1887 the Colombian Society of Engineers was founded. That the Colombian Academy of History was not founded until 1902 underscores the conflict between the new technical knowledge and traditional humanism.

Conflict between the authoritarian state and a Liberal counter-discourse became acute in the 1890s. The Caro administration of the 1890s harassed newspaper publishers. The tensions culminated in the War of a Thousand Days (1899–1903), when Liberals revolted against the rigidly partisan government of President Sanclemente and Vice-President Marroquín. The literary group La Gruta Simbólica opposed the Conservative regime. Although President Rafael Reyes negotiated some compromise during the *quinquenio,* 1904 to 1909, "the war had ensconced men in power from the most authoritarian and Catholic elements of the Conservative party, the military, and the government bureaucracy."[21]

Most of the Conservative ideologues of the Regeneration nourished themselves intellectually in Catholic and Spanish thought. In some ways, the Arcadia had been reinstated. These intellectuals encountered virtue in Colombia's Spanish heritage, its Catholic purity, and the intellectual and literary achievements of its elite.[22] Ironically, this Conservative reaction to Colombia's incipient modernity coincided with the beginning of a new export cycle as Colombians responded to the spectacular rise in world coffee prices which occurred in the late 1880s and early 1890s.[23] Simultaneously, a counterdiscourse of Liberal and new scientific thought survived during the Regeneration, although it would not find nascent expression until the 1930s.

The Conservative Republic (1910–1929)

Conservative dominance of the Athens of South America continued in the early twentieth century, perhaps best exemplified by one of the last major *presidentes gramáticos,* educator, linguist, diplomat, and essayist Marco Fidel Suárez, president from 1918 to 1921. But the Regeneration's ideological project did not go unchallenged; Liberal strength gradually reasserted itself. Indeed, much of the nineteenth-century political structure has remained firmly in place in the twentieth. The traditional political parties in Colombia, Liberal and Conservative, retain the structural form of nineteenth-century politics: They are still rather loosely organized electoral alliances, run at the top by competing elite lineages and drawing support in different regions on a basis of enduring local and seigneurial loyalties.[24] The survival of these two parties into the twentieth century has depended on their ability to reach compromise in moments of crisis, and one such compromise was reached at the outset of the Conservative Republic in 1910. With an agreement between the two parties, Carlos E. Restrepo, who was a leading spirit of the "Republican Union," was able to assume the presidency from

1910 to 1914. He was followed by the conservative José Vicente Concha (1914–1918), previously secretary to President Caro during the Regeneration.

The counter-discourse to the Conservative Republic manifested itself both in political/literary dialogue and in anti-establishment activity. The political dialogue was headed by figures such as María Cano, a leftist organizer of the 1920s who wrote critical essays. The rise of the literary group Los Nuevos and the publication of the literary magazine *Voces* in Barranquilla afforded an alternative to the conservative Hispanism of official discourse. The Indian Manuel Quintín Lane organized political agitation in favor of Indian rights between 1914 and 1918 and intermittently in the following years. The Socialist party was born in Colombia in 1919, and the Communist party was organized during the 1920s. Labor conflicts also characterized the 1920s, the most celebrated of which is the 1928 banana workers' strike in Ciénaga on the Caribbean coast, later novelized by Alvaro Cepeda Samudio and García Márquez. Despite the hermetic ideological positions of the Conservative Republic, pragmatic changes initiated later became predominant features of the 1930s: The transition from an economy of subsistence production to a market-oriented agriculture, for example, occurred during these years.

The Progressive Modern State: The Liberal Republic (1930–1946)

The 1930s and 1940s saw rapid and self-conscious modernization and industrialization under a series of Liberal governments. The Liberal project—the Progressive Modern State—began under Enrique Olaya Herrera (1930–1934), a mildly reformist president who governed a coalition of Liberals and Conservatives known as the National Concentration. He stimulated public housing and welfare and education programs, attempted land distribution, and fostered oil exploration.[25] One of the most striking aspects of the Liberal program, its emphasis on the development of highways, eradicated the historical isolation of Colombia's regions;[26] by the end of the 1940s, new communication systems resulted in the breakdown of striking regional differences. Nevertheless, Bogotá and Medellín, the two largest cities, remained unconnected by direct rail service until 1960.

Alfonso López Pumarejo (1934–1938) undertook the most radical reforms of the Liberal Republic, a program known as La Revolución en Marcha. Such measures as his land reform law of 1936 (Ley 200) attempted to eradicate the final vestiges of Colonial economic and political structures and to accelerate the pace of modernization:

"With the advent of Alfonso López to the presidency of Colombia, Liberal reformism reached a high tide, and the concept of government as director and administrator of orderly revolutionary change made its indelible impress on the nation."[27] After the less progressive "Great Pause" that characterized the Liberal government of Eduardo Santos (1938–1942), Alfonso López Pumarejo's second presidency (1942–1945) found itself engrossed in wartime problems and marred by obstructive opposition and accusations of corruption. Because of a split in the Liberal party, Conservative Mariano Ospina Pérez was elected president in 1946.

The reformist liberalism of the Liberal Republic differed fundamentally from the romantic and philosophical liberalism of the nineteenth century. It represented a radical ideological change, giving voice to heretofore unheard liberal and revolutionary discourse. For example, the founding of the Instituto Etnológico Nacional in 1941 was an attempt to give voice to the largely ignored indigenous population. Literary production, too, particularly the novel, was predominantly the work of Liberals. During the Liberal Republic Diego Castrillón Arboleda produced indigenous novels. Similarly, José Antonio Osorio Lizarazo and César Uribe Piedrahita wrote novels of social protest that played a role within the new discourse of the Liberal Republic. On the other hand, Conservative values continued to be expounded during this period, particularly in the arena of literary criticism.[28]

Modern and Postregionalist Colombia (1947–1987)

This period covers two major events in the nation's history: La Violencia and the National Front. The roots of La Violencia have been traced to conflicts in the 1930s; some social scientists believe the phenomenon still had not subsided in the 1980s. La Violencia is commonly dated, however, from 1946 to 1958. Although figures vary and are difficult to prove, it is generally agreed that 200,000 to 300,000 persons died during this sustained civil war. After the *bogotazo* in 1948 and the increasing violence and disorder of the early 1950s, the Conservative government of Laureano Gómez reached sufficient crisis to precipitate a coup d'état by Gustavo Rojas Pinilla, dictator of Colombia from 1953 until he was overthrown in 1957. From 1958 to 1974 the country was governed under the National Front agreements, struck between the two traditional parties, to alternate the presidency. Liberal Alberto Lleras Camargo assumed the presidency in 1958, followed by Conservative Guillermo León Valencia (1962–1966), Liberal Carlos Lleras Restrepo (1966–1970), and Conservative Misael Pastrana Borrero (1970–1974). Since 1958

Colombian governments have followed policies of capitalistic economic expansion within the framework of a restricted parliamen-
tary democracy dominated by the country's two parties.[29]

The ideological texture and social/political phenomena of the
1950s and 1960s remain difficult to define and are still under intense
examination. La Violencia shaped the national consciousness enor-
mously, an effect comparable in scope only to the War of a Thousand
Days. In 1962 Fals Borda, Guzmán, and Umaña, in the first attempt
to come to grips with La Violencia, stated accurately that "in effect,
the nation lacks an exact idea of what La Violencia was."[30] Their
study, *La Violencia en Colombia*, documenting the macabre national disaster, was in itself a major event for the national consciousness. One issue that virtually no one questions is that the
1950s, under Rojas Pinilla, were years of political repression and
public censorship.

New elements added strength to the counter-discourse during
these years as well. One could mark 1949 as a turning point in the
rejection of the tradition of the Colonial *ciudad letrada* and conservative humanism: Mario Laserna founded the Universidad de los
Andes (after the model of the American private university), purposely excluding a law school. Thus this university became a seminary for a new, modern, technical elite.[31] During the period from
1958 to 1974 Colombia was ruled by the National Front, an agreement providing for alternate governments of Liberals and Conservatives. The 1960s marked the upsurge of leftist guerrilla movements
such as the FARC (Fuerzas Armadas Revolucionarias de Colombia)
and the ELN (Ejército de Liberación Nacional). In the early 1970s the
first groups professing adherence to Trotskyism began to attract notice. García Márquez, whose *Cien años de soledad* was a national
event in 1967, founded the leftist magazine *Alternativa* in 1974. The
National Front was a weakly institutionalized brand of inclusionary
authoritarianism that became increasingly exclusionary and repressive during the 1970s in the face of the regime's deepening legitimacy problems.[32] The transition to exclusionary politics has not yet
been completed nor is the trend irreversible; in fact, during the
presidency of Belisario Betancur (1982–1986) democratic reforms
were instituted.[33]

Colombian Regionalism

As stated in the preface, a fundamental supposition of this study is
that Colombia was essentially four "nations" (or semi-autonomous

regions) for at least a century, approximately from the 1830s to the mid-twentieth century. The nation's political, economic, social, and cultural history supports this proposition. By the 1850s these regional divisions had taken form, finding increased definition throughout the remainder of the nineteenth century. Regional demarcations remained firmly intact during the first third of the twentieth century and then began to disintegrate after the 1930s with the modernization process. Symbolic dates for the beginning and end of this "nation of regions" would be 1830 to 1958, from the collapse of the first Colombian supraregional unity to the National Front.

Modern Colombia consists of four regions with distinct cultural traditions: the Interior Highlands (including the present-day departments of Cundinamarca, Boyacá, Santander, Norte de Santander, Tolima, and Huila); the Costa (Caribbean coastal departments of Magdalena, Bolívar, César, Sucre, Córdoba, and Guajira); Greater Antioquia (Antioquia, Caldas, Risaralda, and Quindío); and Greater Cauca (Valle del Cauca, Cauca, Nariño, Putumayo, and Chocó). The relatively uninhabited areas of the eastern plains, such as Meta and Arauca, have not produced novels; they can be considered cultural extensions of the Interior Highland Region. A political map of Colombia at the mid-nineteenth century reflects this basic division.

Discussions of Colombian society and culture by Colombian intellectuals have emphasized these regional differences. Luis López de Mesa's now-classic essay *De cómo se ha formado la nación colombiana* (1934) portrays the country by region and delineates distinctive characteristics for each. In her oft-quoted sociological/anthropological analysis of Colombian families, *La familia en Colombia* (1968), Virginia Gutiérrez de Pineda studies the family region by region. Novelist and anthropologist Manuel Zapata Olivella has sketched eight "ethnic types" in Colombia, apportioning them into the four regions in this study: the *costeño* of the Caribbean coast; the *antioqueño* of Greater Antioquia; Highlands *cundi-boyacense, tolimo-huilense, santandereano,* and plainsmen types; and Greater Cauca *caucano* and *andino sureño* types.[34]

Colombia's geographic conformation has been a key factor in the development of the nation's regionalism. The mountain ranges of three cordilleras have posed enormous obstacles to any kind of unity. Interregional transportation, economic activity, communication, and cultural activity have always been challenging and frequently nonexistent.[35] Rather than looking to a neighboring region or its capital, the Colombian who has turned outward has traditionally been more likely to look abroad. Notable examples of this phenome-

Colombia in the second half of the nineteenth century

non are two such markedly different cases as the nineteenth-century tobacco industry and the literary career of the twentieth-century's Gabriel García Márquez. The tobacco merchant of Ambalema (a small town in the Magdalena River valley bordering Cundinamarca and Tolima) of the 1850s had more economic contact with German merchants in Bremen than with, for example, capitalists in Medellín or Cali. Similarly, Gabriel García Márquez's fiction is more closely allied with the American William Faulkner than with his Colombian contemporaries from inland Colombia, Manuel Mejía Vallejo and Eduardo Caballero Calderón. Both for the tobacco merchant from Ambalema and for the novelist from Aracataca, the roots are local and the extralocal contact is international, not interregional. Colombia's acute regionalism developed in this fashion.

Many Latin American countries, of course, have regional differences and geographies not conducive to cultural unity, but Colombia's barriers to national integrity have been exceptionally deep-rooted and prohibitive. For example, geographic and political factors have combined to give Colombia a railroad system markedly inferior to that of Mexico, Argentina, or Brazil since the turn of the century: "The real measure of Colombia's slowness to adopt the railways is shown in the period 1880–1910. In that period Colombia built an additional 21 percent of its total; during the same interval Mexico added 79 percent of its railways, Argentina added 59 percent, and Brazil added 49 percent."[36] Ground transportation has always been extremely difficult in Colombia, since the Magdalena River has been the only natural source of interregional connection. As late as the 1920s a reporter from the United States wrote that "the Departments of Antioquia and Cundinamarca are the only ones in Colombia where wagon roads of any length extending outside the towns are found."[37] A concentrated, systematic effort to build the nation's highway system was carried out only from the 1930s forward, with the rise of the modern state. An economic historian describes how the weak transportation system affected Colombia's marked regionalism:

> The effective distance between the cities grew relatively great when compared to that between each city and the outside world. Consequently, internal trade faced increasing relative transport costs when compared to international trade. This tendency was exacerbated by the railways since all lines were built to facilitate external rather than internal trade. Bogotá and Medellín, the two largest cities, were not connected by direct rail service until 1960.[38]

Transportation and communication problems were not the only contributors to Colombia's pronounced regionalism. Regional division colors studies of Colombia's political and economic as well as literary history. A study of twentieth-century Colombian politics demonstrates in detail that "from this fact of Colombian regionalism has stemmed much of Colombia's political strife."[39] An economic history of Colombia focusing on technical education concludes that Colombia's geographic divisions contributed substantially to its problems in modernization: "Its mountainous terrain isolated Colombians from each other and from the outside world, inhibiting the development of a substantial national market or of foreign ones that would have provided incentives for engagements with the process of production and for technical innovation."[40]

Perhaps the most conclusive example of the impact of Colombian regionalism and of its historical base in the nineteenth century is the regionalist legacy of Rafael Núñez.[41] Núñez wrote that Colombia "is not a single nationality, but a group of nationalities, each one needing its own special, independent and exclusive government."[42] The decline of Liberalism and the emergence of Núñez and the Conservatives in the 1880s demonstrate that regionalist tensions were a deep-rooted, permanent feature of nineteenth-century Colombia and not a temporary result of the uneven effect of changes in the international market for Colombian exports.[43] The elections of 1875, for example, were fought along regional lines: "The deep fissures in the Liberal party revealed by the election campaign resulted not from debate of ideological principles but instead from regional rivalries and the desire to end regional hegemony."[44] Though hardly unique in its composition of sections along geographic and economic lines, Colombia "differs from other countries of similar size in the deep imprint its regionalist sentiment has left on the pattern of regional development."[45]

Seen diachronically, the development of Colombian regionalism falls into three basic periods: the Colonial stage from the sixteenth century to the 1830s, the republic's regional division from the 1830s to the 1950s, and the postregional period of the modern state. During the first stage, the regions of the Nuevo Reino de Granada, in geographic isolation, began to develop regional identities based in part on variations in the ethnic mix. During this time the indigenous population was decimated. Relatively small numbers of the indigenous groups remained intact in isolated areas, particularly in the areas of Greater Cauca and La Guajira; a mestizo culture developed in Greater Antioquia, while Antioquia saw the end of any significant indigenous heritage. Entrepreneurs brought African slaves to the Nuevo Reino de Granada, primarily into the lowland regions, but also into the present-day area of Antioquia. The Interior Highlands, meanwhile, maintained a strong Hispanic heritage, and a tri-ethnic racial and cultural situation emerged in the three other regions. Political, economic, and cultural power of the Colonial period was centered in the *ciudades letradas*: Bogotá, Popayán, Cartagena, and, to a lesser extent, Tunja, Santa Fe de Antioquia, Cali, and Mompós.[46] Communication among these Colonial cities and their surrounding regions, even by the standards of the times, remained slow and often treacherous.

In the 1850s certain political, economic, and cultural factors began to change, but with differing levels of intensity and impact in the various regions. In the political area, the two traditional parties had developed a sense of identity by mid-century. The abolition of slavery in 1851 affected the ethnic composition of some regions; for example, Afro-American former slaves in Antioquia tended to move to the Costa. A political scientist points to the development of a regionalist political makeup: "The mid-1850s also saw the realization of the federalist idea in Colombia with the creation of eight self-governing states—Panamá, Antioquia, Santander, Cauca, Cundinamarca, Boyacá, Bolívar, and Magdalena—between 1855 and 1857."[47] The Constitution of 1863 ratified the idea of a nation as a collection of sovereign states; the period of its being in effect, 1864 to 1886, saw the maximum institutionalized political expression of regional autonomy. This autonomy resulted in considerable conflict: "Regional conflict within the [Liberal] party reached a peak in 1875 when Núñez was nominated for the presidency as a frankly regional candidate and his supporters attacked the proposed Northern Railroad on the grounds that the project would benefit only three states at the expense of the other six."[48] The first full-length Colombian novel, *Ingermina*, appeared in 1844 and had a strong regional identity.

Although the political consolidation that took place in 1886 signaled a return to nearly half a century of Conservative rule, national unity was still more a political ideal than an economic, social, or cultural reality. Poor interregional transportation meant that much economic development remained local. And literary activity was typically regional: At the turn of the century the traditional and realist *escuela antioqueña* was opposed to the *modernista* intellectuals in Bogotá. The *costumbrista* writers celebrated regional values.

Colombia's transition from isolated regions to a more unified nation took place between the 1930s and the 1950s. The governments of the Liberal Republic invested heavily in the railway and highway systems; the advent of air transportation in the 1920s opened new possibilities. An unprecedented immigration from the rural areas to the cities, above all Bogotá, began in the 1930s. Bogotá was opening to the outside world as it never had before; as noted, the founding of the Universidad de los Andes signaled a turning away from the pervasive hermetic, Conservative ethos.

The transition from a strictly regionalist to a more national and even international outlook shaped cultural activities. While much of the Antioquian Tomás Carrasquilla's later fiction, published in the 1920s and 1930s, lamented the loss of the traditional values of Antioquia in favor of the growing modernity, other writers such as José Felix Fuenmayor in Barranquilla and José Antonio Osorio Lizarazo in Bogotá novelized themes related to the new, urban settings. If Cartagena had symbolized regional power during the Colonial period, the rise of Barranquilla in the twentieth century was representative of a new, modern order in the Costa. Cultural life began to change radically after the 1930s. One example is the history of newspaper production in small towns. Before 1930 small towns often produced several local newspapers; after 1930, when the roads from Bogotá were completed, many of these regional newspapers disappeared in favor of the national newspaper, *El Tiempo*, available for the first time.

The third stage in Colombia's regional development is the post-regional period from the 1950s to the present, a change reflected in the novel during the 1960s and 1970s. By the 1950s modernization, industrialization, and immigration to the cities had reshaped many of the previous regional boundaries. La Violencia was a national phenomenon that affected the national psyche, not a regional conflict. The formation of the National Front in 1958 contributed to national rather than regional unity and identity. That same year a Ley del Libro was passed, for instance, improving the situation for national book production and distribution.

In addition to the development of a new national unity, Colombia also began to function more fully in the international context. In economic terms the internationalization of the economy has been evidenced in the rapid expansion of multinational companies since the 1950s and in the increased presence of the international underground economy, above all the illicit cocaine traffic of the 1970s and 1980s. In terms of politics, Colombia's active role in the Contadora peace process in Central America under the leadership of President Belisario Betancur (1982–1986) was yet another sign of Colombia's increasingly international presence. Colombia's cultural scene has also been internationalized in several ways in recent decades. In painting, such figures as Alejandro Obregón, Fernando Botero, Enrique Grau, Omar Rayo, and others have achieved world renown. Colombian journalism has changed in accordance with international tastes, with Daniel Samper's investigative unit, for instance. During the 1960s the "boom" of the Latin American novel had an impact on Colombia, bringing the most innovative fiction into the country. The emergence of García Márquez marked the beginning of Colombian influence on the world literary scene, as well as the prominence of the Costa in national letters. Until the 1960s, there had never been a large-scale distribution of Colombian fiction beyond regional boundaries within Colombia. By the mid-1970s the Editorial Plaza y Janés and small presses were publishing and distributing nationally the most recent Colombian fiction. In the early 1980s several multinational publishing companies established operations in Colombia and began contracting Colombian novelists.

Of course, many remnants of regional structures, institutions, and traditions remain strong in Colombia, and some of these regional differences exist in the contemporary Colombian novel. But after the 1950s, regionalism is only one of several important factors in cultural expression in general and in the Colombian novel in particular. By the postregionalist period, Colombia and its novel are predominantly national and international in scope and vision.

In conclusion, both intense ideological conflict and a marked regionalism have left an indelible mark in each of Colombia's six periods of historical experience and four regions of cultural development. The novelistic consequences of the ideological conflict throughout the six periods is the topic of chapter 2; chapters 3 through 6 explore the Colombian novel within a regional context. Literary expression began in the nineteenth century not as the "imaginative literature" we consider it today but as part of a debate between proponents of the Hellenic/Catholic Arcadia and the Liberal Utopia.

Two

Ideology and the Novel in Nineteenth- and Twentieth-Century Colombia

*If art reflects life, it does so
with special mirrors.*
　　　　　—Bertolt Brecht, A Short Organum for the Theater

In Colombia the novel has always been considered a relatively minor genre. The cultivation of poetry and the essay has been a historic ideal for its dominant elite of gentlemen-scholars. Until the 1960s virtually no industry for the production, marketing, and sale of novels had been in operation as it has been known in the industrial West since the nineteenth century. The meteoric rise of Gabriel García Márquez, the advent of the multinational publishing houses, and the arrival of international Latin Americanism, among other factors, have radically transformed the genteel, regional, and provincial literary scenario that in more than a century had produced only three novels of recognized national and international import: Jorge Isaacs's *María* (1867), José Eustasio Rivera's *La vorágine* (1924), and García Márquez's *Cien años de soledad* (1967). *María* and *La vorágine* were written by writers who aspired to be poets and, in fact, had established credentials as poets prior to their celebrity as novelists. Moreover, after the publication of the one novel, each dedicated himself to the affairs of the state in the venerable mold of the Colombian gentleman-scholar.

The cultural heritage still operative in the nineteenth century finds its roots in the Spanish military-bureaucratic culture generally linked to the Iberian *reconquista*, which encouraged the dominance of a military aristocracy and its values over other groups of society, including commercial groups.[1] The one nonnoble sector of Spanish society that could gain aristocratic status was the university-educated *letrado*, who staffed the Spanish royal bureaucracy and then the Spanish Colonial bureaucracy. Nineteenth-century Colombia's upper class imposed many of the Spanish values implanted during the three centuries of the Colonial period. Its future oligarchy was educated almost uniformly at one of the two seedbeds of the upper class, the Colegio del Rosario or the Colegio San Bartolomé, where it tended to seek patents of social honor, in the Spanish tradition, through the pursuit of literary, political, or legal careers.[2] Indeed, Colombia's most brilliant and vigorous *hombres de letras* have frequently pursued two or three of these careers, from the nation's first novelist, Juan José Nieto, to its recent president, writer Belisario Betancur.

The historic privileging of the other genres over the novel is comparable to the attitudes held by the lettered elite and scholars in Europe in the eighteenth and nineteenth centuries. The upper class in nineteenth-century Colombia was both receptive to disparate foreign cultural values and imitative of them, giving preference to the predominant literary modes in France, Spain, and Great Britain. Spanish and British culture were of more importance in the Highland region of Colombia than was the case in most other regions of Colombia and Latin America, which in the nineteenth century tended to reject Spain and ignore Great Britain. During the nineteenth and much of the twentieth centuries, novels were published in small editions and went virtually unnoticed. Innumerable cases could be cited of the young aristocrat who published but one novel, perhaps as a pastime or for social/intellectual accreditation, and then pursued a political or bureaucratic career, from the nineteenth-century statesman-scholar Manuel María Madiedo to the recent president Alfonso López Michelsen.

Given the class values linked to literary production, the relative unimportance of the novel as a genre, and the nation's marked regionalism, the proposition of an "organic" Colombian novelistic tradition is indeed dubious. Instead, one must speak of regional traditions (as outlined in the chapters which follow), of some significant individual novels (even beyond *María*, *La vorágine*, and *Cien años de soledad*) and of some noteworthy novelists. As will be observed in chapter 7, contemporary production can now be viably identified as a modern and postmodern "Colombian novel." Given the class conditions of writing and the historical bias against the novel, the next logical question is, then, Who are the Colombian novelists? Those writers who have actually pursued a career in novel writing, publishing a regular series of novels over a lifetime, usually with little or no financial gain, have almost invariably belonged to the

middle and upper-middle sectors of Colombian society. Often they
have not been part of Colombia's dominant power structure for reasons of either class or gender. If one sets aside the celebrated "intellectual figures" (distinguished men of letters and intellectual/politi-
cal figures who have not dedicated a lifetime to publishing novels)
and the writers who have published only one novel (except for Isaacs
and Rivera), the novelists of Colombia would include Juan José Nieto,
Waldina Dávila de Ponce de León, Eugenio Díaz, Felipe Pérez, Jorge
Isaacs, Soledad Acosta de Samper, Tomás Carrasquilla, Clímaco
Soto Borda, José María Vargas Vila, José Eustasio Rivera, José Félix
Fuenmayor, Ignacio Gómez Sánchez, José Antonio Osorio Lizarazo,
César Uribe Piedrahita, Bernardo Arias Trujillo, Augusto Morales
Pino, Manuel Mejía Vallejo, Eduardo Caballero Calderón, Arnoldo
Palacios, Elisa Mújica, Próspero Morales Pradilla, Manuel Zapata
Olivella, Héctor Rojas Herazo, Gabriel García Márquez, Flor Romero
de Nohra, Fanny Buitrago, Gustavo Alvarez Gardeazábal, Héctor
Sánchez, Alberto Duque López, Albalucía Angel, Marco Tulio Aguilera Garramuño, Rodrigo Parra Sandoval, Germán Espinosa, Jorge
Eliécer Pardo, José Luis Garcés, Alvaro Pineda Botero, Roberto Burgos Cantor, Andrés Caicedo, R. H. Moreno-Durán, and a few other
contemporary writers. One may quibble about the accuracy of this
list, subtracting one name and adding another according to differing
criteria, but one issue is irrefutable: Colombia's elite does not produce its novelists.

Colombia's literary critics and scholarly establishment, on the
other hand, have been closely linked to the oligarchy—the upper
class, the elite universities, and the Catholic Church. Literary criticism has involved the study of the Greek and Roman classics and
philology. Moreover, it has been entirely male-dominated. An important function of this literary criticism in Colombia has been legitimization: Through a complex process of exclusion and inclusion
and a discourse of encomium rather than scholarly inquiry or analysis, the oligarchy has, in effect, annointed its writers. The upper
class has institutionalized literary value.[3] As in the case of the upwardly mobile *letrado* of the Spanish bureaucracy, the middle-class
Colombian writer has presented credentials before the chosen elite,
but the acceptance of novelists (rather than poets/essayists) into the
oligarchical intellectual inner circles has been rare. Each period has
been represented by one or two prominent intellectuals who, in effect, appointed the chosen novelists. Authoritative scholar-critics
who have played this role have included José María Vergara y Vergara, Baldomero Sanín Cano, Rafael Maya, Antonio Gómez Restrepo,
and Gustavo Otero Muñoz, among others. Whereas Colombia's nov-

elists have tended to be Liberals, its literary critics have been mostly Conservatives. Recognizing this situation can help explain why Colombian novelists have always claimed the nation has no critics, while the critics have sustained that Colombia has no novelists.

The formative period of the new nation, from 1810 to 1862, was dominated intellectually by two gentleman-scholars who did not write novels, Julio Arboleda (1817–1862) and José Eusebio Caro (1817–1853). Writers of this period were typically young large landowners and urban aristocrats, most of whom were either actual participants or sons of those who had fought in the battles of independence. Arboleda and Caro, men of letters who distinguished themselves as poets, belonged to the landed gentry. Seen in retrospect, two important novelists of the period were Eugenio Díaz and Juan José Nieto. During their lifetimes, however, they were viewed as social and intellectual upstarts whose work was relatively unimportant as literature, since their novels in particular and the genre in general rendered an insignificant contribution to the ideological enterprises of the upper-class political and literary elite. Political essays, for example, had much more immediate impact; Díaz and Nieto today remain relatively unrecognized as novelists.

The two ideological enterprises, and the corresponding two Colombias which the intellectuals projected in their writings, were the Liberal Utopia and the Hellenic/Catholic Arcadia. During the period from 1810 to 1862, the early years were dominated by the centralists, who followed Simón Bolívar—the future Conservatives of the Hellenic/Catholic Arcadia. The Liberals, under the leadership of Tomás Cipriano de Mosquera, were more powerful near the end of this period. Few utopias and arcadias were actually realized during the 1840s and 1850s beyond the textual—idealistic essays and neoclassical poetry. Rather, continual strife, including the civil wars of 1841, 1851–52, 1854, and 1859 to 1862, carried ideological differences to the battlefield.

Another arena for the conflict between Liberals and Conservatives was the debate concerning the role of public education.[4] This issue determined the literacy of the middle and lower classes, as well as these groups' potential as readers and writers of literature. Given Colombia's marked regional differences, it is logical that attitudes about education varied by region. Greater Antioquia, for example, was consistently in the vanguard of primary education throughout the nineteenth century, a contributing factor to its egalitarian tradition (see chapter 5).[5] The consistencies lie in the upper class's attitudes about education and the relationships between these attitudes and the two ideological projects being promulgated. An important concern of the elite was to "moralize" the philistine masses, and education was viewed as a vehicle to carry out this mission.[6] At the Congress of Cúcuta, the law passed for education accentuated religion and morality; public schools were deemed necessary for youngsters to learn "sacred obligations imposed upon them by religion and Christian morality."[7] For the conservatives, public schools served the function of preparing the future gentlemen-scholars of the Hellenic/Catholic Arcadia—or at the least to enable those less-privileged citizens of the general populace to properly respect the upper class's lofty literary artifices and position in society. Thus, inculcating the upper and middle classes with Greek and Roman classic literature and neoclassic, patriotic poetry made literature ideology. In the 1850s Conservatives tended to believe that people were shiftless because of the disintegration of traditional social values;[8] the literature of the arcadia, as produced by Sergio Arboleda and other like-minded writers, could imbue this fragile society with order. Again, literature was ideology. Conservatives eventually deserted primary education as a useful vehicle for their ideological program, placing a higher priority on the universities, where the elite literary and political dialogue could be carried out with a more receptive audience—the members of their own class.

Given these ideological conditions, it is perhaps surprising that any novels at all were published during this period, much less the approximately two dozen that appeared in print from 1810 to 1862. Nevertheless, Juan José Nieto, Eugenio Díaz, José María Angel Gaitán, and a few others pioneered what today's literary scholars can identify as the first Colombian novels. Most of these works were aesthetic anomalies, particularly when read today as novels: In mid-nineteenth-century Colombia, as in eighteenth-century Great Britain, the concept of literature was not confined as it is today to "creative" or "imaginative" writing.[9] None of these pioneers considered himself a "novelist" but rather an *escritor,* which could refer to the fabrication of something like a novel or a political speech, history, or philosophy. Many of their works, which today are treated as novels, contained elements of each of these genres. In addition, terms such as *personal response* or *imaginative uniqueness,* inseparable for us today from the whole idea of *literary,* would not have made any more sense for Juan José Nieto or José María Samper than they did for Henry Fielding.[10] The ideological enterprise of these mid-nineteenth-century writers pertained less to "imaginative uniqueness" than to the ultimate ideological objectives related to the rationally conceived utopias and arcadias that they aspired to construct in Colombia.

The first novelistic sketch during this 1810 to 1863 period was José Joaquín Ortiz's *María Dolores o la historia de mi casamiento* (1841). Read with today's genre expectations, *María Dolores* seems to be an incomplete outline for a novel. Ortiz was better known for his neoclassic and patriotic poems than this booklet published under the guise of "novel." A devoted Catholic, Hispanophile, and Conservative, Ortiz wrote the famed poem "Los colonos," which fulfilled his ideological mission ideally: It evokes a Hellenic/Catholic Arcadia in the Colonial Reino de la Nueva Granada, a setting in which the Spaniards "civilize" the native population. Nevertheless, *María Dolores* fits within the ideological scheme set forth in his poetry, for this work, with a minimally perceivable social or class context, relates the emotional vacillations of the narrator-protagonist as he pursues, and ultimately marries, his loved one. The reader may conclude that, with pursuit by the proper gentlemen-scholars, the arcadia is possible.

If the Conservative arcadia was possible as fictionalized by Ortiz, the Liberal Utopia finds its novelistic roots in *Ingermina o la hija de Calamar* (1844) by the Liberal *caudillo* from the Costa, Juan José Nieto. In this particular utopia, set in the period of the Spanish conquest, the Spanish conqueror not only weds the Indian princess Ingermina but also instructs her in the refinements of writing culture. Gaining entrance into Cartagena's aristocracy by marriage, the tri-ethnic Nieto aspired to full acceptance into the upper class by writing novels mediated by the conventions of European Romanticism and science. In Nieto's utopia (as in the arcadia), the Indian needed to be "civilized" in order to function in the society Liberals envisioned. Nevertheless, Nieto was the first Colombian novelist to give voice to the New World Indian; *Ingermina* also contains a lengthy anecdote of acculturation (see chapter 4). Moreover, the liberal author offers the consistent subthemes of victimization and liberation. As was the case with *Ingermina*, Nieto's two other historical novels, *Los moriscos* (1845) and *Rosina o la prisión del castillo de Chagres* (1850), were ignored by the Highland literary elite. *Ingermina* and *Los moriscos* (published in Jamaica during Nieto's political exile) as well as *Rosina* (published in a newspaper in Cartagena) have always been marginal to Colombian literary and political history.

A more resonant Liberal voice was Felipe Pérez, brother of the distinguished Liberal political and intellectual figure Santiago Pérez,

who was minister of interior (1868–1870) and then president of Colombia (1874–1876). Felipe Pérez occupied numerous political positions in the Highland region, including governor of Boyacá. His essayistic contributions to the political dialogue were his *Análisis
político, social i económico de la República del Ecuador* [sic] (1853)
and his *Anales de la revolución de 1860* (1862). He was an ardent
believer in such Liberal principles as liberty and progress (the cor-
nerstones of the Liberal Utopia), as his Liberal discourse reveals.[11]
Although better remembered for his more immediate contributions
to the political dialogue than for his novels, his fiction was not as
ignored as Nieto's. Pérez was, in fact, one of the most prolific novelists of the century, publishing the historical novels *Huayna Capac*
(1855), *Atahuallpa* (1856), *La familia de Matías* (1856), *Los Pizarros*
(1857), *Jilma, o la continuación de los Pizarros* (1858), and *El caballero de la barba negra* (1858) during the period under discussion.
The group of novels consisting of *Huayna Capac*, *Atahuallpa*, *Los
Pizarros*, and *Jilma, o la continuación de los Pizarros* are set in sixteenth-century Peru during the Spanish conquest. These novels,
consisting almost entirely of dialogue, depict a clearly dichotomized
world: On the one side are the petty and antagonistic Spaniards and
on the other the idealized Indians. Through their plots and characters, they proffer a Liberal critique of the Spaniards' brutal conquest
in opposition to the Colonial arcadia fictionalized by Conservatives
such as José Joaquín Ortiz. *El caballero de la barba negra* takes
place in sixteenth-century Spain and questions conventional social
customs; more particularly, the parental arrangement of marriages.
The narrator advances his program of social criticism: "Sad the situation of women. Born in dark castles and educated among prayers, they
live far from the world."[12] The narrator also depicts the social norms
in sixteenth-century Spain, thereby criticizing conditions in an excessively conservative nineteenth-century Colombia: "That is the
condition of women in our century and for the most part in our
country."[13] Nevertheless, Pérez always restores the social order momentarily upset in his novels, tempering any real necessity for radical change and assuring his acceptance by the liberal elite into which
he eventually was incorporated by virtue of his achievements with
the pen and the sword.

Manuel María Madiedo, author of the novel *La maldición* (1859),
belonged to the Conservative party but nonetheless was one of its
most virulent critics. A mulatto born in Cartagena and bereft of
eminent family lineage, he published essays on behalf of popular
causes, criticizing the primacy Colombian society accorded to family pedigree. One Conservative contemporary of Madiedo claimed

that he "does not conform because he is not white and rich."[14]
Hardly the gentleman-scholar epitomized by Caro and Arboleda,
Madiedo opposed the most proclerical and doctrinaire faction of the
Conservative party, which was headed by Caro, Arboleda, and José
Joaquín Ortiz. Madiedo's sector of the party espoused a Christian so-
cialism and attempted to promote a spirit of cooperation between
Liberals and Conservatives. His virtually unknown novel, *La maldición*, appeared in serial fashion in a Cartagena newspaper and was
never republished as a book. It relates the story of a Colombian's return to the Costa after a stay in Europe, but the work's most intriguing quality is the fact that it represents the first effort by a Colombian novelist to incorporate Colombia's oral and popular culture
into a novel. In this work, as well as in many of his essays, Madiedo
was ideologically closer to the Liberal project than to the Conservative one. (By the end of the century a not totally unforeseen marriage between the Liberal Utopia and the Hellenic/Catholic Arcadia
will have taken place.)

The most notable novel of this period to emanate from a Conservative voice was *Manuela* (1858) by Eugenio Díaz, who, remaining
distant from the day-to-day political arena, did not fit the classic
mold of the Conservative gentleman-scholar either. The implied author of his major novel, *Manuela*, ridicules the protagonist, a progressive Liberal or *gólgota* from Bogotá visiting the provinces. The
satirical characterization of this protagonist undermines his Liberal
discourse, making it seem naive and ingenuous. The contrast between an authentic and commonsensical oral culture and the Liberal discourse of a writing culture disassociated from national reality makes *Manuela*, in summary, a critique of the Liberal project in
ascendance during the late 1850s and early 1860s.

Judged as aesthetic objects by present-day genre expectations,
none of these books is outstanding as a novel. Nieto's tendency toward the essay, Pérez's weak plots (coupled with excessive dialogues),
and Díaz's detailed attention to the political nuances of ideological positions interfere with the reader's aesthetic experience of a
"novel" as "imaginative writing." José María Gaitán's *El Doctor
Temis* (1851) and Raimundo Bernal Orjuela's *Viene por mi i carga
con usted* [sic] (1858) are imbued with similar aesthetic problems
and ideological propositions. *El Doctor Temis* fictionalizes a situation of social injustice in order to demonstrate, in the end, that justice can prevail. *Viene por mi i carga con usted* ends with a marked
didactic tone, explaining that appearances can be deceiving. On the
other hand, some works had as their primary objective the re-cre-
ation of European models, even though in general they did not prove

to be more successful aesthetically. The subtext of this task was the patriotic proposition that Colombia possessed a novel as well as its own unique national customs comparable to those of European nations. The middle-class readers of much of this fiction found common standards of acceptable and unacceptable behavior based on elitist values, which, in turn, were imitative of Spanish and European values. Juan Francisco Ortiz wrote several novels modelled on the European romantic novel. His first, *El oidor Cortés de Mesa* (1845), is a nineteenth-century Colombian potboiler—an account of its protagonist's obsession with the woman whom he eventually murders. In *Teresa, leyenda americana* (1851), Ortiz turns to legends from regional folklore.

Numerous seemingly irremediable problems were inherent in the idea of a Colombian novel during the period from 1863 to 1885; one of the most grievous was that the novels known could not comfortably accommodate either of the ideological projects being propagated. Neither the Liberal Utopia nor the Conservative Hellenic/Catholic Arcadia lent itself readily to ideologically feasible novelization, at least not as the genre was conceived at the time. Consequently, the essay and poetry were more viable. For example, Arboleda could evoke images of the Hellenic/Catholic Arcadia in his epic poetry set in the Colonial Reino de la Nueva Granada. Of the several extant types of romantic novel prototypes, the romantic novel of social critique (i.e., Hugo's *Les Misérables*) fit neither the concept of the Liberal Utopia nor that of the Hellenic/Catholic Arcadia. It was not ideologically convenient for the proponents of either of these projects to novelize the impoverished and illiterate masses that surrounded them. Many liberals were admirers of Hugo's politics but chose not to follow his example for fiction writing.

The *costumbristas* offered a more acceptable alternative. With the need to incorporate the culturally deficient middle and lower sectors of society into unity with the ruling elite, to diffuse "correct" taste and common cultural standards, *cuadros de costumbres* played a vital role. Vergara y Vergara's most celebrated *cuadro de costumbres*, "Las tres tazas," ridicules Bogotá's customs, concomitantly reaffirming relationships between correct social ritual and proper intellectual behavior. By ostensibly ridiculing the habits of Bogotá's new middle classes (and even the elite), proper taste and common cultural standards were disseminated, primarily through cultural magazines and newspapers. The distinctions we recognize today among newspapers, cultural magazines, literary journals, and scientific journals did not hold in nineteenth-century Colombia.

News, culture, and science typically appeared in one weekly or daily dose of ideologically "correct" *cultura*. Felipe Pérez had founded the *Biblioteca de Señoritas* in 1858; *El Mosaico* and a host of other cultural magazines circulated throughout the nineteenth century.

With the ratification of the Constitution of 1863, Mosquera and the Liberals wrote the Liberal program into the nation's governing document. It was the Liberal Utopia on paper, assuring absolute freedom and humanitarian justice. In this new secular state, the Liberal Utopia intended to replace permanently the Hellenic/Catholic Arcadia as the dominant ideology. For approximately the next two decades the very word *nation*, however, was a questionable term to apply to the autonomous regions that constituted this Federalist system of independent states. Symbolic of the state of affairs was Jorge Isaacs declaring himself "president" of the independent state of Antioquia in 1880. Economic reforms resulted in losses for many landowners, and consequently the nostalgic novel of the rural aristocracy, yearning for a previous order, came into vogue.

Despite the publication of over thirty works of prose fiction, the national novel still had not attained full respectability in comparison with the other genres and the venerable tradition of Colonial letters. When José María Vergara y Vergara published his *Historia de la literatura en Nueva Granada* in 1867, he included no novelists. In fact, the book consists of a panoramic overview of Spanish Colonial writing in the Reino de Nueva Granada, including only a decade of Colombian writing after the independence (his study encompasses up to the 1820s). It was the first of several projects that intended to propagate the idea of an organic national literary tradition and identity, a fundamentally conservative ideological undertaking that would culminate a century later in Antonio Curcio Altamar's *Evolución de la novela en Colombia* (1957).

The most renowned intellectuals of the 1863 to 1885 period were José María Samper (1828–1888), Rafael Pombo (1833–1912), José María Vergara y Vergara (1831–1872), and José Eusebio Caro. None were esteemed primarily as novelists, although Samper produced several novels and Vergara y Vergara wrote some lengthy fiction. A progressive among the Liberals early in his career, Samper was known as a Liberal firebrand and publicist of the Liberal Utopia during the 1860s. He was at the vanguard of the Liberal educational reforms that secularized and expanded public education. For example, Samper proposed a bill in 1864 to reconstitute higher education, institutionalizing a national university with a strong technical orientation.[15] In the late 1870s he joined the Conservative cause in support of Rafael Núñez. His works included novels, plays, several volumes of verse and essays, and treatises on history, government, sociology, travel, and biography. Unlike the flamboyant and unpredictable Samper, Rafael Pombo fit the established mold of the quintessential Conservative intellectual, a gentleman-scholar who translated poetry from Greek, Latin, French, Portuguese, and English. The essayist, literary historian, and fiction writer Vergara y Vergara was also active in the Conservative party, founding the newspaper *La Unión Católica* in 1871 to sustain the concept of a Catholic party.

During the 1863 to 1885 period José María Vergara y Vergara in effect appointed and anointed the novelists into the "national" literature he was promulgating. He admitted new recruits into this essentially male and Conservative national literature club—*El Mosaico*—with the proper class and/or gentleman-scholar credentials, as in the case of Jorge Isaacs, the Greater Cauca's Conservative aristocrat in his twenties. After serving his literary apprenticeship with *El Mosaico*, Isaacs returned to the Greater Cauca to write his only novel, *María*, which appeared in 1867. *María* came into print as a direly needed anomaly for the Conservative ideological project, which was conspicuously deficient in novels, particularly of the aesthetic quality of the European fiction to which Colombia's middle and upper classes were becoming accustomed. Isaacs's regional evocation of the Greater Cauca as earthly paradise in *María*—a regional variant of the arcadia theme—fulfilled the ideological requisites of the period magnificently: It read as a well-crafted romantic novel based on the revered European molds; its "poetic" language compensated for the fact that it was written in the less dignified and still undefined genre of the novel; it was a product of the upper class which contributed to their ultimate objective of transforming Colombia into their vision of a Hellenic/Catholic Arcadia. *María*, for several reasons, then, in addition to being a well-crafted fiction, became Colombia's "national" novel; it is no total coincidence (but rather a sign of the times) that Vergara y Vergara's project for the establishment of an organic national literature, his *Historia de la literatura en Nueva Granada*, appeared in print the same year. In response to the Liberal Utopia, which conceived of Colombia as several autonomous and absolutely free states, the Conservative arcadia, a unified Catholic state, was firmly supported by the ideological subtext of these two "national" works, Isaacs's novel and Vergara y Vergara's history. (Soon thereafter, Isaacs gravitated to the Liberals, but *María* remains, nevertheless, a seminal work of the nineteenth-century Conservative enterprise.) Four years later, in 1871, Vergara y Vergara founded the Academia Colombiana de la Lengua, thereby institutionalizing the notion of a "national" language for this "national" project.

María, many of the Conservative *costumbrista* writings of the period, and the literature of the arcadia project in general were exercises in nostalgia. The progressive writings of José María Samper, however, were free of this nostalgia. A genuine reformer's zeal underlies much of his work, including his fiction. His *artículos de costumbres* express a confidence in progress and the perfectibility of human institutions.[16] This social vision, in addition to his critical attitudes toward the commonplaces of so much of his contemporaries' writing, made Samper an invigorating force in Colombian fiction. He published eight novels during the 1863 to 1885 period, all of which were significant contributions to the political dialogue. *Martín Flores* (1866), as mediated by the romantic novel, promises in the first chapter to make the reader weep (the same promise as in *María*).[17] The protagonist, Martín, is a young intellectual who fights in the political and military battles of nineteenth-century Colombia but who decides to dedicate himself to the priesthood after losing his lover, Dolores. In the chaotic denouement, Colombia undergoes continual civil wars, Martín becomes an educator, and Dolores suffers insanity. By the mid-1860s Samper had converted to Catholicism and begun forging his unprecedented idea of a marriage between Catholicism and social progress, a proposition not acceptable to either Liberals or Conservatives. In *Martín Flores* a priest holds this idea: "Father Ramírez found a profound harmony between religion and progress, between a moderate Catholicism and a democratic republic."[18] *Un drama íntimo* (1870), written in diary form, consists of what the author claims in his introduction is a "true story" and contains Samper's defense of social justice. The unfolding of events in *Florencio Conde* (1875) delineates the paragon of a Liberal (or progressive Conservative) understanding of how Colombian society should operate. The protagonist, Florencio Conde, is the son of a former black slave and a white woman. His father, when a slave in the mines of Antioquia, worked extra on his own time, eventually becoming wealthy and independent. Florencio Conde, a model student, received an excellent education. As a youth, however, the aristocratic family of the woman he loves rejects him. With continued work and discipline, Florencio Conde obtains the social position deemed necessary by her family and in the end triumphantly marries her. Samper questions the prejudices the upper class holds against the mulatto of less social prestige; he also demonstrates an unequivocal faith in education and progress. *Clemencia* (1879) and

Coriolano (1879) are moralistic works that demonstrate the devastating effects of the lack of education, both for individuals and for society as a whole. The title of *El poeta soldado* (1880) embodies the circumstances of most of the intellectuals and politicians of the second half of the nineteenth century whose participation in the ideological dialogue frequently included time on the battlefield. Moreover, the protagonist's role as writer underscores the self-consciousness of much Highland fiction (see chapter 3). *El poeta soldado* appeared during Samper's turn to the Conservatives, and in this novel he propounds Conservative principles: The Catholic and Conservative protagonist, through his own efforts, raises his status in society and fights heroically in the Conservative rebellion of 1876–77. This novel, as well as Samper's other work, emanates from a fundamentally realist impulse, with some romantic clichés in the dialogue and plot.

Felipe Pérez's Liberal critique and progressive vision, as noted in his previous fiction, continued in other historical novels, *Los jigantes* (1875), *Estela o los mirajes* (1877), *El piloto de Huelva* (1877), *Los pecados sociales* (1878), *Carlota Corday* (1881), *Imina* (1881), and *Sara* (1883). *Los jigantes* is set in Colombia, but in the pre-independence period. The author's progressive attitudes are evident when the narrator depicts Bogotá as a city undergoing desirable changes in the 1870s.[19] *Carlota Corday* is a historical novel with romantic overtones set in late eighteenth-century France; Pérez's ideological statement is communicated by means of his implicit critique of problems such as political fanaticism. Pérez uses Colombia as the setting for *Sara*, a denunciation of the 1880s Conservative regime. The unfair recruitment of soldiers to battle in the civil wars is just one of the governmental practices that the narrator condemns in *Sara*. The narrator excoriates the Conservative government with statements such as "Men are equal before the law; nevertheless, the law isn't always equal before men."[20] This injustice is multiplied, as the narrator explains, by the fact that the wealthy can free themselves of their military obligations. According to the implied author's norms in *Sara*, the Liberal Utopia, with an essentially good-willed humanity living in harmony, could be achieved through education. The only mediating factors, providing the novel's romantic overtones, are the contradictions and mysteries of the soul.

European Romanticism was particularly important in the early part of this 1863 to 1885 period and was evident in Temístocles Avella Mendoza's *Los tres Pedros* (1864) and *Anacoana* (1865). Avella Mendoza was a Liberal journalist who, in addition to several brief novels, wrote poetry, history, and political essays. Both novels of this period were brief historical works set in the Colonial era. *Los tres Pedros*, which appeared originally in *El Mosaico*, is based on anecdotes from the tenth chapter of Rodríguez Freile's *El carnero*. *Los tres Pedros* depicts Colonial life as romantic spectacle, relating the horrendous crimes of passion committed in pursuit of the "perverse" woman, Inés de Hinojosa.[21] Colonial society here is basically ideal—a "golden age"—except for the occasional moral infractions that are committed by deviant individuals of the aristocracy. Avella Mendoza explicitly censures the Colonial elite in his brief sketch of a novel, *Anacoana*, in which a Spanish governor attempts to interfere in a Colombian love affair. The atrocities committed by the Spaniards end when the protagonist-lover's men defeat the governor in battle. The Indian princess Anacoana enters in a subplot, which also functions as an ideologeme to denounce the Spanish power structure and to extol the Indians, who, according to the narrator, were "more civilized than the conquerors."[22]

José Caicedo Rojas and José David Guarín were marginal to the political dialogue and militancy cultivated by most of the writers of the period. They were known, above all, as writers of *cuadros de costumbres*, each having composed some of the most memorable sketches of the genre. Despite their marginality to the political process, their brief pieces and their novel-length fiction served the patriotic function of much Conservative writing of the period. Caicedo Rojas was an individual tied to the past whom Rafael Maya described as a "model of correct and Hispanic writers."[23] Spanish heritage is evident in the title of his major novel, *Don Alvaro* (1871), which is set in the Colonial period. As in the case of much historical fiction written by Conservatives and set in the Colonial period, this hierarchical society seems ideal, with the exception of occasional personal excesses that temporarily upset the social order. One of the most elaborate and detailed celebrations of Colonial society, *Don Alvaro* encouraged Rafael Maya to describe it as one of the best historical novels ever written in Colombia.[24] Guarín's *Las tres semanas* (1884), in contrast, celebrates the period contemporary with the author, describing patriotic festivities such as that of the Fiesta de la Virgen del Carmen in Bogotá in 1880, the first year of Núñez's Conservative administration. With respect to the *costumbrista* writing of Caicedo Rojas and Guarín, they were fascinated with the opportunity to write casually and publish quickly and considered writing an end in itself.[25] This attitude concurs with the generally self-conscious tradition of Highland writing cultivated from the nineteenth century (see chapter 3).

Soledad Acosta de Samper, like Caicedo Rojas and Guarín, wrote from a position of marginality to the political process. In fact, she once affirmed in an essay that, as a woman, she should lend her services writing novels, for men took charge of the political sphere: "While the masculine part of society occupies itself with politics, remaking the laws, and tending to the material progress of these republics, wouldn't it be nice if the feminine part occupied itself in creating a new literature?"[26] This statement, published in the 1890s, represented an acceptance, near the end of her career, of her prescribed role in nineteenth-century Colombian society as a woman and as a novelist. Her work, consisting of over twenty novels, has been almost completely ignored by readers and critics, despite its volume and the author's impressive handling of the craft of fiction as it was conceived by nineteenth-century standards. Judging the aesthetic value of Acosta de Samper's *El corazón de la mujer* (1869) according to the same traditional criteria that have been applied to *María*, *Manuela*, and *Frutos de mi tierra* (narrative technique, depth of psychological presentation, and the like) and setting aside political contingencies, the reader would in all likelihood conclude that these are the four "major" novels of the nineteenth century.

Acosta de Samper began her literary career in a secondary role as expected of a nineteenth-century Colombian woman, translating French novels into Spanish. She studied in Nova Scotia and Paris, and from 1858 to 1863 travelled in Europe and Peru with her husband, José María Samper. She was a fervent Catholic who envisioned the ideological function of her writings as teaching polite customs and Catholic moral principles to the Colombian masses less educated and Catholic than she. In an 1895 essay on the mission of the woman writer in Spanish America, Acosta de Samper explained her ideological project: "What is the woman's mission in the world? Undoubtedly to soften the customs, to moralize and to *Christianize* societies."[27] She believed that Colombian women should be educated in these principles and that society should treat these "correctly" educated women equal to men. In 1878 she founded the periodical *La Mujer*, the first Colombian magazine under the auspices of women. Within the context of nineteenth-century Colombia, her positions on customs, morality, and women made Acosta de Samper an exceptional intellectual and even a progressive. Her novel *El corazón de la mujer* relates six interconnected stories of six different women who suffer under the still Colonial order of early nineteenth-century Colombian society. Most of the plots involve women who are punished and suffer because of arranged marriages, a social custom associated in these stories with the Spanish Colonial order. Despite the suffering of these women under the power of patriarchal male figures, of their families, and of the Church, they consistently resist and survive as figures stronger than men. Her novels *Dolores* (1867) and *Teresa la limeña* (1868) offer the same basic ideologeme that postulates a female existence of value only inasmuch as it nurtures males.[28] Her other novels are romantic historical works.[29] *Gil Bayle* (1876) was the first of several historical works set in medieval and Renaissance Spain.

Compared to the prolific Soledad Acosta de Samper, Eugenio Díaz and Próspero Pereira Gamba were of relatively little novelistic importance during the 1863 to 1885 period. Nevertheless, they contributed to the ideological enterprises of the time by publishing novels. Whereas many of the novelists discussed in this 1863 to 1885 period posited a Liberal Utopia, Eugenio Díaz's novels expressed a yearning for the Hellenic/Catholic Arcadia. *El rejo de enlazar* (1873) evokes genteel life on two rural estates, depicting the quaint customs of this rural setting that are brutally interrupted by Liberal revolts. One character in the novel observes that the new Liberal constitutions are attacks against good customs. Melo's revolution of 1854 is the focus of the novel's conflict; by the end peace and order are established and the desired marriages celebrated. *Los aguinaldos en Chapinero* (1873) describes Christmas customs as they had been practiced in middle-class Bogotá. Próspero Pereira Gamba's *Amores de estudiante* (1865), like *El rejo de enlazar*, fictionalizes the consequences of Colombian life interrupted by civil war, but in this case a student love affair overshadows the political conflict.

During the period from 1886 to 1909 a confluence of the utopian and arcadian projects resulted in the political solution identified as the Regeneration and its cultural equivalent, the Athens of South America. Although it is impossible to ascertain exactly when the concept of an Athens of South America originated, it reached broad acceptance at the turn of the century.[30] Many of the distinctions between Liberals and Conservatives that had held in the ideologically lively 1860s were no longer viable; by the time of the Regeneration former Liberals José María Samper and Rafael Núñez had joined the Conservatives and former Conservative Jorge Isaacs had become an active Liberal leader. The ideology of the Catholic Church and Conservative humanist cultural values, symbolized by the very phrase "Athens of South America," were in power.

According to official rhetoric, the basic goals of the Regeneration were to reestablish national unity and to restore the Catholic Church to a prominent institutional role. A standard view of the period has emphasized the conflict between liberty and tyranny or between reason and authority. Certainly Liberals were politically repressed during this period, as demonstrated by the activity of La Gruta Simbólica, later novelized by Clímaco Soto Borda. Nevertheless, a recent reevaluation of the Regeneration argues convincingly that it was not an abstract philosophical conflict between two political parties but a coalition of elites created by specific economic factors, primarily the crisis in the tobacco and quinine economies of the second half of the nineteenth century.[31]

This coalition of upper-class groups undertook the task of civilizing the middle class according to elite tastes by organizing for the first time numerous literary groups and by actively diffusing literature through books and magazines. Such literary *tertulias* met frequently in turn-of-the-century Bogotá and Medellín. The aristocracy had access to European classics and the latest European publications, and during the Regeneration the ruling elite undertook the first of several institutional projects to popularize literature with the middle classes; from 1894 to 1910 Jorge Roa edited the *Biblioteca Popular*, which consisted of 179 titles, 69 by Colombian authors. Most of the Colombian authors included were gentleman-scholars, such as Pombo and the two Caros, rather than novelists, although some fiction writers were included.

The major intellectual figures of the 1886 to 1909 period were Rafael Núñez (1825–1894), Miguel Antonio Caro (1843–1909), Rufino José Cuervo (1844–1911), and José Asunción Silva (1865–1896). Núñez was president and Caro his vice-president who later became president. Both also wrote poetry and have been considered the "official" poets of the period. Núñez composed the "Himno Nacional," the present-day national anthem. This song is a text parallel to the Constitution of 1886, which, in turn, became the instrument for the political legitimization of the Regeneration.[32] These four leading intellectual figures of the Regeneration were not known as novelists but rather as poets and scholars of the language. An exception was Silva's one novel of *modernista* aesthetic, *De sobremesa* (1896).

Eustaquio Palacios, Soledad Acosta de Samper, José Manuel Marroquín, Tomás Carrasquilla, and José María Vargas Vila were the most recognized novelists of the 1886 to 1909 period. Palacios, Acosta de Samper, and Marroquín were writers committed to the Regeneration. An upper-class intellectual from the Greater Cauca, Palacios evoked the aristocratic Colonial order in a rural setting of his region in *El alférez real* (1886), and the novel's denouement reaffirms this order: The protagonist discovers a previously unknown aristocratic pedigree, allowing him to wed the upper-class woman he desires. Acosta de Samper was more concerned with essays and bibliographies than fiction during this period, but she did publish the novels *Los piratas en Cartagena* (1886) and *Una holandesa en América* (1888). She defended fiction rather than the philosophical essay as an expression of ideas.[33] Even though she claims to be writing against an eighteenth-century mindset, this prologue is in fact a defense of the novel during a period when poetry carried social prestige and the essay yielded immediate political impact. *Los piratas en Cartagena* is a historical expression of the Regeneration's ideological program. The early Colombian novels, often written by Liberals, had condemned aspects of the Spanish conquest and its Colonial order. *Los piratas en Cartagena* defends Spain, dramatizing the criminal acts of the British and French pirates during the Colonial period. Acosta de Samper identified her book as a Regeneration project and embellished it with a dedication to President Rafael Núñez "as public testimony of the great admiration and friendship extended to the regenerator of the nation."[34] Núñez's response alludes to the political links that bind the two in their "work of national salvation." The novel then relates a series of historically based anecdotes centered in Cartagena from the sixteenth to the eighteenth centuries. *Una holandesa en América* (a revision of the earlier *La holandesa en América*), set in the 1850s, relates the female protagonist's experiences while travelling from Holland to Colombia and experiencing the political conflicts associated with Melo. In addition to debunking some aspects of the romantic novel, *Una holandesa en América* contrasts an idealized European vision of Latin America with the violent social and political realities of nineteenth-century Colombia.

Marroquín was a Conservative, the acting president of Colombia from 1898 to 1904, a prolific *costumbrista*, and the author of four novels. Described as "always correct" and "probably the best of the Colombian *costumbristas*," Marroquín's work served, among other functions, that of teaching proper manners to the middle-class reading public.[35] Late in his career he wrote the four novels *Blas Gil* (1896), *El moro* (1897), *Entre primos* (1897), and *Amores y leyes* (1898), all of which could also be called uniformly "correct" and *castizo*. In fact, Marroquín's contemporary José María Rivas Groot, in a note on *Blas Gil*, compared him to Spanish writers from Spain's Golden Age as well as Valera and Pardo Bazán. Marroquín's novels respond to a realistic impulse and to a patriotic need to support the

Regeneration project. *Blas Gil*, written in the Spanish picaresque tradition, questions some practices of Colombian politics and government. Nevertheless, the implied author's norms are essentially conservative, for the narrator/protagonist takes a cynical view of the progress of turn-of-the-century Colombia. *El moro* ends on a similar note. On the novel's second page the narrator-protagonist reveals himself as a horse, a technical device that allows for amusing and occasionally irreverent commentary on Colombian society. The narrative situation also allows for the moralization that lays bare Marroquín's ideology. In the end, "Progress: Colombian Transportation Company" replaces the nineteenth-century horse with mechanical transportation. Incipient modernity leaves the narrator-protagonist, as well as Marroquín, nostalgically contemplating a more genteel nineteenth-century life. *Entre primos* also contrasts urban Bogotá with earlier rural life on large estates. In *Amores y leyes* Marroquín, as a Regeneration ideologue, defends Catholic marriages in Colombia.

The early fiction of Tomás Carrasquilla and José María Vargas Vila was not ideologically coterminous with the Regeneration; Vargas Vila's was a strident Liberal voice that wrote in direct opposition to it. Carrasquilla's *Frutos de mi tierra* (1896), like the fiction of Marroquín, communicates an awareness of signs of modernity in Colombia and expresses nostalgic attitudes toward a disappearing rural past. The narrator of *Frutos de mi tierra*, however, is more often satirical about his region's society and more progressive about its local culture, assimilating oral and popular culture into the novel. Vargas Vila not only expressed the irreverent attitudes of anti-Regeneration intellectuals such as Antioquia's Carrasquilla and the Highland's Clímaco Soto Borda but continually offended the upper class. If Marroquín embodied the Regeneration ideal of the gentleman-scholar who wrote well (i.e., manipulated the craft of fiction adroitly in an ideologically acceptable fashion), Vargas Vila was his antithesis. Much of Vargas Vila's "craft" consisted of an amalgam of romantic commonplaces and the language of the *modernismo* in vogue among Bogotá's more cosmopolitan intellectuals. One of Colombia's most fecund and widely read novelists ever, he never wrote a work considered "major." During this period he published *Aura o las violetas* (1889), *Flor de fango* (1895), *Ibis* (1900), *Alba roja* (1901), *Las rosas de la tarde* (1901), and *La simiente* (1905). These novels contain scandalous plots, typically embellished with sexual practices considered taboo during the period, thus making them prohibited reading for generations of Colombian students. They were also viewed as literarily unacceptable for Regeneration intellectuals and their Conservative heirs.

The years from 1910 to 1929 were characterized by Conservative domination and by the empowerment of the Athens of South America as well as its swan song. Following the Regeneration examples and despite such irreverent writers as Vargas Vila and Soto Borda, literature continued in its respected role of moral ideology. The writer and Conservative president Marco Fidel Suárez was perhaps the most prominent example of the socially beneficial effects of writing, as his essayistic production contributed to his own social acceptance by the elite. He was the last president to personify the ideal of the Hellenic/Catholic Arcadia in the Athens of South America. Or, stated in another way, one historian has described Suárez as the last representative of the pastoral nation.[36]

1910 to 1929 was a period of unprecedented peace, never achieved before or after in Colombia, and of vital socioeconomic changes in the 1920s. After the War of a Thousand Days at the turn of the century, no conflicts of national scope took place until the roots of La Violencia began to appear in certain rural areas, such as Caldas, in the 1930s. Signs of modernity were the establishment of the national airline Sociedad Colombo Alemana de Transportes Aéreos (Scadta) in 1919 and the first radio transmission in 1925. With respect to culture, several regional publishing houses began to print novels and distribute them regionally. The national newspaper *El Tiempo* initiated publication of a Sunday literary supplement in 1923 and *El Espectador*, the other national newspaper, made its debut with a weekly literary supplement the following year.

Two generations of intellectuals are often placed in this period— the Generación del Centenario and the Generación de Los Nuevos. Following the Spanish idea of an organic national literature developed by successive generations since the Generation of 98 and in accordance with generational theory as set forth by Juan José Arrom in 1963 in his study published in Bogotá, Colombian intellectuals have assigned to these two generations the task of producing an organic national literature.[37] Abel Naranjo Villegas, for example, in his study of Colombian generations delineates seven generations which supposedly carried forth the task of national leadership and construction from the independence to the 1980s.[38] Ernesto Cortes Ahumada, in a study published in 1968, outlines twelve generations supposedly in control of Colombia's national destiny from 1795 to 1990. Cortes Ahumada identifies numerous intellectuals in power from

1900 to 1930—basically the Generación del Centenario—including, among others, forty-one politicians (including Clímaco Soto Borda), seventy-eight journalists, forty-four poets, twenty-three fiction writers, eighteen essayists, twenty-six historians, twelve orators, and eight members of the ecclesiastical hierarchy. A lengthy list could be made of the generation corresponding to Los Nuevos in the 1920s, headed by the poets León de Greiff and Rafael Maya.

There are several grievous problems, however, with this conceptualization of Colombian intellectual life and literary activity as part of an organic and generational march toward a national literature. The most serious issue, already rehearsed in the first chapter of this study, is Colombia's regionalism. Many intellectuals participating in this generational march of Colombia's presumably national literature in fact had relatively little contact with one another. One reminder of regional dichotomies can be appreciated by recalling that during the presidency of the Catholic humanist Suárez, Ramón Vinyes was publishing the avant-garde magazine *Voces* in Barranquilla, disseminating in the Costa an awareness of the European writers in fashion. Despite the supposed generational unity of the time, enormous differences separated Barranquilla's intellectuals reading the poetry of European Futurists and Highland writers following the intellectual leadership of Suárez. With respect to Los Nuevos, in reality they were a small group of poets, not a truly national literary phenomenon; indeed, several intellectuals well acquainted with the period have questioned the idea of Los Nuevos as a truly coherent literary generation.[39]

No women novelists of the 1910 to 1930 period attained the stature of Soledad Acosta de Samper, but distinguished female writers made notable inroads into Colombia's patriarchal society during the 1920s. María Eastman, Fita Uribe, and María Cano, three important writers from Antioquia, began publishing their political and journalistic articles in the 1920s. In 1924 *El Tiempo* inaugurated its "Feminine Page," and in the same decade the Gimnasio Femenino was founded, thereby offering the same classic education for chosen women as had been the practice for upper-class men.[40]

The major novelist of the period, in accordance with important political contingencies, was unquestionably José Eustasio Rivera. These contingencies revolve around Colombia's nationalism of the 1920s; nationalistic attitudes resulted in attempts to establish a "national culture" of varying expressions. The national hymn was adopted in 1920 and lengthy debates on the existence of a national music were carried out in 1923.[41] Emilio Murillo, Pedro Morales Pino, Guillermo Quevedo, and Luis A. Calvo participated in the debates, fomenting a genuinely national "Colombian" music. Similarly, Antonio Alvarez Lleras, Luis Enrique Osorio, and Rafael Burgos forged a national theater, and in 1927 a national film company was founded. A missing link for a "national culture," of course, was the novel. Rivera's *La vorágine* was the timely response, and the overwhelmingly nationalistic reaction to it has virtually precluded any question in Colombia about its authentic value. Since its publication, *La vorágine* has been the national novel of the Athens of South America; as one respected Colombian critic pointed out in 1924, it was a novel predestined at its birth to be a success.[42] It was, in addition, the novel Colombia had urgently awaited, the one readers were swift and definitive to extol as the finest example of the genre in their national literature. Luis Eduardo Nieto Caballero proclaimed in 1924 that it was one of the "definite books of the tropics" that all patriots should have in their homes.[43] Another of the early reviews concluded with reference to the book's contribution to conserving national culture and to its patriotism.[44] Antonio Gómez Restrepo, one of the most authoritative voices of Colombian literature for several decades, concluded his review, written in early 1925, with the prognosis that *La vorágine* would remain "one of the most typical and original works of our national literature."[45] As the writer seemingly predestined to become Colombia's literary celebrity, Rivera had conceived one of the most self-consciously "literary" works to have been produced in the Highland region (see analysis in chapter 3). A relatively unconnected grouping of regions, suffering from a generally provincial local literary scene, finally had a legitimate "national" novel.

Rivera adroitly exploited the public image of himself as poet and aesthete, a self-characterization he further promoted in his depiction of protagonist Arturo Cova in *La vorágine*. Logically enough for the times, many readers failed to make (the fundamentally New Critical) distinction between author and narrator. In contrast, Carrasquilla's idea of a national novel project was based on an exaltation of regional values, rather than personal image, and as far as he was concerned, Rivera's novel was nothing more than a shambles. Carrasquilla's regionalist attitudes should also be understood as a reaction against the central power exercised by the humanists in the Athens of South America.[46]

In 1906, Carrasquilla proclaimed a national literary independence, calling for a modern, national novel not based on foreign models.[47] Despite the allusions to modernity and newness, Carrasquilla's fictional practice itself was, paradoxically, quite traditional—fundamentally a paean of nineteenth-century rural Antioquian values and its oral and popular culture. His novel *Grandeza* (1910) deals with Medellín's turn-of-the-century nouveaux riches and relates the eventual financial ruin of the female protagonist, who becomes obsessed with her daughters. Negating the elitist aestheticism of the Bogotá intellectuals, Carrasquilla states in his preface that *Grandeza* is a book of few aesthetic concerns—only some notes on his milieu.[48] *La marquesa de Yolombó* (1928), however, synthesizes Carrasquilla's national novel project based on the regional values found in eighteenth-century small-town Antioquia.

Clímaco Soto Borda, unlike Rivera and Carrasquilla, never aspired to write the national novel. Rather than attempting to placate the literary establishment and its political counterparts, Soto Borda engaged in a counter-discourse in opposition to the Regeneration, which was in power when he was composing *Diana cazadora* (1915). Engaging in a literary critique of good taste, liberals such as Soto Borda met regularly for *tertulias* with the group La Gruta Simbólica to speak and write satirically of the Conservative government in power. The characters of *Diana cazadora*, like the participants in La Gruta Simbólica, are oppressed by what the narrator identifies as the *ratonera regeneradora*. Soto Borda also satirizes Bogotá's first signs of modernity, portraying this nascent growth in crisis. In addition, he ridicules the Catholic Church, an institution likewise associated, of course, with the Regeneration.

Other novelists of the 1910 to 1929 period were Antioquians Arturo Suárez and Luis López de Mesa, Highland writers José María Vargas Vila and Daniel Samper Ortega, and Gregorio Sánchez Gómez from the Greater Cauca. Suárez and Sánchez Gómez were prolific, the first generation of mediocre professional craftsmen of fiction who, with the proliferation of printing presses and the growth of a middle-class reading public, forged ahead with careers similar in many ways to those of modern professional novelists. Neither offended middle-class readers. Suárez, setting most of his novels in rural Antioquia, was a defender of the large landowners and the conservative values of the Church.[49] Sánchez Gomez fascinated his reading public with superficial and stereotyped psychological portrayals of individuals who suffered the consequences of breaking society's norms. López de Mesa carried the psychology of characterization to more substantive proportions in his novels *La tragedia de Nilse* (1928) and *La biografía de Gloria Etzel* (1929).

Daniel Samper Ortega and Vargas Vila represented opposite poles of the period's ideological dialogue. Samper Ortega dedicated himself to imparting good manners, fostering the education of the masses. He felt mass education would result in social reform, and he attempted to educate the public through both his pedagogical activity and his novels. Vargas Vila, on the other hand, published several fictions celebrating the social aberrations that his irreverent and sometimes perverse characters practiced. Literature was performing several functions by the early twentieth century, but the novels that received official acceptance functioned as moral ideology. Obviously, Suárez, Sánchez Gómez, and Samper Ortega appeared more frequently in official publications and literary histories than did the contumacious Vargas Vila.

From 1930 to 1946 a series of liberal governments sponsored a process of modernization, Liberal reform being particularly dramatic under Alfonso López Pumarejo's Revolución en Marcha. The most widely recognized literature, however, continued to be elitist, Conservative, and for the most part poetry. And the most venerated poet even into the 1940s was Guillermo Valencia, the turn-of-the-century Conservative man of letters.[50] The novel, often written by Liberals, functioned as a relatively minor genre, for Colombian literature was viewed primarily as a generational succession of poets destined to communicate their immutable and universal message. After the national frenzy generated by *La vorágine*, some writers attempted to imitate it.

Following literary history as it is often conceived, the reader of Colombian literature will conclude that the literature of this period was carried forward by the generation of Piedra y Cielo and soon thereafter by the generation of Cántico. The poet Jorge Rojas in effect launched the Piedra y Cielo group in 1939 by publishing an ongoing collection of poetry using the same name. The poets Rojas, Eduardo Carranza, Arturo Camacho Ramírez, Carlos Martín, Tomás Vargas Osorio, and Gerardo Valencia are commonly placed in this generation of writers, who espoused inspiration from the poetry of Juan Ramón Jiménez, Rafael Alberti, and Gerardo Diego.[51] Already in 1944 the Cántico group (in obvious homage to Jorge Guillén) was established by Jaime Ibáñez. One result of such established generations or groups is that they often provoked "national" polemics, thereby offering the opportunity to justify their identity—a process of self-institutionalization. Consequently, polemics around the Piedra y Cielo poets, such as the debate fomented by Juan Lozano y Lozano in 1940, only contributed to the group's legitimacy as authentic representatives of Colombian literature of the time.[52] Those who questioned this legitimacy maintained that these poets were narcissistically obsessed with poetry and marooned from history. Whatever one's position with respect to these two groups may be, it should be kept in mind that in reality they were a relatively small group of poets based in culturally powerful Bogotá.

Coterminous with these poets, a small group of almost uniformly Conservative critics came forth during this period with a body of work, all of which espoused an organic national literary tradition in a land historically divided by region and a multiplicity of other factors. On the one hand, a series of national literary histories appeared: José Joaquín Ortega Torres's *Historia de la literatura colombiana* (1935), Antonio Gómez Restrepo's *Historia de la literatura colombiana* (1938–1945), Javier Arango Ferrer's *La literatura colombiana* (1940), Baldomero Sanín Cano's *Letras colombianas* (1944), Rafael Maya's *Consideraciones críticas sobre la literatura colombiana* (1944), Gustavo Otero Muñoz's *Historia de la literatura colombiana* (1945). The most authoritative of these books of traditional literary history and critical essays, the Conservative Gómez Restrepo's history of Colombian literature, carries such implicit suppositions as the following: The literature written during the Spanish Colonial period marks an important (perhaps the most important) period of Colombian literature; the Colombian novel is a minor genre; the contemporary Colombian novel is virtually nonexistent. The publication of the one hundred volumes of the *Selección Samper Ortega de Literatura Colombiana* from 1935 to 1937 attempted to reaffirm the existence of an organic national literary tradition. However, because most of these volumes contained revered poetry and essays inscribed by the Conservative cultural elite, it contributed little to the idea of a contemporary Colombian novel.

Given the Conservative shadow of Valencia's poetry, the visibility on the cultural scene of the different generations of poets, and the resonances of *La vorágine*, it is logical that the Colombian novel in general did not fit the political contingencies necessary for its blossoming on the national scene. Colombia certainly did not provide favorable ground for the cultivation of the modern, innovative fiction that began to appear in the 1940s throughout Latin America, from the stories of Borges to the novels of Asturias and Carpentier. In 1941 a polemic did arise when Tomás Vargas Osorio advanced a set of nationalistic and essentially traditional principles as a paragon for Colombian fiction, negating any foreign influences. "Foreignness," of course, was a key word for European modernity. Paradoxically, Vargas Osorio's own fictions were among the most modern and cosmopolitan to be written during the period, but some less capable writers used his nationalistic principles as a justification for their own anachronistically traditional production.[53] Colombia would not have a truly modern novel until García Márquez, following the lead of European and North American moderns, published *La hojarasca* in 1955.

Active novelists during the Liberal Republic were César Uribe Piedrahita, Eduardo Zalamea Borda, Bernardo Arias Trujillo, and José Antonio Osorio Lizarazo. Uribe Piedrahita, Zalamea Borda, and Arias Trujillo sustained patterns established by Rivera and other Latin American *criollistas.* All three addressed issues of national identity and social conflict in a rural setting. Unlike Rivera, however, who virtually ignored one of the most essential elements of national culture, its oral component, Uribe Piedrahita, Zalamea Borda, and Arias Trujillo exhibit a sharp awareness of oral culture and interest in assimilating it into their national novel projects. Rivera, like many Highland writers, was far too fascinated with his self-conscious act of participating in writing culture to accept the predominant orality that surrounded him. Even though Zalamea Borda has moments of self-consciousness in *Cuatro años a bordo de mí mismo*, he also displays a fascination with the oral culture of the Costa.

José Antonio Lizarazo and Luis Tablanca questioned the ideological underpinnings of the power structure. They wrote novels of social protest. Osorio Lizarazo was prolific, publishing some twenty books, including a dozen novels. During the 1930s and 1940s he was fully committed to fiction of denunciation; in 1938 he published the essay "The Social Essence of the Novel," proposing that the only legitimate function of the novel is social.[54] It was a function that Osorio Lizarazo carried out in *La casa de vecindad* (1930), *La cosecha* (1935), and *Hombres sin presente* (1938). In *La casa de vecindad* the narrator-protagonist, living at the margins of society in a pension home for the destitute, is totally destroyed by his milieu. At the beginning of the novel he is unemployed, desperate, and suffering solitude. Unable to establish a relationship with a woman and to support a young girl he adopts as a daughter, he ultimately becomes demoralized and a beggar. He never reaches an understanding of his situation and concludes that a socialist revolution is not the solution because "the world is made poorly."[55] Like much Highland fiction, *La casa de vecindad* is also a self-conscious novel. *Hombres sin presente* has an urban setting too but is more clearly didactic and programmatic in its social message: It is a defense of urban workers and their right to strike. Set in a coffee-growing region, *La cosecha* is a denunciation of rural violence and land manipulation by the upper class.

Luis Tablanca also wrote novels denouncing social injustice, his *Una derrota sin batalla* (1933) having been called "one of the best novels to have come out of Colombia in recent years."[56] It relates a story of political corruption and thus functions as part of the ideological dialogue in which Tablanca, Osorio Lizarazo, Uribe Piedrahita, and others participated during the 1930s. Deceitful and unscrupulous politicians involved with local provincial politics cause such disillusionment on the part of the protagonist that he resigns from his political position almost immediately. Consequently, his career and Colombian politics of the early 1930s are indeed "una derrota sin batalla" (a defeat without a battle).

Tablanca's novel and a series of works that appeared in the 1940s seriously questioned the ideological underpinnings of the supposedly dynamic and progressive modern state, López Pumarejo's Revolución en Marcha. The authors of these works, including Rafael Gómez Picón, Ernesto Camargo Martínez, Jaime Ardila Casamitjana, and Jaime Ibáñez, address middle-class concerns to a middleclass readership, for rather than novelizing social issues directly, in the fashion of Osorio Lizarazo and Tablanca, they communicate a sense of the emotional and psychological experience of Colombia's middle class in this period. Unfortunately, their fiction did not fit the political contingencies of either the cultural right (with its generations of poets) or the Liberals in power. Gómez Picón's *45 relatos de un burócrata con cuatro paréntesis* (1941) deals with the tedious and stultifying life of a small-time bureaucrat; the suffocation the protagonist feels—if seen as typical of the lower middle class—was unleashed in 1948 with the *bogotazo* and the ensuing violence. *De la vida de Iván el mayor* (1942) by Camargo Martínez relates the process of the protagonist's psychological disintegration. And in Ardila Casamitjana's *Babel* (1943) a young intellectual continually questions his role in a society still dominated by the rhetoric of the Athens of South America.

Gabriel García Márquez claimed in 1960 that Colombian literature was a national fraud.[57] This comment should be read exactly as it was intended: as a political statement about a literary establishment that has supported its mediocre poets—such as Guillermo Valencia—as national monuments and as an assault upon a weak critical tradition that has been either unable or unwilling to recognize works of genuine value. During the 1947 to 1974 period the century-long insecurity over the status of the novel persisted. In his 1960 essay, García Márquez maintained that the Colombian novel had reached a point of nothingness; the late 1950s, indeed, were not fruitful years for the genre. In defense of those novelists who had been writing, a foreign scholar observed in 1947 that "with an almost blind regard for their great lyric poetry, Colombian critics in their treatises on literature have been willing to accord to the novel only a minor place."[58]

Among the most significant events in the field of the novel during the 1947 to 1974 period were the publication of Antonio Curcio Altamar's *Evolución de la novela en Colombia* in 1957, the explosion onto the scene of García Márquez's *Cien años de soledad* in 1967, and the rise of the first modern publishing firms for novels. Curcio Altamar's now classic study of the Colombian novel legitimized the concept of an organic literary tradition—just the opposite of his contemporary García Márquez's view of Colombian literature as a fraud. Upon its publication in 1957, *Evolución de la novela en Colombia* was the most ambitious and complete study on the subject. As its title suggests, a theoretical assumption that underlay Curcio Altamar's concept of the Colombian novel is that it has undergone a constant process of "evolution" or "development," a teleological formulation that carries questionable cultural and ideological baggage. It assumes the existence of an organic and always forward-moving "Colombian novel" as a national cultural product without taking into account the issues of regionalism, class, and the political contingencies involved in cultural power. Despite these divisions, Curcio Altamar presents a Colombian novel evolving through the different periods of literary history (realism, Romanticism, etc.) as if Colombia's political and literary history were a replica—albeit a consistently inferior duplication—of that of European nations. This use of the concept of "development" corresponds chronologically to the importation of foreign ideas of "development" in Colombia, in the political and economic spheres, during the late 1940s and 1950s.[59]

The immediate and overwhelming success of *Cien años de soledad*, initially in the Hispanic world from 1967 forward and then in the international community in the 1970s, profoundly shook the foundations of Colombia's literary establishment. Colombian novels had been historically legitimized (or, in most cases, delegitimized) by Conservative literary scholars, or more recently, since the 1950s, in the literary supplement of the major liberal newspaper *El Tiempo*. García Márquez, a middle-class *costeño* without credentials in Colombia's self-perpetuating literary elite, was proclaimed a major writer in the West by an international community of literary scholars, Latin Americanists, and a broad general readership. Even though Isaacs, Rivera, Carrasquilla, and Mejía Vallejo had been recognized beyond Colombian borders, never before had a Colombian writer received such reception abroad. Colombia was overwhelmed by the phenomenon of García Márquez—the best-selling novelist, the jet-set celebrity, the leftist intellectual. The "boom" hit Colombia with a vigor and intensity even more forceful than in the United States and Europe. By the early 1970s the young novelists were publicly lamenting the shadow of García Márquez that weighed on novels seemingly doomed to be either too similar to Macondo or unable to measure up to it. Young writers such as Gustavo Alvarez Gardeazábal, Fanny Buitrago, and Marco Tulio Aguilera Garramuño and later Rafael Humberto Moreno-Durán and Albalucía Angel all responded to this shadow of García Márquez in a different way. By the mid-1970s several postmodern alternatives to the fiction of Macondo began to appear.

The rise of two modern publishing houses, Tercer Mundo Editores and the Editorial Plaza y Janés, enabled Colombian novelists to address a truly national (rather than regional) and even international reading public for the first time. Tercer Mundo began operation in the early 1960s, publishing in the social sciences and literature. The multinational Plaza y Janés took interest in the Colombian novel in the early 1970s and in 1974 published Gustavo Alvarez Gardeazábal's best-seller *El bazar de los idiotas.*

Other factors contributed to the deregionalization (or "nationalization") and modernization of the Colombian novel. The cultural magazine *Mito,* modern and cosmopolitan in impulse, published modern Latin American and European writers from 1955 to 1962, including García Márquez, Alvaro Cepeda Samudio, Octavio Paz, Julio Cortázar, Carlos Fuentes, Alejo Carpentier, Henry Miller, and Vladimir Nabokov. A national prize—the Esso Novel Prize—was awarded to a series of modern novelists during the 1960s, including Alberto Duque López for his experimental and postmodern *Mateo el flautista* (1968). A group of defiant poets, known in the 1960s as the *nadaistas,* rebelling against literary and societal convention, sponsored a prize for innovative novels such as Germán Pinzón's *El terremoto* (1966) and Humberto Navarro's *Los días más felices del año* (1966).

The modern novel was inaugurated in Colombia with the publication of three patently Faulknerian works: García Márquez's *La hojarasca* (1955), Alvaro Cepeda Samudio's *La casa grande* (1962), and Héctor Rojas Herazo's *Respirando el verano* (1962). Each of the three relates stories of the Costa's decadent aristocracy, adopting a plethora of Faulknerian narrative stratagems. *La hojarasca* and *La casa grande* relate to the presence of the American Fruit Company in the Costa: The first deals with the effects of this foreign presence in a formerly traditional town; the latter dramatizes the massacre of striking banana workers by government soldiers (a historical event of 1928).

Other significant contributions to the modern novel in Colombia during this period were Manuel Mejía Vallejo's *El día señalado* (1964), García Márquez's *Cien años de soledad* (1967), Rojas Herazo's *En noviembre llega el arzobispo* (1967), Fanny Buitrago's *Cola de zorro* (1970), Albalucía Angel's *Dos veces Alicia* (1972), and Alvarez Gardeazábal's *Dabeiba* (1973) and *El bazar de los idiotas* (1974). Additional titles include the experimental works *Después de la noche* (1964) by Eutiquio Leal, *El terremoto* by Pinzón, *Los días más felices del año* by Navarro, and *Mateo el flautista* by Duque López.

During this period the political dialogue was effected predominantly in novels of La Violencia, a type of fictionalization so prevalent in the 1950s and 1960s that until the advent of García Márquez's Macondo, the contemporary novel in Colombia was virtually synonymous to "the novel of La Violencia." Over forty such works were published during this period. Generally speaking, readers either uninformed about the political dialogue or uninterested in it will find these novels faulty. Four exceptions to such a generalization were Manuel Zapata Olivella's *La calle 10* (1960), García Márquez's *La mala hora* (1962), Mejía Vallejo's *El día señalado* (1963), and Alvarez Gardeazábal's *Cóndores no entierran todos los días* (1972), all of which communicate experience through narrative strategies that allow the reader the active participation expected in the modern novel. In *La calle 10* and *La mala hora*, Zapata Olivella and García Márquez use the setting of La Violencia but do so by indirect allusion rather than by naming specifics. Many of the earlier novels of La Violencia had been documentary in impulse and frequently laden with crude violence. Zapata Olivella and García Márquez, writing after many of these novels had been published, create more distance between the reader and the concrete historical data. *La calle 10* consists of a series of unrelated scenes; a sense of unity is created by making a peripheral character or event of one scene central to another.[60] After portraying the conditions of the urban poor, *La calle 10* develops a series of circumstances similar to those surrounding the assassination of Gaitán in 1948. The reader of *La mala hora* observes virtually no physical violence; rather, the power in this novel is wielded by language. The oppressive life in an unnamed Colombian town is depicted over a period of seventeen days; the strife between individuals and groups is articulated through conflicts of language in a novel rich in heteroglossia.[61]

Mejía Vallejo and Alvarez Gardeazábal approach La Violencia in a more Faulknerian fashion, both with regard to technique and also to the visibility of physical violence. In *El día señalado*, Mejía Vallejo, like Faulkner, obtains reader involvement by means of structure and changes in point of view. It is not only the tale of a town overtaken by La Violencia as government soldiers pursue rural guerrillas but also relates a personal story of violence. In the end, Mejía Vallejo undermines any strictly partisan interpretation of La Violencia by communicating a sense that the determining factor is not partisan politics but acts of human irrationality. Similarly, in *Cóndores no entierran todos los días* Alvarez Gardeazábal questions previous interpretations of La Violencia as exclusively a Liberal-Conservative conflict. Here the crude brutality of La Violencia is part of a family tradition that often results in inexplicable human behavior.

Some readers have been tempted to identify these four well-crafted novels as nonideological. They are, of course, as ideological as any text, but unlike much of the fiction of the period they communicate their ideological dicta through strategies that eschew explicit statement; functioning as an equipoise of contending attitudes, they invite the reader to reflect upon and accept or reject the then extant interpretations of La Violencia. Most novelists of the period, less distanced from the events at hand, were as directly engaged in the political dialogue as was Eugenio Díaz in *Manuela* and Osorio Lizarazo in his dissonant fiction of the 1930s. The documentary impulse was particularly evident in the early novels of La Violencia such as Pedro Gómez Corena's *El 9 de abril* (1951), which is better read as historical document and essay than as novel. It deals with Gaitán's assassination and the subsequent violence in a land called "Risolandia." Gómez Corena's position on the events at hand is evident from his prefatory note referring to the "nefarious assassination of Doctor Jorge Eliécer Gaitán." In contrast, Alfonso Hilarión Sánchez defends the Conservatives in *Las balas de la ley* (1953), whose narrator-protagonist describes the violence perpetrated by the Liberals during the 1930s and 1940s. Ignacio Gómez Dávila's *Viernes 9* (1953) begins as a story of human relationships among the members of an urban family, but with the assassination of Gaitán the second half becomes an account of human carnage and death. *La ciudad y el viento* (1961) by Clemente Airó is also an urban, small-screen novel that eventually relates episodes of violence, but it ends with a self-conscious note suggesting that the events were perhaps a dream, a fiction.

According to one theorist, violence, when appeased, seeks and always finds a surrogate victim.[62] The culture that excited violence's fury abruptly replaces its victims, who are chosen only because they are vulnerable and close at hand. In novels such as Daniel Caicedo's *Viento seco* (1953) rural violence finds numerous victims as well as surrogate victims; this novel and Alvarez Gardeazábal's *Cóndores no entierran todos los días* contain some of the most powerful passages of victimization in fiction dealing with La Violencia. *Quien dijo miedo* (1960) by Jaime Sanín Echeverri involves a complex interaction among ideologically motivated guerrillas, criminals, and surrogate victims.

Eduardo Caballero Calderón's three novels of La Violencia portray individuals whose lives are affected directly or indirectly by socioeconomic phenomena; they too become victims or surrogate victims of La Violencia. In *El Cristo de espaldas* (1952) a liberal son is accused of having killed his conservative father, and the town's novice priest becomes a surrogate victim when he attempts to defend the son's just cause. The protagonist in *Siervo sin tierra* (1954) succumbs to violence, having died without ever attaining his objective of possessing his own land. *Manuel Pacho* (1962) sets forth its thesis in its epigraph and the epilogue: Any person, no matter how humble, has at least one opportunity in life to achieve hero status.

A review of the fictional treatment of La Violencia provides yet another example of why the novel has always been considered a minor genre in Colombia. Whatever the partisan position or the human condition portrayed in these novels, they were not the kind of literature the upper class preferred to read and disseminate. Most of these novels were written by Liberals and have either passed unnoticed or been adamantly censured by the Conservative critical establishment. Since the 1840s, when the first brief fictionalized political pamphlets were published as novelas, aesthetic value has always been determined to a great extent by political contingencies, from the initial projections of arcadias and utopias to recent radicalized interpretations of La Violencia—a fact which readers must bear in mind when approaching any of the supposedly "major" or "minor" (or known or unknown) Colombian novels. Similarly, one should approach with caution the concept of an organic national literary tradition. From Colombia's history of exceptional regionalism to García Márquez's admonition about the fraud of Colombian literature, many factors render such teleological formulations highly questionable.

Part Two

The Novel in Its Region

Three

The Interior Highland Tradition: From *Manuela* (1858) to *El buen salvaje* (1966)

Bogotá and the Interior Highland Region have been a privileged writing center since the Colonial period and dominant in most areas of literary production since independence. From the beginning of the Colonial era, "culture" in this region's context has implied a literature produced by a relatively small but hypersophisticated lettered elite often active in political life. As former president Alfonso López Michelsen once explained, the presidency of Colombia has always been the ultimate prize for its writers.[1] Bogotá and Tunja flourished as *ciudades letradas*—to use Angel Rama's term once again—and as centers of Spanish literary activity during the Colonial period.[2] One of the major literary figures of that era, Juan de Castellanos (1552– 1607), was a priest in Tunja and remained there his entire life. Tunja also hosted renowned poetry contests. Under the influence of the Jesuits and Dominicans, literary culture blossomed in the monasteries and universities of Tunja and Bogotá. Although largely isolated from cultural movements outside Colombia until well into the twentieth century, Bogotá, the Athens of South America, grew in population to become Colombia's cultural center.

Characteristics of Highland culture are a dominant Spanish heritage, a sophisticated writing culture (frequently self-conscious), and a sparse presence of oral culture in literature. The latter is particularly the case in the twentieth-century novel. The region's indigenous population was decimated during the conquest and Colonial period, and Colombia's Afro-American population has never been, relatively speaking, demographically or culturally significant in Bogotá. Directly linked to Spain's literature, the Highland writers have been relatively uninvolved with the oral and literary cultures of Colombia's other regions. Until the advent of García Márquez's fame in the late 1960s, writers outside of Bogotá have usually been ignored by Highland intellectuals. Jorge Isaacs was the one prominent exception.[3] Consequently, even *Cien años de soledad* was a bestseller in Buenos Aires prior to its arrival in Bogotá.

Bogotá's role as a center of literary activity in the nineteenth century was promoted by literary magazines such as *El Alacrán* (1848). In the 1860s José María Vergara y Vergara founded *El Mosaico*, a seminal literary organ, important not only for the literature it published but also because it brought together writers of diverse tendencies and provided a literary arena for a "national literature" in a nation totally divided by region. An important contribution to the formation of a national literature was the 1867 publication of Vergara y Vergara's history of Colombian literature, the first attempt at synthesizing literature written in Colombia.[4] The literary production of the period was dominated by a *costumbrista* current inherited from Spain which proliferated in the Highland area. Vergara y Vergara and José María Samper were its chief exponents.

The Highland novelistic tradition has been conservative; it produced no novels, for example, equivalent to the avant-garde experimental fiction written by the Contemporáneos in Mexico or their peers in Cuba, Argentina, Chile, and Peru during the 1920s and 1930s.[5] The literary magazines most closely allied with the cultural avant-garde were published in Barranquilla (*Voces*, see chapter 4) and Medellín (*Pánida*, see chapter 5). What can be identified as the nation's most "official" literary language—that of the Highland—has been essentially Hispanic: During the first quarter of the twentieth century, the discourse of power was Hispanic, Conservative, and associated directly with the political hegemony that had as its intellectual component the humanists of the Regeneration.[6] During the Regeneration, to be sure, a contestatory language also persisted, a counter-discourse often censured or ignored, embodied in the writing of José María Vargas Vila and Clímaco Soto Borda.[7]

Highland novelistic production offers four key moments: Eugenio Díaz's *Manuela* (1858), Clímaco Soto Borda's *Diana cazadora* (1915), José Eustasio Rivera's *La vorágine* (1924), and Eduardo Caballero Calderón's *El buen salvaje* (1966). These four novels therefore form the core of this chapter, which takes as its object a consistently self-conscious novelistic tradition.

Manuela (1858) by Eugenio Díaz

The Colombian novel was still in its infancy when Eugenio Díaz began publishing *Manuela* in serial fashion in *El Mosaico*. Literary culture in Bogotá placed more emphasis on printing magazines and newspapers than on publishing novels—no Colombian novel had as yet captured the national consciousness. The few novels published in the Highland region before *Manuela* were simple sketches, more outlines of novels than fully developed fictions. José Joaquín Ortiz's *María Dolores o la historia de mi casamiento* (1841), which Otero Muñoz has identified as the first Colombian novel, was a fifty-page series of abbreviated chapters published in Ortiz's magazine *El Cóndor*. José María Angel Gaitán's *El Doctor Temis* (1851), Felipe Pérez's historical novels *Atahuallpa* (1856), *Huayna Capac* (1856), and *Los Pizarros* (1857), and Juan Francisco Ortiz's *Carolina la bella* (1856) were the only memorable full-length novelistic antecedents to *Manuela* in the Highland region. Anxiety over the novel as a genre was in fact the subject of the lead article of an 1858 issue of the literary magazine *Biblioteca de Señoritas*. The anonymous article, titled "De la Novela," questions the possibility of developing a national literature in Colombia: "Is it possible . . . to raise the building of our national literature? Our country has never excelled in anything other than poetry."[8]

Neither Díaz or his contemporaries in Bogotá clarified *Manuela's* genre status. Díaz himself described *Manuela* simply as a collection of sketches, a statement widely publicized by José María Vergara y Vergara.[9] Even worse, Vergara y Vergara portrayed Díaz as a simple rural type, "a man dressed in a poncho"—a kiss of death in the Highland's elite literary circles, particularly in Bogotá during the subsequent years. Salvador Camacho Roldán, in praising *Manuela*, nevertheless questioned its authentic literary merit, suggesting that its only saving quality was in the veracity of its descriptions.[10] Díaz has been partially vindicated by readers of subsequent generations.[11]

Generally speaking, and with the exception of Bogotá's Conservative elite, mid-nineteenth-century Colombia was more oriented toward the Anglo-American world and France than to its own Spanish heritage. The complex political circumstance of the period reflected the influence of romantic ideas. Romantic and utopian political thinking was predominant.[12] Manuel María Madiedo, an influential intellectual of the period, was a romantic utopian whose political thought was based on vague romantic ideas.[13] The French Revolution of 1848 was the source for a heterogeneous set of ideological concepts, including several that may be called romantic: Bastiant's economic harmony, Lamartine's romantic republicanism, Lammenais's liberal Christianity.[14]

Some of the attitudes demonstrated by Demóstenes, the protagonist in *Manuela*, are typical of the period. *Manuela* appeared in 1858 precisely during a time of intense ideological conflict, but one in which liberalism predominated. The Liberals began with tentative reforms, met formidable resistance in the 1850s, and insisted on their power by writing "their own Liberal world view into the Constitution of 1863."[15] This program contained a standard set of nineteenth-century liberal ideas: the abolition of slavery; freedom of speech, religion, and the press; universal public education; and a laissez-faire economy.[16] In the second half of the century in Colombia, ideology conflicted with sociopolitical reality. Liberals imbibed an integral world view fundamentally at odds with the structure of the society in which they lived.[17]

Demóstenes is a *bogotano* intellectual who arrives in a small provincial town as a representative of the more radical faction of the Liberals, or the *gólgotas*.[18] He is characterized from the opening chapter as, above all else, a man of letters. He soon meets the unlettered Manuela, who is being pursued and persecuted by Tadeo, a *draconiano* or moderate Liberal. Tadeo makes amorous advances, but Manuela loves Dámaso. The basic plot of *Manuela* revolves around Demóstenes' presence in this rural area of Cundinamarca and his observation of the Manuela-Tadeo-Dámaso affair. The narrator provides both occasional scenes of a *costumbrista* nature and lengthy dialogue between Demóstenes and others, usually on political topics. The novel ends with Manuela dying from the fire that Tadeo sets on the day of her marriage to Dámaso, which falls on July 20, the anniversary of Colombian independence.

The melodramatic denouement, in which Manuela desperately marries Dámaso moments before expiring, is only one of the novel's several romantic qualities. To be more precise, *Manuela* contains three typical clichés of the romantic novel: its characterization of women, its presentation of the relationship between man and nature, and some aspects of romantic plot structure. Women are characterized as possessing an ideal female beauty and as weak and helpless victims of destiny and other forces. Human beings and nature are depicted as inextricably bound. Díaz uses some of the conventional techniques of the romantic novel to construct the plot, the most noteworthy being premonitions or auguries of evil.

Díaz's use of these devices, however, is limited: *Manuela* is not preeminently a love story in the romantic tradition. To be a true romantic hero, Demóstenes would have been destined to a passionate love affair, probably with the heroine Manuela; rather, he is consistently granted an intellectual distance from the Dámaso-Manuela-Tadeo affair. Demóstenes becomes infuriated with Tadeo, moreover, for reasons that seem inappropriate in a romantic novel: Rather than being offended for sentimental reasons by Tadeo's intervention, Demóstenes continually expresses outrage over what Tadeo represents ideologically. *Manuela*, then, is not a novel of the conflicts based on love affairs but one of ideological conflict posited in the novel with sufficient clarity for Curcio Altamar to conclude that Díaz did nothing more in *Manuela* than present the ideological battles of the country.[19] The novel conveys ideological conflicts of the Colombia of the 1850s through the protagonist's lengthy political discussions, from commentary by the narrator, and in the characterization. The protagonist's political dialogues are the most unmediated vehicle for conveying ideology. At the outset (in chapter 3), when Demóstenes engages in a dialogue with a priest, he sets forth clearly his Liberal principles with respect to the church. Chapter 9, which, according to its title, "Lecciones de baile" ("Dance Lessons"), should be a *costumbrista* episode, is transformed into a lengthy discussion of the radical Liberal Demóstenes' principles of liberty and equality. It is common to begin with chapter titles and introductory paragraphs that would seem to indicate a romantic or *costumbrista* intention and then to focus the entire chapter on ideological issues; chapter 14 begins, for example, with the romantic title "Lo que puede el amor" ("What Love Can Do") but ends with ideological debate.[20] In chapter 10 Demóstenes expounds one of his favorite global topics, the unjust feudal economic and social system whose Colonial remnants have been left intact in nineteenth-century Colombia.

The treatment of the main characters underscores, above all, their ideological commitments: *All* the principal characters embody political positions. Demóstenes represents the *gólgota* viewpoint and Tadeo the *draconiano*. In an introduction to characters in chapter 9, the narrator clarifies ideological stances, as well as his ideological agenda as storyteller, by describing in detail each character's political leanings.[21]

The significant elements in *Manuela* are not those of Romanticism or *costumbrismo* but the dynamics of oral and written culture that are the vehicle of ideological encounters. On the one hand, Demóstenes epitomizes the *bogotano* intellectual who represents writing culture: His perceptions, modes of thinking, and world view are totally circumscribed by written texts. In contrast, Manuela represents a primary oral culture. She views all situations in an entirely different fashion from the writing culture's Demóstenes.

The conflict between writing culture as embodied in Demóstenes and its oral counterpart surges at the outset. Upon his arrival at an inn, Demóstenes is inscribed as a reader: He reads Eugene Sue's novel in fashion at the time, *Los misterios de París*, and transports in his trunk "los libros y la ropa" (books and clothes; we note the order of these two elements). He reads throughout his evening at the inn, and when he discovers a used book there he exclaims "O Gutenberg! Your sublime discovery has even arrived here!" (Díaz, 14). More signs of the difference between Demóstenes and the local scene appear in the second chapter when the protagonist, absorbed in his books, fails to notice the human contact in the streets (Díaz, 17). Notably, an essential object of the nation's writing culture, the newspaper *El Tiempo*, fails to arrive from Bogotá. In contrast, the local culture emphasizes personal greetings, human contact, popular folk music, and other customs typical of a primary oral culture. When his opponents come to arrest Demóstenes in chapter 17, they take not him but, appropriately enough, his books. Deeply immersed in literary culture, Demóstenes consistently views writing as a panacea for the problems depicted in the novel. Two specific examples of this vision appear in chapters 23 and 24.[22]

Manuela, on the other hand, as the novel's counterpoint to Demóstenes, represents an oral culture. In one of the most indicative passages in the work, in terms of both her oral culture vision and her diction, she responds to a statement of Demóstenes: "Sir, one thing is to crow and another is to lay eggs. I don't believe a lot in those who make noise" (Díaz, 124). This statement exhibits both the commonsensical attitudes and the homeostatic perception that are essential to oral cultures.[23] From this condition, she cannot understand the *historias* that Demóstenes subsequently explains to her: "What are these *historias?* Aren't they stories? Didn't you have some stories on your table?" (Díaz, 312).

The dynamics of oral and written culture are played out in the form of a persistent conflict throughout the novel. Despite his superior formal education, Demóstenes frequently appears inferior to illiterate speakers when this conflict surfaces directly. Manuela's sweet and forceful voice, for example, can communicate ideas better than literate students of rhetoric (Díaz, 89). In another confrontation between these two cultures, Demóstenes fortuitously encounters some peasants on a rural path and speaks with them briefly, exhibiting kindness and respect. Nevertheless, the peasants are suspicious of written ideas (a common response in oral cultures), distinguishing in a commonsensical fashion between abstract ideas and concrete acts: "This city slicker is always talking about equality" (Díaz, 105). Differences between the two cultures appear in one of the novel's most entertaining passages, a dialogue between Demóstenes and an Indian, when it is apparent that Demóstenes' educated vocabulary is incomprehensible to the Indian, who simply repeats what Demóstenes says rather than responding to his questions (Díaz, 321).

As the ingenuous Demóstenes gains experience in the everyday life of rural mid-nineteenth-century Colombia, he begins to understand the differences between the Colombia he knows in written forms—the laws and constitution—and the radically different nation of the oral culture in the rural areas. For instance, he admits that he is surprised to have learned that the laws the lawmakers have approved in Bogotá are not the norm in rural Colombia (Díaz, 218). Although the statement offers no resolution of the conflict between oral and written culture, it suggests Demóstenes' gradual departure from a rigid perception of Colombian reality based exclusively on written texts. The denouement also indicates modification on his part. At the end, he decides to leave for Bogotá, realizing that his very presence is an anomaly and a disturbance (Díaz, 436). The priest with whom he speaks at the end judges the value of his experience in the rural area, his immersion in an oral culture—a value superior to his formal book-bound education abroad. In 1850s Colombia, the local, oral, and concrete reality has predominated over the foreign, the written, and the abstract.

Even the elements of the romantic in *Manuela* serve the ideological confrontation expressed in the opposition between oral and written culture. Authors associated with Romanticism, such as Sir Walter Scott, Espronceda, and Zorilla, are directly linked to the dynamic conflict between cultural ideologies. Romantic literature in this novel is the reading domain of *women:* Females are uniformly the readers of Scott (Clotilde and other women), Espronceda, and Zorilla (Marta and other women). The males in *Manuela* are associated with the highly rational, explicitly political component of writing culture—the Enlightenment texts that inform Demóstenes. For Eugenio Díaz, the ideology seminal to his writing was the exclusive domain of men; women remain romantically idealized as readers of escapism—or as simple preliterates like Manuela.

Manuela presents the story of a nascent republic in which the new nation is conceived as a post-Enlightenment writing culture in the process of developing beyond both an oral culture (the rural Colombia of Manuela) and a traditional writing culture (a "feminine" Romanticism and a conservative Hispanic tradition). Obviously confident in writing, Eugenio Díaz portrays a nation as written document, as Archive.[24] Near the end of *Manuela*, Dr. Jiménez concludes, appropriately enough, that the town and the nation are portrayed in Tadeo's archive, which contains "all the political and religious factions in the country" (Díaz, 432). In the end, post-Enlightenment writing culture is a transient phase in the total written archive: Defeated, Demóstenes leaves for Bogotá.

The protagonist of *Manuela* can be seen as a personification of the transient phase of Liberal domination in Colombia from the 1850s through the 1870s. Even one of the foremost exponents of Liberal politics in Colombia during the period, José María Samper, has described it as an era of "theories and only theories."[25] The ideological dialogue presented by Eugenio Díaz, together with Samper's comment, confirms the proposition that the Liberal worldview of this period was not in touch with the political, social, and economic realities of the time. Unequivocally, *Manuela* represents a rejection of both the aristocratic Colonial order and Romanticism. The more significant domain of conflict in *Manuela* is found, however, in the complex dynamics between oral and writing culture, revealing Liberal ideological underpinnings not fully accommodated in the novelistic world of Eugenio Díaz nor in nineteenth-century Colombia.

Transition (1859–1914) and *Diana cazadora* (1915) by Clímaco Soto Borda

Between the publication of *Manuela* in 1858 and *Diana cazadora* in 1915, momentous literary and political events took place in Colombia; both inform the construction of *Diana cazadora*, which was written at the turn of the century and published later. Jorge Isaacs's *María*, an anomalous novel which surpassed regional and even national boundaries, appeared in 1867. This romantic idyll of the Greater Cauca would serve either as model or as intertextual referent for many writers of all regions of Colombia (and much of the Hispanic world) for the remainder of the century. No other novel, even from the Interior Highland Region, had as much impact in Bogotá as *María* during the second half of the nineteenth century. The major political event, within a constantly turbulent scenario, was the ratification of the Constitution of 1886 and the establishment of the Regeneration. This constitution proclaimed Catholicism the official national religion, following more than a quarter-century of Liberal attacks upon the Church's position.

The constitution and the Regeneration, headed by Rafael Núñez and Miguel Antonio Caro, were also a triumph for centralization, placing the nation's political and cultural power in Bogotá—hence the Highland—and the hegemonic culture of the neoclassical humanists. The links between ideology and culture and the continued political power of the lettered elite are evident in the roles of Caro as one of the authors of the Constitution of 1886 and of Núñez, also a writer, as president from 1880 to 1882 and again from 1886 to 1892.

The Bogotá of 1886, at the outset of the Regeneration, was the largest city in Colombia, with a population of 80,000. It could boast ten public schools, four banks, the Casa de Moneda, a national and municipal theater, a library, and the National Museum.[26] Industrialization and incipient modernization were marked by the foundation in 1891 of one of Colombia's most powerful industries, the Cervecería Bavaria. In a travel book written during this period, visiting Argentine writer Miguel Cané described the intellectual caliber of Bogotá's elite as being of unmatched superiority.[27] He found the neoclassic tradition, based on the study of classical language, literatures, and rhetoric, to be flourishing in Bogotá. The Argentine writer was uniformly impressed by the witty and cosmopolitan *bogotanos* who invited him to their soirees. The Athens of South America was successfully establishing its identity. The prominent intellectual Caro found it intolerable that his contemporaries were losing interest in venerable Latin models (another sign of the times in Bogotá); one of the notable books to appear in print during 1886 was his *Gramática de la lengua latina.*

Writing culture was fostered in the eleven newspapers and several literary magazines published in the capital in the mid-1880s. Daily newspapers featured not only standard news items of a political and social nature but also articles pertaining to letters. The *Papel Periódico Ilustrado,* founded in 1881 by Alberto Urdaneta, used European illustrated magazines as its model. *El Repertorio Colombiano* functioned as an influential cultural organ from 1878 to 1899, and *La Siesta* began publication in 1886. One Colombian literary critic well versed in the period has maintained that despite the isolation of Bogotá's inhabitants its bookstores disseminated foreign literature well.[28]

The fiction of the 1890s, as practiced by José Manuel Marroquín and Soledad Acosta de Samper, revealed both romantic and realist impulses; it was often descriptive of local customs. In accordance with the Interior Highland's reverence for the Hispanic tradition, realism was influenced not only by the French but also by the Spaniards Pereda and Pérez Galdós, who were in vogue in turn-of-the-century Colombia. A sense of the times is apparent in the reviews of *Entre primos* (1897), the recently published novel by José Manuel Marroquín. In one review, the influential Rafael María Carrasquilla begins by referring to four Spanish writers, Fernán Caballero, Alarcón, Pereda, and Pérez Galdós; he affirms that Marroquín takes the best from the Spaniards.[29] In another reaction typical of the times, the Antioquian intellectual (and later president) Carlos E. Restrepo, in a letter to Marroquín, affirmed that *Entre primos* had caused as much weeping as *María*.[30] As late as 1897 Restrepo still used *María* as the measuring stick of literary merit: "I don't hesitate in placing *Entre primos* next to *María*."[31] Whereas both the editors of the *Bibliotecas de Señoritas* and Eugenio Díaz had been unsure about what a Colombian novel might be, in turn-of-the-century Bogotá some specific models were being articulated—European novels and the single Colombian novel, *María*.

The *modernistas* influenced local literary activity in Bogotá, as evidenced in the poetry of Guillermo Valencia, José Asunción Silva, Víctor M. Londoño, and others. On the one hand, they were reacting against what they perceived as the vulgarity of turn-of-the-century Bogotá, replete with incipient modernity, represented by its new financiers and new stock markets. Just as well, they were rejecting their literary predecessors—lingering Romanticism and the realist-naturalist tradition in the novel. Silva published a noteworthy novel of *modernista* aesthetic, *De sobremesa* (1896), unquestionably among the best examples of the self-conscious aesthetics of turn-of-the-century Colombia's writing culture.[32] It relates the story of José Fernández, a wealthy, neurotic Colombian poet who cultivates interests in the esoteric and pursues the mysterious and unattainable Helena. Juan Loveluck maintains that *De sobremesa* construes better than any other Spanish-American novel the rarefied intellectual atmosphere of that exquisite and problematic era.[33] Fernández's story, written in diary form, consists of a series of episodes, incidents, and even essays which find their unity in the presence of the narrator-protagonist himself.[34] Rather than turning to the realist-naturalist tradition, Silva appropriates techniques from his French contemporaries, characterizing individuals as if he were painting instead of narrating and making ample use of other standard *modernista* techniques, such as synesthesia. Fernández is a self-conscious storyteller who sets forth propositions about aesthetics and the novel.[35]

Another novelist who wrote against the predominant literary mold of the time in Colombia was José María Vargas Vila, fecund author of seven novels during the period under discussion: *Aura o las violetas* (1889), *Flor de fango* (1895), *Ibis* (1900), *Alba roja* (1901), *Las rosas de la tarde* (1901), *La simiente* (1905), and *La caída del Cóndor* (1913). The early works, such as *Aura o las violetas* and *Flor de fango*, reveal an author anxious to offend society's norms, even though he reverts to some of the norms established in *María* as his model. Most of the novels, however, are even more critically anti-establishment, a true counter-discourse, involving an anomalous combination of *modernista* aesthetic, ungrammatical use of language, and scandalous plots. The frequently anticlerical positions set forth in these novels were also in direct opposition to the ideology of the Regeneration.

The Conservative Regeneration was able to centralize cultural and political power in Bogotá successfully only through the continued repression of Liberals and, in turn, Liberal literary voices. A circle of writers rejected by the regime of Rafael Reyes (president, 1904–1910), La Gruta Simbólica, met regularly for literary *tertulias.* Some seventy intellectuals participated in the meetings, among them poets, prose writers, and satirists, many of whom never published some of their most witty pieces of brief prose. The satire often targeted the government of Reyes. Along with Jorge Pombo and Alfonso Caro, Clímaco Soto Borda was deemed among the most brilliant in these verbal encounters.[36]

Soto was an energetic intellectual and witty participant in Bogotá's lively and precious literary scene. He edited the magazine *La Barra* and wrote a volume of short stories titled *Polvo y ceniza* (1906) consisting of seven humorous stories satirizing Bogotá society. The book constituted quite a novelty, printed in vertical lines in blue ink.[37] Critics were swift to praise Soto Borda's first novel, *Diana cazadora.* Luis E. Nieto Caballero, an influential intellectual of the time, immediately proclaimed it an outstanding work.[38] Set in Bogotá during the Regeneration, *Diana cazadora* is an account of a young man's disillusionment, failures, and ultimate death. It is a novel of personal and national crisis. The characters suffer under the policies that the narrator calls the "ratonera regeneradora" (Regeneration thievery).[39] The narrator also reveals a specific, critical attitude about the Regeneration throughout the text.

The characters who suffer under the Regeneration are Liberals such as Alejandro Acosta, who is actively involved in the political scene. The protagonist is his brother Fernando, who suffers from the state of affairs of Colombian society, his infatuation with Diana, and his alcoholism. Consequently, in Genette's terminology, the basic plot of *Diana cazadora* could be reduced to the nuclear sentence "Fernando suffers personal and national tragedies."[40] The novel unfolds in the militarized and repressive setting of the War of a Thousand Days, a period when Liberal and Conservative forces once again battled for political power. The Liberal-Conservative conflict which Soto Borda delineates and the narrator's critical language were typical of the period.

Fernando's suffering is also, in part, a crisis of modernity, the initial signs of which began to appear in conservative Bogotá at the turn of the century, and Soto Borda is among the first writers to utilize these indicators in the setting of a novel. Having returned from Europe, Alejandro notes the "progress" of Bogotá, including the new gas lights, the new water system, the foreign communities, the sicknesses, the secret police, the sudden deaths, the sermons, and other items (Soto Borda, 16). The narrator places in doubt the very idea of modernity, speaking with obvious ironic overtones about the "heights of civilization" that Bogotá has reached (Soto Borda, 16). Just as modernity is arriving in Bogotá "at a snail's pace," its objects fit uncomfortably into the Bogotá of Soto Borda. Although this novel differs radically in tone from *De sobremesa*, Soto Borda shares Silva's fundamental attitude in rejecting a new but vulgar society.

Fernando's suffering, in fact, represents a crisis of its nascent modernity in Bogotá. An excessive participant in a newly decadent world, he ruins the family's finances in his attempts to impress Diana—the modern woman par excellence. Fernando becomes an escapist consumer upon his return from Europe; increasingly he needs to flee from a harsh reality into alcohol. Near the end of the novel, when Alejandro is alcoholic, the narrator describes him as desperate and violent (Soto Borda, 143). In the end, Fernando dies of his excesses, perhaps as a metaphor for modernity in a Bogotá become too excessive for a conventional society. Fernando does not fit, and neither do the signs of Western modernity that he and others have brought to Colombia from abroad.

Despite this critique of incipient modernity, *Diana cazadora* should not be construed as an argument for traditional values. To the contrary, the narrator frequently satirizes a society still obsessed with custom and convention. The Catholic society of the Regeneration, for example, is the target of the narrator's observation that "that home was a little piece of old Santa Fe [Bogotá] with its clean customs, its ambience purified by virtue and sanctity" (Soto Borda, 30). The butt of Soto Borda's satire is the very conventional society of the Regeneration that was beginning to experience the growing pains of modernity, a process that will not be placed fully into motion until the 1930s.

In addition to the satirical tendencies already noted, Soto Borda employs other techniques to create the humorous effects that are essential to the experience of *Diana cazadora*. One such procedure is the constant juxtaposition of literary and colloquial language. For example, the narrator characterizes Diana as a Greek goddess, then describes her growing fame with a paragraph that begins with the following colloquial phrase: "Diana empezó a subir como espuma"

(Diana began to rise like foam) (Soto Borda, 47). The narrator also engages in caricature for humorous effects. José Lasso ("Pelusa") appears as a buffoon whose primary role in the novel is comic relief. Similarly, the narrator caricatures a *costeño*, whom he identifies as *bulldog* and whose Caribbean language patterns are reproduced in dialogue.

Diana cazadora does not fictionalize the ambiguities and conflicts between oral and written culture noted in *Manuela*. For the most part, both the text itself and its characters are immersed not only in writing culture but in the latest literary fashion: They could feasibly fit into the scenario of *De sobremesa*. *Diana cazadora* is a celebration of writing itself. It is a self-conscious literary work, inasmuch as it plays with language and parodies other texts; the playfulness of *Diana cazadora* takes the form of neologisms and witticisms. Soto Borda portrays himself as an intellectual lost in the playfulness of words in a poem quoted in the prologue which refers to him being "lost in word play" (Soto Borda, 9). In his initial characterization of Alejandro, the narrator invents a humorous neologism: "No es ropólogo" (He isn't a "clothesologist") (Soto Borda, 12). The narrator coins another untranslatable neologism (*sobremulares*) to describe the extraordinary effort two mules make to pull a derailed trolley back on its track (Soto Borda, 116). In yet another playful move, the narrator cedes the pen, in a way, to a painter for a description of Fernando's moribund state (Soto Borda, 159).

The parody in *Diana cazadora* targets the literature in fashion: Romanticism (again, *María* was still the major text in Colombia), neoclassic humanism, and *modernismo*, as embodied in Silva. In his description of Fernando's entrance at a party, the narrator offers a brief and compact one-line parody of the romantic conception of love that probably would have provided anecdotal material for endless tirades in a romantic text (Soto Borda, 60). One of the most humorous parodies of romantic literature appears after Fernando has received a love telegram from Diana, and the narrator has the trees leaning toward him and the leaves kissing him passionately (Soto Borda, 122). In a dramatic moment of anti-Romanticism, Fernando sets fire first to his own poems and then to the complete works of Marroquín and finally to a lengthy series of romantic clichés (Soto Borda, 108).

Soto Borda clearly uses images and descriptions beyond the predominant romantic mold of *María* and the realist/*costumbrista* impulses still in vogue at the end of the nineteenth century. When Antonio and Velarde observe the sky, for example, the stars they see are "pálidas y tristes como ojos de enfermos" (pallid and sad like the eyes of the sick) (Soto Borda, 127). The description of Fernando's death is systematically antiromantic: It begins with the already quoted painterly portrayal of his moribund body and is underlined by one brief statement by the doctor referring to the little blood he has remaining (Soto Borda, 159). The doctor then writes the death certificate and runs out, jumping on the bloodstains. In the end, death, like the invented neologisms, is a playful work of art, and the narrator presents the funeral ceremony as theater (see Soto Borda, 166).

This work does not depict a fully modern society, nor is *Diana cazadora* a truly modern novel. Both phenomena are still decades away from Soto Borda. Nevertheless, there are some signs of modernity in this self-conscious and parodic text, as there were in the other noteworthy novel of the period, Silva's *De sobremesa*. Modernity, self-consciousness, and parody were not fully exploited in the Interior Highland until the publication of *El buen salvaje* and then, in the 1980s, with the arrival of R. H. Moreno-Durán. *Diana cazadora* is a well-conceived critique of Regeneration values and an effective parody of literary fashion at the turn of the century. It represents a substantial transformation of literary culture from the ambiguous period of *Manuela* in the 1850s. Only a sophisticated writing culture can parody itself. As Fernando burned the clichés of the romantic novel, he opened the doors to a new type of literature, such as that of José Eustasio Rivera's *La vorágine*.

Transition (1914–1923) and *La vorágine* (1924) by José Eustasio Rivera

Two significant literary phenomena took place in the Interior Highland between the publication of *Diana cazadora* in 1915 and *La vorágine* in 1924: the continued rise of José María Vargas Vila to international prominence and the birth of *La novela semanal* in 1923. During this period Vargas Vila was one of the most widely acclaimed writers of the Hispanic world; one example of his stature is the reception he was given in Mexico by then-president Obregón. Among his novels during the second decade of the century were *María Magdalena* (1917), *El huerto de silencio* (1917), *Salomé* (1918), and *Vuelo de cisnes* (1919). His liberal political positions, critique of the Catholic Church, and generally iconoclastic attitudes resulted in his being totally rejected by the conservative literary establishment of the time. The appearance of *La novela semanal*, meanwhile, did not necessarily signal a weekly outpouring of outstanding works of fiction, but it was a noteworthy contribution to a Highland writing culture with respect to the novel. The very publication of a weekly novel inaugurated an unprecedented role in Colombia for prose fiction. These were short pieces of fiction, usually fifteen to thirty pages in length, rather than fully developed novels. They ranged in quality from the most sophisticated writing of the time to popular fiction, with a predominance of the latter.

The 1920s witnessed for the first time the mass production of the Colombian novel. A prominant literary critic noted in 1928 the increased publication and availability of books.[41] If Soto Borda symbolically burnt the remainders of Isaacs's romantic model, he and his contemporaries left little in its place as the basis for a "new" Colombian novel. There were Vargas Vila's irreverent and often scandalous fiction and traditional stories of love and customs, such as those published by Luis Enrique Osorio and Daniel Samper Ortega in Bogotá or Arturo Suárez and Roberto Botero Saldarriaga in Antioquia. In a period of growing nationalism, however, the attitude arose that fiction should somehow contribute to the definition of Colombian identity. This concern led to a general trend toward *criollista* or New World literary projects in Colombia and Latin America in general. Given this new nationalism, it was a propitious time for an exciting event to take place on the Colombian literary scene, and the book that responded to the situation was *La vorágine.*

Rivera was born and reared in Huila at the western extreme of the Interior Highland. Like most intellectuals from the Huila/Tolima region, he was educatcd in Bogotá and interacted with Highland intellectual circles. Like Soto Borda, Rivera stood at a distance from orality; he is strictly an exemplar of writing culture. Issues of oral and writing culture are, in fact, unimportant in this period of Highland writing, because by the 1920s the Interior Highland was essentially a self-conscious writing culture. Rivera had been in contact with Highland intellectuals and had been writing poetry (*Tierra de promisión,* 1921) and short fiction for approximately a decade when he published *La vorágine.* The initial responsc was polarized; in subsequent years, scholarly approaches to this novel have varied widely.[42] Many scholars have pointed to *La vorágine*'s place in Spanish-American literary history, its formal characteristics, and its denunciation of social injustice.[43] More recent readings have addressed similar issues in the light of sociological and poststructuralist literary theory.[44] There is no common agreement, however, on such basic questions of narratology as precisely who narrates and what the subject of this narration is.[45] (As will be discussed, Rivera's treatment of orality is minimal and indirect.)

Extant critical readings of *La vorágine* portray a flawed work with multiple sources: romantic, realist, realist/naturalist, or realist/*crio-*

llista. One critic, for example, has claimed that it is in turn "vision-
ary, mystic, realist, modernist, and melodramatic."[46] Many readers
have pointed out the work's defects, stressing problems with the
plot and with the protagonist, Arturo Cova: Some readers find Cova
unbearable, while a contemporary of Rivera, Tomás Carrasquilla,
described *La vorágine* as a shambles.[47] More recent readings embody
a similar range of reaction concerning the novel's quality: Randolph
Pope salvages Rivera's text by viewing Cova's narrative as the story
of a decadent intellectual; Sharon Magnarelli, on the other hand,
criticizes the depiction of woman as a "malevolent being in collabo-
ration with the evil forces of the universe."[48] One assertation can be
made on the basis of these readings: Cova functions exclusively
within a plane of writing noetics; he is, that is to say, a Western intellectual, a product of a cosmopolitan writing culture.

The narrator-protagonist Arturo Cova has been described as a romantic poet.[49] Certainly much of the text fully supports such a characterization, beginning with Cova's initial portrayal as a free spirit
who flees society in search of the ideal. The characterization as romantic poet, however, is only a partial portrayal of the total person.
Pope has forcefully demonstrated that Cova also shares many qualities of the decadent intellectual.[50] For Magnarelli, Cova is a "seriously demented character"; both she and others consider him an
"unreliable narrator."[51] In fact, Cova is neither "demented" nor "unreliable" and the characterization as romantic poet/decadent intellectual is also quite limiting. These characterizations project the
image of a "writer." The reader observes a patently literary character
creating a self-conscious "literary" text.

The first matter to consider, then, is Cova's supposedly "demented" character. Several readers have described him as unstable,
irrational, or unreasonable.[52] Indeed, his relationships with women
and reactions to his surroundings do indicate unorthodox behavior;
his decision to flee from Bogotá with Alicia, for instance, is not totally reasonable, given the social context. What is unique about
Cova's supposed irrationality and instability, however, is its self-
consciousness. Cova himself often qualifies his actions as irrational
or his thoughts as malevolent (Rivera, 35). Two questions arise when
observing such commentary: How literally should it be interpreted?
What could possibly motivate a self-characterization as an insane
person? The answer to both questions lies in Cova's identity as
writer. Interpreted literally, Cova must be dismissed as a ludicrous
madman, as indeed many critics have considered him. He should be
seen, rather, as a narrator who employs a series of strategies in order
to effect his characterization as a writer. At the end of the "Primera

Parte" Cova watches Franco's house burn and comments: "In the middle of the flames I began to laugh like Satan!" Magnarelli claims that the fact that he reports this personal reaction highlights his instability.[53] When Cova makes this oft-quoted statement, however, Cova the narrator should not be seen as either diabolical or unstable but rather as attempting to characterize himself as a literary figure. (We should also recall that he is a protagonist created in the Athens of South America.) He uses similar imagery soon thereafter: "A tragic demon insisted on slowly and darkly taking over my conscience" (Rivera, 66). In both cases Cova situates himself in a literary context, portraying himself metaphorically as a devil. It is important to read Cova not as literally insane but as part of a venerable tradition of literary devil-figures and madmen; the devil here is not a sign of malevolence or instability but of difference. Cova also quotes other characters to enforce the characterization of himself as the unorthodox writer-type (Rivera, 25). Indeed, he insists incessantly on his role in writing culture.

Cova's irrationality not only corroborates his characterization as a writer but functions as a positive antidote to the excessively rational modern world developing in Colombia. An implied criticism of the rational arises, for example, when, after a *caudillo*'s greed-driven excesses are described, two characters end the section with the ironic comment "Logic triumphs! Long live logic!" (Rivera, 134). Here the modern world of commerce and rationality is placed in opposition to a romantic world of the "irrational" writer. As such, the authentic Cova is not a demented individual who abuses women (as Magnarelli would have us believe), for this status would require the presence of a human being; lacking the ontological status of being, Cova is only the figure of a writer. Far from functioning as unreliable narrator, Cova is a paradigm of the model romantic-decadent writer: self-centered, horrified by a world both vital and decaying around him, constantly vacillating among multiple duplicities. The telltale indicator of Cova's genuine stability, however, is his consistent insistence on his instability. He states in paraphrase of Franco: "All this because I'm an unbalanced person who is impulsive as well as theatrical" (Rivera, 75). Rather than observing an unreliable narrator, the reader encounters a character in the process of characterizing himself as a literary figure—the unstable and theatrical writer.

What, then, is the subject of this writer's writing? Readings have stressed the portrayal of the New World as one of three classic *criollista* texts: civilization versus barbarity, "the evil forces of the universe," social injustice. Such forces do indeed operate in the fictional world of *La vorágine*. The *costumbrista* cockfight scene and the revelation of exploitation of *caucho* workers are two of several examples of subject matter that supports such readings. The question, however, is whether these are the primary subject matter—the thematic core of this *criollista* text. The predominant subject of *La vorágine* is not a fictional representation of rural Colombia in 1924, with its concomitant vacuous women and bedraggled workers, but rather the self in the process of writing. Read in this light, the novel fits squarely in the realm of a self-conscious writing culture.

Several problems arise with reading *La vorágine* as a fictionalized replica of Colombia's rural story; one basic difficulty with such a reading of this novel as a fictionalized simulacrum of Colombia's rural story is, simply stated, the absence of story. As narrator, Cova constantly vacillates between his role as creator of story and narrator of himself. Many of the novel's narrative segments begin not with the subject matter of the external story (that is, Colombia's rural story) but with intrusions about the self. The reader observes Cova reacting to the world rather than fabricating a story. The novel's first sentence sets the tone and typifies what will take place in the remainder of the work: "Antes que me hubiera apasionado por mujer alguna, jugué mi corazón al azar y me lo ganó la Violencia" (Before falling in love with any woman, I took my chances with my heart, and Violence won) (Rivera, 5). In this sentence five basic elements are in operation with respect to the self and story: three references to the self ("me," "jugué mi corazón," and the second "me") and two references with the potential of developing the external story, these being the "mujer" (love story) and "la Violencia" (a Colombian story).

Given the overwhelming presence of the self in this novel, the story is not essentially of a *vorágine*, of natural phenomena in a New World, but of a self in the process of writing, of establishing a writerly identity that interrupts the narration of a story. Interruptions can appear at the most inopportune moments of the narrative's potential as a story. When a group of Indians drowns, Cova's reaction is: "The spectacle was magnificent" (Rivera, 74). This oft-quoted passage has led Pope to the logical conclusion that Cova, as intellectual, has an aesthetic vision of the world. The importance of this passage with respect to the story, however, is its radical shift of focus from an adventure story to a writer's story: The Indians' death is a relatively unimportant event at the end of a narrative segment; Cova's emotional reaction to it turns out to be the subject of the entire first part of the following narrative segment, centered upon this vision of mass death as "spectacle." The potential story of an adventure had been subverted by Cova's presence from the beginning of the "Segunda Parte." The narrator does not present the Indians as human beings but as the literary figures about whom Cova-the-writer has read: He characterizes them all as being strong, young, and with Herculean backs (Rivera, 56). Indeed, with respect to the orality–writing culture dichotomy, Cova's attitude epitomizes a writing culture appropriating an oral culture strictly for literary purposes.

Refusing traditional subject matter and subverting the New World *histoire* from transformation into *récit*, Cova develops as his central subject writing itself; the novel's dynamism is found in the narrator's striving for *écriture*. In addition to his reiterative identification of himself as writer, as member of writing culture par excellence, the narrator signals the literariness of his text at the outset with the use of exclusively literary constructions such as the Spanish "pidióme" (he asked me, rendered in special literary form) (Rivera, 7). He then proceeds to announce explicitly that his narration has been informed by writing rather than observation of external reality: "In what code, in what writing, in what science had I learned that prejudices predominate over reality" (Rivera, 12). This questioning is strictly rhetorical; all of Cova's actions betray an individual whose "prejudices," acquired from writing culture, underlie his actions and his interpretation of the world around him.[54]

The narrator exploits his subject matter of writing in three ways: by the use of metaphor, by means of literary allusions, and by dramatizing the very act of writing itself. Cova's language is consistently metaphorical: Rather than naming the world, he relates what it is "like" (*como*). Cova's inconsistent story also strives to acquire the status of *écriture* by means of association with classic literary texts or by direct allusions to them. Clemente Silva, for example, refers to their trip as "our Odyssey" (Rivera, 82), and Cova himself characterizes his experiences and the book he is writing similarly, referring to them as "my Odyssey" (Rivera, 128). In addition to a series of parallels between *La vorágine* and Dante's *Divine Comedy*, references relate the text to Dante's *Inferno* and Virgil's *Aeneid*.[55]

The third manner in which the novel self-consciously seeks the status of *écriture* is the drama of writing that Cova develops. "José Eustasio Rivera" initiates this drama in the prologue, which features as its preeminent subject neither Arturo Cova nor the unjust life of *caucheros colombianos* but a manuscript. In the final sections of the novel the significant drama is not Cova's struggle with nature, for neither he nor nature has a sufficiently important fictional status. Rather, the tension involves Cova's completion of his writing. Since he has acquired his status as writer, thus assuring his text's

status as *écriture*, the only question remaining is the novel's denouement as fiction: Precisely how and under what circumstances
will the text be completed? This drama involves Cova's mental condition under the adverse conditions of the jungle. He assures the
reader, for example, of his superb mental functioning, despite the
situation: "My brain was burning sharper than the lamp" (Rivera,
140). He also explains the mechanics of his text's development: "Today I write these pages in the Negro River" (Rivera, 141). Near the
end the threats to his life increase, but he defends himself: The text
survives and progresses. At the end of Cova's writing, the drama of
the text culminates in its being left for Clemente Silva. Cova concludes: "They are our history, the desolated history of the *caucheros*. So many blank pages, so much left unsaid" (Rivera, 149). The
statement that this manuscript is either the story or history (*historia* in Spanish) of the *caucheros* is misleading, a distortion of a book
which has had as its real subject a writer and his writing. This fact is
implied in the sentence that follows: The "so much left unsaid"
would indeed be the *cauchero* story, which had been told only by
Clemente Silva as a sidelight to Cova's obsessive focus upon himself. The news in the epilogue that Cova has been devoured by the
jungle is of little consequence: The writer has disappeared, as was
promised in the prologue, but his writing has survived.

The multiple ambiguities with respect to author, writer, narrator,
story, and text are a function of the ambiguous genre status of the
novel in 1920s Colombia. Oddly enough, Rivera's most significant
predecessor and literary model was the romantic classic *María*, a
situation which contributes to an understanding of the romantic
elements in *La vorágine*. Published some six decades after Isaacs's
María, *La vorágine* shares approximately the same temporal distance from *María* as does *La vorágine* from readers today. Having
been published in several successive editions and read throughout
the Hispanic world, *María* was still an understandably viable presence in Colombia during the 1920s.[56]

Modernization, industrialization, and a growing middle class in
Highland Colombia during the 1920s fostered a growing reading
public. *La vorágine* did, indeed, become a bestseller in its time.[57]
Any further statement about this novel's status is more problematic.
In *La vorágine* a plethora of literary conventions and languages is
also at work, including realism, *costumbrismo*, decadentism, *modernismo*, and *criollismo*. The text suggests that the empirical author Rivera was unsure or ambivalent about the basic elements of
the novel: his own role as author, the narrator's relationship to author and character, and *La vorágine*'s relationship to society. An am-

biguous attitude toward rural orality is present in the colloquial language of the dictionary at the end. Realist/naturalist suppositions about the verisimilitude and utility of the novel lead Rivera to a contrived sense of social obligation when he has the narrator imply at the end that this novel about writing is "our history" or "our story."

The contradictions and ambiguities in *La vorágine* result from its complex dynamics of writer and narrator. It is evident that the function of these elements was not entirely clear to Rivera: He was patently insecure in his role as author. The role of the author, the novel, and the reading public was still in many ways undefined in Colombia. Thus, the first edition of *La vorágine* included a supposed *photograph* of the protagonist Arturo Cova![58] The reader must recall, nevertheless, that, rather than simulacra of people, novels are universally composed of language.[59] *La vorágine* is a text about writing—the ambiguities, contradictions, and metaphors are all part of a text striving to attain the status of *écriture*. Despite Carlos Fuentes's admonition that all these early twentieth-century novels were simply variations on the same theme of "they were devoured by the jungle," *La vorágine* does not play out this pattern in a significant way. The meaningful drama is not the death of Cova or anyone else but rather the survival of the text. The fictional José Fernández had stated in *De sobremesa*, "And now I write my adventure." Similarly, *La vorágine* is Arturo Cova's adventure in the Highland novel's most pervasive topic—writing itself.

Transition (1925–1964) and *El buen salvaje* (1966) by Eduardo Caballero Calderón

Soto Borda's satire and Rivera's adventure in writing had diminished the importance of classical rhetoric and the influence of the Regeneration humanists in the Interior Highland Region. Within that context, three important phenomena occurred between *La vorágine* and the publication of *El buen salvaje* in 1966. The first was the rise, during the 1940s, of five Highland fiction writers whose interests were more cosmopolitan and whose fiction was more interiorized than had been the case previously: Tomás Vargas Osorio, Rafael Gómez Picón, Ernesto Camargo Martínez, Jaime Ardila Casamitjana, Jaime Ibáñez. The second important phenomenon was the outbreak of La Violencia in the streets of Bogotá on April 9, 1948. The third was the rise of the modern novel in Colombia and Latin America, accompanied by the international recognition or boom of the 1960s.

A noteworthy novelistic antecedent to these three major events was Eduardo Zalamea Borda's publication of *Cuatro años a bordo de mí mismo* (1934), another ostensibly *criollista* Highland project. This novel does bear the imprint of *La vorágine* again, of the New World adventure. In this case a trip from Bogotá to the "uncivilized" Caribbean region of La Guajira is of less importance than the adventure in writing. The narrator/protagonist in *Cuatro años a bordo de mí mismo* is a Highland intellectual who experiences four years of the Costa's tri-ethnic and oral culture. After initial chapters of a predominantly introspective nature, the narrator pursues his New World adventure with the native population, for the most part an exercise in exoticism. During some moments this experience involves the type of inspiration from the special qualities of the land itself with which New World protagonists typically develop a unique relationship. For instance, the narrator describes it as "land of thirst, of sun, and of dreams."[60] At the end, he bids goodbye to the trees he personifies. Despite these occasional *criollista* gestures, *Cuatro años a bordo de mí mismo* is preeminently an intellectual's exercise in sensory perception and the creation of metaphors.[61] He is scrupulously sensitive. The self-consciousness of this writer's exercise is evident in the novel's final line, which appears in parentheses: "(Here I place the last period, but from all periods a new sentence is always born)."

A significant change of direction for Highland fiction—away from the pseudo–New World model established by Rivera and continued by Zalamea Borda—was signaled by the rise of five fiction writers in the 1940s: Vargas Osorio published *Vidas menores* in 1937, after which followed Gómez Picón's *45 relatos de un burócrata, con cuatro paréntesis* (1941), Camargo Martínez's *De la vida de Iván el mayor* (1942), Ardila Casamitjana's *Babel* (1943), and Ibáñez's *Cada voz lleva su angustia* (1944). Known for his cosmopolitan interests, Tomás Vargas Osorio also wrote a set of outstanding short stories. The fiction of this group expressed concerns and displayed methods of fictionalization unimaginable by the traditional writers of the Athens of South America. A reverence for Spanish tradition and a self-conscious literary culture nevertheless remained prevalent in the Highland region through the decades until the 1960s. Germán Arciniegas's fictionalized essay *El estudiante de la mesa redonda* (1932) celebrates the Hispanic *letrado* of the Spanish, Spanish Colonial, and Spanish Highland traditions. Vargas Osorio, although often European in vision, also finds roots in a Hispanic and Highland tradition, the latter represented in the figure of Guillermo Valencia, about whom he wrote. Eduardo Caballero Calderón wrote in 1947 that "in *Don Quixote* I learned to read and to dream."[62] Elisa Mújica also published two introspective novels dealing with human relations, works of "small screen" scope, *Los dos tiempos* (1949) and *Catalina* (1963).[63]

The outbreak of La Violencia with the assassination of Gaitán left its imprint on more than one generation of writers from the Interior Highland. Besides Caballero Calderón, other Highland novelists who fictionalized experiences set in the context of La Violencia include Pedro Gómez Corena, Ignacio Gómez Dávila, Eduardo Santa, and Clemente Airó (see chapter 2). Jorge Zalamea's *El gran Burundún Burundá ha muerto* (1952) satirized military dictatorships such as the one that governed Colombia for much of the decade. The major cultural organ of the period, the magazine *Mito*, was founded in 1955 by two poets, Jorge Gaitán Durán and Hernando Valencia Goekel, with the following statement as a doctrine of sorts for the generation: "Words are in their situation. It would be vain to demand for them univocal or ideal positions. In order to accept them in their ambiguity, we need words *to be*."[64] Writing culture had become progressively internationalized in the Interior Highland by the 1950s: *Mito* published writers such as Sartre, Borges, Robbe-Grillet, Henry Miller, and Jean Genet.

Caballero Calderón has not only been the perfect embodiment of a Highland *letrado*, but his total work compares in volume to Eugenio Díaz, Soto Borda, and Rivera combined. By the mid-1980s he had published ten novels, four volumes of short fiction, eleven books of essays, and numerous translations and journalistic essays. In his essay on *Don Quijote,* Caballero Calderón demonstrates his knowledge not only of this classic novel but also of the entire Hispanic literary heritage from the *Poema de Mío Cid* through the Golden Age and twentieth century. As a participant in the Highland tradition, Caballero Calderón is also acutely aware of his Colombian predecessors, as demonstrated by his mentioning *La vorágine* in his book on *Don Quijote*. His connections with the Highland tradition are deep-rooted: When he was seven years old he read a speech at school in homage to José María Samper; his first literary essay was on the humanist president Marco Fidel Suárez.[65] Caballero Calderón's novels *El cristo de espaldas* (1952), *Siervo sin tierra* (1953), and *Manuel Pacho* (1962) are related to La Violencia and have received substantial critical attention.[66] *El buen salvaje*, which received Spain's Nadal Prize in 1965, represents the culmination of a self-conscious novelistic tradition in the Interior Highland Region.

The idea for *El buen salvaje* had interested Caballero Calderón from early in his career—1947—when, referring to the romantics, who were inspired by Rousseau, he wrote: "Some fall in love with this *buen salvaje*. . . . This *buen salvaje* (too literary to be authen-

tic) is a kind, educated, sentimental man."[67] Some two decades after
making this observation, Caballero Calderón was in Paris (perhaps
in some ways himself the Latin American *bon sauvage* in Europe);
there he wrote his novel concerning a twenty-seven-year-old student
in Paris aspiring to be a writer.

El buen salvaje consists of fourteen numbered *cuadernos*, the
notes of the narrator/protagonist who relates his projects for writing
and anecdotes of his personal life in Paris. In a general sense, these
projects appear in chronological order. While his plans for fictions
abound, his ability to complete any given project is problematical.
He conceives some thirteen possible designs for a novel, but in the
end, psychologically unbalanced and desperate for a continued relationship with his Chilean friend Rose-Marie, he leaves Paris with no
novel completed. During the initial chapters the plot moves forward
primarily on the basis explored by Rivera in *La vorágine:* the drama
of writing. The protagonist has imaginative ideas for a novel and
would seem to offer the promise of completing an interesting book.
His economic problems, his excessive consumption of alcohol, and
the continual excuses he contrives to avoid writing, however, soon
render the project doubtful. He incessantly reproaches himself for
his writing and other acts. By the fifth *cuaderno* he obviously possesses absolutely no story to write and the reader realizes that he
probably will not complete a novel. Rather than a "writer," he is
what Barthes has denominated a "scribbler."[68] During the final chapters he becomes more erratic and frenetic about his novelistic plans
and concurrently more intense in his relationship with Rose-Marie.
By then he is a pathetic individual who is totally immersed in writing culture but who commands neither the motivation nor a viable
reason to write the novel that would supposedly transform him into
a literary celebrity.

The distance established between the narrator/protagonist (extra-
diegetic-intradiegetic) and the figure of an implied author, similar in
several ways to the empirical author Caballero Calderón, permits
satire of the Latin American intellectual in Europe. The narrator/
protagonist and the empirical author share certain experiences, such
as stints in Europe and lengthy meditations on Latin American culture. The distance between these two entities revolves around the
issue of writing: The narrator/protagonist is the eternal "scribbler";
the empirical author, Eduardo Caballero Calderón, has published
both essays on Latin American culture and novels, some of which
are actually similar to the plans proposed by the young narrator/pro-
tagonist in Paris.

The implied author's satirical attitude toward the narrator/protagonist is evident from the first paragraph, where he explains that he is "resolved" to write a novel superior to the "bad" ones he has read, and he is going to do so in the ten days he now has free.[69] The implied author—apparently an experienced professional writer—thus begins by presenting a young novelist who innocently believes that with ten free days he is going to realize significant progress on a novel. The next two statements also resound with amateurish enthusiasm: The young man is "resolved" to write this work precisely because he has read so many "bad" novels in recent months. He thus establishes certain conditions for writing (ten free days; resolution to compose fiction superior to the "bad" novels he has read) but offers no viable project.

The naive writer/protagonist, upon confronting pen and paper, faces the most basic problems of novelization. He contemplates a variety of possible approaches to his book without ever realizing that his meditations deal with the most essential questions of narratology. In his first two *cuadernos* he evokes six basic issues of storytelling that could almost have been abstracted from a manual on fiction such as Brooks and Warren's *Understanding Fiction.*[70] The first question that concerns him is how the novel should begin (Caballero, 10). A second essential problem is what Genette calls *histoire*, or the basic anecdotal material. At the outset the protagonist is confident of having his own anecdotal material without having to search for sources: "Besides, I don't have to read the newspaper in order to find a theme" (Caballero, 10). Later in the novel, however, he contradicts this statement by indeed turning to a newspaper for material. Empirical author Caballero Calderón, who in this case can be associated easily with this figure of the implied author, does in fact utilize newspapers: "I'm a dedicated reader of the social pages because they are a good source of suggestions and lessons."[71] A third basic narratological issue is order. The narrator/protagonist addresses this issue in the first *cuaderno:* "I think of two things simultaneously. Which should come first?" (Caballero, 11). He writes, "In any novel the ambience . . . is fundamental" (Caballero, 12) and then proceeds to describe a setting which will supposedly serve for his novel. The fifth problem he confronts is perhaps the most essential: Who will narrate and in what person? This fundamental problem causes one of the numerous interruptions in his plan: "Now what is keeping me from writing . . . is a problem of technique. . . . I need to decide if I should write in first person" (Caballero, 25). In the second *cuaderno* he faces the narratological issue that Brooks and Warren call selection. For the narrator it is a matter of deciding which details to include and which to exclude, and he believes he has resolved the

issue: "I can't lose myself in insignificant details" (Caballero, 39).
Nevertheless, most of his notes are precisely the insignificant details that never lead to a consistent story line.

Even though the narrator/protagonist never actually completes
his novel, he certainly holds a more developed conceptualization of
what the genre of the novel is or should be than did Eugenio Díaz a
century before. The narrator/protagonist in *El buen salvaje,* a product of a literary culture, is fully aware of the many classical books
that this culture has produced. Consequently, he does not share
with Eugenio Díaz the problem of dealing with a strong oral culture
in a written text. Nevertheless, the technology of writing per se is a
significant element in *El buen salvaje,* and some residual orality
plays a role in its fabrication.

The dynamics of *El buen salvaje* are based on the vital interplay
of writing, speaking, and thinking as acts carried out by the narrator/
protagonist. His writing consists of several levels of fictionality:
notes about his daily life that he inscribes in diary fashion, ideas or
plans for novels, and actual pieces of "fiction writing" for these novels. Several kinds of speaking appear within these *cuadernos* too: dialogue that is transcribed mimetically in the text and conversations
from the past which the narrator relates indirectly. Also within the
realm of the *cuadernos'* "writing" is the act of thinking. Two particular types of thinking that the narrator feels he needs to conscien-
tiously control in order to be a successful novelist are imagination
and memory. The technology of writing and its relationship to speaking and thinking are not as clearly understood and controlled by the
narrator as are the basic narrative techniques of novelization.

Persons who have interiorized writing not only write but also
speak literately, which is to say that they organize, to varying degrees, even their oral expression in thought patterns that they would
not know unless they could write.[72] The narrator/protagonist, a
well-read young intellectual, embodies the quintessential characterization of a person whose writing, speaking, and thinking have been
determined by the noetics of writing. With respect to the relationship between writing and thinking, in fact, the narrator/protagonist
is a recurrent victim of the very noetics of writing he has mastered
so well. By taking on conservative functions, the text frees the mind
of certain tasks, that is, of its memory work, and thus enables the
mind to turn itself to speculation.[73] This is the narrator/protago-
nist's predicament. Once his ideas for one particular novel, or even a
passage of the novel, are written, this act allows him to slough off
these memories and obsessively turn to new speculation, the next

possible novel. The situation also leads to other kinds of thinking—of the past (memory) and of the unreal (imagination).

How to use memory and imagination in the creation of his novel are perplexing matters for this narrator. At the beginning of his book he claims to have no memory: "Proust pulled them from his microscopic memory, but I don't have memory. I live in the present, leaning toward the future, which represents an advantage for a future novelist" (Caballero, 10). Several noteworthy ideas and contradictions stand out in this passage. Despite his claim to lack memory, he recalls reading a Proust of some five decades in the past. Moreover, he is so deeply immersed in his writing that he fails to realize that past readings, as well as events from his past, are indeed a part of his active memory. He does not explain exactly why living in the present and the future would necessarily represent an advantage for the novelist. Nevertheless, the text does provide the basis for some reasonable speculation concerning this issue. The statement implies a privileging of immediate real-life experience over the historical or the literary as the anecdotal material for a novel. It also suggests the possibility that living in the present liberates the novelist from the literary specters and traditions of the past, thereby freeing the imagination and fostering the "originality" of the post-romantic writer. The opening statement about living in the present also reveals an implicitly oral-culture concept of storytelling. Rather than being a Proustian "literary" storyteller, the narrator implies that he lives and narrates only in the present, a typical position of an oral storyteller: Oral cultures are homeostatic, tending to slough off memories of the past and live in a constant present. Thus, already in the first *cuaderno*, the narrator attempts to reject the literary sources of writing culture in favor of a "pure imagination" (an implied orality). He states that he writes only with his imagination, sitting in the Bibliothèque Nationale (Caballero, 17). An additional factor here is the image of the Bibliothèque Nationale in Paris, a monument of writing culture and the apex of the literary tradition of the West, which the narrator openly rejects.

His immersion in the noetics of writing impedes the creation of his novel at other moments as well. In several instances he explains how writing makes thinking difficult and vice-versa. Thus, the mechanics of writing obliges him to stop writing in order to think (Caballero, 22). He insists again that his writing somehow requires him neither to think nor to remember (Caballero, 36). He also returns to his idea that his imagination predominates over his memory (Caballero, 69). A related idea, almost an obsession for him, is that a writer should somehow be ahistorical. It fits his concept of the homeostatic—living in a constant present and rejecting memory.

The narrator also deals with the issues of writing and speaking. There is no way to write "naturally"; anyone with sufficient knowledge of writing culture to be capable of writing already carries grammar rules, structures, and the like. Nevertheless, this Latin American *buen salvaje*, immersed in writing culture and a novelistic tradition, wants to write "naturally," rejecting both his predecessors and contemporaries. One form this rebellion takes is an escape into speaking: "I like engaging in dialogue more and more and I find it an excellent exercise to sharpen my style" (Caballero, 62). The idea is that an oral exercise can improve upon writing. Another assumption implied here is that orality somehow embodies a classic form of culture and, once written on paper, can represent a more "classic" or lasting form of literature than "written" stories. Indeed, the protagonist invests much of his time in dialogue itself, often relating novels in spoken fashion rather than writing them. For example, in *Cuaderno No.* 7 he relates to Rose-Marie his plans for a novel on the Caribbean. At no point, however, does he consider himself an oral storyteller; his oral anecdotes are always told with the intention of converting them into written texts. One of his most grievous problems is possessing certain unconscious oral impulses, causing him to reject literary tradition, at the same time that he is attempting to function in a writing-culture environment.

Analysis of the relationships among writing, thinking, and speaking in *El buen salvaje* leads to the conclusion that the narrator/protagonist is an obsessive thinker (immersed in the thinking of writing culture) and teller of stories (with impulses of oral culture) but not a novelist. He fails both in the writing culture in which he is unable to function and in the feeble efforts he makes to reactivate modes of an oral culture of which he is not consciously aware. Although a sophisticated participant in writing culture, he is not able to complete a written narrative within the bounds of its genre expectations.

The anxiety of influence contributes to his failure.[74] The narrator/protagonist not only feels the weight of both a Western and a Highland tradition, but he also sets forth his own work as an intertextual dialogue with some of their most recognized texts.[75] He sits in a café, contemplates the fact that Sartre and Simone de Beauvoir wrote there (Caballero, *Cuaderno No.* 1, 11), and immediately states that he detests existentialism. In the same first *Cuaderno*, still in the planning stage, he meditates on Western classics such as *Don Quijote*, *War and Peace*, and *The Brothers Karamazov* and thinks about

Proust's style. He is also sensitive to his Highland predecessors. For example, without specifically naming *La vorágine*, he notes that "el paisaje es un devorador de escritores hispanoamericanos" (landscape is a devourer of Spanish-American writers) (Caballero, 84), thus incorporating intertextually the now-famous verb *devorar* from Rivera's final page. In addition, the narrator does offer a critique of rhetoric, thereby criticizing Regeneration scholars without ever naming Caro or Cuervo.

The matter of literary fashion is essential to the functioning of this novel. From the publication of *La vorágine* through the period of the boom of the Latin American novel of the 1960s (drawing attention precisely when Caballero Calderón was writing *El buen salvaje*), reading and writing Latin American novels had become fashionable. Rivera had published the first Colombian bestseller in the 1920s; by the time *El buen salvaje* appeared, Carlos Fuentes, Mario Vargas Llosa, and Julio Cortázar had published their bestsellers *The Death of Artemio Cruz* (1962), *The Time of the Hero* (1963), and *Hopscotch* (1963), respectively. The Latin American novel, even in Latin America, was in fashion. The protagonist of *El buen salvaje* is more attracted to the fashions of writing and the celebrity associated with its success than he is to literary communication. He imitates the life-styles of trendy writers and fantasizes about the glory of being a recognized intellectual. For example, he decides to take notes on the table of a bistro formerly occupied by prize-winning novelists. He imagines his future books on display in bookstores. His ultimate goal is not just to communicate a story but to be an international celebrity. A counterpart of his anxiety of influence is his urgent need for fame—of the type the very masters he attempts to reject have enjoyed.

El buen salvaje consists of a series of proposed spoken novels ("spoken" in cafés) related by the narrator to other characters but never completed. The protagonist fails as a creator of novels in a writing culture that only values the printed word. He assumes several roles as a product of a writing culture: reader, thinker, teller of stories, potential writer, potential literary celebrity. In the end, despite the multiple roles he plays, he does not achieve the one he desires—writer of stories. In a sense he is the victim of a particular Western and Highland tradition that weighs upon him. He also insists upon a self-willed ahistoricism, an anomalous decision in a writing culture as imbued with history as Colombia's. In several ways, *El buen salvaje* culminates the Highland's self-conscious novelistic tradition. It seems only appropriate that a book which satirizes a

Highland writer should mark the culmination of a tradition whose focal topic of the twentieth century has been self-conscious writing. In contrast to a novel with a strong oral base, such as *Cien años de soledad*, *El buen salvaje* has no memorable characters beyond the protagonist. It is a work structured entirely by the technology of writing, from its diarylike *cuadernos* to its strictly writing-culture meditations and speculation. The writing of Caballero Calderón is of a superannuated elite, and *El buen salvaje* epitomizes a self-conscious Highland literature of exhaustion.[76]

What is *El buen salvaje*'s status as metafiction? The text fits within Alter's general definition of the self-conscious novel as one that systematically flaunts its own condition of artifice and that, by so doing, probes the problematic relationship between real-seeming artifice and reality.[77] The distinction Pérez Firmat has made between "discursive metafiction" and "narrative metafiction" would place *El buen salvaje* in the former category: This work contains discursive theorizing about fiction itself, the novel which ironically never comes into being as theorized.[78] Spires proposes a metafictional mode which results when the member of one world—that of author, of story, or of text-act reader—violates the world of another.[79] The violations in *El buen salvaje* involve those of a fictional author—the narrator/protagonist—and multiple stories. In this case, as frequently occurs in metafiction, the violations themselves become the pivotal events of the story: The plot of *El buen salvaje* is a story of proposed stories and failed plots. Caballero Calderón's culminating work effectively satirizes the obsessions of many Highland writers, from Eugenio Díaz to Eduardo Zalamea Borda and beyond.

Conclusion

The predominant concern and thematic focus for Highland novelists has been writing, culminating in Caballero Calderón's metafiction. In contrast to the novels of the Costa and Greater Antioquia, after *Manuela* there has been no equivocating in the Highland text concerning the privileging of writing over orality. If anything, Eugenio Díaz's rustic ways and doubts about the value of intellectuals (and their writing culture) are at least partially responsible for his relative anonymity. Even though it is a major nineteenth-century Colombian novel, *Manuela* has passed relatively unrecognized, yet it was an early exercise in self-conscious tendencies.[80] Thereafter, the major Highland novels tend to be ironic reflections on the fate of intellectuals and writers and on the act of writing.[81] Silva's *De sobre-*

mesa, Soto Borda's *Diana cazadora,* Rivera's *La vorágine,* Zalamea Borda's *Cuatro años a bordo de mí mismo,* and Caballero Calderón's *El buen salvaje* are novels of writer-figures who, in essence, relate their respective "adventures of writing" under a variety of guises. *Cuatro años a bordo de mí mismo* carries the subtitle "Diary of the Five Senses"; to varying degrees, each of these novels could have the same subtitle. As the form of the novel evolves over the century, Highland novelists are acutely sensitive to these changes and often make their ambivalent feelings about the form and limits of the genre a part of the reader's experience.

Despite the predominance of writing culture in the Highland region, there remain some traces of oral residue in its novel. In *Manuela,* the character of Manuela herself brings orality to the novel and places into question the values of writing culture. Soto Borda gives some oral effects to *Diana cazadora,* integrating colloquial language, thereby creating humorous effects in the juxtaposition of oral and written diction. The protagonist of *Cuatro años a bordo de mí mismo* observes an oral culture. In *El buen salvaje* we have noted an idealizing of certain concepts associated with oral culture. Orality, however, does not inform the Highland novel in a significant way.

The technology of writing, of course, developed markedly during the four periods represented by these novels. Díaz published *Manuela* not as a "novel," in the fashion novels are mass-produced today, but as some sketches that appeared in serial fashion in *El Mosaico.* At the turn of the century Soto Borda was undertaking radical experiments with the technology of writing, publishing stories in vertical lines with blue ink. Rivera participated in a nascent technology of mass-produced bestsellers, even though the volume of mass production was relatively modest by contemporary standards. His book fulfilled an important ideological function for a broad readership awaiting the fulfillment of Colombia's nationalistic project (see chapter 2). In *El buen salvaje,* the technology of writing gives structure to and often impairs the telling of a story. By 1966, the technology of writing, taken together with other factors of Highland intellectual culture, had made the possibility of just telling a story in novel form a challenging proposition indeed.

Writing in the Highland, of course, does not end with *El buen salvaje* in 1966. After that, with the advent of the young writers Albalucía Angel and R. H. Moreno-Durán, among others, novelists from the Interior Highland Region are most appropriately described not as Highland regionalists but as Colombian and Latin American writers. All of them, for instance, produced their fiction during lengthy stays in Europe. But the Highland tradition has also left an imprint on these writers, particularly on Moreno-Durán. Consequently, the most adequate context for discussing these cosmopolitan writers of a new generation is within the broad scope of contemporary modern and postmodern fiction in Colombia and Latin America.

Four

The Costa Tradition: From *Ingermina* (1844) to *Cien años de soledad* (1967)

Still to varying degrees many cultures and subcultures, even in high technology ambience, preserve much of the mind-set of primary orality.
—*Walter Ong*, Orality and Literacy

Gabriel García Márquez has claimed that *Cien años de soledad* is nothing more than an attempt to write a 450-page *vallenato*.[1] Both García Márquez and Alvaro Cepeda Samudio have emphasized the importance of the *vallenato*—a popular music form—in the Costa's culture. Germán Vargas, another prominent member of García Márquez's Group of Barranquilla and its most knowledgeable chronicler, has even stated that García Márquez himself was once the best singer of *vallenatos* of the group.[2] The *vallenato* is a music, accompanied by the accordion, which grew from popular roots on the Costa (first in the region of the present-day Department of Magdalena) in the late nineteenth century.[3] Before the modernization brought by telegrams, telephones, and nationally distributed newspapers, which arrived in the small towns of the Costa in the 1930s and 1940s, a primary source of information and news was a form of oral culture: the *vallenato*.[4]

The major composer of *vallenatos* in the twentieth century, Rafael Escalona, appears in *Cien años de soledad* as the character Francisco the Man and has been described by Alvaro Cepeda Samudio as a "great singer of tales" and "a chronicler whose only precedent in Colombia is Juan Rodríguez Freyle."[5] In the last thirty years the *vallenato*, like most forms of popular culture, has been assimilated by modern technology and is now produced on the records and cassette tapes that are a part of technology identified by Ong as secondary orality. *Cien años de soledad* is also the product of a modern, writing culture. However, both the *vallenato* and *Cien años de soledad*, quite likely the two most successful artistic phenomena to have been produced in the Costa in the twentieth century, find sources in the premodern, primary oral culture of the Costa of García Márquez's youth. Both García Márquez and Escalona were born in the 1920s, when forms of primary oral culture were still a viable and lively tradition in the small-town Costa.

Since the publication of Juan José Nieto's novel *Ingermina* in the mid-nineteenth century, *costeño* literature has been a part of both the writing and established oral traditions of that region.[6] *Costeño* artists who appropriated oral culture included the poets Candelario Obeso (1849–1884), Luis Carlos López (1879–1950), and Jorge Artel (1909–), the composer Escalona, and the novelists Cepeda Samudio and García Márquez. Nieto, José Félix Fuenmayor, and Héctor Rojas Herazo should be located in writing culture, although all three employ some oral effects. García Márquez, in addition to belonging to the first group, can be identified with the second: He can be placed with both groups because he participates fully in both the oral and writing cultures of the Costa. The novels to be analyzed in this discussion of the *costeño* novelistic tradition are Nieto's *Ingermina* (1844), Fuenmayor's *Cosme* (1927), two novels of 1962 (Cepeda Samudio's *La casa grande* and Rojas Herazo's *Respirando el verano*), and García Márquez's *Cien años de soledad* (1967). The novel as Archive, as defined by Roberto González Echevarría, will be considered as an important factor in the *costeño* novelistic tradition.[7]

While Highland culture has a predominant Spanish heritage with its venerable Hispanic literary tradition representing an elitist writing culture, *costeño* culture is tri-ethnic in heritage and represents a popular and oral culture.[8] The Highland has been conservative, closed, and unreceptive to change. The Costa, on the other hand, with its port cities, has been more receptive to outside influences and innovation. From Colonial times the Costa has even benefited intellectually from its strategic location for contraband.[9] *Costeño* oral culture has co-existed with writing culture, the former located primarily in the small towns and rural areas in the Costa and the latter in the cities. The vast differences between the culture of a town such as Aracataca and a city such as Barranquilla in the 1920s, for example, or between Cartagena and Chimá in the 1880s, correspond to the phenomenon that Fals Borda has described as the uneven development of the Costa.[10] Some areas of this region, especially before the nineteenth century, were predominantly a primary oral culture of people who were illiterate; in the twentieth century many of the areas of primary orality have become a residual oral culture that has strongly affected literary production.[11] A closer look at the uneven chronological and geographical development will bring this unique juxtaposition of cultures into better focus.

The Costa has origins in both Spanish literary tradition and a local primary oral culture, and both these origins center historically on the port of Cartagena. Cartagena was one center of the Spanish bureaucracy during the Colonial period, a *ciudad letrada* with a small, lettered elite.[12] The Spaniards also brought with them an influential form of oral tradition, the *romance*.[13] At the same time Cartagena was one of the main centers of slave traffic in the New World; some 150,000 slaves passed through Cartagena destined for either the Reino de Nueva Granada or other parts of the Spanish empire.[14] Cartagena fell into economic decadence during the nineteenth century, but a small writing elite remained, as did the oral tradition of the *romance* and the tri-ethnic, popular culture of the Costa, which was strongly influenced by Afro-American culture. In the Costa the black slaves would eventually work in the Magdalena River mining towns of Guamocó, Simití, Norosí, and Loba. The city of Mompox on the lower Magdalena River, a *ciudad letrada* of Colonial splendor, was a distribution center of slaves to these other inland *costeño* towns.[15] This region centered around Mompox became a center for Afro-Colombian culture strong in oral traditions. Fals Borda has documented the presence of oral culture in the region in considerable detail, describing, for example, the popular image of the "tortoise-man" (*hombre-hicotea*) in the San Jorge areas of Mompox, a perfect example of the real human lifeworld vision typical of oral cultures.[16] Fals Borda also points out that in San Jorge "the main concern is the present moment," an example of what Ong has described as the homeostatic nature of oral cultures.[17] Numerous other specific examples of a living oral culture in the Costa can be cited from Fals Borda's four-volume study and the anthropological writings of Manuel Zapata Olivella.[18]

The black presence in the Costa relates directly to the slave rebellions during the Colonial period that led to the founding of villages of black rebels, *palenques*, some of which have survived for centuries, such as Palenque de San Basilio, a village located between Mompox and Cartagena. Palenque de San Basilio can be seen as the opposite pole from Cartagena's Spanish and lettered aristocracy: It has consisted entirely of runaway African slaves, virtually isolated for over three centuries from the writing culture of the Costa's cities. Even as late as 1924, the year *La vorágine* was a bestseller in the remainder of Colombia, contact between Palenque de San Basilio and the nation was tenuous.[19] Only after 1945 did Palenque de San Basilio begin to have regular contact with the outside.[20] This isolated Afro-Colombian culture has developed its own language, *palenquero*, the only Spanish-based creole language in the Western hemisphere.[21] The case of Palenque de San Basilio is perhaps the most extreme example, but certainly not the only one that could be cited that points to the heterogeneity and uneven development of the oral-based tri-ethnic culture of the Costa.[22]

In curious juxtaposition with this tri-ethnic popular and oral culture are the modern and progressive elements of the Costa. This juxtaposition is best understood first in geographic terms. One key to an understanding of the phenomenon, as suggested already, is what Fals Borda has identified as the uneven development of the Costa.[23] A primary oral culture remains in areas such as Palenque de San Basilio, the Mompox lowland region, and in varying degrees in the small towns in the inland area. The context for modernity has been larger cities, most prominently the three port cities of Barranquilla, Cartagena, and Santa Marta.[24] Barranquilla was an unimportant village during the Colonial period but grew progressively throughout the nineteenth century, becoming the largest metropolitan center in the Costa by the beginning of the twentieth century. The first steamboats connected Barranquilla to the interior in the 1830s via the Magdalena River, and this fluvial transportation made Barranquilla the major exporter when coffee from the interior became Colombia's principal export from the 1880s.[25] By the 1920s Barranquilla was becoming a modern city with an expanding middle class. An example of Barranquilla's modernity is the fact that Colombia's first radio stations and movies arrived there in the 1920s. (At the same time, small towns in the Costa did not yet have highways connecting them to major cities or even electricity, yet another example of the Costa's uneven development.) Cartagena and Santa Marta also grew significantly in the twentieth century.

Unlike the comparatively isolated and conventional Bogotá, Barranquilla of the twentieth century, perhaps because it is a port city, has been more progressive and receptive to foreign influences, literary and other. Ramón Vinyes, a Spaniard from Catalonia, brought much modern European literature and the latest avant-garde cultural trends to Colombia by publishing the cultural magazine *Voces* in Barranquilla from 1917 to 1920.[26] Another foreigner, the American Karl C. Parrish, contributed in the 1920s to the modern architectural layout of the El Prado neighborhood, still present in Barranquilla. During the 1940s and 1950s José Félix Fuenmayor functioned as a literary father figure for a group of artists and intellectuals, later to be designated the Group of Barranquilla, which consisted of García Márquez, Cepeda Samudio, journalist Alfonso Fuenmayor (1917, son of José Félix), and journalist and critic Germán Vargas (1919).[27] They were avid readers of Faulkner, Kafka, Borges, Cortázar, and other modern writers still of relatively little import elsewhere in Colombia. The Barranquilla newspaper *El Heraldo* (and in recent years its Sunday cultural supplement) has played an active role in *costeño* writing culture since the 1940s, regularly publishing the work of García Márquez, other members of the group, and the latest European and North American writers. From the 1950s to the 1980s *El Heraldo* has contributed significantly to the diffusion of *costeño* literature in Colombia, always maintaining an open and cosmopolitan attitude toward the contemporary international cultural scene.

One of the most striking features of the Costa's economic and political history lies in the fact that it is the only region of Colombia with a formerly dependent export economy of foreign ownership.[28] The most frequently cited and best-known case is the United Fruit Company's presence in Colombia. In 1899 the Colombian Land Company merged with the Boston Fruit Company, and the resultant United Fruit Company began operations in the Costa; two years later United Fruit had consolidated all banana production in Colombia. In 1928 striking workers of the United Fruit Company were massacred by Colombian soldiers, an event that not only left an indelible mark on the collective memory but also informed the novels of Cepeda Samudio and García Márquez four decades later. The United Fruit Company, however, was not the only foreign enterprise to establish operations in the Costa. The French Compañía Francesa del Alto Sinú was established in the upper Sinú River region in 1844 and was followed by several foreign companies: the George D. Emory Company of Boston, which exploited wood in the Sinú region; the Colombia Company, which acquired land in the Sinú area in 1892; the South American Gulf Oil Company, which was in the Costa in 1920.[29] In addition to the celebrated banana workers' strike in 1928, the 1920s in general were years of conflict between workers and ownership in the Costa. The Sociedad de Obreros y Artesanos was founded in Montería in 1918.[30] The participants in the Group of Barranquilla were born during a decade of intense social conflict in the Costa, and popular legend and collective memory kept these conflicts alive until they were inscribed in written form in *La casa grande* and *Cien años de soledad*. As a result of living in a dependent export economy, among other factors, the *costeño* writer has expressed a notable social and historical conscience.

The Costa at present consists of seven departments: Guajira,

Magdalena, Cesar, Atlántico, Bolívar, Sucre, and Córdoba. La Guajira is predominantly indigenous and mestizo, with a historically strong oral tradition and a relatively inactive writing culture, with the exception of *La casimba* (1959) by Isaac López-Freyle. The remainder of the Costa is best described as tri-ethnic. In the present-day Department of Magdalena, the cities of Santa Marta and Valledupar were founded by Spanish conquistadores in the sixteenth century. Valledupar later became renowned as a center of the *vallenato*. Many small towns of Magdalena were founded in the late eighteenth century.[31] The train line from inland passes through Valledupar and Aracataca, García Márquez's boyhood town, to Santa Marta. Near Santa Marta is Ciénaga, the site of the 1928 banana workers' strike. Contiguous with Magdalena is Atlántico, the capital of which is Barranquilla, the setting for the fiction of José Félix Fuenmayor, Abraham López-Penha, and Manuel García Herreros.

The departments of Bolívar, Sucre, and Córdoba—one state until the twentieth century—resemble each other in their cultural heterogeneity. Cartagena and Mompox, two Colonial *ciudades letradas*, produced the writers Juan José Nieto, Manuel María Madiedo, and Candelario Obeso. Bolívar and Sucre keep alive another popular music form with functions like the *vallenato* in the Department of Magdalena, the *porro sabanero*. As one inhabitant of this area has explained, "My *porro* has the taste of all the best in my region."[32] The Magdalena River lowlands, discussed above, share the region with the writers Manuel Zapata Olivella (born in Lorica, with fiction located in parts of Córdoba and Bolívar) and Héctor Rojas Herazo. Rojas Herazo's native town of Tolú functions as the setting for *Respirando el verano* and *En noviembre llega el arzobispo*.

Finally, it should be noted that Fals Borda's monumental *Historia doble de la costa* is in itself a tribute to the Costa's simultaneous development of oral and writing culture. The verso pages of this book are Fals Borda's compilations of the Costa's oral and popular culture, the "other history" frequently forgotten or left untapped in conventional written histories. The recto pages of the text are the sociologist/historian's formal research, the product of writing culture. Oral culture was a vital force in nineteenth- and early twentieth-century *costeño* Colombia (as well as in isolated pockets of the Costa today), always co-existing in juxtaposition with writing culture. It was not until the advent of the commercialized *vallenato* (on records and cassettes) and the publication of books such as *Cien años de soledad* and *Historia doble de la costa* that the Costa's rich oral and popular culture, as well as its unofficial "other history," became accessible to the writing culture's Bogotá, Mexico City, and New York. This "other history" is a factor in making *costeño* fiction what has been identified as "novel as Archive."

Ingermina (1844) by Juan José Nieto

In the second volume of his *Historia doble de la costa*, dedicated entirely to Juan José Nieto (1804–1866), Fals Borda describes a figure of humble origins who married into Cartagena's upper class, went into political exile in Jamaica, where he wrote four books, and enjoyed regional political success in the 1850s and 1860s as a *caudillo* in the Costa. Prior to his exile he had published one of the first books of *costeño* regionalism, his *Geografía histórica, estadística y local de la provincia de Cartagena* (1839), described by Fals Borda as the first regional geography written in the country.[33] In exile in the 1840s, Nieto wrote a *Diccionario mercantil* and three novels: *Ingermina* (1844), *Los moriscos* (1845), and *Rosina o la prisión del castillo de Chagres* (published in serial fashion in Cartagena's newspaper *La Democracia*, (July 11 to October 10, 1850). Nieto represented a new type of *letrado* of the nascent republic which would have been impossible in the *ciudades letradas* of Cartagena and Mompox during the Colonial period. In addition to his nonelite origins, Nieto was tri-ethnic and autodidactic.[34] His novels have been generally ignored in critical studies on the Colombian novel.[35]

Ingermina is a historical novel set during the Conquest and Colonial period, as announced in the book's full title: *Ingermina o la hija de Calamar: novela histórica o recuerdos de la conquista, 1533 a 1537 con una breve noticia de los usos costumbres i religión del pueblo de Calamar*. This complete title reveals the author's archival source ("with a brief notice on the customs and religion of the people of Calamar").[36] The novel is basically the story of Alonso de Heredia (brother of the conquistador Pedro de Heredia) and Ingermina, an orphan Indian princess with whom Alonso falls in love and marries. After depicting confrontations with the Indians and political intrigue among the Spaniards, *Ingermina* concludes happily with the uniting of Ingermina and Alonso.

Ingermina is divided formally into four parts: a two-page dedication; a thirteen-page introduction to the customs of the Indians of Calamar; a ninety-three-page "Tomo I"; and a one-hundred-page "Tomo II," the latter published as a separate volume. In addition, there is a one-page list of twelve "subscribers," a noteworthy page in terms of the technology of writing.[37] The first two parts provide con-

siderable insight into Nieto's intentions and view of his mission as
novelist. The first part, a two-page dedication, is titled "Gift to the
señora Teresa Cavero de Nieto" and is written in epistolary form to
Teresa. The narrator begins by stating in the first line that he is unsure why he writes.[38] He speaks of an "impulse" here that he then
maintains recalls that of the romantic writer. On the one hand, he
uses the romantic argument that his writing is the product of an obscure force which he cannot control (Nieto, iii). He also positions
himself as the suffering romantic. The author offers an observation
which questions the political function of literature by denying that
writing has any concrete effect outside the artifice of fiction: "Letters aren't rocks with which one can break heads, although they
have a magical power over the spirit" (Nieto, iii). Unlike Eugenio
Díaz in Bogotá a decade later, who claimed to have written some
simple sketches (never mentioning the word "novel"), Nieto does
conceive of his work unequivocally as a novel, as he explains (Nieto,
iii). This explanation is then signed "Juan José Nieto," thus fictionalizing Nieto as a romantic and literary figure. According to this
fictionalization, Colombia's first novelist might or might not exert
some direct political effect by writing.

The second part, the thirteen-page introduction to Indian customs, has the following title: "On the customs and religions of the
people of Calamar. Taken from the fragments of an ancient unpublished chronicle of the Augustinians of Cartagena, by Fray Alonzo de
la Cruz Paredes. Serving as introduction to this work." The title of
this introduction reveals a double intention. On the one hand, the
narrator assumes the role of nineteenth-century scientist, in the tradition of Alexander von Humboldt, José Celestino Mutis, and other
Enlightenment figures, whose descriptions of the New World were
embodied in scientific discourse, as "science" was then understood.[39]
Nieto takes this "scientific" approach to storytelling, describing in a
scientific discourse and considerable scientific detail exactly how
Calamar's Indians governed themselves, how they organized their
society, what they ate, their religion, their economy, and their physical appearance. The scientific discourse that mediates this language
contributes to a reading of the novel as Archive.[40] In addition, the
title of this section reveals the function of *Ingermina* as Archive,
that is, a novel with sources in Colonial chronicles, supposedly
based on an unpublished chronicle of the Augustinians of Cartagena, written by Fray Alonzo de la Cruz Paredes.[41] The narrator concludes this section as Archive by adding a final note of historical veracity: The Spaniard Rodrigo Bastidas was on the Caribbean coast in
1501, and Alonzo de Ojeda and Juan de la Cosa were there in 1509.

What has been identified as the third part consists of "Tomo I," narrated almost entirely by an extradiegetic-heterodiegetic narrator who assumes a role of omniscience. There are two exceptions to this narrative situation. The narrator occasionally interrupts the narrative to inject brief editorial or essayistic comments. For example, he enters directly near the beginning of Tomo I to justify his deviation for nationalistic reasons: "But I have deviated because of you, my country, which I love so much" (Nieto, 5). The second exception appears in the last chapter of Tomo I (chapter 8), in the form of a framed story told by Velásquez, a shipwrecked Spanish soldier who also relates his own account of learning the ways of Indian life and becoming integrated into Indian society. The anecdotal content of Tomo I consists of the following: the conquest; plans among the Calamar Indians to marry Ingermina to the Indian Catarpa; Alonso de Heredia's "civilizing" of the Indians, particularly Ingermina; the falling in love of Alonso and Ingermina; the rebellion of the Indians, which is quelled; Alonso's conquest of Sinú and return to Cartagena; and finally, Velásquez's story, which he himself narrates.

Tomo II, the fourth part, is told almost in its entirety by an extradiegetic-heterodiegetic narrator who assumes a role of total omniscience. The following exceptions occur: Velásquez's wife relates a six-page narration of being victimized by the barbarous Spanish tyrant Marcoya, who took her as a slave; and Gambaro, the son of a cacique, relates a seventeen-page narrative about his love for Armosala, not accepted by his father, and the battle against the Spanish conquistadores.

Several unique features of this narrative situation operate in the novel. On the one hand, the narrator assumes the role typical in nineteenth-century narratives of the all-knowing scientist. If science is the discipline that mediates nineteenth-century Spanish-American fiction, as González Echevarría has suggested, then *Ingermina* exemplifies the novelist-scientist at work, especially evidenced in the introduction, the numerous footnotes, and the editorial comments. On the other hand, the narrator cedes the narration to some unique characters of New World storytelling, and in doing so Nieto presents the voice of the New World, not of the Spanish conquistador, for the first time in the Colombian novel. The shipwrecked Velásquez's story is, above all, one of assimilation, the first process of acculturation to take place in the Colombian novel. His wife's story offers the underlying theme of victimization and liberation, a constant topic throughout the book, for it connects with Pedro de Heredia's conquest in the initial pages of Tomo I, only now offering a view of the conquest from an Indian perspective. The vision of the

Spanish conquistadores set forth by Nieto is fundamentally one of the benevolent civilizer. Nevertheless, he privileges the Indian and New World side of the story by providing the narratives of Velásquez, his wife, and Gambaro. It should be noted that the most lengthy of the three is that of the Indian Gambaro—the "other history" of which many contemporary Latin American novelists have spoken.

The final unique feature of the narrative situation concerns the implied reader.[42] This postulated reader is a *woman* who may have been in love before. In Tomo II, when Badillo has jailed Alonso, separating him from Ingermina, the narrator makes the following statement to this implied reader: "Tú, amable lectora, si alguna vez has amado de veras, dirás si tenía razón la hija de Calamar" (You, kind reader, if you have truly loved, can say if the daughter of Calamar was right) (Nieto, 19). Unlike the masculine *lector*, which can include readers of both genders, the feminine word *lectora* establishes Nieto's (and 1840s Colombia's) hierarchy clearly: *Writing* is the domain of the authoritative male figure implied in the narrator's role in the text; *reading* is the passive role of females.

Ingermina is the first of three *costeño* historical novels related to the Archive in this chapter, reaffirming Carlos Fuentes's statement that the gigantic task of Latin American literature has consisted in giving voice to the silences of its history.[43] Raymond D. Souza has pointed out that, with the Independence, the Spanish-American writer was interested in helping the new nations define themselves, and part of this process was the examination of the past.[44] Souza also observes that the theme of the *buen salvaje*, taken from the Europeans, coincided with the admiration for the Indian heroes, an anti-Spanish phenomenon produced by the independence movement. (See also chapter 3 concerning the *buen salvaje* theme.) Nieto does not fit exactly into either of Souza's generalizations concerning Spanish America as a whole, but some notable connections can be made. With respect to defining national identity, in this Colombian case Nieto did not command a truly national vision. Rather, he was more concerned with defining a regional identity for the Costa. His 1839 geography was not of Colombia but of the province of Cartagena. Nieto's attitude toward the Spaniards was not based on the typical nationalism of the period either. He does depict the unfortunate indigenous population as losing its *patria* to the Spanish invaders, and the Badillo of Tomo II is the stereotype villain. Nevertheless, Alonso de Heredia and the Spaniards in general appear not as the "civilizers" of the Indian population but as the outsiders. A basis of the plot and the ultimate felicitous denouement depend on Alonso "civilizing" Ingermina to his satisfaction. In Genette's terms, the

nuclear phrase which summarizes the novel's action could be for-
mulated as follows: "Alonso civilizes Ingermina." The expansion of
this verb would be the entire conquest and civilizing of the Indian
population in the novel. A constant theme in this process, at both an
individual and a group level, is freedom: Ingermina, the Indian population, and even certain Spaniards (Alonso and Velásquez) lose and
gain freedom during the process. Metaphorically speaking, *Ingermina* is a reworking of the freedom theme of the Independence. For
Nieto freedom from Spain, the individual freedom being contested
in 1840s Colombia (during Nieto's own limited freedom), and the
Costa region's freedom from central authority are being elaborated
in this multithemed novel, which depicts the conquest as the process of civilizing and the parallel process of attaining and losing
freedom.

As a historical novel, *Ingermina* shares some characteristics of
the novel as Archive.[45] The *récit* begins with an intriguing historical
context: "Acababa la Aurora de anunciar al pueblo de Calamar el
hermoso sol del día 14 de enero de 1533* [*sic*] cuando el Adelantado
Don Pedro de Heredia, después de haber pasado revista al ejército, se
aproximaba con sus Castellanos † [*sic*]" (The Aurora had just announced to the people of Calamar the beautiful sun of January 14 of
1533*, when Don Pedro de Heredia, after having reviewed his army,
approached his Spaniards †). The novel's opening sentence is replete
with the facts of time and place. An equally typical opening for a
nineteenth-century Spanish-American novel, and frequently used in
Colombia, would have been more or less the following: "The Aurora
had just announced to the people of C*** the beautiful sun of January 14 of 15***, when Don Pedro de Heredia . . ." The typical nineteenth-century novel feigned historicity and flaunted its fictionality
by using a procedure such as this, purposely avoiding the precise
date, the place, and the names of historical figures. Nieto, however,
having provided his "Brief Historical Note" prior to the *récit*, continues with an ostensible historian's approach, including the exact
location, date, and historical character involved with the events at
hand. The reader also notes deviations from historical discourse:
"Aurora" carries the capital *A*, announcing a literary rather than scientific discourse, as does the phrase "the beautiful sun."

In contrast, in what appears to be a historian's strategy, the narrator includes two scholarly footnotes, one interrupting the sentence with an asterisk, and the other appearing at the end of the sentence indicated with a dagger. These two footnotes create a patently
ambiguous dimension of the historical/fictional discourse noted up
to this point. The footnote corresponding to the asterisk reads sim-

ply "Historical." The reader may ask if only the year is historical or
if the entire date is. And, by logical extension, the reader may won-
der how historical the phrase "the beautiful sun" might be. Patently
ambiguous and hardly a model of scholarly documentation, the footnote places in doubt the narrator's role and capacity as "historian"
per se. (Numerous other ambiguous footnotes which say only "Historical" appear throughout the text.) The footnote corresponding to
the dagger, appearing at the end of the sentence, does not offer scientific or historical discourse either but rather a narrative that relates
Pedro de Heredia's story as a seven-and-one-half-line narrative to expand the *récit* from the initial four and one-half lines. Upon completing the first sentence, along with its corresponding footnote, the
reader has read twelve lines of *récit* concerning Pedro de Heredia's
background and arrival to Calamar, in addition to one ambivalent
note indicating the supposedly "historical" nature of this story.

Throughout the remainder of the text the footnotes provide the
novel with a facade of Archive (as in the initial footnote/asterisk)
and develop the *récit* (as in the footnote/dagger). González Echeverría has set forth three basic characteristics of the novel as Archive:
the presence not only of history, but of previous mediating elements
through which it was narrated, be they legal documents of Colonial
times or scientific documents of the nineteenth century; the existence of an inner historian who reads, interprets, and writes the
texts; the presence of an unfinished manuscript that the inner historian is trying to complete.[46] The documents that implicitly fulfill
the first category are those footnotes. They all appear as asterisks or
daggers but number a total of twenty-five. The exact source of each
note is not indicated, but it is implied that the Colonial archives represent the source of all information offered in the text, particularly
the footnotes, from the initial subtitle to the "Brief Historical Note,"
a reference to the Augustinian friar's unpublished chronicle. Of the
twenty-five notes, almost all are historical or scientific in nature.
Three are basically extensions of the *récit*.[47] The remaining twenty-
two notes can be divided into three categories. Eleven of the notes
are historical in nature, seemingly from the friar's Colonial archive.[48]
Another three could be labeled nineteenth-century science, because
they are based on supposedly "scientific" observation, in the tradition of von Humboldt and Mutis.[49] Similarly, two notes could be
classified within the social sciences today.[50] Finally, the author includes six footnotes which supposedly belong in the category of Colonial archive—historical document—but which, in reality, are ambiguous notes that identify passages as "Historical."[51]

Nieto has created an Archive with respect to González Echevarría's first characteristic, both the presence of history and the previous mediating documents. However, no character appears as an inner historian who reads, interprets, and writes the texts (as does Melquíades in *Cien años de soledad*). The individual who fulfills this role in *Ingermina* is the narrator. An inner historian as character or an unfinished manuscript implies a level of self-consciousness and play not present in *Ingermina*. It is a work with some elements of the historical novel, which González Echevarría has identified as Archive, but the fully developed historical novel will not appear in the Costa until the 1960s. Like García Márquez, nevertheless, Nieto relates the forgotten and now inaccessible documents of the Colonial archives and succeeds in making them an integral part of the *costeño* story. The new republic, now democratic (the sign of freedom so often evoked in the novel), allows for the revelation of previously secret documents. In several ways, then, Nieto's partially developed Archive initiates a *costeño* novel which intends to tell the "other history." This partial Archive culminates in the more successful historical novel and complete Archive, *Cien años de soledad*.

Nieto's sources in *Ingermina* are derived almost exclusively from writing rather than oral culture. Unlike Eugenio Díaz, who attempted to deal with the dynamics of orality and writing of nineteenth-century Colombia in *Manuela*, Nieto constructed a novel conceived entirely within the writing culture of the aristocratic Cartagena in which he aspired to be accepted.[52] Consequently, in accordance with the political contingencies he faced, he excluded almost entirely the enormous potential of vital orality of the 1840s Costa. A portion of the novel is dedicated to what could be called once again (as seen in *La vorágine*) the drama of writing. Alonso's "civilizing" of Ingermina (again, the nuclear verb) is essentially teaching her to read and acquire the subsequent knowledge associated with writing culture. For Alonso and Ingermina, knowledge is exclusively the content of writing culture. Even when Alonso defends his choice of Ingermina to Pedro, expressing his view of the equality of all humans, the language is still of "ignorance" (i.e., oral culture) versus "knowledge" (i.e., writing culture). He explains that Ingermina's "ignorance," as compared to a Spanish woman's "knowledge," does not negate the fact that all women have the same "nature." His defense of *mestizaje* depends on the assumption that the assimilated Indian can learn what is worthwhile of written culture, as Ingermina ("Christian and educated") has successfully done.

Nieto reveals no intention of novelizing the oral culture that would represent an anthropologically sound version of the indigenous presence of the sixteenth century or the nineteenth-century tri-ethnic and oral culture in which he lived. The Indians in *Ingermina*, rather, are presented in favorable terms because they seem to govern themselves and behave according to European models. Above all, they possess a nineteenth-century European sense of *patria*. Nevertheless, an implicit (probably unintentional) text contains the other half of the Costa's culture—its oral culture. The narrator/ anthropologist observes this oral culture but fails to allow its recognition in his narrative. It has already been noted that some of the footnotes are those of a nineteenth-century social scientist who observes society "scientifically." The narrator fails, however, as observer of "the stupid simplicity" [sic] of these Indians (Nieto, 24). Behind the "ignorance" of orality, nevertheless, is Rousseau's ideal of the natives' innocence, an ideal orality implied throughout the text. This idealization is communicated in several ways: in the characterization of Ingermina and the description of the Indians "of such beautiful condition" (Nieto, 70); rewriting Rousseau, Indian life is described as a "life filled with innocent delights" (Nieto, 70). These citations imply an idealization of a premodern, prewriting orality, a nostalgia to be fully exploited in *Cien años de soledad.*

In his expansion of the nuclear verb "Alonso civilizes Ingermina," Nieto assumes the role of novelist or, as he would write it, "Novelist." In contrast to the Highland novel, where the subject of fiction has always been, above all, writing and where the novel itself has been consistently problematized, in the Costa the novel is born as history and story. From Nieto forward, the Costa writer assumes the role of historiographer and storyteller unabashedly. In addition, the Costa writer proceeds with no visible signs of the weight of the Hispanic tradition so often expressed in the Highland. *Ingermina*'s characters are engaged in a series of roles in search of freedom, and by playing out his plot of oppressor and oppressed (in its multiple variations of binary oppositions), Nieto fulfills the role that the contemporary Latin American novelist has assumed, that of the creator of the "other history." As a tri-ethnic writer attempting to matriculate into Cartagena's lettered elite by means of the pen, Nieto is only vaguely interested in what might be called the "other culture"—the oral culture that surrounded him outside the walled city of Cartagena. He does not have the means for assimilating oral culture (any more than the typical Spanish-American writer of his time did), and even the orality of his dialogues is totally influenced by the noetics of writing. Not until García Márquez would the means be available to *costeño* writers to fully assimilate both the fertile oral and writing cultures of storytelling (both linked to oral storytelling) and history (which depends on written documents).

Transition (1844–1926) and *Cosme* (1927) by José Félix Fuenmayor

The transition from *Ingermina* to *Cosme* is radical; no region in Colombia experienced as drastic a transformation as the Costa, particularly in the city of Barranquilla, during these eighty-three years. Social and economic development transformed Barranquilla from a village to a modern city and, as novelized by García Márquez in *La hojarasca*, several foreign companies arrived and departed from the region. Two novels of national importance, *María* and *La vorágine*, were read among small groups of literati in the Costa, despite their isolation from most of the cultural activity in other regions. In the Costa, as elsewhere, intertextual resonances of *María* and *La vorágine* were present in later novelistic production. Several local writers, such as Abraham Zacarías López-Penha and Víctor Manuel García Herreros, also published novels. The most significant literary event between *Ingermina* and *Cosme*, however, was the creation of the cosmopolitan magazine *Voces*.

After the publication of *Ingermina*, novelistic production was relatively sparse in the Costa in the nineteenth century; both the printing presses for fiction and an ample middle-class reading public were lacking. Nieto published two more novels, *Los moriscos* (1845) and *Rosina, o la prisión del Castillo de Chagres* (1850). *Los moriscos* is set in Spain during the expulsion of the Moors, but Nieto relates the situation to his own project for freedom in Colombia: "Exiled from my country because of one of those excesses of power which are so common in politics, it was natural that I often identified with the Moors when I was writing."[53] In his prologue, Nieto also cites as sources of this novel both the "chronicles," as Archive and the oral tradition of the *romancero* from Spain. Interestingly enough, he begs the indulgence of "enlightened men" for offering them a book with oral sources; in effect, this is an apology to the heirs of the once noble *ciudad letrada* of Cartagena for using oral and popular sources from the *romancero*.

The three significant novelists to appear between Nieto and *Voces* were Manuel María Madiedo, Candelario Obeso, and Abraham Zacarías López-Penha. Madiedo and Obeso dealt with aspects of the Costa's tri-ethnic culture absent in Nieto's fiction. Madiedo's *La maldición* (1859) represents the first attempt in the novel of the Costa to fictionalize elements of this culture. The protagonist, Carlos, returns to Colombia from Paris after a twenty-year absence. His journey up the Magdalena River is a classic encounter between European writing culture (represented by Carlos, who has been educated by "able professors" in Paris) and the oral culture of the Costa (represented by Diego, the elderly and wise fisherman who accompanies him). Diego's spoken language is the first attempt in the Colombian novel to imitate the speech patterns of orality, the same language of the Magdalena River lowlands that Obeso popularized in his colloquial poetry. A crucial moment in *La maldición* occurs when the reader can observe Carlos's transformation from a person of a writing culture to someone starting to integrate himself into an oral culture. The narrator explains how the protagonist begins to lose his distant manners and talk like the local inhabitants.[54] In the remainder of the novel he will learn more of the region's vital oral culture.

Abraham Z. López-Penha was less interested in oral culture in *La desposada de una sombra* (1903), but he clearly delineates the regional locale in a city of the Costa in his depiction of "B***," obviously Barranquilla. The initial pages portray the city's renowned celebration of popular culture, the annual carnival.[55] Later the same popular music will appear in the background. López-Penha's anomalous novel, however, is by no means a tribute to oral culture. Rather, it relates a bizarre story of the narrator/protagonist's spiritual tribulations as he pursues the ephemeral love of an even more ephemeral woman.

The importance of the magazine *Voces* in Barranquilla during the second decade of the twentieth century (1917 to 1920) cannot be overemphasized. The intellectuals involved with *Voces* formed what could be called the first Group of Barranquilla.[56] Germán Vargas has explained that *Voces* differed from other publications in its consistent humor and its presentation of new writers from Colombia and abroad.[57] In view of the Costa's regular contact with foreign sources, it was scarcely surprising that the founder and de facto director of this magazine was the Catalonian Ramón Vinyes. The sense of humor noted by Vargas contrasts with the solemnity and sobriety of the Highland tradition. This playful humor will be a constant in *costeño* fiction from Fuenmayor to García Márquez. On one level, *Voces* served as a regional organ, publishing the most accomplished *costeño* fiction writers at the time: Fuenmayor, García Herreros, and the short-fiction writer and poet Gregorio Castañeda Aragón. Modern and avant-garde figures to appear in the cosmopolitan *Voces* included Chilean poets Vicente Huidobro and Gabriela Mistral, Mexican José Juan Tablada, Peruvians Abraham Valdelomar and José María Eguren, and R. B. Cunninghame Graham.

Two of Fuenmayor's contemporaries in the Costa during the 1920s were García Herreros and Pedro Sonderéguer. García Herreros wrote two short novels which represented the two principal options open to a writer of that decade: His *Lejos del mar* (1921) relates a trip to Meta—a discovery of the New World—and his later book, *Asaltos* (1929), is set in Barranquilla—the urban option. Sonderéguer chose the first alternative (the same as *Lejos del mar* and *La vorágine*) with his *Quibdó* (1927), a story set primarily in an exotic Chocó. As in *Lejos del Mar* and *La vorágine*, the protagonist in *Quibdó* finds himself occasionally overwhelmed with the New World experience, feeling "plastered by the marvelous view of the gulf."[58] Gregorio Castañeda Aragón, in a novelette titled *Náufragos de la tierra* (1923), also chose to fictionalize a conflict between man and nature. In both its sparse style and theme, *Náufragos de la tierra* can be seen as a precursor to García Márquez's *La hojarasca*.

José Félix Fuenmayor clearly chooses the urban setting—his native Barranquilla—rather than New World experience. His first literary creations were poems, *Musa del trópico* (1910). After collaborating with Vinyes on *Voces* in the late teens, he directed the newspaper *El Liberal* in Barranquilla in the 1920s when he also wrote his major fiction, *Cosme* (1927) and *Una triste aventura de 14 sabios* (1928). His short stories *La Muerte en la calle* (1967) appeared posthumously. The advent of García Márquez and the Group of Barranquilla has unquestionably contributed to Fuenmayor's recent recognition in Colombia. Nevertheless, it should be noted that *Cosme* did achieve some recognition at the time of its publication.[59]

Alvaro Cepeda Samudio, in referring to the writers of the Group of Barranquilla, once said that "we all came from Fuenmayor."[60] Consequently, it is logical that the humor of *Cosme* resembles that found in *Voces* and *Cien años de soledad*. Fuenmayor's novel is the entertaining and tragic story of the protagonist Cosme growing up in the new, modernizing Barranquilla of the 1920s. The novel begins humorously with Cosme's future parents, Damián and Ramona, receiving advice from the physician, Dr. Patagato, concerning the sexual practices they will need to carry out in order to conceive their son. The playful second chapter tells of Cosme's birth, developing from a "little microscopic animal" to a young baby. The early chapters deal with his youth. He becomes a voracious reader and experiences adolescent rites of passage involving fights with classmates and an infatuation with a young girl. It is also a novel of crisis: Cosme's father is unable to establish a stable life and he must work on a ship, where he meets and falls in love with Srta. Tutu; the family problems sharpen when Damián loses the mortgage to their home. Cosme's encounters in the later stages of the book include the one with Srta. Tutu and another with his friend Remo Lungo, who explains to Cosme the novel he has written. Damián dies near the end of the novel, and Truco, captain of the ship on which Cosme worked, attacks Cosme because of his relationship with Srta. Tutu, apparently leaving him dead.

Cosme appeared three years after the publication of *La vorágine*, while the national sensation created by Rivera's novel was still raging. Consequently the light tone and antirhetorical language of *Cosme* are particularly notable. Though an anomaly on the national scene, it fit perfectly in a humorous and irreverent *costeño* culture.

Cosme can be seen as an expansion of the nuclear sentence "Cosme suffers." The expansion of this verbal action relates Cosme's suffering from multiple causes: as an adolescent, his suffering in the struggle for affection and for employment, his suffering the loss of his family, and, finally, his suffering the attack of Captain Truco. The basic plot is prefigured in each chapter by a brief résumé of the content, which appears in the form of lengthy subtitles. The résumé of the first chapter differs from the others in that it relates a verbal action, using two verbs, the first of which relates directly to Damián's suffering.[61] Chapter 2 uses a brief description rather than a verbal action, and the remaining chapters contain verbless descriptions and consequently do not relate directly to the expansion of the nuclear verb.

The narrator of Cosme's suffering is located consistently outside the story (extradiegetic-heterodiegetic), narrating from an assumed omniscience. His attitude and tone are contributing factors to the novel's humorous effects. However, the narrator does not assume a role of total omniscience and sobriety in storytelling, at one point playfully claiming to be unsure of a character's whereabouts (Fuenmayor, 143). The narrator often assumes a humorous attitude toward the events at hand; his description of Cosme's prenatal state ridicules scientific discourse, depicting his "biological state" similar to that of a crocodile (Fuenmayor, 24). His description of Cosme's learning to walk also reveals a humorous attitude, using the animal-human comparison once again (Fuenmayor, 28). Foreshadowing García Márquez's *Cien años de soledad*, the narrator occasionally employs understatement.

Cosme is not a novel of elaborate characterizations or profound psychological development. In contrast to the excessive emotion in *La vorágine*, in *Cosme* the characters function as an element of the novel's play, entering with little or no introduction on the narrator's part. The one exception is Cosme, whose lengthy introduction, even from a prenatal state, is part of a satire of the scientific details of human evolution and results in a humorous treatment of the subject. Much of the humor is situational. In one instance, the narrator describes Cosme "crossing the street . . . with his butt hanging out" (Fuenmayor, 57). Cosme often appears as a caricaturesque person, as do others. Barbo, for example, is described as leaving Cosme with wings like a penguin (Fuenmayor, 214). This situational humor, in addition to other varieties of humor, will be exploited by García Márquez several decades later.

The Costa's oral culture is integrated into *Cosme* in a significant way, even though Fuenmayor and his novel are prominent elements of the writing culture of 1920s Barranquilla, with its eyes on the European avant-garde. Nevertheless, a certain awareness of orality is communicated by means of the colloquial, spoken language, in opposition to a written, literary language. Even more important are the attitudes toward written culture expressed in the novel. The issues of writing culture, debated for decades in Colombia, and more specifically classic humanism, practical education, and modern science are all dealt with in *Cosme*.[62] The scientific discourse that had mediated the nineteenth-century novel in general, as proposed by González Echevarría, and *Ingermina* in particular has become the object of parody. In addition, it should be kept in mind that the 1920s marked the waning years of the Conservative hegemony with its intellectual counterparts, the classical humanists.

The revealing chapter with respect to these issues is chapter 12, which contains a discussion of Cosme's education. Here Cosme has just completed his *bachillerato*, or high school education. One of his teachers, Dr. Colón, praises Cosme's academic performance and then discusses education in general with his father, Damián, and Dr. Patagato. Dr. Colón points out that Cosme has not enjoyed a classical education—"he doesn't read or write any dead languages" (Fuenmayor, 78). When Colón explains that he has exposed Cosme to modern litcratures, Damián responds with a statement questioning the valuc of the classics. Dr. Patagato then contributes another element which also questions the real value of classic humanism. Patagato relates the story of a Greek scholar who lived in an unhappy home. In general, the content of their conversation questions the authentic value of a classical education and favors a more modern and practical preparation. Colón maintains that wisdom (*sabiduría*) is not a characteristic of classical scholars, who, according to him, are "maniacs" and "wise men" (Fuenmayor, 80). Dr. Colón's conclusion is notable in both content and diction: "Finally, I'll add that, as far as your son is concerned, Cosme is well prepared to not be a Greek lover, as well as hc is to embrace without risk of error the art of shoemaking" (Fuenmayor, 83). On the one hand, Colón clearly

undermines classical scholarship as an ideal. To make this statement in favor of practical knowledge, he uses the term *chambona-
das* (errors), a colloquial term from the Costa. In effect, he valorizes
the "art" of shoemaking. The entire chapter and the statement by
Colón in particular can be seen as metaphors for a debate concerning
the value of writing culture (with classic humanism as one of its
most sophisticated forms) and oral culture (common-sensical attitudes and colloquial language having their roots in oral culture).
Cosme himself is little concerned about his formal education and
classic humanism. In every sense, chapter 12 is one which emphasizes the modern, the practical, and the immediate over the written
classics of the past.

After this chapter, Cosme has nothing to do with the superannuated classic humanism, but he does become something of an intellectual. As a modern intellectual his interaction with writing culture is noteworthy. The first signs of his intellectual activity are the
love poems he writes as an adolescent upon being rejected by Lucita,
and the narrator depicts this writing as a parody of the anguished
romantic poet. Cosme's father, Damián, finds some of his poems, is
alarmed by their content, and discusses his concern over them with
Dr. Patagato. Their conversation (chapter 11) reveals a misunder-
standing of poetry and more of the deep-seated suspicion of writing
culture which had been suggested in the previous discussion of the
classics. The father's solution to Cosme's problematic activity is to
involve his son in the business world.

The intellectual in this novel, Cosme appears as the antihero representative of writing culture. He is characterized as an inefficient
and dreamy intellectual who at times aspires to be a hero but always
fails; he is unsuccessful in the basic rituals of his relationships with
women, and in this regard is the opposite of Cova, the hero and
womanizer in *La vorágine.* Just as Cosme fails with Lucita as a
youth, he is unsuccessful with Srta. Tutu as an adult. Rather than
the traditional hero as portrayed by Arturo Cova, Cosme is the modern, intellectual antihero. Near the end of the novel, when Cosme's
family has lost its household belongings, Cosme wanders direction-
less through the streets of the city, epitomizing the antihero.

Cosme is an epistemological dialogue with connections to both
oral and written sources. The narrator expresses a constant suspicion of the most sophisticated forms of writing culture, as demonstrated in the attitudes toward the classical humanist tradition,
modern science, and the modern writer. The modernity of *Cosme* is
not so much in its use of the narrative techniques of modernity as in

its dialogue on the conflict between tradition and modernity in the Costa. The modern novel is integrated into *Cosme* only through the presence of Remo Lungo, who appears in chapter 35 to explain his own novel, a fantastic work with no geography and no clearly delineated time frame.

The exceptionality of *Cosme* is to be found not in its modernity but in its absences. Absent is the traditional hero in a nation where all male protagonists were heroes. The rhetorical and emotive language of most early twentieth-century Colombian narrative, still laden under the weight of both Romanticism and *modernismo*, are also lacking. *Cosme* does not contain the traditional lengthy introductions to characters and descriptions of setting. The formula for the fully elaborated *récit* is pure anecdote (or pure *histoire*, excluding complements such as description) and dialogue.

The priority of pure anecdote, the humor, and the playfulness of *Cosme* all link Fuenmayor to later *costeño* fiction and García Márquez. Consequently, it is understandable that Cepeda Samudio would state that the writers of the Group of Barranquilla (Cepeda and García Márquez being the most prominent) all come from Fuenmayor. Some specific passages from *Cosme* also associate it directly with García Márquez. Doña Ramona's death, for example, culminates with the same understatement used in the otherwise hyperbolic story of a legendary matriarch in García Márquez's "Big Mama's Funeral." The description of Saturita's disappearance at the end of a chapter is similar to many inexplicable events in García Márquez's fiction, including one of his favorite phrases, "para siempre" (forever or for always) (Fuenmayor, 150). The Archive is identifiable in *Cosme* only as the object of parody. However, *La casa grande* and *Respirando el verano* are, above all, rewritings of *costeño* history.

Transition (1928–1961) and *La casa grande* (1962) and *Respirando el verano* (1962)

The period from *Cosme* to the publication of *La casa grande* and *Respirando el verano* witnessed the interaction among members of the Group of Barranquilla and the writing of García Márquez's early fiction. *La hojarasca* marked in 1955 the beginning of the modern novel not only in the Costa but also in Colombia. During this period García Márquez also published his first stories (1947 to 1952) and a decade later *El coronel no tiene quien le escriba* (1961) and *La mala hora* (1962). *La hojarasca* was the most important novel of this period, and the most significant literary event, other than the publication of this novel, was the rise of the Group of Barranquilla. The fiction of Zapata Olivella and Amira de la Rosa also appeared during these years.

The late 1920s and 1930s saw the growth of printing houses in the Costa, a phenomenon enhancing culture in each region. In Barranquilla the Imprenta Mogollón and Editorial Mundial began publishing authors from that area. Neither operated as a publishing house in the modern sense, lacking techniques used today for contracting, marketing, and distributing novels. They simply printed books. Mogollón also operated a small regional chain of bookstores. The rise of these printing houses did result in an increased number of novels published in the Costa from the late 1920s forward. Fuenmayor, in fact, published his second novel, *Una triste aventura de 14 sabios*, in 1928 with the Editorial Mundial in Barranquilla. This novel is still something of a curiosity in Colombia—one of the rare cases of science fiction written there.

The continued modernization of Barranquilla and the growth of printing houses were the most important cultural developments in the Costa during the 1930s—more significant than the fiction of that period. Juan B. Fernández, Alberto Pumarejo, and Luis Eduardo Manotas founded the newspaper *El Heraldo* in 1933. Dionisio Arango Vélez, Aquileo Lanao Loaíza, Marzia de Lausignan, and José Ramón Lanao Loaíza also published novels, but the most notable developments with respect to modern fiction in the Costa during this period took place with the appearance of the first stories by García Márquez, in addition to fiction of Amira de la Rosa and Manuel Zapata Olivella. Amira de la Rosa wrote mostly short pieces of prose fiction but also published a novelette titled *Marsolaire* (1941). This story demonstrates a superb control of narrative technique and well-handled transitions between the interior and exterior worlds of the story. For *costeño* fiction, the late 1940s marked a turning point, for Zapata Olivella published his first novel, *Tierra mojada* (1947), and García Márquez began publishing his first stories. Zapata Olivella's *Tierra mojada* deals with workers' experiences in rural plantations. The young García Márquez, a law student in Bogotá in 1947, published his first story, "La tercera resignación," an experiment with the techniques of modern fiction. It is evident in this and his other early stories that he was a reader of Kafka and was seeking to create some kind of "other reality" in his fiction.[63] After García Márquez's departure from Cartagena for Barranquilla, he became affiliated with *El Heraldo* and was introduced to additional modern writers, including Faulkner, primarily through his association with Germán Vargas, Alvaro Cepeda Samudio, and Alfonso Fuenmayor. Zapata Olivella, who lived in Cartagena, occasionally socialized with the group in the Café Colombia in Barranquilla.[64] García Márquez was the only writer of the group who was a friend of the musician Rafael Escalona and met with Escalona and Germán Vargas in the Café Roma to hear Escalona sing his latest *vallenatos*, based, of course, on *costeño* oral tradition.[65]

The reception of Faulkner and other foreign writers in the Costa during the late 1940s and early 1950s was an important factor in the unique juxtaposition of a traditional orality and Western modernism. Contrary to the general situation of Colombian intellectuals of the period, the Group of Barranquilla was fervently antinationalistic and in favor of an openness to foreign literatures.[66] In the 1950s, for example, the only mention of Julio Cortázar in Colombia appeared when he was alluded to by a member of the Group of Barranquilla.[67]

The 1950s were marked by one novel of central importance, *La hojarasca*, and several lesser-known titles of relatively limited artistic achievement. Daniel Lemaitre opened the decade with *Mompós, tierra de Dios* (1950), a novel set in the city of Colonial splendor, Mompox. Since the novel takes place there, the emphasis on historical description and the reciting of *coplas* of oral tradition is not surprising. *La casimba* (1959) by Isaac López Freyle represents another effort to capture Guajira Indian history and culture with the written form of the novel. Novels such as it are indicators of the interest in conveying the specialness of the Costa's tri-ethnic culture and, in this particular case, from an Indian point of view.

The publication of García Márquez's *La hojarasca* marks a new direction for the *costeño* novel, although it contains elements from the past—Cosme, the Faulkner discovered by the Group of Barranquilla, *costeño* history. *La hojarasca* also points to García Márquez's subsequent fiction as well as *La casa grande* and *Respirando el verano*. The Faulknerian overtones in *La hojarasca* are abundant, from the language to the structure: It is clearly modeled after *As I Lay Dying*, with three main narrators who alternate in telling the story, which is preceded by a brief section with both historical and mythical overtones, told by an extradiegetic-heterodiegetic narrator.

Like *La hojarasca*, *La casa grande* and *Respirando el verano* are books of similar origins (Faulkner and *costeño* history), comparable dimensions (each are family stories of approximately 150 to 200 pages), and an identical focus (a home, *casa*). They were the first novels for each of the respective authors, although Cepeda Samudio had published *Todos estábamos a la espera* (1954), a volume of short stories, and Rojas Herazo had been publishing poems since 1952. Cepeda Samudio, who was born in Barranquilla and lived there most of his life, wrote only one novel, situating it in the *costeño* area of Ciénaga, the site of the 1928 strike and massacre of banana workers. Rojas Herazo was born and spent his childhood in the *costeño* town of Tolú, which is the location of all three of his novels, beginning with *Respirando el verano*. Rojas Herazo has never been considered a part of the Group of Barranquilla, but he was personally acquainted with its participants in the 1950s.[68]

In addition to the 1928 banana workers strike, *La casa grande* presents the story of a family that dominates the town and occupies *la casa grande* (the big house). A tour de force in narrative technique, the novel consists of ten unnumbered chapters, each containing a different method of developing a story set in a time frame immediately preceding and following the massacre. The principal characters are the family that has dominated the entire town from the *casa grande*, an imposing edifice visible to all. The first chapter, "Soldados," consists almost entirely of dialogue between two unidentified soldiers travelling to a zone in rebellion. Ten of this chapter's seventeen sections are the soldiers' dialogue (strictly voices with no intervening narrator), and seven are sections conveyed by an extradiegetic-heterodiegetic narrator. The first sixteen sections take place prior to the massacre, and the last after the event. This handling of events is Cepeda Samudio's first surprise of narrative technique: The history and story of the massacre are told without ever actually depicting the major event itself, a technique radically different from the typically violent and sanguinary novel of La Violencia. The second chapter, "La hermana" (the sister) consists of an interior monologue of one sister, directed in the form of *tú* to another. The time frame for this chapter is after the massacre. The third chapter, in which the populace kills the father, begins with an omniscient narrative about the father and then moves to nine numbered sections of dialogue among unidentified members of the population who speak of killing the father. In the tenth section of this chapter, instead of relating the father's death directly, the extradiegetic-heterodiegetic narrator relates what *la muchacha* (the girl) hears—in effect, the father's death. The fourth chapter, "El Pueblo" (the town or the people), contains two and one-half pages in which an extradiegetic-heterodiegetic narrator describes the town, always in simple and direct language. The fifth chapter is unique: It is a textual reproduction of "Decreto No. 4," dated December 18, 1928, and is the only historical document in the novel. Elsewhere, the conflict is generalized with no specific names, places, or dates. This decree begins with the heading "Magdalena, diciembre 18 de 1928." "Jueves" (Thursday), the sixth chapter, consists of three sections: Two feature extradiegetic-heterodiegetic narrators and the third is exclusively dialogue. The time frame is immediately before the massacre. The seventh chapter, "Viernes" (Friday), contains six sections related by an extradiegetic-heterodiegetic narrator, and the last of these six sections presents the generalized reaction of the townsfolk. This last section can be seen as a counterpoint to the dialogue between the soldiers in the first chapter; here is the view of the townspeople, who know nothing of the dialogue or the intentions of the soldiers. Yet another narrative technique appears in the eighth chapter, "Sábado" (Saturday). Here a dispassionate and objective extradiegetic-heterodiegetic narrator provides a minute-by-minute account from 5:10 A.M. to 10:00 A.M. of the morning of the massacre. "El hermano" (the brother), the ninth chapter, is narrated entirely by a "brother" in the family. The nine sections of this chapter alternate between the brother's account in the present (an "experiencing self") and his relating of past events (a "narrating self").[69] The last chapter, "Los Hijos" (the children), is exclusively dialogue, identical to the beginning of the novel, but the speakers are children, consisting of the generation that has survived and will be the future of the *casa grande*.

Like *La casa grande* and *La hojarasca*, *Respirando el verano* is a family story. In *La hojarasca* and *La casa grande*, the generalized hatred of the townsfolk against the respective families is evident. *Respirando el verano* is also similar to *La casa grande* since both works deal with intense hatreds, but these powerful emotions in Rojas Herazo's work are among members of the same family. The two central characters of Rojas Herazo's novels are Celia, the aging matriarch, and her grandson Anselmo. Celia lives a bitter life of solitude, apparently hating virtually everyone except one of her children, Horacio. She also appears to be fond of one of her sons-in-law, a Lebanese who marries Julia. The grandson Anselmo is portrayed during the years he is discovering the world through the description of some of his special experiences. In this connection, an important passage occurs in the fourth chapter, when Anselmo climbs the church tower to observe his town as a whole for the first time. *Respirando el verano*, like *La casa grande*, contains Faulknerian techniques, but technically it falls short of Cepeda Samudio's masterpiece. *Respirando el verano*'s twenty-three numbered chapters are divided into two parts, "Las Cosas en el Polvo" (things in the dust) and "Mañana Volverán los Caballos" (tomorrow the horses will return), which are conveyed for the most part by an extradiegetic-heterodiegetic narrator. (The two exceptions are chapter 11, which contains an interior monologue by Celia, and chapter 20, which is entirely her interior monologue.) In addition, Rojas Herazo evolves characters through the use of synesthesia. For example, one character is described "listening to the mist in the patio."[70] Rather than literally seeing or hearing events, characters often feel them intuitively: "She felt more than she saw" (Rojas Herazo, 95).

As *costeño* novels published the same year, *La casa grande* and *Respirando el verano* share striking similarities that invite parallel analyses. A central structuring element in both novels is the house. In *La casa grande* this image functions in opposition to the people of the town, representing, above all, the center of authority and power. The image of the house is evoked from numerous perspectives in *La casa grande*, from the soldiers encountering it in the first chapter to the children's continuation of the family traditions, as its inheritors, as noted in the last chapter. The house is a more complex element in *Respirando el verano*. The stories and the lives of Anselmo are intimately related to the *casa* and its heart, the patio. The child Anselmo contemplating the patio is the novel's first image. One of his most moving emotional experiences occurs when he climbs the church tower with Falcón to meditate on his *casa*—its windows, its roof, and the details of its colors. The narrator explains that Anselmo feels a "human concern" prior to this scene (Rojas Herazo, 33), then observes that Anselmo's feeling has a special meaning, suggesting that he is in the process of discovering the meaning of the concept of *casa*. Celia's life is also inextricably bound to the *casa*. After her arrival at the home from Ovejas in 1871 she only leaves once for two months to be at a hospital in Panama and "the rest was her house and the patio" (Rojas Herazo, 131). She develops a symbiotic relationship with the house, which is exactly her age, and it survives the same number of years as she does, falling apart three days after her death. The narrator states that "she and the house became one organ" (Rojas Herazo, 132). In both Cepeda Samudio and Rojas Herazo the vitality of life, with its conflicts and hatreds, centers on the *casa*.

Set in the Costa of the early twentieth century, *La casa grande* and *Respirando el verano* evoke a premodern, oral world. In both cases the narrative techniques are fundamentally of a Faulknerian modernity, but the fictional world is premodern and oral. (This simultaneous incorporation of the modern and traditional will be exploited masterfully in *Cien años de soledad*.) Cepeda Samudio stresses orality in two ways. On the one hand, he privileges the spoken word from the first chapter, which is exclusively dialogue. From this chapter forward, reality will be defined to a large extent by what people say. (In a world in which written history is an act of exercising political power, what is [subversively] said rather than what is [officially] written becomes essential to an understanding of reality.) Cepeda Samudio also uses a patently oral technique: the repetition of key images and themes. In the first chapter, for example, there is not a lengthy enumeration of several images but rather the repetition of a limited number of them, such as the image of the soldiers' boots and rifles. Similarly, in the last section of the seventh chapter (Rojas Herazo, 105–106) the narrator repeats the words *el pueblo* (the town) at the beginning of each chapter. *Respirando el verano* is set in an essentially traditional and premodern oral world in which the mindset of orality is omnipresent. In the fictional world of Rojas Herazo there are readers, such as Celia's husband (who constantly rereads *The Iliad*, a text, interestingly enough, based on oral tradition), but many of the characters think and react as members of the Costa's late nineteenth- and early twentieth-century primary oral culture. Characters in *Respirando el verano* are often guided in their actions not by the norms of a writing culture, with its modern science, but rather by inexplicable intuition or impulses. It is an oral-culture reasoning that a person in a writing world would identify as irrational.[71] Berta intuitively perceives her sister María's sadness, for example, rather than comprehending it in rational terms (Rojas Herazo, 95). When Celia leaves her home in Ovejas to begin her life anew with her husband, she sets out alone on a horse without asking any directions and arrives without mistake, apparently through instinct (Rojas Herazo, 131). The narrator occasionally assumes a role as a person in an oral culture (a role García Márquez assumes throughout *Cien años de soledad*); the narrator's description of Celia as one organism with the *casa* is how an oral-culture person would view the situation, exhibiting the tendency to conceptualize and verbalize all their knowledge with more or less close reference to the human lifeworld.[72]

The orality of *La casa grande* and *Respirando el verano* is one aspect of the heterogeneity that typifies the novel as Archive. Both represent a heterogeneous synthesis of orality, history, and myth, in addition to other factors. They are constructed around a real historical setting. In *La casa grande* it is 1928 Ciénaga (even though the town is never named) during the days preceding and following the massacre of the striking banana workers. In *Respirando el verano* the empirical historical setting is the region of Sucre and Bolívar during the second half of the nineteenth century and early twentieth century. The town of Tolú in Sucre, which is never named, is the focal point of the action, and the nearby towns of Ovejas, San Onofre, and Sincelejo are named, as is the nearby region of Sinú. The prosperous tobacco economy of the region during the late nineteenth century is mentioned as part of the socioeconomic background.

González Echevarría identifies the presence of previous mediating elements in the novel of Archive through which the story is narrated, a type of inner historian and a particular place such as a special room where the Archive is located. In *La casa grande* the previous mediating element is the "decree," the one historical document in the nation's archive which is the important difference between a story of human conflict and this particular story as Archive. The only inner historian in *La casa grande* is the figure of the narrator, who has rewritten history by organizing oral history and this document. In *Respirando el verano* there are no real documents but instead an inner historian and a special location for history. The inner historian is Celia, the voice of the past that explains family history to the young Anselmo (Rojas, 23). Under the influence of Celia, Anselmo begins to sense the "secret history" of the house (Rojas, 23), the patio functioning as the special place from which history emanates. The way history and the inner historian are present in these two novels is an example of González Echevarría's observation that the Archive is not so much an accumulation of texts as it is the process whereby texts are written, a process of repeated combinations, of shufflings and reshufflings ruled by heterogeneity and difference.[73]

The presence of myth in these heterogeneous texts is associated with orality and the characterization process. In *La casa grande* Cepeda Samudio creates characters of mythic dimension by repeatedly portraying them as larger-than-life types, a common occurrence in the oral story. Thus a conversation between the father and a girl who works in the home becomes a dialogue between "El Padre" and "La Muchacha," an encounter between two types as well as between the forces of power and the elements of submission and passivity (see the third chapter, "El Padre"). In *La casa grande* virtually no characters are named; Cepeda Samudio sets forth conflicts of broad, mythic dimension. Rojas Herazo does name his characters and endow them with specific human qualities, but Celia and her absent husband also take on mythic dimensions. Menton has appropriately described *Respirando el verano* as a precursor to *Cien años de soledad*.[74] This observation is well taken; more specifically, García Márquez's previous fiction, along with *La casa grande* and *Respirando el verano*, with roots in the Costa's premodern orality and modern Faulknerian techniques, were all antecedents to *Cien años de soledad*, the epitome of the Archive novel.

Transition (1963–1966) and *Cien años de soledad* (1967)

During the years 1963 to 1966, the most significant novelistic production consisted of three titles by Manuel Zapata Olivella, Fanny Buitrago's first novel, and Rojas Herazo's second. Zapata Olivella's fiction of the early 1960s depicts the Costa's tri-ethnic, oral culture. *En Chimá nace un santo* (1964), set in the region of Sinú and the towns of Chimá and Lorica, relates stories of the Costa's prodigious happenings and captures some of the magic of this oral culture before it was popularized internationally by García Márquez. Zapata Olivella is aware of the specialness of the culture he is fictionalizing, beginning with an epigraph on myths and magic in primitive cultures.[75] The story concerns religious fanaticism, but to depict the cultural milieu the author juxtaposes the superstitious and magical religion of an oral culture with the official religion of writing culture. The consequences of the cultural conflict in this particular novel are the worst, producing an ignorant and dangerous fanaticism. Zapata Olivella published two other novels during this period, *Chambacú, corral de negros* (1963) and *Detrás del rostro* (1963). The former deals with Afro-Colombians struggling for survival in Chambacú, a neighborhood of Cartagena. *Detrás el rostro* treats both rural and urban life with greater narrative sophistication. As Marvin Lewis has explained, Zapata Olivella uses a process of interiorization of experience instead of mere descriptions of series of occurrences.[76]

Fanny Buitrago and Rojas Herazo also anticipated some of the magic of Macondo. Buitrago's first novel, *El hostigante verano de los dioses* (1963), portrays a decadent and emotionally fatigued youth but also integrates elements of *costeño* culture. In *En noviembre llega el arzobispo* (1967) Rojas Herazo continues the family chronicle begun in *Respirando el verano*, further developing his use of Faulknerian technique.

García Márquez published three books after *La hojarasca* (1955) and before *Cien años de soledad* (1967): the stories of *Los funerales de la mamá grande* (1962), which were written in the late 1950s; and two short novels, *El coronel no tiene quien le escriba* (1961) and *La mala hora* (1962). Several of the stories reveal García Márquez's roots in *costeño* oral and popular culture. The title story of *Los funerales de la mamá grande* draws from this popular culture to satirize antiquated institutions by including descriptions of *costeño* culture to humorous extremes.[77]

The two novels represent the period of García Márquez's fiction when his writing was most overtly political,[78] the setting for this being, though unstated, La Violencia. *El coronel no tiene quien le escriba* is a novel of silences—of that which is not said in an environment of repression and violence. *La mala hora* dramatizes what is said at a popular level when public political discourse is stifled. Political discourse survives in *La mala hora* only at the level of the *pueblo*—the orality of "lo que se dice" (that which is said). Posters embody a part of this language, serving as a metaphor for literature in the form of resistance or protest. The public display of the posters is a unique example of the Archive—secret document—made public. The common roots with rumor are one characteristic that these posters share with literature. This multilanguaged novel contains the residual idiom of a society both in flux and in a process of decay.[79]

Cien años de soledad represents both a synthesis of the Macondo cycle initiated with *La hojarasca* and the culmination of *costeño* fiction with its roots in the oral culture and the tendency toward the novel as Archive. It is the total story (and history) of Macondo from an oral, prewriting society to its development as a sophisticated writing culture in the final chapters.

Cien años de soledad is the story of both the Buendía family and of Macondo. In terms of Genette's nuclear sentence, the novel's plot can be reduced to the basic sentence "The Buendía family persists" (seen as a family story) or "Macondo persists" (seen as the history of a town, nation, or civilization). In both cases the verb "to persist" (despite the town's ultimate disappearance) indicates the basic verbal action in the novel, from José Arcadio Buendía's persistent creation and Colonel Aureliano Buendía's equally persistent military uprisings to Macondo's survival in the face of national calamities and persistent development despite all the forces of tradition, as well as its maintaining of tradition in the face of modernity.

The narrator consistently and systematically employs a series of temporal strategies to expand this basic verb into an elaborate narrative. The two fundamental techniques are analepse and prolepse, and both are present in the novel's first line: "Many years later, as he faced the firing squad, Colonel Aureliano Buendía was to remember that distant afternoon when his father took him to discover ice."[80] The first three words, "Many years later," posit a prolepse which will be a consistent feature of the novel's temporal construction: The narrator will take the reader forward in time regularly, and in the first line of the tenth chapter he repeats the prolepse in a fashion basically identical to the first: "Years later on his deathbed Aureliano Segundo would remember the rainy afternoon in June when he went into the bedroom to meet his first son" (García Márquez, 174).

The orality of *Cien años de soledad* could be placed in two general categories: the orality of the folk tale, similar to the tradition of the "tall tale" in the United States,[81] and primary orality. The tradition of the tall tale connects with García Márquez's youth when he heard stories from his grandparents in the Costa's town of Aracataca. García Márquez claims to have discovered the key to handling the narrative voice in this novel when he remembered how his grandmother used to tell him stories. His discovery was that he should tell his story of Macondo as she told hers.[82] One consistently used technique which this narrator has in common with the teller of the oral tall tale is an absolute coolness or understatement when describing incredible situations and, on the other hand, a penchant for exaggeration when dealing with the commonplace.[83] In the ice episode of the first chapter, for example, the narrator's language shares the characters' exaggerated reaction to Melquíades's new object.

In contrast, the narrator regularly reacts to the most marvelous and fantastic things with absolute passivity—the lesson in technique García Márquez supposedly learned from his grandmother. Again, in the same first chapter José Arcadio and his children experience the disappearance of a man who becomes invisible after drinking a special potion. Neither the narrator nor the characters pay particular attention to this incredible occurrence. There are other similarities between this novel and the tall tale in the United States.[84]

Ong has observed that many cultures and subcultures, even in a high technology ambience, preserve much of the mind-set of primary orality. García Márquez, in a sophisticated product of writing culture, juxtaposes with writing culture much of the mind-set of the residually oral milieu of his youth in Aracataca. Both a primary oral culture and a sophisticated writing culture permeate *Cien años de soledad*, often in hilarious juxtaposition. Much of this novel recreates precisely the shift from orality to writing, changes hitherto labeled as shifts from "magic" to "science" (or Lévi-Strauss's "savage" mind to "domesticated" thought), which can be more cogently explained as shifts from orality to various stages of literacy.[85]

This transition from orality to various stages of literacy is essential to the experience of *Cien años de soledad* and is particularly evident when one compares the initial chapters with the ending. In the first chapter the mind-set of a primary orality predominates; in the last the most intricate exercises of writing culture are carried out. In the first chapter these two extremes are represented by Melquíades of a writing culture from the outside and by Ursula with a mind-set of orality. The Macondo of the first paragraph is one of a paradisiacal primary orality in which stones are "white and enormous, like prehistoric eggs." The use of the word *prehistoric* associates it with a prehistory, prewriting stage. It is not only a prewriting stage but borders on prespeaking: "The world was so recent that many things lacked names, and in order to indicate them it was necessary to point" (García Márquez, 11). José Arcadio Buendía, between the two extremes of Melquíades and Ursula, occupies a special link in this chapter between oral and writing cultures as he paradoxically belongs to both, reacting in some circumstances as an oral-culture person and in others as the only writing person in the predominantly oral milieu. José Arcadio Buendía is literate. Nevertheless, he reacts to science with the same ingenuousness of an oral person, conceiving Melquíades's magnets, for example, as a "weapon of war" (García Márquez, 12). Also typical of an oral-culture person's reaction to a writing mind-set is José Arcadio Buendía's response to Melquíades: "Even José Arcadio Buendía himself considered that Melquíades's knowledge had reached unbearable extremes" (García Márquez, 17). Oral-culture persons tend to view many of the modes and concerns of writing culture as irrelevant or even ridiculous.[86] Similarly, Ursula, in the first chapter, is uninterested in definitions and loses her patience with José Arcadio Buendía when he defines the world as round like an orange.[87] The oral mind is also situational rather than abstract,[88] the former being Ursula's constant mode of operation. When José Arcadio Buendía attempts to convince her to move from Macondo with his (abstract) fantastic stories and the (abstract) promise of a "prodigious world" (García Márquez, 22), her response is to bring him down from his high level of abstraction to the concrete reality of this situation: "Instead of going around thinking about your crazy inventions, you should be worrying about your sons" (García Márquez, 22). Thus, the world of the first chapter emerges as orality (Ursula), writing (Melquíades), and a humorous semi-orality (José Arcadio Buendía) that bridges the gap between the two.

After the first chapter Macondo moves from preliteracy to literacy. The narrator's mind-set also shifts from the feigned pre-orality of the first chapter to the historicity of the second. In the first chapter he had used the preliteracy image of "prehistoric eggs"; in the first line of the second chapter he uses the historical discourse of writing—"When the pirate Sir Francis Drake attacked Riohacha in the sixteenth century, Ursula Iguarán's great-great-grandmother became so frightened with the ringing of alarm bells and the firing of cannons that she lost control of her nerves and sat down on a lighted stove" (García Márquez, 27). In the final chapters *Cien años de soledad* announces itself not only as writing but as an example of the highly sophisticated forms of self-conscious fiction: It incorporates characters from other contemporary fiction and García Márquez's literary friends and characterizes Aureliano as reader in the act of deciphering parchments, which tell the story the reader has been reading.[89]

Cien años de soledad contains several qualities typical of oral noetic processes. One of these, also typical of the tall tale, is the use of "heavy characters," persons whose deeds are monumental, memorable, and commonly public.[90] The extensive litany of José Arcadio Buendía's exploits after his return from sixty-five trips around the world (fifth chapter) and Colonel Aureliano Buendía's military exploits (including losing thirty-two battles) are perhaps the best example of this particular oral noetic process.

A second typical oral process, already alluded to in the case of Ursula, is the use of concepts in situational frames of reference that are minimally abstract in the sense that they remain close to the human lifeworld.[91] The narrator assumes this role as an oral-culture person throughout much of the novel, often using down-to-earth and animal imagery, thus remaining close to the living human lifeworld. In some cases the narrator, when he takes such positions, is assuming a role similar to the characters. For example, he describes Amaranta at birth using the following animal imagery: "She was light and watery, like a newt, but all her parts were human" (García Márquez, 37).

The narrator assumes other roles typical of an oral mind-set. His treatment of Remedios the Beauty is that of an oral person both in form and content. The narrator regularly employs the epithet *la bella* for her in Spanish, a form common in oral storytelling. The scene in which Remedios rises heavenward is a typical description of how a person in an oral culture would view such an event.[92] Another characteristic of this narrator's storytelling is his copiousness. Oral performance demands flow: Hesitancy is always a vice, and the copious flow of oral performance is effected through repetition and redundancy.[93] The repetition in *Cien años de soledad* has been well documented.[94] García Márquez has conceived a novel with the copiousness and flow demanded in oral performance, one of the best examples being Fernanda's two-page, single-sentence diatribe (García Márquez, 298–300).

In addition to the narrator and Ursula, the most prominent examples of oral-culture individuals, other characters in this novel are either oral-culture persons or persons who occasionally react as such. By the twelfth chapter, for example, Macondo's inhabitants seem to be lettered and modern. Nevertheless, the chapter begins with a hilarious episode describing an oral-culture person's reaction to a modern apparatus: The people of Macondo become outraged and break the seats in the movie house because an actor who died and was buried in one film reappeared later in another alive as an Arab.

Oral cultures are also verbally agonistic. The Buendía family history begins as a result of Prudencio Aguilar's verbal challenge to José Arcadio Buendía, questioning the future patriarch's masculinity. The female characters are a special case with respect to orality and literacy. As is common in many traditional cultures, the males of Macondo are the lettered characters, beginning with Melquíades and José Arcadio Buendía,[95] whereas, in contrast, Ursula thinks and expresses herself consistently as an oral-culture person. In the latter parts of the novel Macondo's women do begin to read, usually finding themselves unfit for life in the masculine writing culture. The loss of the feminine oral culture affects the novel's denouement: The lettered Amaranta Ursula and Aureliano conceive a baby with the pig's tail not only because he abandoned his studies of the parchments at the point where he would have uncovered their blood relationship but also because neither of them remembers "Ursula's frightened admonitions." Their failure also represents the final defeat of a lost oral culture.

What has often been identified by the now overused and frequently vague term *magic realism* in this novel is more precisely described as a written expression of the shift from orality to various stages of literacy. The effects of the interplay between oral and writing culture are multiple. García Márquez has fictionalized numerous aspects of his youth in the tri-ethnic oral culture of the rural Costa. The unique traditionalism and modernity of this novel are based on the various roles the narrator assumes as oral storyteller in the fashion of the tall tale, as narrator with an oral person's mindset, and as the modern narrator of a self-conscious (written) fiction.

Conclusion

Like García Márquez, Nieto, Fuenmayor, Rojas Herazo, and Cepeda Samudio demonstrated historical impulses, but they did not develop the novel fully as Archive. *Ingermina* displays the nineteenth-century scientific discourse that becomes the object of ridicule in *Cosme*. *La casa grande* contains the historical document of the Archive, while *Respirando el verano* offers the heterogeneity of the Archive. González Echevarría, in his discussion of how myth and history coexist in *Cien años de soledad*, has proposed the three basic characteristics already outlined in this chapter, each of which is present in *Cien años de soledad:* the presence of historic and mediating documents through which the novel was narrated; the existence of an inner historian; and the presence of an unfinished manuscript that the inner historian is trying to complete.[96] History, of course, is amply present in the novel, from the nineteenth-century civil wars in Colombia to the 1928 banana workers' strike in Ciénaga.[97] In this case the Archive is in the Buendías' room, which is full of books and manuscripts and has its own time.[98] The unfinished manuscript, of course, is Melquíades's parchments, which are being deciphered at the end of the novel.

González Echevarría concludes that the most salient characteristic of *Cien años de soledad* is heterogeneity,[99] his point being the coexistence of history and myth within its pages. In addition, the heterogeneity of *Cien años de soledad* involves the coexistence of a conservative primary oral culture[100] based on the rural Costa's triethnic oral culture and a progressive modernity of a group of readers of modern literature—the Group of Barranquilla. At least in a metaphorical sense, as a masterful appropriation of orality, García Márquez's novel is a 450-page *vallenato*.

Cien años de soledad represents a culmination of two major tendencies in the novel of the Costa. It is a stunning synthesis of oral and writing traditions only partially achieved in the previous *costeño* texts, particularly in the novel, and, in this sense, is an expression of the Costa's uneven development. It also represents a synthesis of *costeño* history which had been striven for since *Ingermina*. After *Cien años de soledad*, both the work of García Márquez and novels such as *Mateo el flautista* (1968) by Alberto Duque López and *Changó, el gran putas* (1983) by Zapata Olivella indicate new directions for the *costeño* novel, well beyond regional traditions and boundaries.

Five

The Greater Antioquian Tradition: From *Frutos de mi tierra* (1896) to *El día señalado* (1964)

This awareness of writing culture is agony for persons rooted in primary orality, who want literacy passionately but also know very well that moving into the exciting world of literacy means leaving behind much that is exciting and deeply loved in the earlier oral world.

—*Walter Ong*, Orality and Literacy

Todavía se recuerda con gastronómico deleite el espesor de aquel mondongo, la suculencia de aquellos tamales! [We still remember with gastronomic delight the thickness of that mondongo, *the succulence of those* tamales!]

—Frutos de mi tierra

One of the most salient characteristics of the Antioquian tradition in the novel is a preponderance of nostalgia. From the region's early works by Tomás Carrasquilla to many of the modern novels, nostalgia permeates Antioquian fiction. *Frutos de mi tierra*, published in 1896, celebrates traditional, nineteenth-century Antioquian life and values. Social, political, and economic factors in Antioquian history can contribute to an understanding of Antioquian attitudes toward its past. A factor to be explored in the present chapter is precisely what Ong has described as the process of leaving behind much that is exciting and deeply loved in an earlier oral world.

Many Colombian and foreign intellectuals have attempted to define *antioqueños*, and adjectives such as "hard-working," "independent," and "adventuresome" frequently appear in their definitions. These adjectives are also associated with Antioquia's twentieth-century economic success. Well-intentioned or not, some of these explanations have fostered unfortunate racial stereotypes.

Greater Antioquia has not been as geographically isolated from the remainder of the nation as the Costa. Nevertheless, the culture of that region (including the present-day departments or states of Caldas, Risaralda, and Quindío) has been willfully independent of the remainder of Colombia and quite often in direct opposition to it. An indigenous population of approximately 600,000 inhabited Antioquia at the time of the conquest, but conflicts and disease swiftly reduced their numbers. The *antioqueños* of the Colonial period lacked the capital necessary to bring African slaves from Cartagena. Consequently, gold seekers from Antioquia went searching as independent prospectors: Many of the Spaniards, as well as the later generations of *criollos*, were thus forced into productive labor on their own account.[1] This situation gave an early impetus to Antioquia's egalitarian work ethic. The tradition of independence and egalitarianism, however, did not contribute to Antioquia's cultural development during the Colonial period. On the contrary, most observers were struck by the general backwardness, illiteracy, and poverty of the province until the end of the Colonial period. The situation was decisively improved in the late eighteenth century, when the Spanish crown appointed as administrator Oidor Juan Antonio Mon y Velarde. During the three years of his administration (1787–1790), he directed a cultural and economic renaissance.[2]

Antioquia's major city, Medellín, founded in 1616, was little more than a village during the first half of the nineteenth century. The image and memory of Medellín-the-village and the traditional life around it became one source of much nostalgic fiction in Antioquia. Key factors in Medellín's transformation from village to city were the markedly increased coffee production from the 1880s forward and the foundation of the textile industry by the end of the century. Nascent industrialization was further indicated by Antioquia's ten factories in place by 1900. A direct relationship operated between increased coffee production and industrialization: Coffee created the market and the capital for the subsequent industrialization.[3]

Three major elements are crucial to an understanding of Antioquian culture and its fiction. The first, to which we have already alluded, is Antioquia's egalitarian tradition. This tendency has fomented a literature based on popular tradition, regional custom, and oral storytelling rather than on the more elitist models of writing culture that were important in the Highland. The second major element is the presence of a strong primary oral culture in rural areas in the nineteenth century. This oral culture has influenced written culture in several ways, including the oral residue and oral effects connected with the late nineteenth-century writing of Tomás Carrasquilla. The third major element is a pervasive reaction during the twentieth century against modernity. This reaction can be explained in several ways: as a movement against industrialization and industrialized-culture values, as a nostalgia for the nineteenth century evoked in rural, small-town Antioquian life, and as a desire on the part of the elite to maintain the paternalistic society that was disappearing with industrialization.[4] A nostalgia for a lost oral culture is a factor in all these issues.

Perhaps the most telling example of Antioquia's root in oral culture and its nostalgic attitude toward its premodern past is a recent artifact of writing culture, a book entitled *Testamento del paisa.* (*Paisa* is a colloquial term for *antioqueño.*) Compiled by Agustín Jaramillo Londoño, this 572-page volume is a compilation of Antioquia's rich oral culture and popular traditions. Jaramillo explains in his prologue that all the material of the volume "is first hand, collected directly from the aged illiterates who, in turn, learned it as children from other aging men with good memories, from who knows when." As such, the volume functions as homage to the "old oral storytellers" who are now disappearing in writing culture. The volume contains an ample offering of oral and popular culture filtered through the medium of writing: oral tales, oral verse, "refranes" or oral sayings rooted in popular tradition, and other selections from folkloric traditions. The publication of such a volume, of course, does not actually preserve oral culture or popular tradition per se but rather serves as a method for keeping intact an artifact in the form of a simulacrum of what that oral culture was. It also functions as an exercise in nostalgia. This nostalgic impulse is revealed in the compiler's prologue to the fifth edition: He explains that his motive for publishing this book was the depressing spectacle of seeing the roots of popular culture disappearing forever.[5] This volume and its nostalgic function have been kept alive by Antioquia's readers with the publication of seven editions of the *Testamento del paisa* from 1961 to 1986.

Upon gaining independence Antioquia did not have a well-established intellectual elite such as that in the *ciudades letradas* of Bogotá, Popoyán, and Cartagena. In 1825 Medellín was a provincial town with a population of little over 6,000. Antioquia's literary production in the early nineteenth century was limited to an unimpressive set of political speeches, patriotic poetry, and parochial essays. Antioquia's most renowned nineteenth-century poet, Gregorio

Gutiérrez González, once boasted that he did not write in Spanish but in *antioqueño*. He published the voluminous and prosaic poem *Memorial científica sobre el cultivo del maíz en los climas cálidos del Estado de Antioquia por uno de los miembros de la Escuela de Ciencias; Artes; dedicado a la misma Escuela* (1866). Written in the popular language of the region, it is a detailed and realist description of the agriculture and land of Antioquia. In accordance with the region's work ethic and egalitarian tradition, this poem also celebrates the common man working the land.

Literary culture began to take form in Antioquia during the 1860s and 1870s. In addition to the publication of Gutiérrez González's poetry in the 1860s, Antioquia's first printing press for literature began operation in 1868, and the literary magazine *El Oasis* was founded in Medellín. Another sign of Antioquia's nascent literary culture was the publication of a volume titled *Antioquia literaria* by Juan José Medina in 1878. Its content of mostly essays and political speeches is less important than the fact that Medina conceived of the idea of an *antioquia literaria*. The most important prose writer of the nineteenth century to precede Carrasquilla was Emiro Kastos (pseudonym for Juan de Dios Restrepo, 1823–1894), author of numerous *artículos de costumbres*. Kastos's brief pieces of prose portrayed local customs, often in a light, humorous tone. Carrasquilla's predecessor in the novel, Juan Clímaco Arbeláez, published *Adelaida Hélver* in 1868, a short work unrelated to Antioquia; it is a first-person account of the narrator/protagonist's trip to Italy and acquaintance with a woman named Adelaida Hélver.

Frutos de mi tierra (1896) by Tomás Carrasquilla

The first major Antioquian novelist, Tomás Carrasquilla, typifies the middle-class Antioquian writer who did not belong to the elite that had formerly dominated Colombian literature, an aristocracy based primarily in the Highland region. Carrasquilla produced realist-regionalist fiction in considerable volume between 1896 and 1935. During the 1890s he began publishing short stories; his three most renowned novels were *Frutos de mi tierra* (1896), *Grandeza* (1910), and *La marquesa de Yolombó* (1926). In contrast with the cosmopolitan tastes of the turn-of-the-century *modernistas* (mostly elite writers located in Bogotá), Carrasquilla defended a realist-naturalist type of fiction which carefully located characters in their regional environment. *Grandeza* depends primarily on quaint character types, although it has a more intricate structure than most of the *costumbrista* work of the period.

In *La marquesa de Yolombó*, a historical novel set in the late eighteenth and early nineteenth centuries, Carrasquilla creates the impression of oral storytelling by using a loose and casual tone. He explains in his prologue that the principal source of his story is oral tradition: "All these recent circumstances are known only by verbal tradition." As such, he positions himself as a communicator of the oral tradition to a writing culture. Carrasquilla once described in a letter to Max Grillo his project as a novelist as follows: "My ideal is clear, Maximiliano: a national work with modern information; artists of the house and for the house. I dream of a literary 20th of July."[6] This statement reflects the content and discourse of his novels. First, he proposes an ambitious "national" novel which would somehow recognize the modern (with "modern information"). He then changes to a more colloquial discourse: "artists of the house and for the house." This phrase seems to imply a local or regional focus. The reference to Colombia's independence day, July 20, evokes nationalism once again. In its totality, the statement alludes to a number of ambivalences, including those produced by the interaction of oral and writing cultures.

Frutos de mi tierra has been appropriately described as one of the most outstanding Spanish-American novels of the realist tradition.[7] It deals with an Antioquian family in late nineteenth-century Medellín. The two principal characters, Agustín and Filomena Alzate, inherit from their mother, Señá Mónica, enough money to pursue their commercial enterprises and flaunt their wealth among Medellín's upper middle class. The basic plot centers on two love affairs: between the older Filomena and the younger César Pinto, the educated man of letters from Bogotá, and between the *caucano* Martín Gala and the local Pepa Escandón. The characters from these two plots never speak to each other, and there are only two occasions in which the two plot lines directly connect.[8] Sidetracks from these basic story lines involve sections of chapters, and occasionally whole chapters, on local customs—festivities, celebrations, songs, and dances. The two love-affairs result in marriages, although Filomena dies on the last page of the novel.

The referent for *Frutos de mi tierra* is a Medellín in transition. The growth of the coffee industry in Antioquia from the 1880s forward contributed significantly to Medellín's transformation at the turn of the century from small town—*pueblo*—to city. The growth of industry produced a new class of entrepreneurs who generated a radical change from the traditional agricultural economy of the *campesino paisa*. These transformations represented a parallel change from a strong oral culture in nineteenth-century rural Antioquia to a predominant writing culture in turn-of-the-century Medellín. This shift was accompanied by a national debate between those who defended the traditional, humanistic training in letters and those who favored the English model of technical education.[9] The latter obviously had exerted considerable impact in Antioquia by the end of the century, as is evidenced in *Frutos de mi tierra*.

Agustín and Filomena represent Medellín's new middle class and its values. Agustín's initial characterization emphasizes, above all, his bourgeois obsession with order: "exactness," "symmetry," and "polished" are three adjectives applied to him in his initial characterization.[10] Soon thereafter, the narrator observes how Agustín acts "with the equilibrium and parallelism which Agustín puts in everything" (Carrasquilla, 8). Filomena's values also represent well her class status and commercial interests. The narrator even describes the two siblings' relationship in commercial terms: "The case is that the two siblings complemented each other to form, in admirable unity, mercantile genius" (Carrasquilla, 25).

The nuclear verb which best summarizes the novel's action is "Agustín and Filomena acquire objects." This sentence includes the protagonists' varied acts of acquisition. On the one hand, it encompasses their enthusiastic acquisition of material wealth. This nuclear sentence also includes Filomena's relationship with César, which she conceives in commercial terms: Her declaration of her love to him includes giving him an expensive gift, implying future economic benefit in exchange for his wedding vow. The narrator explains what might be called her writing/business noetics: "Filomena's intellect, directed always toward mercantile business" (Carrasquilla, 205). As active participants in Medellín's new bourgeoisie, they dedicate themselves primarily to the act of acquiring, as their upwardly mobile name, "Alzate," implies.

The extradiegetic-heterodiegetic narrator, similar in some ways to the narrator in *Cien años de soledad*, assumes multiple roles as participant in both writing and oral culture in *Frutos de mi tierra*. As obvious participant in writing culture by virtue of his act of narrating, the narrator refers to classical literature either directly or indirectly. He creates parallels between such classic texts as the Bible and *Don Quijote* and characters and events in this novel.[11] More interesting are some of the narrator's attitudes toward this writing culture. He presents Martín's love affair as ridiculously determined by the noetics of writing—the writing of romantic poetry. In reference to the love-struck Martín, the narrator asks: "Wasn't love always made by the poets?" (Carrasquilla, 100). Following the literary model of Lord Byron, Martín pursues a "literary" love with Pepa, always presented in a humorous tone by the narrator.

Certain phrases also reveal the narrator's distanced position and critical attitude toward writing culture. The narrator explains the *bogotano* accent by ridiculing the erudite speech patterns used by *bogotanos* and promoted by the turn-of-the-century philologists Caro and Cuervo (Carrasquilla, 277). His description reveals some of his own oral-culture values. Although firmly located within writing culture, the narrator at times questions this culture's values by using an oral-culture's perspective.

Similarly, the narrator at times assumes the role of oral story-teller, employing either oral noetics or oral effects. The procedure frequently used to simulate an oral-culture person's vision is to employ phrases or words that Ong would identify as close to the human lifeworld. These words and phrases usually are associated with the animal world. The narrator uses María, a neighbor of the Alzates, as focalizer in order to present the following description of Filomena: "Suddenly and unconsciously [María] raised her head to look at Filomena and, within the view of that macaw biting grapes" (Carrasquilla, 54). What María sees—a macaw instead of a person—is that which an oral person sees. The narrator's text is replete with this type of animal imagery (see pages 174, 237–238, 313). These phrases represent the narrator's assimilation and simulation of an oral-culture person's language and thought processes.

The narrator fictionalizes a reader who appreciates and is skeptical of both writing and oral culture. This reader is called upon frequently to assume the role of a rural and traditional *antioqueño*: The references to "our flowers" (Carrasquilla, 17), "our gardens" (Carrasquilla, 131), and "our Antioquian towns" (Carrasquilla, 197) each fictionalizes a reader who is indeed one of "us" appreciating "our" Antioquian things. In a subtle fictionalization of an Antioquian reader, the narrator portrays a scene in a church using the demonstrative adjective "that" three times (Carrasquilla, 93), assuming a reader who is indeed acquainted with "that sound," "that movement of handkerchiefs," and "that general movement." These strategies fictionalize a reader, and in this case an Antioquian reader acquainted with such church scenes in Medellín.[12] This fictionalization corresponds to Carrasquilla's regionalist project, which celebrates Antioquia's traditional life and culture.

The implied author who orchestrates these varieties of position for the narrator and the reader incorporates both writing and oral culture into *Frutos de mi tierra*, frequently maintaining distance and a humorous, critical attitude toward both. What these multiple positions imply for the author, Carrasquilla, is his understanding of the transitions the culture was undergoing, above all the transformation from oral to writing culture in the Antioquia region.

As suggested, the implied author's position toward writing and oral culture is somewhat ambiguous. The ideological consequences of this ambiguous position are contradictory. The fundamental contradictions address issues of regionalism (and its related nostalgia) and ideology. On the one hand, this realist-regionalist fiction represents an encomium of traditional, nineteenth-century Antioquian values, from its oral culture to its work ethic. Regionalist interludes throughout the novel affect this encomium. The privileging of oral culture and its values is also an indirect praise of the traditional Antioquia that preceded the rise of modernity and the new bourgeoisie portrayed by the protagonists of *Frutos de mi tierra*. The narrator, from his position of "today," looks back to this past and comments nostalgically: "We still remember with gastronomic delight the thickness of that *mondongo*, the succulence of those tamales" (Carrasquilla, 20). From this same contemporary position signified by "today," the narrator describes the main plaza of Medellín (Carrasquilla, 22), nostalgically evoking images of the past which contrast with the present. He juxtaposes the quaint main plaza of the past (with the pleasant aromas coming from the store) with the now modern setting ruined by its modern stores. This narrator will continue to describe an approaching modernity (culminated in "today") which represents life and values inferior to the nostalgic past.

Contradictions arise when one considers the ideological subtext implied in this novel. As a point of departure, it is difficult to accommodate the above-noted nostalgic overtones with Carrasquilla's extratextual affirmation that his fiction would ideally include "modern information." The narrator describes Medellín as a modern, Liberal paradise (Carrasquilla, 31), replete with all the industry-produced textile products a consumer could desire. Logically enough, it is the same paradise that has constructed the modern stores that now ruin the formerly quaint plazas. In celebrating Antioquia, the narrator is also celebrating contradictory values, both those of the traditional oral culture and those of an increasingly commercial writing culture.

This supposedly Liberal narrator's attitudes toward class, race, and gender are even more contradictory: Predictably enough for a nineteenth-century text, they are consistently classist, racist, and sexist. The reader acquainted with these attitudes in nineteenth-century Spanish-American texts is not surprised. Nevertheless, it is difficult to accept both the narrator's celebration of the *pueblo's* popular culture and his sexist remarks about Pepa's grace and charm.

In conclusion, in *Frutos de mi tierra* Carrasquilla makes use of a formula from the writing culture—the established practices of the realist novel—and "nationalizes" it, so to speak, to produce an Antioquian realist-regionalist novel. This regionalism has roots in both form and content in a premodern and oral culture often presented nostalgically in this novel (and other later Antioquian fiction). In accordance with Antioquia's famed egalitarian tradition, Carrasquilla's text often privileges oral and popular culture. Nevertheless, the ideological subtext—which is classist, racist, and sexist in attitude—contradicts and subverts Carrasquilla's Antioquian and regionalist project. The implied author's position is as ambivalent about both oral and writing culture as it is about the class structure of the fin de siècle Antioquia.

Transition (1897–1932), *Toá* (1933) by César Uribe Piedrahita and *Risaralda* (1935) by Bernardo Arias Trujillo

The years between the publication of *Frutos de mi tierra* and *Toá* saw the production of a substantive portion of Carrasquilla's work and a nascent psychological fiction in Antioquia written by Luis López de Mesa and José Restrepo Jaramillo. Antioquia never had a true avant-garde in fiction comparable to the *Contemporáneos* in Mexico or the *Martín Fierro* group in Argentina. Nevertheless, Antioquian intellectuals produced magazines and some literature with modern impulses, the most important of these being *Pánida* and *Cyrano* and *Antioquia*. *Pánida*, which began publication in 1915 under the direction of the avant-garde poet León de Greiff, featured writers as diverse as Juan Ramón Jiménez and Oscar Wilde. The magazine *Cyrano* (1921–1923) contained writings of the prominent female intellectuals of the time—María Cano, Fita Uribe, and María Eastman—in addition to figures such as León de Greiff. Fernando González published the cultural magazine *Antioquia* irregularly during the 1930s and 1940s, with the conviction that "the only limit to our daring is lying."[13] At the same time, during the 1920s and 1930s an increased social awareness resulted in fiction of social protest, as evidenced in *Toá*.

After *Frutos de mi tierra*, turn-of-the-century Antioquia saw the first regular publication of novels by an entire group of writers. The most important of these new novelists were Samuel Velásquez, Eduardo Zuleta, Francisco de Paula Rendón, and Gabriel Latorre.

Their work falls within the realist-naturalist tradition, and some of their fiction confronts the same transitions from traditional rural life to modernity (and from a predominant orality to a predominantly writing culture) observed in *Frutos de mi tierra*. Velásquez published four regionalist novels: *Al pie del Ruiz* (1898), *Hija* (1904), *Madre* (1908), and *Al abismo* (1910). The works of more impact in Antioquia during the period were *Al pie del Ruiz* and *Madre*. *Al pie del Ruiz*, set in the Antioquian town of Manizales, has a disperse and rambling plot, portraying a region in crisis. The novel deals with the challenge to rural values of Antioquia, the effects of the recent civil wars, and ideological tensions. It does not contain as much oral, colloquial language as *Frutos de mi tierra*, although the characters do speak this language in the dialogues. The narrator does employ occasional rural imagery in descriptions.[14] The tensions between the new and the old—and oral versus writing culture—operate through the presence of the character Manuel, who learns a sophisticated writing culture in Bogotá, and the other characters, who are typically suspicious of writing culture's knowledge. (As has been mentioned in earlier chapters, Ong has pointed out that the common-sensical attitudes of oral-culture people usually result in a cynical attitude toward the exercise generated by writing culture.) *Madre* is set in Antioquia's countryside, telling the story of the dying breed of *arrieros* and thus responding to a fundamentally nostalgic impulse.

Zuleta and Rendón are comparable to Carrasquilla and Velásquez with respect to their handling of orality and writing in a regionalist setting, whereas Latorre is more cosmopolitan in approach, affected by the *modernistas*. In writing about Zuleta's *Tierra virgen*, Carrasquilla claimed that "what Zuleta writes, so similar to life, isn't a novel: it doesn't entertain."[15] Indeed, in comparison to the playfulness and humor found in *Frutos de mi tierra*, neither the works of Velásquez nor of Zuleta are attractive novels. Zuleta's *Tierra virgen* (1897) is too realist in approach and not playful enough for Carrasquilla's tastes: It narrates the story of three generations of an Antioquian family, from the mines of a small town called Remedios to its end in London. The narrator uses a strictly literary language. A culture in transition is appreciated in a female character, doña Juana, who had to hide from others to learn reading and writing autodidactically: "They refused to teach me to write because this was a 'temptation,' as my grandfather always said."[16] Antioquia's egalitarian tradition is signaled in this novel by the implied praise of the *antioqueño* work ethic and by the presence of Afro-Colombians in one chapter, considered by one critic as the novel's best chapter.[17] Rendón's *Inocencia* is equally realist in impulse and sober in tone as

Tierra virgen but drew the acclaim of many local intellectuals in Medellín because of its strong characterizations and scandalous plot for such a still conventional turn-of-the-century society: The protagonist Inocencia expires upon seeing her mother wed the man she loves.

The literary magazines *El Montañés, La Miscelánea,* and *Alpha* contributed significantly to the new literary dialogue in turn-of-the-century Antioquia. *El Montañés,* which began publication in 1897 under the direction of Gabriel Latorre, described itself as a "magazine of literature, arts, and the sciences." The first issue (September 1897) is noteworthy in the context of the status of writing in late nineteenth-century Antioquia. This issue featured a picture of Samuel Velásquez on the cover, a semiotic communication which privileges regional over national or foreign literatures. Under the picture, the editor portrays a situation in which amateur writing predominates over professionalism, offering the statement that Colombian writers rarely are more than *aficionados.*[18]

During this period, between 1896 and 1935, Carrasquilla wrote three novels (*Grandeza, La marquesa de Yolombó,* and *Hace tiempos*) and five short novels.[19] Kurt Levy has proposed that Carrasquilla's slogan as a writer was "to remember is to live."[20] Interestingly enough, Ong has pointed out that memory carries great importance in oral culture (knowledge is memory), a coincidence which suggests the seminal importance of orality in Carrasquilla's total vision. Much of Carrasquilla's remembering, as demonstrated in the analysis of *Frutos de mi tierra,* implied a nostalgia for the lost oral culture and rural life of nineteenth-century Antioquia. *Grandeza* (1910) shares several similarities with *Frutos de mi tierra.*[21] The most important in the context of this study is the implied author's satirical attitudes about writing culture. In the author's "Several Words," which precede the text, he assumes the unpretentious role of the storyteller who is not really a novelist.[22] *Grandeza* is set in Medellín and tells the story of Juana de Samudio's obsession with her daughters, a situation which eventually leads to her financial ruin. The main subject of this novel is the new aristocracy in early twentieth-century Medellín.

La marquesa de Yolombó (1927), as has been indicated, has sources in oral culture. It is Carrasquilla's culminating work in the sense that he fully exploits his interest in orality and traditional and rural Antioquia. He creates the impression of oral storytelling by using a colloquial language and by suggesting the narrator's presence without his actually entering to participate in the action.[23] Also in the tradition of oral storytelling, the narrator has absolute control of the story and gives the impression of regaling his listeners (and not readers). Set in small-town Antioquia at the end of the eighteenth century, *La marquesa de Yolombó* relates the story of the "self-made woman" in the sense that she teaches herself to read and write and becomes successful in the mining business. All this takes place in a culture where women were typically illiterate and not managing businesses; consequently, she attains the Antioquian ideal of independence. Both in its exploitation of Antioquia's dying orality (in the 1920s) and in its celebration of Antioquian popular culture and customs, *La marquesa de Yolombó* is one of the region's most notable products of the nostalgic impulse.

Carrasquilla's five short novels offer many of the same thematic concerns, types of characters, and handling of oral and writing culture of his full-length novels. The author consistently employs colloquial language with strong regional flavor, both in the voice of the narrators and the characters. *Ligia Cruz* (1920), one of the more complex short novels, deals with another exceptional woman who has entered the precarious world of writing culture. In fact, the female protagonist becomes so obsessed with novels that she changes her name from Petrona to Ligia Cruz in homage to her favorite novel, *Quo Vadis*.

Carrasquilla, writing squarely within the realist-naturalist tradition, was obsessed with the material world. The initiators in Antioquia of a more interior, psychological fiction were José Restrepo Jaramillo and Luis López de Mesa. Restrepo Jaramillo's *David, hijo de Palestina* (1931) is a psychological portrayal of its protagonist, with an occasionally moralistic tone. His later *Ventarrón* (published posthumously in 1984) is both a psychological study of a youth's maturation and a celebration of traditional Antioquian independence and the work ethic. Luis López de Mesa, renowned in Antioquia for his historical and sociological essays, also wrote two novels, *La tragedia de Nilse* (1928) and *La biografía de Gloria Etzel* (1929), both of which reveal an interest in essayistic writing. Urbane dialogue and occasionally long speeches by the characters are López de Mesa's principal vehicles for depicting the spiritual and psychological lives of his characters.

Restrepo Jaramillo and López de Mesa explored new possibilities for fiction in Antioquia and produced results that differed from the predominant realist-naturalist model established by Carrasquilla. Nevertheless, much Antioquian fiction of the first four decades of the twentieth century, instead of looking forward in the manner of Restrepo Jaramillo and López de Mesa, preferred to look back to the established model of Carrasquilla and back to Antioquia's past as exercises in nostalgia. The traditional novels of Arturo Suárez, such as *Montañera* (1916), *Rosalba* (1918), *El alma del pasado* (1920), *Así somos las mujeres* (1928), and *El divino pecado* (1934), responded to this traditionalist and nostalgic impulse.

The 1920s and 1930s saw the rise of a new social awareness and sociopolitical conflicts. An intellectual figure and prose writer who did not publish novels but who did represent this social activism was María Cano (1887–1967). A controversial figure in her time, she published journalistic works and short fiction during the 1920s at the same time that she was active in the new socialist movement. Novels such as Rafael Jaramillo Arango's *Barrancabermeja* (1934) and César Uribe Piedrahita's *Mancha de aceite* (1935) are of social protest, both works denouncing the exploitation of workers by foreign oil companies. *Barrancabermeja* (portrays a sordid world of ugly oil fields and bordellos. Uribe Piedrahita's less strident *Mancha de aceite* contains a series of documents and fragments to allow the reader the discovery of the social inequities in an oil operation in Venezuela.

Two important and representative novels of Greater Antioquia during this period, Uribe Piedrahita's *Toá* and Arias Trujillo's *Risaralda*, are also novels of social criticism. They are directly associated with the social reality of the New World experience. In this connection, both works can be related, as a point of departure, to the classic works of this type—*La vorágine, Don Segundo Sombra*, and *Doña Bárbara*. Uribe Piedrahita and Arias Trujillo also reveal the egalitarian impulses often noted of writers in this region.

Uribe Piedrahita typifies the stereotype of the *antioqueño* as adventuresome and of independent spirit. He studied medicine at the University of Antioquia, where he completed a thesis titled "Apuntaciones para la geografía médica del ferrocarril de Urabá" (1922), thereby demonstrating an interest in both the intellectual and the practical that he would pursue throughout his career. In 1924 he went to Venezuela to direct a hospital for a U.S. petroleum company, an experience which led to the writing of *Mancha de aceite*. He also travelled on several occasions to the jungle region of Caquetá, acquiring personal experiences which were used in the creation of *Toá*. Although this novel has not become part of the canon of Latin American literature, it has, nevertheless, drawn the serious attention of several critics of the Latin American and Colombian novel.[24]

Toá is the story of Antonio de Orrantia's experiences in the jungle, where he is sent by the central government to write a report. There he encounters the problem that comprises the central plot: The Colombian *caucheros* and the indigenous groups are in conflict with

Peruvians who are encroaching on the official border of Colombia and abusing the Colombian workers and Indian groups.[25] The *huitotos, sionas, carijonas, boras,* and *andoques* are Indian groups which are victimized throughout the novel. A subplot involves Antonio's love affair with Toá, a mestizo who has lived with the *huitoto* Indians. In the end Toá dies and Antonio, physically and psychologically exhausted, wanders aimlessly through the jungle.

The basic narrative situation involves an extradiegetic-heterodiegetic narrator who relates a story which could be essentialized in the sentence "Antonio searches." The verb "to search" includes both aspects of the plot—his search for an authentic identity in the jungle and his search for Toá. In fact, he loses her, searches for her, finds her, and then loses her again when she dies. Like many texts dealing with the New World experience, however, *Toá* is also a novel of a protagonist's learning. Following a common model for such New World novels of the period, a young protagonist (in this case twenty-eight years old) leaves the city to go to the country, where he begins a "new life" and receives "lessons."[26] Seen in this fashion, a more appropriate reduction of the plot would be "Antonio learns," since the verb "to learn" essentializes his action as New World protagonist.

Uribe Piedrahita's project is similar to many of that period in Latin America in that the author contributes to the New World identity by focusing on a social group that is "less sophisticated, less cultivated (in the European sense) than the city-dwelling members of the ruling class."[27] Sophisticated and cultivated in the "European sense" here refers to one's knowledge of writing culture. In *Toá* the basic model is clearly set forth: The outsider Antonio (to whom the narrator refers even late in the novel as "visiting doctor") experiences a series of lessons as a part of his possible integration into this New World. Early in the novel the differences between this world and his previous cosmopolitan life are vividly delineated, as the narrator explains how the protagonist desires to experience the "strange landscapes of that new world."[28] The adjectives "strange" and "new" obviously promise the reader a New World encounter. Initially, Antonio's lessons are with New World objects with which he had been previously unfamiliar: In chapter 3 the Indians introduce him to *casave* and, later in the chapter, he learns about the local use of the accordion. He also experiences fervent Indian rituals, which the narrator describes in lively detail.

Despite Antonio's fascination with this new world, his sympathy for its exploited people, and his love for Toá, his process of "learning" is, in fact, a failure. During the second half of the novel, when he is active in this new context, he does not fit comfortably with the

locals nor is he strong enough to withstand the physical environment. For example, when invited to participate in an Indian dance,
he turns cold and refuses (Uribe Piedrahita, 87); he is physically
weak and sick throughout the second half of the novel. Near the end
of the work the narrator describes Antonio as "exhausted from the
trip in the jungle" (Uribe Piedrahita, 130). *Toá* follows a typical
model of the New World protagonist who becomes so lost in nature
that he ceases to function as a social human being.[29] As Brushwood
has pointed out, this work is considerably closer than many Spanish-
American novels of the period to the *criollista* novel.[30]

Antonio's presence in the New World is likewise an encounter between writing and oral culture. He leaves for the jungle as a sophisticated product of writing culture, even thinking of writing a book on
the basis of the information he collects. The people he encounters in
the jungle are either illiterate, such as the Indian groups, or apparently semiliterate, such as the *caucheros*. The narrator describes the
latter as "crude and simple people" (Uribe Piedrahita, 41), a key
word for either illiterate or semiliterate. In addition, they demonstrate several traits typical of oral cultures.[31] They also have to
explain their regional, colloquial language to Antonio, who does
not fully understand it. The Indians, who are a constant presence
throughout the novel, of course, represent a strictly oral culture.
One of the notable passages in this context is an explanation of how
Antonio explains writing culture to Toá: "It was true that Antonio
spent hours with Toá, explaining to her life in populated cities and
talking of the sea and of the ships and of a thousand things that the
young girl listened to with astonishment" (Uribe Piedrahita, 100).
Generally speaking, the narrator assumes the role of a writing culture narrator, leaving oral language and oral culture to the characters. Similar to the case of many texts of the period, *Toá* contains a
dictionary at the end to explain regionalisms, thus representing an
attempt at legitimizing the presence of an authentic orality in this
New World text.

The intertextual relationships between *Toá* and *La vorágine* are
announced by the placement of Rivera's name in the dedicatory. The
protagonist's trip to the jungle, his discovery of the rubber workers'
problems, and the novel's ending also remind the reader of patterns
in *La vorágine*. More subtle intertextual relationships involve a
similar evocation of the descent into hell and classic myths related
to this descent, as delineated in *La vorágine*.[32] The narrator refers to
the setting as a *vorágine infernal* (infernal vortex) (Uribe Piedrahita,
130), and characters refer to it as an *infierno* (Uribe Piedrahita, 132,
137). Classic myths are evoked by references to an *odisea* (Uribe

Piedrahita, 25) and *escenas dantescas* (Uribe Piedrahita, 57). Nevertheless, *Toá* is not a repetition of *La vorágine*.[33] Antonio perceives the jungle in a far more objective manner than does Cova in *La vorágine*. Cova's destruction comes from the jungle; Antonio's is from the pressure of the culture to which he belongs.[34]

Uribe Piedrahita participates in Greater Antioquia's egalitarian tradition in ways heretofore unseen in the region's novel. An egalitarian attitude is evidenced in *Toá* from the dedicatory, which includes a *huitoto* Indian chief, through the many chapters which privilege the indigenous groups throughout the story. If it were not for the narrator's constant position as outsider to this culture, *Toá* could even be seen as an indigenist novel. The implied author rejects European (writing) culture, which is unable to comprehend this new world. In the end, oral culture predominates over writing; Antonio fails in the jungle of Caquetá. In this sense too *Toá* is radically different from *La vorágine*, a novel obsessed with writing. As a New World novel, *Toá* is a more authentic expression of national reality, successfully integrating indigenous and oral culture.

Bernardo Arias Trujillo's participation in the region's egalitarian tradition was based on an interest in the Afro-Colombian rather than Indian contribution to its culture. The author had established himself in Greater Antioquia's writing culture by publishing two short novels in 1924, *Luz* and *Cuando cantan los cisnes*, and a volume of essays, *Diario de emociones* (1938), a set of semifictional and poetic vignettes on writers ranging from Cervantes to Wilde. In the tradition of the *paisa aventurero*, he traveled throughout much of Latin America and resided in Buenos Aires. He was seen in Colombian society as a liberal and heretic.[35] After living a life of a hedonist who willingly broke society's norms, according to one critic and friend, he died at the age of thirty-four.[36]

Arias Trujillo's *Risaralda* promises in its subtitle to revolutionize the local obsession with classical humanism, announcing itself as a "film written in Spanish and spoken in *criollo*." He only partially delivers on this promise. With respect to the film, the promise remains virtually unfulfilled. The only exception is chapter 30, which features the subtitle "(Projected in slow motion)" and does change in narrative technique. The extradiegetic-heterodiegetic narrator in this chapter describes a flood in the detail that could be perceived as a slow-motion film and which ends with an allusion to slow motion: "The land is purified slowly, with water of pain."[37] The remainder of the novel's subtitle is accurate: The narrator writes a standard Spanish and the characters speak a regional, colloquial language, thus making it a novel "spoken in *criollo*."

Risaralda is set in the valley of Risaralda in the Department of Caldas in a town originally called Sopinga by its black inhabitants but which the white pioneers will later name La Virginia. The first eleven chapters are descriptions of the ideal life of the blacks in Sopinga, with lengthy passages about Afro-Colombian customs and anecdotes about two of its main characters, Juancho and Pacha Durán. The novel undertakes a radical change in the twelfth chapter, when white pioneers, *colonizadores paisas*, enter the area and begin to transform it. The Antioquian of independent spirit, the *paisa aventurero* Juan Manuel, becomes the central character of this portion of the novel to its end, chapter 31.

Arias Trujillo, like Carrasquilla and Uribe Piedrahita, was interested in defining a national identity by appealing to regional values. In this sense *Risaralda*, like *Toá*, is an Antioquian New World project—in this region's context, what could be called *criollismo antioqueño*. Following Antioquia's egalitarian tradition, Arias Trujillo's point of departure is a recognition of the Afro-Colombian element in this New World culture. In fact, he dedicates the book to its Afro-Colombians: "For you, blacks of Colombia, this book of . . ." (Arias Trujillo, 21). The first eleven chapters represent an encomium of Afro-Colombian culture to such a degree that life for Sopinga's blacks is consistently idealized. This "little *criollo* town," as the narrator identifies it (Arias Trujillo, 29), is described with the adjective "happy" (Arias Trujillo, 42).

This profoundly nostalgic novel idealizes a region as being vastly superior in the past. The Valle de Risaralda, inhabited by blacks, is described from the novel's first paragraph as a paradise. The new order to replace the society of Sopinga is equally idealized. The Valle de Risaralda remains ideal even when inhabited by *antioqueños* (*caldenses*). Similarly, in the entire second half of the novel idyllic *criollo* life is idealized. The narrator praises the value of such *criollo* objects as the *poncho* and *aguardiente*; by the end of the novel the authentic *criollo* Juan Manuel Vallejo acquires hero status.

As in Carrasquilla's *Frutos de mi tierra*, *Risaralda* assumes an Antioquian reader who shares with the narrator an acquaintance with these regional values and esteems them. A reference such as the one the narrator makes to "our *bambuco*" creates this complicity between narrator and reader. Similarly, in a description of Juan Manuel Vallejo the narrator fictionalizes a reader who recognizes and appreciates the assumed proper family lineage of Antioquians from Caldas: "Like all *caldenses*, he was a man of good blood" (Arias Trujillo, 125).

Arias Trujillo's New World project privileges oral culture as part of what is authentically *criollo*. Both the illiterate blacks and the *antioqueños* use oral, colloquial language in the dialogues, a language minimally affected by writing. The paradisiacal world of Sopinga is an oral culture. For example, it is a verbally agonistic society in which males confront each other in battles as *trovadores*; several of these confrontations take place in the novel's initial chapters. The Antioquian story of the second half also reveals the implicit superiority of orality over writing: Juan Manuel Vallejo gained the respect of the local folk by winning in a verbal confrontation with another *trovador*, and as the classic *paisa aventurero* (adventuresome *antioqueño*), he abandoned his studies "and took off to see the world" (Arias Trujillo, 137). Although literate, he is valued by others because of his capacity to survive in the oral culture.

The narrator vacillates between a position of superiority to this oral world and, in other instances, participation in it. The superiority of writing culture is evidenced in his occasional references to the elitist literary tradition of the West. References to the blacks' emotions with phrases such as "savage passions" also reveal a narrator who envisions these people as inferior.[38] Just as Uribe Piedrahita views the Indian world from the outside, the position of narrator in *Risaralda* is usually outside the Afro-Colombian culture. Nevertheless, the narrator uses certain strategies to bring himself closer to this world. Other techniques allow him to occasionally assume the role of oral storyteller. The narrator creates a closeness to the fictional world when he employs the informal, colloquial tone of spoken language. His characterization of some youths as *mocosos carisucios* (snotty, dirty-faced kids) (Arias Trujillo, 48) is one of the more humorous examples of such an effect. As in *Frutos de mi tierra*, the narrator occasionally assumes the role of an oral storyteller, although less frequently. Near the end of the novel the narrator employs a series of repetitions at the beginning of several paragraphs, thus using the repetitive strategies of the oral-culture *trovadores*, who are oral-culture characters in his novel.[39]

Arias Trujillo resembles more the predominant twentieth-century model for Antioquian fiction—Carrasquilla—than does Uribe Piedrahita, both in tone and in his appropriation of oral culture. *Risaralda* expresses nostalgia for an ideal world that is premodern and prewriting. Risaralda, both in its Afro-Colombian and *criollo* stages, was a regional paradise in which traditional values and traditional orality were yet to be lost to Antioquian progress. As sophisticated participants in writing culture themselves, Arias Trujillo and Uribe

Piedrahita effect their New World projects by using educated persons (one semi-educated and the other highly educated) as interpreters of a highly valorized oral culture—Juan Manuel Mejía and Antonio de Orrantia.

Transition (1936–1963) and *El día señalado* (1964) by Manuel Mejía Vallejo

The three most important phenomena to occur in Greater Antioquia from 1936 to 1963 were the continued publication of novels of social protest through the 1940s, the growing rural violence (dating from the 1930s), culminating in La Violencia during the 1950s, and the rise of Manuel Mejía Vallejo. By the 1950s Antioquia's strictly regional culture was undergoing radical transformation. By then Medellín was a fully industrialized city with a population of over 400,000. The arrival of television in 1955 placed Antioquians in daily contact with their nation and the world. That same year Belisario Betancur founded the cultural magazine *Prometeo*, more national and international in vision than strictly Antioquian.

The publication of novels such as Luis Carlos Flórez's *Llamarada, novela obrera anti-imperialista* (1941) was an indicator of the continued thrust of social protest fiction as practiced by Uribe Piedrahita. The writer who most actively cultivated this type of fiction was Iván Cocherín, whose settings are western Antioquia, the present-day State of Caldas. The circumstance of workers in the mines in the town of Marmato in Caldas and similar scenarios are to be found in his novels *Túnel* (1940), *Esclavos de la tierra* (1945), *El sol suda negro* (1954), and *Carapintada* (1959). For Cocherín, the denunciation of social injustice obviously was a higher priority than the aesthetic quality of the writing. Antonio J. Arango's *Oro y miseria* (1942), set in the mines of Marmato, and Victoriano Vélez's *Del socavón al trapiche* (1958) also deal with miners and denounce their exploitation.

Antioquia and its fiction were deeply affected by La Violencia and its antecedents in the form of social and political conflict during the 1930s and 1940s. One of the authoritative studies on La Violencia notes that the nation in general has been relatively ignorant about the intensity of the violence in Antioquia, one of the most affected regions.[40] The Antioquian novels of this period that deal with the experience of La Violencia most successfully were Arturo Echeverri Mejía's *Marea de ratas* (1960),[41] Euclides Jaramillo Arango's *Un campesino sin regreso* (1959), and Jaime Sanin Echeverri's *Quién dijo miedo* (1960). Echeverri Mejía's *Marea de ratas* denounces political repression and injustice in small-town Antioquia during the 1950s. In addition, much of Alonso Aristizábal's fiction published during the 1970s and 1980s, both short stories and novels, deals with the historical conflicts between Liberals and Conservatives in the 1930s in the town of Pensilvania in Caldas; these conflicts predate La Violencia but are directly related to it.

Two novels varying from the norm to appear during this period were Alejandro Vallejo's *La casa de Berta Ramírez* and Fernando González's *Don Benjamín, jesuita predicador*, which were published in 1936. *La casa de Berta Ramírez* captures the vitality and energy of a new generation of Liberals who arose in the 1930s. It tells the story of a young student discovering the excitement of Colombia's nascent modernity and some of its ideological counterparts, from Marx to modern European thinkers. Just as Liberals such as Vallejo rejected the Conservative Republic, the language he employs is free of the traditional rhetoric frequent in much early twentieth-century Antioquian fiction. The narrator successfully creates the atmosphere of a student pension in the first chapter. Fernando González's novel was quite radically different: The author describes *Don Benjamín, jesuita predicador* as a book without a plot or denouement, and this philosophical narrative essay is a notable novelistic experiment of the period.

During the late 1930s and 1940s the literary supplement *Generación* arose in Medellín, directed by Miguel Arbeláez Sarmiento and Otto Morales Benítez.[42] This organ represented an opening toward modernity in several respects. Besides publishing the writings of Antioquia's new generation of intellectuals, such as Belisario Betancur (later to be president) and Otto Morales Benítez, *Generación* included Highland writers of cosmopolitan vision, such as the Highland fiction writer Tomás Vargas Osorio and poet Fernando Charry Lara. In addition, a wide range of writers, such as Benjamín Jarnés, Heinrich von Kleist, and Oscar Wilde, cross the pages of *Generación*.

Manuel Mejía Vallejo claims to have begun writing as a youth. While studying in high school in Medellín, he wrote letters home and his parents commented to him how pleased they were to receive such well-written letters. In the 1940s he became more enthused with writing while pursuing studies at the Boliviariana University in Medellín. While studying there he wrote for a small local newspaper and composed his first novel, *La tierra éramos nosotros*. Looking back on that first amateurish novel, Mejía Vallejo stated years later, "I don't defend that work except in the sense that it was made honestly, with characters I had lived with on my parents' farm. I tell the story of my youth, and with so much innocence that I didn't even change the characters' names. They are still alive with the names that appear in the book."[43] *La tierra éramos nosotros* is a first-person account (extradiegetic-homodiegetic) of Mejía Vallejo's childhood in rural Antioquia. The narrator-protagonist writes in an immediate present (i.e., "I contemplate the church through the window") his experiences with the *campesino* life upon returning to his region after an extended absence. The absolute peace and tranquility of this life contrast with the decaying nation he leaves behind in the city. From the moment he returns to the farm he begins making systematic connections between himself and the land.

In the stories of *Tiempo de sequía* Mejía Vallejo captures the essence of rural life in Antioquia. For example, in the story "La muerte de Pedro Canales" he uses a narrator-protagonist (extradiegetic-homodiegetic) who confesses having assassinated the hero at the same time he insists on "simply" telling a story. (The character Pedro Canales will later appear in *El día señalado*.) In the story "Al pie de la ciudad" the reader finds the first pages of what later will be the novel of the same title: the anecdotal material of this story of humble folk in the neighborhood of "Los Barrancos" in Medellín who live, as the title indicates, at the foot of the city. The title story, "Tiempo de sequía," deals with characters who barely survive, in absolute misery and without the most basic necessities.

In 1958 Mejía Vallejo published the novel *Al pie de la ciudad*, once again the story of the humble people who live in the neighborhood of "Los Barrancos," from the story of the same title. The novel is divided into three parts, offering the reader three perspectives of the events. In Part One the focus is on Los Barrancos and the process of maturation of a boy in a poor family that lives there. The perspective totally changes in Part Two: The same problems of Los Barrancos are seen through the eyes of Dr. Salomón Arenas of the upper middle class. These two perspectives are synthesized in Part Three, which contains stories from both of the previous story lines. Because of its denunciation of social injustice and its concomitant incorporation of the modern and the traditional, *Al pie de la ciudad* is quite similar to Miguel Angel Asturias's *El Señor Presidente*.

El día señalado is a synthesis of various elements that had appeared in Mejía Vallejo's previous fiction. The narrator develops two story lines: one told by an extradiegetic-heterodiegetic narrator dealing with a priest in the small town of Tambo, and another told by a character (intradiegetic-homodiegetic) who arrives at Tambo to commit an act of revenge. The novel begins with a six-page prologue narrated by an extradiegetic-heterodiegetic narrator which relates the life-story of a common boy with a common name (José Miguel

Pérez) who lives, as indicated in the novel's first line, from December 1936 to January 1960. He experiences a typical childhood and is instructed by his mother from an early age that he must *ser alguien* (be someone) in his life. Nevertheless, he dedicates himself to the simple pleasures of rural life. Both guerrillas and soldiers pass through his land, and soldiers steal his horse. He decides to pursue them and recover his horse. In the countryside he sees the visible evidence of La Violencia: mutilated bodies of guerrillas. Then the perspective changes to the townsfolk and José Miguel's mother: Several cadavers are brought to the town, including José Miguel Pérez's. This prologue sets the tone and an atmosphere of irrational violence that will be developed later in the text.

José Miguel Pérez becomes a background character mentioned intermittently in the remainder of the novel, which is developed in three parts, each preceded by a prologue. The extradiegetic narrator relates the story of the priest in a town embroiled in the conflicts of La Violencia: The power structure, associated with the government and soldiers, is in conflict with the rural guerrillas. The intradiegetic story tells of the final stages of the narrator's life-long search for his father in order to murder him as an act of revenge. The narrator's search is presented in the text as both an obsession and an inevitable process destined to result in an encounter between father and son. The narrator's only emotions throughout the story, in fact, are related to the hatred he feels for his father and his obsession with revenge. He states that he was "destined" to be "born for revenge." The structure reaches a turning point at the end of the second part: The son encounters the father, Chútez, setting the stage for the seemingly inevitable violence of the third part. This story culminates in only metaphorical violence: The son's fighting cock kills Chútez's prize-fighting cock, but the son leaves the town after deciding not to kill his father.

A basic verb and sentence which synthesizes the novel's action is "The protagonist becomes a man." This sentence refers to the son, whose search for his father and encounter with him represent an act of maturation, of becoming the complete person he feels he will not be until he finds his father. In the end, his decision not to kill his father represents a rational process uncommon in a setting of continuous and irrational violence. Becoming a man is a theme developed on other levels of the narration. José Miguel Pérez's story in the prologue underscores his becoming a man: His mother instructs him as a youth that he must *ser alguien* and his entire story relates to his attempt to fulfill the mother's desire. In addition, becoming a man is a theme which resonates throughout the text. The son explains his travels throughout little towns: "This is why I followed roads from town to town, from farm to farm, gathering experiences that made me more of a man."[44] His rural experiences—living among fighting cocks—also were part of his becoming more of a "man": "I was reared with them, and they showed me the road to the men" (Mejía Vallejo, 23). He uses a similar concept, explaining to a young girl, Marta, that her brother Antonio Roble, a guerrilla, will become a man when he attacks: "Your brother, little girl, is going to be a man" (Mejía Vallejo, 59). The priest also reminds another character (*alfarero*) that his father "was a complete man" (Mejía Vallejo, 64). In synthesis, the protagonist and other male characters perceive their lives as a process of "becoming men" in traditional Antioquian masculine roles.

The two principal narrators of this novel, one extradiegetic-heterodiegetic and the other intradiegetic-homodiegetic, employ a variety of strategies whose norms suggest an implied author of notable interest within the context of the Antioquian tradition. The extradiegetic-heterodiegetic narrator of the prologue uses a series of résumés to relate José Miguel Pérez's entire life story in six pages. From the prologue's outset the narrator establishes an editorial tone, offering a precise explanation of the totality of Pérez's life. The prologue begins with several of the narrator's generalizations about Pérez and life in general. Such statements establish the narrator's right to make generalizations, a right which will be exercised throughout the novel. Only with this understanding is it possible for the reader to accept the extradiegetic narrator's interventions when narrating the priest's and the town's story. One of the most salient examples of this tendency is a statement such as the following: "Man acts according to whom he is around" (Mejía Vallejo, 156). Later this narrator sets forth an essay on violence and humanity (Mejía Vallejo, 202). The generalizations and essays cited here, slightly out of context, would not appear to be successful rhetorical strategies. The narrator's position is generally more neutral, however, and he often filters the narrative action through characters who are focalizers. The beginning of the first chapter, for example, functions with the gravedigger as focalizer, a much more subtle technique for presenting the fictional world than the explanations cited above. Even the use of a focalizer can sometimes lead to more than obvious communication, such as the following use of the priest as focalizer to explain the character of Tambo's inhabitants: "The priest saw in the gravedigger the shadow of Tambo's inhabitants" (Mejía Vallejo, 32).

Some readers have pointed out other inconsistencies in the two narratives. For example, it has been commented that often there is not enough difference between the language used in the two narrative lines.[45] The reader may conclude that the author has failed to differentiate properly and consistently between the two narrators. On the other hand, the reader may maintain that the narrator-protagonist has a sense for detail, for associations, and for a metaphorical perception of reality usually ascribed to writing culture's novelists and poets. For example, when this narrator hears the sound of drums, he makes the following detailed associations: "I remembered the leather of cattle on the outside, the bellies of iguanas and crocodiles" (Mejía Vallejo, 51). Similarly, this narrator often begins chapters with the kind of language and description used by the extradiegetic narrator. The questions raised by these observations concerning the narrators can be resolved by considering the role of the implied author. This fictional entity employs two narrators who have in common two equally traditional roles as storytellers. They are highly authoritarian roles in both cases: The extradiegetic narrator assumes the authority from the first paragraph to explain the nature of things; the intradiegetic narrator assumes the authority to be, in effect, a writer. In accordance with the basic verb discussed above, the implied author is indeed a "man"—the patriarchal authority figure. In this sense *El día señalado* has a distant resonance of nostalgia. Beneath the overt trappings of modernity—under the guise of the modern novel's structure—lies a nostalgia for the traditional authority of narrating associated with the nineteenth-century writer, such as the Carrasquilla whom Mejía Vallejo so admires.[46]

Issues of writing and orality also bring forth vague resonances of nostalgia. *El día señalado* is conceived strictly as a product of writing culture. Certainly it bears a closer relationship to writing culture's modern novel than it does to oral storytelling. The basic structure of this novel—with prologues and dual story lines—belongs to writing culture. This structure and the two narrators' metaphorical method of perceiving the world belong to writing and not oral noetics.

Nevertheless, *El día señalado* does carry a distant relationship with orality—more a case of vague oral effects than assimilation of primary orality or oral residue. As in *Frutos de mi tierra*, the narrator occasionally privileges orality by communicating reality in terms of what is generally said—"lo que dicen." For example, the narrator-protagonist sets the atmosphere in Tambo early in the novel by explaining what the common and anonymous people are saying (Mejía Vallejo, 39). Such procedures, within Antioquia's egalitarian tradition, privilege—albeit in a minor and relatively insignificant fashion—communication on an oral level. Authority is momentarily centered in speaking, not writing.

In many cases, this novel's distant and vague relationship with orality is best described as resonances of orality. It is possible to conceive of the two story lines as representing writing and oral noetics, the former being the extradiegetic story and the latter being the intradiegetic one. In accordance with this conception of the novel, the intradiegetic story is related to oral noetics because of its agonistic relationships and because of the narrator's proximity to the human lifeworld. This narrator's tendency to refer constantly to the land and objects around him emphasizes his closeness to the human lifeworld. In addition, the protagonist's situation is in some ways similar to someone living in an oral culture: He inhabits a closed, unchanging world, which recalls Ong's observation that oral cultures are fundamentally conservative, unwilling to change. These comparisons, however, indicate only distant parallels with a vaguely residual oral culture, occasionally evoked by the characters or the narrator's use of sayings and epithets.

El día señalado signals the entrance of the modern novel into Antioquia. This novel represents the most successful incorporation of the techniques of the modern novel heretofore seen in the Antioquian novelistic tradition. Mejía Vallejo's unique synthesis of modernity and tradition—in some ways comparable to García Márquez's similar achievement in *Cien años de soledad*—has resonances of premodern orality. The basic theme of "becoming a man" in *El día señalado* coincides with the implied author's characterization of narrators who are authoritarian in impulse. They tell their stories with the authority formerly conceded to oral storytellers. These oral resonances function as part of the nostalgia frequently present in Antioquian fiction, from Carrasquilla to the modern period. As the culmination of the *antioqueño* tradition in the novel, *El día señalado* marks the ending of an orality and popular tradition—an ending left behind with nostalgia—and the unequivocal beginning of the modern or new novel in Antioquia. Now distant from the traditional regionalism of Carrasquilla, Mejía Vallejo appropriates the discourse of modernism to create what has been identified as a transcendent regionalist fiction.[47]

Conclusion

The nostalgia of the Antioquian tradition is pervasive from Carrasquilla's desire to return to the small-town, rural, and oral culture of Colonial and nineteenth-century Antioquia. These nostalgic attitudes are present in the novels of many of the writers of Antioquia and particularly so in one of its most important novelists, Bernardo

Arias Trujillo. Of course, any use of oral culture in twentieth-century writing culture implies a type of nostalgia, and this implicit nostalgia can be noted even in Mejía Vallejo.

Carrasquilla's project, self-defined as a "modern novel" with regional qualities, was not only consummated by him in his several novels but also became the predominant model for fiction in Antioquia for most of the twentieth century. (It should be understood that his novels were not at all "modern" in the contemporary use of the term *modern novel*.) The possible intertextual relationships between Carrasquilla and those who followed him are numerous and complex, although in some issues it would be difficult to determine to what extent Antioquian writers are responding to Carrasquilla's writing and to what extent their cultural backgrounds simply coincide with Carrasquilla's. Whatever the case may be, Bernardo Arias Trujillo successfully appropriated Carrasquilla's strategies for his own purposes.

Compared to the Interior Highland Tradition, the novel in the Greater Antioquia region is a nonelitist form of literary expression. Whether or not one accepts the idea of Antioquia's famed egalitarian tradition, its novel does reveal egalitarian tendencies, from Carrasquilla's interest in the region's rural folk and its values to Mejía Vallejo's prologue to *El día señalado* highlighting the plight of the *campesino* in the context of La Violencia. The New World projects of Uribe Piedrahita and Arias Trujillo attempt to define a national identity by associating the common person with regional values, emphasizing the value of orality over writing. In accordance with Jean Franco's observation about the relationship between orality and the *criollista* novel in general, orality is recuperated by these two writers as a popular and folkloric element and consequently as an indication of authenticity.[48] The presence of orality in the novel of Greater Antioquia ranges from oral residue noted in *Frutos de mi tierra* and *Risaralda* (habits of thought and expression tracing back to preliterate practices) to the oral effects in *El día señalado* (colloquial and other informal speech patterns). Whatever the influence of orality in Greater Antioquia, after Carrasquilla it became difficult for the fiction writer to ignore the region's rich and vital oral traditions. The exaltation of regional values, fictionalized with the narrative techniques of the modern novel, produce the culminating work in Antioquia's novelistic tradition.

Six

The Greater Cauca Tradition: From *María* (1867) to *El bazar de los idiotas* (1974)

Oral memory works effectively with "heavy" characters, persons whose deeds are monumental, memorable and commonly public.
—*Walter Ong*, Orality and Literacy

The Greater Cauca, centered in the Valle del Cauca but including Popayán (founded in 1535) to the south and Chocó to the north, has developed a tradition of cultural heterogeneity. Since the Colonial period Popayán has been a bastion of elitist writing culture. The Jesuits founded the University of San José in Popayán in 1774. The Valle del Cauca, with Cali (founded in 1536) as its largest city, has felt the influence of an opulent aristocracy and also of the populist forces represented by the minority Afro-Colombian population and the Antioquian pioneers who settled northern and eastern parts of the Valle del Cauca in the nineteenth and twentieth centuries. The Chocó (northern) area of this region, geographically and culturally isolated and sparsely populated, has been a stronghold of oral and African traditions with relatively little production of written culture. (Nevertheless, the novelist Arnoldo Palacios is from Chocó.)

The egalitarian traditions of Antioquia can be contrasted with a vastly different situation in Greater Cauca. Until well into the twentieth century this region's society had a markedly stratified class structure with a small lettered elite and generally illiterate masses. This generalization echoes the description of the Highland. Indeed, one of the *ciudades letradas* of the Colonial lettered power structure was centered in Popayán, a city that compares favorably to its counterparts Tunja and Bogotá in both its colonial architectural splendor and its venerable literary tradition. Popayán also represented a similarly conservative Hispanic model. Despite these similarities, one must avoid the facile and superficial conclusion that the Greater Cauca is a western Colombia replica of the Highland model discussed in chapter 3. The historical and cultural denominators are far too complex in the Greater Cauca to allow for such a simplification. The region's complexity is marked by the presence of Cali, a town with a small elite in the nineteenth century which became a modern, industrialized city in the twentieth century, the strongly Afro-Colombian region of Chocó, and a tri-ethnic racial makeup whose indigenous presence is the most pronounced of the four regions during the last two centuries.

The indigenous and black African populations of the Greater Cauca have lived with the Hispanic inhabitants since the sixteenth century, suffering differing degrees of exploitation or extermination depending on the period and the specific area of the region. By 1511 the Spaniards knew of the gold in the Department of Chocó, and African slaves were the primary source of labor in the mines. Of the approximately 150,000 African slaves that passed through Cartagena to be shipped, in turn, to other parts of the Spanish colonies, many were sent, from the mid-sixteenth century, to the distribution centers of Popayán and Cartago in the Greater Cauca. *Palenques* (towns founded by runaway slaves) were common throughout Colombia, and by 1575 there was such a town—Nechí—in the Greater Cauca.[1] There is a considerable black population in all parts of the Greater Cauca region today, including 84 percent of the population in the Department of Chocó. The greater Cauca is renowned for the memory of its slave estates in the eighteenth and nineteenth centuries, such as those of the Arboleda family.[2] The genteel life of the estate owner was evoked, though in different ways, in Isaacs's *María* and Palacios's *El alférez real*. The Indian population present throughout most parts of the Greater Cauca was rapidly decimated. In Chocó, for example, an indigenous population of 60,000 in 1660 was reduced to 15,000 by 1783 and then to only 4,450 by 1808.[3] Nevertheless, the Department of Cauca has the largest Indian population of any department in Colombia, with 101,000 of the approximately half-million Indians in the nation.[4] Indigenous groups in the Greater Cauca region today include the Emberá, Noanamá, Páez, Guambiano, and Coconuco. Compared to countries such as Perú and Ecuador, Colombia has never produced a flourishing movement of indigenous novels. Nevertheless, a few novelists from the Greater Cauca, notably Diego Castrillón Arboleda, have attempted to fictionalize the Indian situation.

For nineteenth-century visionaries, whose hopes for regional prog-

ress were constantly being swept away by political chaos and economic instability, the Greater Cauca of today would appear to be a
promise fulfilled. The vibrant and progressive city of Cali is for
many—particularly for civic-minded *caleños*—a veritable monument to the possibilities of modern urban development in Latin
America. The region's vast expanses of abundant land, fertile for agriculture and rich in minerals, have afforded the area economic pros-
perity. The Valle del Cauca is one of only three regions in the world
that can produce sugar year-round. Wealthy families of the Valle del
Cauca's large landowning elite, with names such as Caicedo, Garcés,
and Lourido, some of which are the mainstays of the region's elite
today, were financially prosperous and politically powerful during
the seventeenth and eighteenth centuries.[5] Cali's aristocracy considered itself "noble": One local account of the population of 5,000 in
1777 read as follows: 74 *religiosos* (clergy), 1,200 *nobles*, 2,078 mes-
tizos, and 1,962 *pardos* (blacks).

The Greater Cauca's heterogeneity was stimulated by a series
of factors in the nineteenth century which radically changed the
makeup of the region's society and culture. A key turning point was
the abolition of slavery in Colombia in 1851, a severe blow to the
interests of the large-landowning elite. The region suffered economic stagnation during much of the second half of the nineteenth
century.[6] The 1890s saw an economic recovery. Nevertheless, as in
the Costa, it was a case of uneven development. For example, one
observer has spoken of the curious juxtaposition of the modern and
the ancient; the majority of the populace in the 1880s was illiterate.[7]
During the 1920s, Cali, like Colombia's other major cities, underwent a process of modernization. The train line connecting Cali to
the port city of Buenaventura, completed in 1915, was an important
predecessor to this transformation. Modern technology for sugar re-
fining was introduced to the Valle del Cauca in the 1920s. The clear-
est indicator of Cali's industrialization was the presence of seventy-
seven factories in the 1930s, compared to only one at the turn of the
century. An exceptional factor in the region's twentieth-century history was the intensity of La Violencia, particularly in Tuluá and
Caicedonia. The 1950s also saw conflict between workers and own-
ers in the sugar industry.

The heterogeneous Greater Cauca culture offers strong writing
and oral traditions. Writing culture produced its most prominent literary monuments in the works of the novelists Jorge Isaacs and Eustaquio Palacios and of the poets Guillermo Valencia (1873–1943)
and Rafael Maya (1897–1983). In juxtaposition with this writing are
oral traditions based on indigenous and Afro-Colombian cultures

and widespread illiteracy among the population at large until well into the twentieth century. The oral tradition does not have a representative such as Carrasquilla in Antioquia or García Márquez in the Costa to assimilate this primary orality into the novel, probably because of the Greater Cauca's more elitist tradition in literary production. Nevertheless, scholars have compiled into written form stories from the region's oral culture. One anthology includes stories told by a bilingual Embera Indian who learned to read in the early twentieth century and who explained later: "When I learned to read, no black in Baudó knew how to yet and the Indians even less because they didn't even know Spanish."[8] This Indian's stories have "heavy" characters, to use Ong's term, and other characteristics of oral storytelling.[9] Modern writers such as Arnoldo Palacios and Gustavo Alvarez Gardeazábal, more distant from orality than this Embera Indian but less elitist than Isaacs and Eustaquio Palacios, show some traces of the Greater Cauca's residual orality of the twentieth century in their fiction.

María (1867) by Jorge Isaacs

Isaacs's only important literary production was his now classic novel of Latin American Romanticism, *María*. Before 1867 he had become acquainted with the intellectuals of *El Mosaico* in Bogotá and published some poetry, *Poesías* (1864). Near the end of his life he began writing two historical novels, *Camilo* and *Fania*, which never were completed. He also published a study of indigenous groups in the Costa, *Las tribus indígenas del Magdalena*. In addition, scholars have recently discovered some manuscripts of popular poetry left by Isaacs and published in 1985 as *Canciones y coplas populares.*[10]

Isaacs was born into the Valle del Cauca's landed aristocracy and supported the Conservative party during the early stages of his career. In 1854, at the age of seventeen, he enlisted in the army of General Tejada, joining Conservatives against the dictatorship of Melo. Six years later he joined those attempting to overthrow Mosquera's dictatorship, actually battling on the bridge of Cali in 1860. For Isaacs, the 1860s were intense years, and he underwent a series of radical changes. His father died in 1861, leaving the twenty-four-year-old Jorge in charge of the family's wealth, including several estates. At this time the Valle del Cauca's general economic crisis began, and within two years the family's finances were in ruin. In 1864 Isaacs went to Bogotá to negotiate financial matters, and there he met José María Vergara y Vergara, who introduced him to the group of *El Mosaico*. During the years 1864 and 1865 he held several government positions, but he spent much of his time from 1864 to 1866 in isolation writing *María*. In 1866 he was elected a representative of the Conservative party to the national congress, despite his incipient interest in Liberal Doctrine. During the next two years the radical changes in Isaacs's career became evident: He published *María* in 1867 and became a member of the Radical party the following year. For the remainder of his life he continued to be involved in Liberal causes, from his direct participation in politics to his support of education and of indigenous groups in Colombia.[11]

María is unquestionably the product of the Greater Cauca's sophisticated and elitist writing culture. The predominant oral culture of 1860s Greater Cauca was a matter of relatively little interest for Isaacs the novelist in the years from 1864 to 1866 when he was writing. Less than an issue of interest (or elitist lack of interest) is the problem of how to assimilate a predominant oral culture into a novel, particularly when a writing culture product is still in its infancy. This was the same problem confronted in the cases of *Manuela* in the Highlands and *Ingermina* in the Costa. Isaacs did have the audacity to write a "Colombian novel" (something many of Colombia's intellectuals of the time considered a hopeless enterprise) some two decades after Nieto and nine years after Díaz had begun this national project. The difference in maturity and quality between these two foundational novels and *María* is evident.

The Greater Cauca's tri-ethnic and predominantly oral culture is in the background, as an occasional subtext, evident in *María* only to the reader who is aware of the novel's setting and context. The characters who are uneducated peasants, such as Emigdio, do use some colloquial language in the dialogues, but far less frequently and far less convincingly than, for example, their rural counterparts in *Frutos de mi tierra*. Isaacs's major concession to orality is the four-chapter story which the illiterate black Feliciana relates on her deathbed (chapters 40 to 43). Her story, however, is not by any means an oral tale in style and conventions. Rather, she speaks the Spanish of an educated writing-culture storyteller, in diction, syntax, and story structure, an anecdote mediated by literate culture's romantic tradition.[12] With the exception of a few colloquial phrases employed by the narrator and uneducated peasants, *María* represents in its totality a product of writing culture. Consequently, it should be considered primarily within this literary context.

The assumptions underlying critical thought on this novel have been quite traditional. During much of the twentieth century, studies were limited to the sources of the book, comparisons or influences of European models (in effect, the mediation of writing culture), or thematic and biographical investigations.[13] A moribund line of thought maintained that its numerous deviations from the principal story line undermined its effectiveness as a coherent novel.[14] A more recent reading has meticulously diagrammed relationships demonstrating the book's unity.[15] The least traditional of these analyses is a Barthesian exposition of codes of character definition.[16]

The fundamental assumption underlying many readings of *María* is the desire and necessity for unity. Hispanists writing in defense of one of Latin America's most widely read products of writing culture argue convincingly that Isaacs did indeed effect an organizational plan, fundamental to quality writing-culture products, in this case conceived to evoke tears in a way comparable to the most capacious and renowned literary structures of the West.

A first step toward the problematization of this writing product's organizational plan—novel as unity—is a consideration of the first-person narrator (extradiegetic-homodiegetic). The distinction which Franz Stanzel has made between a "narrating self" (a first-person narrator who tells a story in retrospect) and an "experiencing self" (a first-person narrator who tells the story as he or she experiences it) is a useful point of departure.[17] The first-person narrator in *María* is, technically speaking, of the "narrating-self" type: He tells his story of losing María with the advantage of hindsight. Several matters, however, complicate the narrative situation. These include the narrator's use of retrospection, the presence of a fictional editor, the changing relationship between the narrator and his surroundings, and the fact that the novel is partially autobiographical.

The basic narrative situation is as follows: An adult narrator relates in retrospect the story of his adolescent love affair with María. Despite this perspective, he does not use this temporal advantage to analyze his past circumstances. Rather, the narrative is a chronological reconstruction of the events and feelings of the moment. Isaacs does not write in a diary-present contemporary with the main events.[18] A dedication "A los hermanos de Efraín" (To the brothers of Efraín) suggests that an unidentified editor fabricated the novel from Efraín's memoirs. There are a few deviations from Isaacs's basic method. These variations appear in the form of interruptions in which the narrator reacts to these past events in the emotional framework of the present. For example, near the beginning of the novel the narrator interrupts his description of María's voice with the following response, a reaction to the situation he is describing: "Ah! How many times in my dreams . . . have I seen her . . . so beautiful that August morning!"[19] In most of the novel he reacts intimately to the natural world to which he belongs, but during his trip returning to the Valle del Cauca his descriptions are more distanced.[20] During his trip up the river the story is technically Efraín's, but the tone is different from that in other parts of the novel. Here the voice takes on an objective quality and, unlike the sensitive reactions to the land that characterize the earlier narration, seems to be describing something new.

By taking this consideration of the intricacies of the narrative situation a step farther, the reader approaches the problematics of the self in writing culture, from technique to ideological-based structures and a questioning of the assumptions mentioned earlier. An examination of the self further places the idea of unity in doubt. It should be noted once again that Isaacs wrote *María* from 1864 to 1866 while living in the mountains, often isolated.[21] There is little question that he integrated experiences and anecdotes from his own personal life. For example, as a child he was sent to Bogotá to study, just as the protagonist. Setting aside the difficult, and perhaps unimportant, issue of the precise level of autobiographical content, we can note the textual evidence of instabilities created by the confluence of autobiography and the creative process. The problematics of the self are established in the novel's first line: "Era yo niño cuando me alejaron de la casa paterna para que diera principio a mis estudios en el colegio de xxx, establecido en Bogotá hacía pocos años, y famoso en toda la República por aquel tiempo" (I was still a mere boy when sent away from home to study in xxx college, founded a few years before in Bogotá, and then well known all through Colombia). First, we note the subject-verb relationship in this initial establishment of the *yo* (I) as the supposed central object of the text. It would have been possible to begin the novel, of course, by inverting the subject and verb, probably a more natural structure: "Yo era niño . . ." Such a beginning would locate the *yo* as the primary and central focus of the written text. Other inversions similar to the first sentence occur throughout the book. The third word of the sentence, *niño*, presents more problems. Isaacs has confused the biographical and the narrating self: He identifies the narrator *niño* because he has failed to distinguish clearly between the fourteen-year-old fictional character and the Jorge Isaacs who once studied in Bogotá at the age of eleven. At this point a reader familiar with the novel notes there is considerable ambiguity with respect to the self: It neither asserts itself as a well-defined entity who is the protagonist (as would be the case in "Yo era . . .") nor is it capable of identifying itself properly. The self functions in an ambiguous area which the narrator seems unable or unwilling to define.

An additional factor complicating the basic narrative situation is the presence of a fictional editor at the beginning of the book. This invented editor indicates that the manuscript is dedicated "A los hermanos de Efraín." The written text in theory contains both the sender and the receiver, narrator and narratee. Two important points relate to the narrative situation.[22] This first-person narrator certainly does not address himself exclusively to a group of sibling readers, because he makes many references that would be gratuitous if he were thinking only of members of his household. For example, most of the physical descriptions of María and the family would be unnecessary for siblings. These observations lead us back to the speaker. If the receiver is unclear, the burden for this ambiguity ultimately leads the reader to question the identity of the sender. The term *hermanos* (brothers) can also include persons like Efraín. Just as the sense of the dedication vacillates between the literal and figurative meanings, the reader's sense of the narrator has a similar ambiguity: Is this narrator a brother or one of those creators with the broad vision of writing culture's epic? The answer to this question will be the former if read literally; on the other hand, those who suffer loss as Efraín did can consider themselves his "spiritual" siblings.

The confluence between personal biography and literary experience reaches a literal level of expression when one observes the changes effected by Isaacs in the four editions of the book. The author focused his revisions in the four editions on precisely the issue under consideration: the presence of the self in the novel. An examination of the successive editions reveals a tendency to transform personal pronouns to impersonal ones (i.e., "my dream" to "the dream").[23] Significantly, the revisions include the omission of the personal pronoun *yo* from the text. Just as the author consciously or unconsciously chooses to mask his presence from the beginning with the misuse of the term *niño*, his relationship to the narrating self is blatantly unstable and even progressively more so in the later revised editions. Considered within the context of the basic narrative situation, any unity of the self is questionable.

With respect to the relationship between the author and the narrating self and to the relationship between this self and the fictional world, one encounters more obstacles to the unified and coherent text proposed in the standard readings. The structure that establishes this assumed unity operates from the assumption of an Efraín who is a clearly defined self and juxtaposes this self with other characters in the fictional world. The psychological complexity in fiction is often tolerated as long as it does not threaten an ideology of the self as a fundamentally intelligible structure unaffected by a his-

tory of fragmented, discontinuous desires.[24] Our reading reveals desires and desiring impulses sublimated into emotional "faculties" or
passions and thereby the basis for the notion of a distinct and coherently unified personality. Rather than considering *María* an aesthetic failure as a novel because of the techniques which disrupt
unity, we should see this text and its standard readings as part of a
Western cultural habit of referring all experiences to centers or
beginnings.[25]

The complex network of relationships among Efraín, his parents,
and María creates the tension between the fulfillment and the sub-
limation of desire in this novel. The Oedipal structure is played out
according to the most basic triangular model involving the father,
the son, and the mother, in addition to certain variations involving
substitutions. The horror of mother-son separation is announced in
the first lines of the novel and repeated often in the first chapter.
The first line deals specifically with the protagonist's separation
from home. The remainder of the chapter deals with the emotional
trauma involved with this separation. For example, the night before
his departure to Bogotá he wept in suffering: "I fell asleep sorrowful,
filled with a vague foreboding of coming trouble" (Isaacs, 11). The
characterization of María in the initial chapters also emphasizes
separation—the loss of her family. More specifically, in the sixth
chapter the narrator explains the family history that resulted in
María's loss of her parents in the Antilles and her being sent to Colombia to live with her uncle's family. Separation from the mother
will remain a constant underlying threat and consequently function
as part of the Oedipal structure throughout the novel.

The playing out of the Oedipal triangle portrays the following
situation: a son who spends the entire novel in an ambiguous state
between boyhood and manhood (as suggested already in the analysis
of the first line); a father who plays an overbearing role as domi-
nator; a mother who subtly encourages incest; and, finally, a moth-
erlike María who functions as Efraín's substitute for the desired
mother. Efraín's characterization as a child rather than as the adult
figure that he wishes to embody is a constant part of the book's dynamics. The following scene near the beginning of the story is revealing: "Then my mother kissed me good-night, and Emma gave
me her hand; María too, yielding me hers for an instant, smiled upon
me; it was the dimpled smile of my childhood loves—like the smile
one detects on the face of a Virgin of Raphael's" (Isaacs, 15). First, we
note that this mother embraces him in reaffirmation of the mother-
child as opposed to mother-adult relationship. Then the narrator-
protagonist associates María's smile with "childhood loves." This

image refers ostensibly to María; the substitution of "childhood love" for love of one's mother, however, is not an illogical or surprising substitution. In addition to this rather overt Oedipal revelation, the total context of the paragraph communicates an idealization of childhood; the ideal love is represented by a return to childhood and the security of the mother-child relationship.

Numerous incidents and remarks by the narrator in subsequent chapters underscore his characterization as a child. At times he describes childhood as an ideal state. The protagonist evokes a similar idealized vision of childhood when he describes an idyllic scene of country life (Isaacs, 70). Efraín's institutionally acceptable situations for overcoming childhood and assuming an adult role are his displays of masculinity while hunting in the wilderness. His prizes of ferocious beasts seem impressive proof of what social ideals deem genuine manliness. A brief analysis of these masculine adventures, however, reveals a character who is not convincingly effective in this traditional masculine role. Once in the wilderness, for example, Efraín does not seem to measure up to the hearty Emigdio. When the protagonist picks some flowers, Emigdio warns him, "Do you want everything to smell of roses? Men should smell like goats" (Isaacs, 62). We note here, in addition, the contrast between a writing-culture value (Efraín's flowers in poetry) and an oral-culture value (Emigdio's human lifeworld of goats). Once involved with the actual hunt, his prize is not the awesome bear that Efraín's father had demanded but an effeminate cat. It is described in the diminutive (*gatico*) and is wounded and weakened before Efraín finally delivers the death blow. This act clearly does not measure up to the aggressive dominance that Efraín desires and believes he needs in order to fulfill his traditional role. Rather, he reacts spontaneously to the tiger's attack, happening to be the one with a rifle.

On the return trip from the hunt, his instrument of supposed aggression, his firearm, is appropriated by the person who substitutes the true masculine role, José, who carries it on his shoulders (Isaacs, 76). Having completed the adventure, the men unpack and restore order at home. Efraín, meanwhile, finds comfort in the return to the mother, explicitly evoked in nature: "Nature is the most loving of *mothers* when pain has taken possession of our souls; and if happiness caresses us, she smiles on us" (my emphasis, Isaacs, 77). The female-mother functions as a type of surrogate for the active male.

The second important character in the Oedipal triangle, the father, is an overwhelmingly dominant competitor for the childlike Efraín. Indeed, this father would represent formidable competition for even the most masculine and mature of Oedipally inclined sons. One critic

has observed that Efraín consistently speaks to his father in rever-
ential language.²⁶ This language maintains a clearly defined distance
between Efraín as child and the father as adult. The father is ever
present as a barrier to Efraín's potential advances toward the mother/
María. His presence is a threat that remains constant throughout the
novel. The father communicates the threat of María's death and remains associated with this possibility (Isaacs, 39). The father's absence, in contrast, allows for the possibility of incestuous contact:
Scenes in which the father leaves the premises are those in which
Efraín initiates dialogue with María. The father unequivocally de-
termines the direction and limits of Efraín's incestous desires: He
decides the necessary waiting period before any marriage can take
place; the father announces the inauspicious notice with respect to
María's health; he plays the role of "dictator"—he who dictates to
his son, who writes passively. (Emigdio appears as a model of a
dominant oral culture type, and Efraín plays the role of the passive
writing-culture character.) Finally, the father sends the son to En-
gland, definitely ending the threat of the son's consummation of his
desire.

An understanding of Efraín's behavior with respect to his mother
depends upon the already-established association between the
mother and María. This relationship is created, as already noted,
from the first chapter, which ends with the image of María standing
among the flowers adorning the mother's bedroom (Isaacs, 12). In opposition to the father's rigid and ever-hovering control over the triangle, the mother encourages Efraín's repressed and feeble initia-
tives. After the father has fixed stern regulations to control Efraín's
relationship with María, the mother communicates her disapproval
to the son. We note, importantly enough, within the context of a
Freudian reading of this scene, that she breaks through the symbolic
space of the son's bedroom to protest about the situation (Isaacs, 48).
The isolation from María has been too extreme, according to the
mother; that is, it is too excessive to permit the symbolic incest. At
the end of the novel Efraín's relationship with his mother, despite
his age and experience, is still that of mother-child.

The relationship with María, of course, is considerably more developed in the text. The protagonist evokes images of María at the
outset which associate her with the joy of childhood; she is also
characterized as a mother-figure. She will appear, once again, as the
ideal mother in the third chapter (Isaacs, 14–15).

Two key chapters, 20 and 30, are revealing with respect to the relationship between María and Efraín. In chapter 20 the intimacy of
the relationship is solidified. Until then it has been only a poten-

tially intimate and incestuous union. First, the father leaves the space occupied by the pair, creating the opportunity for the son to express his desires. In terms of action, the chapter stands out as the one in which the duo articulate love vows for the first time. On a more subliminal level of exchange, it is important to note that María initiates a type of physical contact while observing Efraín with his rifle. In this scene she serves him coffee, insists that he not load his rifle at that moment, and touches his cup. He assures her that he will respond to her contact with the cup by getting rid of the threatening rifle (Isaacs, 65). With all danger of the phallic object removed, they exchange vows of love.

Chapter 30 elaborates the full Oedipal triangle, with father, son, and María (the mother-substitute) present. María cuts the father's hair, while he controls the entire situation. The scene has been read symbolically but as a ritual of symbolic self-punishment,[27] beginning with the classic dominant-father/passive-son situation: "In the morning my father dictated and I wrote while he was shaving" (Isaacs, 118). The father extends the domination to María with the demand that she cut his hair while he continues dictating to the passive and subservient son. His utter domination of María, parallel with the humiliation of his son, occurs at the end of the scene. His comments to the diligent Efraín are patronizing: "Be careful, child, with making mistakes" (Isaacs, 120). When María stoops obediently to clean up the father's hair trimmings, a rose falls from her hair. The father picks up the rose (symbolically dominating once again over Efraín) and places it in her hair, substituting for the enamored youth. Then the narrator notes that she "appeared anxious to leave because of her fear of what he might add" (Isaacs, 120). What he might "add" is left ambiguous, but María's growing anxiety over this exchange makes it, symbolically at least, an unmistakable sexual affront. The father not only diverts any incestuous contact with the two mother figures but also symbolically flaunts his sexual prowess before his helpless son.

Considering its date of publication, *María* is indeed an impressive novel, particularly when compared with its counterparts in other regions, *Ingermina* and *Manuela*. Discoveries of a certain level of unity and dualities attest to Isaacs's mastery of the traditional craft of writing fiction. The function of the narrator and the self, however, depends on deeper structures that place into question the proposition of ultimate unity. The narrator's striving for anonymity and ambiguity is one sign of his fragmentation. An analysis of his characterization, moreover, reveals a protagonist who is far from the unified personality which the traditional unified text would require. The superficial psychic coherence of the type Efraín maintains involves a crippling of desire. He operates as the eternal child, even within the rigid and traditional nineteenth-century societal structures. As such he remains incomplete—the potential writer who never dictates, the lover who never consummates his desires.

As the potential writer who never writes except when receiving dictation, Efraín fails to fulfill his potential as a participant in writing culture. Isaacs, similar to Nieto in the Costa, fails in his attempt to novelize a New World experience beyond the mediating documents of writing culture. Isaacs is more confident in incorporating elements of oral culture but remains equally incapable of presenting a viable orality. His peasants, like Nieto's Indians, speak educated writing-culture Spanish. *María*, published in eight hundred copies in its first edition, is a text that emanates from the Greater Cauca's Conservative elite and that has as its readership that same European-oriented aristocracy. It is safe to assume that most of those eight hundred copies circulated among Isaacs's aristocratic acquaintances in Cali, Popayán, and Buga (in the Greater Cauca) and among a few intellectual friends in Bogotá. Only after publishing *María* and his conversion to Liberalism would Isaacs begin to recognize the presence of the nonelite sectors of Colombian society and to discover the heterogeneity of the Greater Cauca and the authentic tri-ethnic oral culture fictionalized by Carrasquilla in Antioquia and by other later writers.

Transition (1868–1886) and *El alférez real* (1886) by Eustaquio Palacios

As was the case in the Costa, the Greater Cauca produced relatively little fiction in the nineteenth century. The only notable literary activity between 1868 and 1886 consisted of the publication of two novels by Adriano Scarpetta, *Julia* (1871) and *Eva, novela caucana* (1873), both of which, like much fiction produced after *María*, hold unequivocal intertextual relationships with Isaacs's novel.[28] *Julia*, for example, is a romantic tale of the narrator/protagonist's love affair with Julia. One of the oft-used codes established in *María*, of the Valle del Cauca as earthly paradise, is evoked in the novel's initial pages in a description of Julia: "Her body seemed to rise straight and gently like a palm tree from the Valle."[29] The narrator proceeds to set forth a set of symbolically incestuous relationships, introducing three women unknown to the reader in the second chapter as his mother, his sister, and an orphan girl who will later become his beloved. The suggestion of mother–male child incest, as evoked in *María*, is also pursued from the outset of *Julia*. Scarpetta likewise exploits other codes from *María*, such as separation.[30]

Eustaquio Palacios, like Isaacs, was the author of only one novel, but he also published *Elementos de gramática y literatura castellana* and a study of the classics, *Explicación de las oraciones latinas*, and some short fiction and poetry. Palacios was also born into the Valle del Cauca's aristocracy and was educated in the Greater Cauca's most prestigious educational institutions. He completed his secondary education at the convent of San Francisco de Cali and received his degree in law and political science in Popayán. Palacios lived the remainder of his life in Cali, where he was active in local politics as a Liberal and held several governmental positions. One biographer claimed that his contribution in politics "spread his name throughout the Cauca."[31] After 1864, nevertheless, he dedicated himself solely to literature and pedagogy. He also wrote journalistic articles in his own newspaper, *El Ferrocarril*, which he founded in 1878.

El alférez real is not only the product of the Greater Cauca's elitist writing culture but seems to represent an attempt to function as a strictly writing-culture creation.[32] As it is in *María*, the Greater Cauca's tri-ethnic and oral culture is relegated to the background. Even more than in Isaacs's romantic idyll, *El alférez real* embodies elitist values. It is the story of Daniel and Inés de Lara's love and eventual union. The two are orphans, and the action is centered on the hacienda of the wealthy Manuel de Cayzedo y Tenorio, who has agreed to rear the two protagonists after the death of their parents. The main problems with the pair's eventual union is class difference: Daniel is from a common family, but Inés belongs to the Greater Cauca's local aristocracy. The novel's denouement produces the revelation that hidden in Daniel's obscure origins was his consanguinity with the noble Henrique de Cayzedo, thus enabling him to marry Inés.

In *El alférez real* the Greater Cauca's oral culture is totally ignored or systematically mediated by writing culture. The author promises in the "Dedicatoria" to relate some *tradiciones populares*, but the only popular traditions to appear in the novel's several costumbristic interludes are the aristocracy's holiday diversions and the like. In fact, the Greater Cauca's oral culture appears only as a parenthesis. In one reference to a female character named Magdalena, the narrator states the following: "Salió a recibirlos al corredor de la casa la señora Magdalena (ña Magdalena) en compañía" (ña Magdalena went out to receive them in the corridor).[33] This is the only passage in the novel where oral culture appears, virtually hidden between the beginning and the end of the parentheses: "(ña Magdalena)." Nowhere else in the novel are there any traces of language so obviously mediated by orality.

El alférez real is best located within writing culture's realist tradition. Like Carrasquilla in *Frutos de mi tierra*, Palacios rehearses the standard conventions of the realist novel, carefully operating on the basis of cause and effect and systematically introducing the characters and setting in considerable detail before placing the plot into motion. In addition, the narrator not only regularly reminds the reader (and perhaps himself) of the time frame but also becomes increasingly concerned with time. Consequently, in the latter parts of the novel the narrator obsessively announces the exact date and even the time of the events at hand.[34] Like other nineteenth-century Colombian novels, such as *Ingermina* and *Frutos de mi tierra*, *El alférez real* reveals an author lacking confidence in the act of novel writing and insisting too much on the use of the conventions of verisimilar storytelling.

The narrator in Palacios's work assumes the role of an elitist and authoritarian storyteller, emerging as an extradiegetic-heterodiegetic figure who tells a Colonial story, set in 1789, from the perspective of a "today" (late nineteenth-century Greater Cauca), which is also regularly evoked. The narrator's elitist attitudes are communicated consistently by means of his allusions to classical Greek and Latin literature as points of reference. This procedure is begun in the "Dedicatoria," in which the narrator humbly expresses his wish to have produced a work such as the *Iliad*, the *Aeneid*, or *Paradise Lost*. In addition to using citations in Latin, this narrator describes the Valle del Cauca's physical beauty by comparing it to idyllic scenes in classical literature. In contrast to these frequent references to classical literature of the West, the narrator labels as "barbarous" the manner in which the Africans speak (Palacios, 50).

The narrator communicates his ethnocentric and authoritarian attitudes by frequently offering similar editorial comments as, for example, the categorical statement about women and fashion: "But this was the fashion, and it is known that fashion has always been and always will be women's torment" (Palacios, 85). After having established the elitist proposition that all of Cali's women during the period were Spanish (Palacios, 112), the narrator notes: "We believe that of all the world's nobility, Spanish nobility is the most charitable" (Palacios, 113). Later he makes another stereotypical and deprecatory generalization about women: "Three things excite woman's sensibility and make her communicative and obliging: dancing, bathing, and horseback riding" (Palacios, 140).

The narrator projects himself as a historian figure who, with the special knowledge of the historian and access to historical archives, relates the sequence of events within the late eighteenth-century historical context. This narrator regularly explains, with the historian's precision and detail, the Valle del Cauca's social and governmental structure, including direct citation from archives. Despite the historian's intention, the narrator unmasks himself as a figure often giving an account, in fact, of the nineteenth century instead of the eighteenth. For instance, both the narrator's and the characters' generalized obsession with objects and material possessions is really more a reflection of nineteenth-century bourgeois values than those of the eighteenth-century Colonial elite. Similarly, Daniel's interest in commerce and technical education is more typical of the new bourgeois values of the late nineteenth century—also fictionalized by Carrasquilla in *Frutos de mi tierra*—than of those of the Colonial elite.

Like Scarpetta's *Julia* and many other novels subsequent to *María*, *El alférez real* needs to be read within the context of the mediating text through which it was written—*María*. Indeed, the impact of *María* was so enormous that the novel of the Greater Cauca in its entirety must be read in its intertextual relationship with *María*. In using the concept of intertextuality, we refer here not simply to the imitation of one text by another, as seen in Scarpetta's *Julia*, but rather to the system of codes that Kristeva and others have used to define the term.[35] The intertextual relationship between *El alférez real* and *María* is best understood by considering certain codes present in much Greater Cauca fiction from *María* forward: codes of characterization, codes of plot development, and codes of setting. With respect to the codes of characterization, there are direct parallels in the two novels between the female protagonists, María and Inés. The characterization of Inés involves an identical code: Like María, she is an orphan who nevertheless, despite this personal misfortune, truly belongs to the elite because she is both sensitive and well read. In addition, both María and Inés are systematically characterized as virginal Mary figures throughout their respective texts. For example, the narrator explains that Inés prefers to dress in white (Palacios, 101). With reference to Daniel, the main similarity to Efraín is his characterization as the eternal child, since all the other characters refer to him in this fashion throughout the novel.

A code of separation similar to the one in *María* operates throughout *El alférez real*. Both protagonists are separated from their parents from the beginning of the novel, a situation which poses a threat of other separations. The remainder of the novel presents a separated love-struck couple whose misfortune is caused by three basic factors: class differences, which are the most serious threat to the couple's possible union; Inés's desire to become a nun; and Daniel's disappearance in chapters 17 through 21. However, unlike *María,* the ominous threat of permanent separation is never realized.

One of the most frequent intertextual links between these two novels could be identified as the code of the "Valle del Cauca as earthly paradise." The strong ties in *María* between María as the ideal woman and the Valle del Cauca as the ideal region have been pointed out.[36] In *El alférez real* the narrator elaborates a code suggesting that the Valle del Cauca is indeed a paradise: It is repeated as beautiful, fertile, and rich. The actual setting of the Daniel-Inés affair, the Cañasgordas hacienda, is, of course, larger, richer, and more productive than any of the others (Palacios, 21). The narrator's description of Cali, the exclusive topic of chapter 7, depicts an ideal town in which absolute happiness reigns, with the possible exception of some minor class differences. Generally speaking, the populace enjoys a perfect life, fervently following traditional religious customs (chapter 9). Perhaps the most extreme portrayal of the Valle del Cauca as an earthly paradise appears in chapter 14, classically titled "Una Nueva Arcadia." For example, the narrator explains how the Pance River in the Valle del Cauca is more beautiful than the most eulogized European rivers (Palacios, 138). The only element this "new Arcadia" lacks, according to this narrator, is a writer to legitimize it (Palacios, 138). The Hellenic/Catholic Arcadia, as discussed in the first two chapters of this study, was feasible, according to the vision of the Valle del Cauca fictionalized by Eustaquio Palacios.

The Greater Cauca's heterogeneous and tri-ethnic culture has a direct or mediated presence in *El alférez real.* Cali has been proud of its Colonial "nobility," and Eustaquio Palacios portrays this small elite as an authentic Spanish nobility at the crown of the Greater Cauca's hierarchy. A broad range of the social structure is introduced in the first chapter, from the sophisticated readers of classical literature of the local elite to the unlettered black slaves. Daniel, of course, appears throughout the novel, before the felicitous denouement, as less than noble. Nevertheless, his credentials as a potential noble are presented in the form of writing: By chapter 14 he does not appear to have the pedigree necessary to marry his beloved, but he does have the ability to recite the elite's poetry of Garcilaso de la Vega. The Afro-Colombians, on the other hand, are not only presented as illiterate but are characterized in accordance with racial stereotypes. Fermín, for example, is described as a "pleasant" mulatto who is also "happy, agile, and valiant" (Palacios, 36). The orality implicit in the indigenous and Afro-Colombian cultures is never expressed.

In short, *El alférez real* repeats some of the incestuous patterns— yet another intertextual code—observed in *María*. On the one hand, the plot line leads to a denouement that entails a symbolic incest: By discovering that he truly belongs to the closed family of the nobility, Daniel is allowed to consummate his thus incestuous marriage. On the other hand, writing's primary function is to reaffirm one's place in this nobility. Literary culture in the Greater Cauca, in *El alférez real*, turns upon itself to incestuously reproduce writing about a writing culture. Not until the twentieth century are *María*'s incestuous schemes to be broken and the Greater Cauca's rich cultural potential more fully exploited in the novel.

Transition (1887–1948) and *Las estrellas son negras* (1949) by Arnoldo Palacios

María and *El alférez real* were products of an elitist writing culture published primarily for its own consumption. A modern reader will observe with amusement that the theme of incest, consciously used at the level of plot in these novels, also reveals itself in the cultural codes of that class, and even in the literary mode of production. A more popular literary culture with its roots in oral tradition also thrived in the Greater Cauca at the turn of the century. The creators of this popular literature were poets considered "minor," such as Pedro Antonio Uribe (1854–1934). Uribe's simple verse, *décimas* and sonnets, was sometimes recited on the street corners of Tuluá, a town in the Valle del Cauca north of Cali. On other occasions some of this verse was written. Uninterested in the classical themes in vogue in literary circles of the time, from the Greater Cauca to Bogotá, Uribe wrote a light verse concerned with the topics of daily life in Tuluá and nearby towns. His poems, similar in function to the Costa's *vallenatos* of the same period, often served as newspapers, relating the news orally to an illiterate populace. Consequently, as oral tradition they serve as unofficial oral history of the region; they were published posthumously as *Los juglares de Tuluá: don Pedro Uribe*.[37]

Despite the presence of this popular oral culture, the elite models of literary culture conceived by Isaacs and Eustaquio Palacios persisted. One of the Greater Cauca's most respected turn-of-the-century intellectual figures, Luciano Rivera y Garrido, wrote eloquent homages to Isaacs and Eustaquio Palacios. Rivera y Garrido wrote in 1899 that *El alférez real* was one of the best Colombian novels.[38] In his praise of *El alférez real* Rivera y Garrido compares its descriptions to those of Walter Scott, implying, of course, that the legitimizing factor for the novel is the European romantic model. Within the regional context, it is also interesting to note that, according to Rivera y Garrido, *El alférez real* was, after *María*, the book most read by the Greater Cauca's inhabitants.[39] Rivera y Garrido praises Eustaquio Palacios as an eminent regional figure rather than a national one,[40] and, similarly, the poet and novelist Isaías Gamboa read an elegy in honor of Eustaquio Palacios at his funeral.

Rivera y Garrido, Gamboa, and others continued the Greater Cauca's novelistic tradition of their models Isaacs and Eustaquio Palacios. Rivera y Garrido published some short fiction in the 1870s, followed by the brief novel *Dónde empieza y cómo acaba* (1888), a seventy-eight-page story evoking some of the images and codes from *María* and *El alférez real*. Mercedes Gómez Victoria followed Palacios's model with her historical novel *Misterios de la vida* (1889), a work described by Rivera y Garrido as "destitute of literary pretensions and foreign to the scientific procedures of Art."[41] *La expiación de una madre* (1894) by José Rafael Sañudo, set in the Department of Nariño in the southern part of the Greater Cauca, repeats the plot of the adopted child seen in *María* and *El alférez real*. The descriptions in Sañudo's work, however, are not of the paradisaical Valle del Cauca but of the similarly luscious and fertile coffee region of Matituy in the Department of Nariño.

Two novels attempting to continue the basic model of storytelling set forth by Isaacs and Eustaquio Palacios are *La tierra nativa* (1904) by Isaías Gamboa and *Eufrosina de Alejandría* (1924) by Francisco María Renjifo. The intertextual relationships between *María* and *La tierra nativa* are uncanny. Even though Gamboa uses many of the same romantic clichés in developing the love story of the narrator-protagonist and the heroine, Marta, the plot is less intense and compelling than in *María*. The strong intertextuality is evidenced in the use of the identical codes present in *María:* The codes of separation, of the Valle del Cauca as earthly paradise, of incest, and of the female character as virtuous Mary-figure are present throughout *La tierra nativa*. The protagonist, Andrés del Campo, returns to his native Valle del Cauca after a stay in Chile and, like Efraín returning from Europe, is overwhelmed by the beauty of the Valle and the experience of returning to his native region. When Andrés first sees this land again, the narrator describes it as "marvelous" and "stunning."[42] Numerous other descriptions such as this constitute a code which portrays the Valle del Cauca as an earthly paradise.

Gamboa's self-conscious evocation of *María* required a modification of the codes found in Isaacs's classic; the cycle of proto-*María*s had logically reached an exhaustion by the time Gamboa was portraying love relationships as literary affairs in repetition of acts by Efraín and María. A culmination of the elitist humanist project as novel, initiated in *María* and *El alférez real* in the Greater Cauca, was Renjifo's *Eufrosina de Alejandría* (1924), a historical novel set in the Near East in the fifth century. The impressive historical research such a project presents could only have been carried out by a scholar of the classics like Renjifo. The simple plot is overshadowed by the implied author's classical erudition.

With the modernization of Cali in the 1920s and the rise of a middle class and the first small publishing houses, a commercial novel began to appear. Ramón and Guillermo Franky were among the first commercial writers for this new reading public, but Gregorio Sánchez Gómez was the most prolific. Generally speaking, their novels contained the conventional narrative techniques of the nineteenth-century novel and relatively simple plots.

The sign of the novel's new commercial possibilities beginning in the 1920s was the phenomenon of Gregorio Sánchez Gómez, who by 1949 had published over ten novels. Many of these were published in Cali in new publishing houses such as Editorial América, Casa Editora Palau, Velásquez y Cía, and Imprenta de Relator. As in the other regions, these were locally and regionally based printing houses rather than "publishers" in the modern sense, and most were short-lived. Nevertheless, their growth in the 1920s and 1930s provided an outlet for writers such as Sánchez Gómez, and this growth corresponds to the needs of a new middle-class reading public. It was not a particularly demanding readership. Some of Sánchez Gómez's work is psychologically sophisticated, usually presenting characters in conflict with the social norms. Frequently the characters find themselves in conflict over the norms of the Greater Cauca's formerly conventional, patriarchal nineteenth-century society and the new norms of the modernity which transformed Cali and the region so rapidly and forcefully in the 1920s and 1930s.[43] Sánchez Gómez tends to defend the old values.

The 1940s witnessed the conception of a more serious fiction based on the region's awareness of sociopolitical and cultural realities. The fiction of Guillermo Edmundo Chaves, Diego Castrillón Arboleda, and Arnoldo Palacios represents this new consciousness and new novelistic project. Chaves's *Chambú* (1946) is an ambitious search for identity which in some ways recalls similar New World projects such as *Doña Bárbara*, *Don Segundo Sombra*, and *La vo-*

rágine (or *Risaralda* in Antioquia), but the *tierra* is now the southern region of the Greater Cauca. Chaves demonstrates not only an awareness of this region's tri-ethnic oral and writing culture but is fascinated with it as the material for establishing an identity. The protagonist, Ernesto, who often serves also as focalizer, sees the black and indigenous cultures from the outside, and in this sense *Chambú* is not comparable to the anthropological and sociological projects of authentic *indigenismo* as practiced by José María Arguedas and others in Latin America during the period. The implied author, however, does demonstrate a reasonably sophisticated knowledge of indigenous cultures and respect for them, integrating both Quechua and Caribe Indian language and culture into the novel. *Chambú* was already an anachronism by the mid-1940s, both as a tardy evocation of the problematics of *La vorágine* and as a nostalgic critique of modern progress. Nevertheless, it represented an affirmation of the Greater Cauca's tri-ethnic culture as a collective identity, as set forth in the novel's final lines, which tell of the importance of mestizo culture in the region.[44]

Diego Castrillón Arboleda also pursued a fictional project related to the Greater Cauca's indigenous, black, and mestizo cultures as an outsider to the culture, producing the novels *José Tombé* (1942) and *Sol en Tambalimbú* (1944). In both novels a strictly writing culture is the frame of reference for telling stories intimately related to the region's tri-ethnic culture. *José Tombé* deals with the exploitation of the indigenous population by the local power structure in the hands of whites. Exploitation in this novel follows classic schemes in Latin America, from the illegal methods of stripping the Indians of their land to forcing the purchase of products from the company store. The main character, the Indian José Tombé, leads a failed rebellion. Nevertheless, Castrillón Arboleda fictionalizes Tombé as a mythic character, associating him with the mythical Tupac Amaru: "He has a spirit of revenge. . . . Perhaps he carries the same warrior blood as Tupac Amaru."[45] *Sol en Tambalimbú* does not deal with indigenous issues but represents Castrillón Arboleda's consideration of the future the Greater Cauca's tri-ethnic culture may hold for Colombia seen in an ideological context. The author's conclusion is affirmative to the point of simplistic idealism. He portrays three models of political action, one represented by a mulatto, one by a white, and one by a mestizo. The mestizo, Gabriel, holds the key to Colombia's bright future, as suggested throughout the novel and reaffirmed at the end.[46] Unfortunately, the characterization of the nonmestizo characters involves simplistic racial stereotypes. Castrillón Arboleda's interest in an authentic language is reflected in the two-page dictionary of regionalism which appears at the end of the book.

The work of Arnoldo Palacios should be seen as a continuation of the new social awareness among writers in the Greater Cauca which surfaced in the 1930s and 1940s, signaled by the work of Chaves and Castrillón Arboleda. Arnoldo Palacios is from the Department of Chocó, a predominantly black population located in the northern part of the Greater Cauca region. He spent his youth in his native Chocó and much of his adulthood in Bogotá and Europe, mostly the latter. Palacios has published two novels, *Las estrellas son negras* (1949) and *La selva y la lluvia* (1958), neither of which has gained much critical attention in Colombia.[47] The second novel represents one of the better syntheses produced thus far of the Greater Cauca's tri-ethnic culture, integrating oral culture through a specific character (Rentería) who preserves the oral tradition. In addition, *La selva y la lluvia* is an effective counter-discourse to the official language of power.

For one authority on Colombia's Afro-Colombian novelists, Arnoldo Palacios is one of five major Afro-Colombian prose fiction writers in Colombia, along with the Greater Cauca's short story writer Carlos Arturo Truque and the Costa's Jorge Artel, Juan Zapata Olivella, and Manuel Zapata Olivella.[48] *Las estrellas son negras* is particularly impressive for a writer's first book. In this connection, the work's maturity supports the contention that "Arnoldo Palacios is well versed in literary theory and its application to fiction."[49] The novel deals with a day and a half in the life of Israel, a black in Chocó who suffers from poverty and the physical pain of hunger. Israel (usually referred to as "Irra") is the first-born son of five children in a family headed by the mother. With respect to the region's tri-ethnic culture, it is a novel which sets forth an authentic vision of the region's Afro-Colombian presence, with some residue of its oral culture. The narrator's characterization of Irra, for example, with repetitive use of crude bodily functions, involves what Ong has identified as the "heavy character" typical of oral storytelling.

The story is related consistently by an extradiegetic-heterodiegetic narrator who presents a text with narrative characteristics never seen before in the novel of the Greater Cauca. This narrator is located close to Irra: He follows Irra's thoughts and actions closely during the novel's relatively limited (day and a half) time period. In addition, the narrative is frequently filtered through Irra himself. For example, in the following passage the reader gradually follows Irra's eye by the end of the passage: "Irra se detuvo un instante, disparando una mirada hacia la casa, enfocándola. El sol reverberaba bajo el cielo azul, cruzado de algodonosas nubes errantes. La casita estaba separada de las demás de la acera, sobre la callejuela inclinada" (Irra stopped a minute, taking a glance toward the house, focusing it. The sun reverberated under the blue sky, crossed with cottonlike errant clouds. The little house was separated from the rest of the sidewalk, on the slanting little street).[50] This oft-used type of narrative procedure makes the reader an intimate part of Irra's circumstances as he suffers hunger and depredation. It also provides the reader with an insider's view into black culture. The relative closeness to the character also permits the presentation of ideas that otherwise might appear to be editorial interventions on the part of the narrator. For example, the narrator poses a question that the reader interprets as the focalizer's interrogation. Generally speaking, *Las estrellas son negras* is an intense text, filtered subtly through either the narrator-focalizer or Irra-focalizer.

The novel's thematic focus is conveyed by observing the nuclear verb around which the plot is developed: "Irra suffers." Irra's suffering is first and foremost an individual act, for he is hungry and destitute throughout the novel. The narrator successfully communicates this suffering by attacking the reader's sensibility in the context of the physical: The narrator places considerable emphasis on bodily functions.[51] Irra's conceptualization and understanding of this suffering and his reaction to it are keys to the novel's ideological positions. At some moments his understanding of his circumstances is limited to bewilderment. He questions why he and those close to him suffer hunger, but he is unable to reach any comprehension of his situation, be it in terms of either class or race. In at least two different moments of the novel, in fact, he betrays his own class and race, reacting in disgust to the beggars on the street who lack the ambition he still has for self-improvement (see pages 82 and 149). Despite these moments of confusion, he often perceives that at least a part of his situation is related to race.

Some of the most interesting moments of the novel with respect to this thematic development—in effect, this analysis of Irra's consciousness—occur in those passages when he realizes that his situation is part of a general condition, caused by domination but not limited to any specific class or race. For example, early in the novel Irra-focalizer observes not only black poverty but the impoverished houses of the blacks and the whites (Palacios, 30). In the final pages, when his experiences have led him to a clearer understanding of the situation, he concludes that whites suffer poverty too (Palacios, 166). With this observation, *Las estrellas son negras* is no longer a novel exclusively about Irra or the black circumstance in Chocó but about human suffering in general as experienced by one historically oppressed racial group in Colombia.

Las estrellas son negras is a dialogic novel of at least five heterogeneous and conflicting discourses.[52] It is one of the most successful novels of the Greater Cauca in incorporating the oral language of Chocó's Afro-Colombian culture. The dialogues are direct transcriptions of the illiterate speech patterns: "Deben de sé laj tré" is how the first such dialogue is transcribed for "Deben de ser las tres" (It should be three). The dialogue consistently reads in this fashion, and the narrator's language, although standard speech, includes enough regionalisms to require a three-page vocabulary at the end of the book. The oral language of the blacks, as spoken by the characters and filtered through the discourse of the narrator, contrasts with the more official discourses, such as the written language of the newspapers and the official written language of the power structure, both of which originate from the outside. The language of the newspapers reporting political conflict in Bogotá brings the only national consciousness to Irra. On the other hand, he is confounded by the official language of power, which speaks of "consecrated figures," a concept utterly foreign to him.[53] The narrator also employs the language of Christianity, not as parody but as a constant presence which eventually leads to self-awareness. The novel opens with an epigraph from the Sermon on the Mount, and traces of this language appear throughout the work. This language suggests the theme of humanity being forsaken by God.[54]

In the end, within this context of heterogeneous discourse, it is the language of orality and of Christianity which predominates.[55] In the novel's last part, "Libro Cuarto: Luz Interior," Irra undergoes a self-affirmation which represents, in turn, an affirmation of his own language—the unofficial oral language of the blacks of Chocó. The language of Christianity is clearly articulated in this last part, especially in the work's concluding paragraphs. The narrator states: "Irra felt his soul fill with confidence" (Palacios, 178). Irra's discovery takes place, significantly, near water, which suggests the unconscious, purification, and the Christian concept of redemption.[56]

Las estrellas son negras in several ways is a pioneer work in the Greater Cauca. It is the first novel in this region to create an experience of transcendent regionalism; it can be described as such because both in terms of ideology and discourse it transcends its regional base in Chocó. The representation of poverty (not limited by class or race) and liberation transcends geographical, social, and racial boundaries.

The intextextual relationship between this work and the two previous landmarks of the Greater Cauca's novelistic tradition—*María*
and *El alférez real*—figure as what Riffaterre has defined as an antonym rather than a synonym.[57] Novels such as *El alférez real*, Scarpetta's *Julia*, and Gamboa's *La tierra nativa* seemingly exhausted
the viable intertextual possibilities as synonym. *Las estrellas son
negras*, on the other hand, functions in relationship to these novels
as antonym—along the lines of difference. In the rarified world of
María and *El alférez real*, subtle love relationships are developed
around symbolic gestures that cautiously avoid physical contact
with the virtuous Mary-figure heroines. In *Las estrellas son negras*
the one male-female relationship is the polar opposite: a relationship reduced strictly to the physical. In the novels by Isaacs and Eustaquio Palacios emphasis is placed on the spirituality of the main
characters: They are not only readers who live in the world of literature but tend to read the most lofty romantic texts. Their relationships are encounters of kindred spirits, of souls seemingly destined
to be united either on earth or in heaven. In contrast with these idealized characters, Irra and the others in *Las estrellas son negras* are
physical entities who carry out bodily functions and other physical
acts. Sexuality in this novel is strictly a response to a physical drive.
Rather than responding to their souls, the characters respond to
their flesh. The culminating novelistic product of this heterogeneous tradition, *El bazar de los idiotas*, also emphasizes physicality
over spirituality in a contemporary writing against *María*.

Transition (1949–1973) and *El bazar de los idiotas* (1974) by Gustavo Alvarez Gardeazábal

The most significant of the relatively few notable literary events
to occur between *Las estrellas son negras* and *El bazar de los idiotas*
was the publication of three important novels of La Violencia: Daniel
Caicedo's *Viento seco* (1953), Fernán Muñoz Jiménez's *Horizontes
cerrados* (1954), and Alvarez Gardeazábal's *Cóndores no entierran
todos los días* (1972) (see chapter 2).

A later work by Arnoldo Palacios, short fiction by Carlos Arturo
Truque, and a novel by Rogerio Velásquez represent a continuation
of the Afro-Colombian portion of the Greater Cauca's tri-ethnic culture as initiated in *Las estrellas son negras*. Arnoldo Palacios's second novel, *La selva y la lluvia* (1958), begins as a youth's story of the
Chocó region and ends as "public service literature."[58] Despite the
work's structural weaknesses, it is interesting in the context of oral
culture: The characters have kept their oral tradition alive, and

Rentería, an oral storyteller, preserves the oral tradition by resisting the outside and dominating culture. Carlos Arturo Truque, a short story writer from the Chocó region, published a volume of stories in 1953 and another posthumous book in 1973, both of which are valuable contributions to the Greater Cauca's tri-ethnic culture.[59] Rogerio Velásquez's *Las memorias del odio* is a brief novel (108 pages) in which a black protagonist in the Chocó at the turn of the century writes his tale of enduring prejudice and injustices inflicted upon him by the white power structure. As the title suggests, it is marked by resentment and hatred. The protagonist speaks as an insider in a poverty-stricken black world. He observes an oral culture and occasionally thinks like an oral-culture person (probably a phenomenon of residual orality), but he belongs to a writing culture. Like Arnoldo Palacios, Rogerio Velásquez writes against *María:* The intertextuality is found in the codes which Velásquez subverts. It is also one of the early works to question the "progress" that had gone unquestioned since the national modernization project set in motion in the 1930s.

Gustavo Alvarez Gardeazábal initiated a "cycle of Tuluá" with the publication of short stories in the early 1970s, followed by three works set in the Valle del Cauca's town of Tuluá—*La tara del papa* (1971), *Cóndores no entierran todos los días* (1972), and *Dabeiba* (1973). *La tara del papa* deals with three generations of the Uribes, an important family in Tuluá. One of the main achievements of this novel is the dramatization of La Violencia at various levels by means of specific narrative techniques. Here La Violencia is experienced more as a conflict of deep-rooted traditions than as conflict exclusively of ideologies or social classes. In certain historical segments, La Violencia is seen as part of a long tradition prior to its intensification in the 1940s and 1950s. In intradiegetic sections the reader experiences the importance of family tradition in the sense that each one of the Uribes fulfills his or her personal "destiny" within this tradition.[60] *Dabeiba* is written with the copious flow Ong attributes to oral storytelling and occasionally creates other oral effects. It deals with the inhabitants of the town of Dabeiba during a time frame of only a few days. Several of these inhabitants are what Ong would identify as "heavy" characters. A thread that links the descriptions of the numerous characters is the constant threat of a natural disaster. A principal source of information in the story has its roots in one of the most oral fonts: rumor. A series of temporal strategies associated with the writing tradition, however, creates one of this novel's principal successful effects: the dynamics of expectation.

The oral tradition of Pedro Antonio Uribe, the bard of early twentieth-century Tuluá, can be associated directly with Alvarez Gardeazábal's fiction. A level of communication expressed by the frequent use of the word *dizque* (it is said) in addition to other elements of orality form this link between the popular poetry of Pedro Antonio Uribe and the fiction of Alvarez Gardeazábal. In addition, the reader should keep in mind that Alvarez Gardeazábal began writing after the publication of García Márquez's *Cien años de soledad*, which in a sense legitimized the incorporation of oral culture in Colombian fiction and exerted a strong impact on Alvarez Gardeazábal's generation.

El bazar de los idiotas (1974), Alvarez Gardeazábal's fourth novel, relates a bizarre story focusing on a pair of miracle-producing adolescents in Tuluá. The humor and magical quality of some of the events of the novel recall similar qualities in *Cien años de soledad*. In accordance with Genette's concept of the nuclear verb, the novel is an expansion of the basic sentence "Two masturbating idiots become heroes in Tuluá." The use of "become" emphasizes the importance of inventiveness (the elaboration of this becoming) as fundamental to the novel.

A cursory overview of the expansion of this nuclear verb and its sentence provides a summary of the *histoire*. The point of departure of this "becoming" is the relating of the events that lead to the idiots' birth. Tuluá's priest, Father Severo Tascón, cohabits with Manuela Barona, despite protest from the local women's religious organization. Their offspring, Marcianita, suffers a degree of ostracism but does eventually marry Nemesio Rodríguez, who fathers two idiots, Bartolomé and Ramón Lucio. Becoming heroes involves their discovery of the fact that, despite their mental deficiencies and inability to cope with life in conventional terms, through masturbation they can miraculously cure illnesses. As their fame grows in the process of their becoming heroes, so does the economy of the surrounding area, which becomes a tourist center. A significant aspect of their becoming involves the people they cure in order to attain this popularity—a gallery of types ranging from a paralyzed ex–beauty queen to a homosexual suffering from "sickness of the soul" after losing his lover. Each of these sufferers represents the "heavy characters" typical of oral storytelling. The idiots attain "hero" status in their becoming when their feats achieve such fame that national and foreign experts converge upon Tuluá. Their process of becoming ends on the last page of the novel when they die, assassinated by their bastard half brother. It should be noted that the "in Tuluá" portion of the proposed sentence is significant: As the culminating work in the Greater Cauca's regionalist tradition, the specific place is important to the experience of the novel.

Fundamental to the experience of the expansion of the verb in *El bazar de los idiotas* is the basic structure as an element of transformation. This expansion manipulates time and anecdote in a way that does not correspond to a mimetic description of the spatial and temporal boundaries it covers. Two opposing structural tendencies effect the transformation of the perception of reality: a tendency toward short story technique in which individual chapters function as entities within themselves, and within these entities individual sequences which function as units (this characteristic underlines the anecdotal orality of the novel); a tendency toward overall cohesion in which the manipulation of time creates structural unity.

The first tendency, the formation of entities and then sequences within these anecdotes, can be seen by considering the individual chapters as units or as one of a series of anecdotes. The even-numbered chapters, those in which individuals are characterized, correspond most closely to a closed system or a cycle of short stories. The first chapter is special in this respect because its circular structure clearly reveals the nature of the closed system. The first two and one-half pages are narrated from a temporal position that creates an initial analepsis. From a position marked as "today," the narrator comments briefly on the past events that are to take place in the novel. These events are seen as part of a cycle which, after these two and one-half pages of introduction, the narrator begins as follows: "The cycle that just closed today."[61] The beginning of the cycle related in the remainder of chapter 1 involves the cohabitation of Tascón with Manuela, the protests by Paulina Sarmiento and her group, the appearance of a mysterious mare, and the departure of Tascón. After these anecdotes the chapter comes to a close within the same analepsis-creating present with which the narrator began (Alvarez, 20). The structural makeup of the chapter created through this temporal indicator contributes to the cohesion of the chapter.

All the even-numbered chapters function similarly. In almost every case they constitute complete systems which close with a reference that relates them to the rest of the novel. Chapter 2, the story of Andrés, opens with his arrival in Tuluá, and his story reaches its logical conclusion as he apparently nears death. The chapter ends: "It was in this moment when someone decided to take him to the idiots" (Alvarez, 42). When he appears again it will be in the context of the idiots' rise to fame, their becoming. The next chapter of this type, chapter 4, characterizes Isaac Nessim, whose story will be slightly more developed than Andrés's in chapter 17, but again the chapter can stand as an independent unit. Chapters 6, 8, 10, 12, and 14 follow the established pattern.[62]

In the odd-numbered chapters the close correspondence to a closed system is not as apparent. These chapters, however, like the characterization chapters, do contain a strong anecdotal base, making the anecdotal sequence an important factor in the experience of the novel. Considering the development of this anecdote in detail, we can see the novel as a series of eighty-six narrative sequences.

The importance of the independent units is emphasized also through the repetition of the same information in different sequences, a technique typical of oral storytelling. For example, Andrés's complete story is related in chapter 2 up to the announcement that he will visit the idiots. In chapter 13, however, the information about Andrés is repeated. He could almost function in this chapter without previous characterization in chapter 2. A similar type of reiteration occurs to a lesser degree with the other characters. As in oral storytelling, information is often repeated in the form of the epithet or short phrases describing the character. Nemesio Rodríguez carries several epithets, all of which emphasize his masculinity as an officer in the army and builder of the Ferrocarril del Pacífico. (This railroad, built in the Greater Cauca in the late nineteenth century, was also one of Eustaquio Palacios's extraliterary obsessions.) Another example of reiteration is Toño González, Inesita's brother. He appears or is mentioned only a few times, but in three chapters an allusion is made to his having studied in Switzerland (Alvarez, 155, 195, 250). In this case the reiteration is particularly evident because this information is the only thing known about him.

Each of these factors—the chapter as an individual unit, the sequence, and reiteration—contributes to the episodic experience of *El bazar de los idiotas.* Together they also create at least an impression of orality. Nevertheless, the second structural factor—related to writing culture—unifies these anecdotes. The main factor involved in this unity is the manipulation of certain elements of time.

The overall structure is based on a manipulation of time in the sense that the events of the novel are the completion of a cycle in the past which is recounted as an analepsis. The opening two and one-half pages establish this present, which is maintained as a point of reference throughout the novel. The beginning pages provide a retrospective overview of all the events that will take place. With this overview completed, the narrative begins as a movement that has already been completed "today." After other similar references throughout the novel, in the last chapter there are several references that point to this present time, referring to the events of "yesterday," "today," and "tomorrow." When the explosion occurs on the last pages, the cycle that "today" had begun in the first chapter has been completed in the same "today" with which it began. Thus, this use of analepsis for the basic narrative—by means of the references noted above—imposes an order and unity on what would otherwise be chaotic. Another effect of the analepsis is that its progressively increasing use toward the end creates a sense of climax and culmination.

Beyond this basic expansion of the nuclear verb, a more detailed examination of time reveals other aspects of Alvarez Gardeazábal's transformation of reality. As has been suggested with the use of analepsis, the novel's *récit* does not correspond to a strictly lineal development of *histoire*. In terms of chronology, the *histoire* covers a span of approximately fifty-eight years, from 1915 to 1973. The cohabitation of Father Taxcón and Manuela occurs in the years 1915 and 1916 (chapter 1). The second chapter tells of Andrés from approximately the mid-1950s to 1973. Chapter 3 deals with Marcianita from 1916 to the 1930s. Chapter 4 has the broadest temporal scope of all, this being the story of Isaac Nessim from 1917 to 1972. Marcianita's later youth and her romance and eventual marriage to Nemesio Rodríguez in chapter 8 correspond approximately to the years from the 1930s to the early 1950s. The remaining chapters run from approximately the 1950s to the narrative present of about 1973. Two exceptions are the chapters of Nina Pérez and Chuchú, the former covering these years but also moving back to the 1920s and school with Luisita Tascón, and the latter also probably extending back in time beyond the 1950s (depending on her age, which is unknown).

As the highly anecdotal nature of the novel suggests, "becoming" and its elaboration are as important as the act of becoming itself, if not more so. The two structural tendencies, one emphasizing the independent narrative unit and the other the novelization of these units, create a certain lack of equilibrium in the expansion process, transforming *histoire* beyond the limits of mimesis. The consideration of time indicates the rupture with objective chronology and the importance of the manipulation of these temporal factors in the inventive process. The creation of a cyclical structure through the manipulation of time and the use of the "present" as a point of departure create a distance from the events at hand instead of the closeness to the reality that the traditional regionalist novel—*El alférez real*—depended upon for its nostalgic effects.

The narrator in *El bazar de los idiotas* is extradiegetic-heterodiegetic; the manner in which this narrator regulates information is a fundamental part of the experience of the invention and humor of this novel. It is by no means a profound psychological analysis. The narrator does have the capacity, however, to penetrate the characters' thoughts and feelings, often using words like "[he] understood" and "[he] felt" in brief descriptions rather than extensive elaboration. One source of the novel's inventive humor is the rupture with this standard procedure. The narrator has the characters "decide" things, for example, that would not normally be decisions or at least would not be referred to as such. This technique is used at least three times in the opening chapter. First, Marcianita "decides" to be born (appear between her mother's legs; Alvarez, 8). Then Paulina Sarmiento "decides" to die (Alvarez, 11). The narrator creates a similarly humorous effect in describing women who are experts "en hacer vomitar hasta un tornillo a quien decidiera embarazarse" (in making whoever should decide to become pregnant vomit up even a screw) (Alvarez, 13). This change in narrative procedure recalls the incongruities already noted involving the use of time (detail within the general context).

When the narrator's focus moves nearer to that of the perception of the characters, the effect is ironic. When Paulina Sarmiento leads her group in the campaign against Marcianita, the narrator describes them using the term *reencarnación demoníaca* (satanic reincarnation) (Alvarez, 44), which corresponds more closely to the perception of the group than to his own. In addition, the language is the colloquial language of orality. At other times this use of language reflects more than the pettiness of the inhabitants of Tuluá. The narrator compares Inesita González with other candidates using a colloquial, oral language that humorously reflects Tuluá (Alvarez, 149).

Similarly, the narrator inverts the normal terms of language, using a commercial language to describe the workings of the Church and the language of the Church to describe the activities of the idiots. In reference to the Church, the members are called "clients" (Alvarez, 241). The language used in reference to the idiots tends to be ecclesiastical. The people that come to be cured are referred to as "pilgrims" who make their "pilgrimage." At other times they are a biblical "multitude."

One basic function of the narrator is that of organizer. His role is significant because he is the only source of memory of the events in Tuluá and consequently is their only possible organizer. Ong has pointed out that, in oral cultures, one knows only what one remembers. In the case of *El bazar de los idiotas*, Tuluá's typical inhabitant seems to be an oral-culture person who has forgotten; the narrator-organizer belongs to writing culture and has remembered. As a participant in this writing culture, the narrator-organizer is highly cognizant of time and treats time with precision. The narrator notes from the beginning of the novel that the lack of understanding of the events that have occurred in Tuluá results from a problem of memory: Tuluá has forgotten about Father Tascón and the origins of the idiots' cult. The narrator's task, thus, is remembering and rewriting Tuluá's forgotten history. Tuluá's reality is determined as much by the way it is remembered (or forgotten) as by the facts of its real history. The narrator's act of organizing and narrating is to an extent a denunciation of modernity and its technology because it is this modernity—brought about by writing—that causes Tuluá to forget its real past. "Civilization" has conveniently caused Tuluá to forget Marcianita's past and, as such, is typical of Tuluá's memory: Things are forgotten when it seems convenient. As Ong has noted, oral cultures are homeostatic and they tend to slough off memories that are not useful or necessary. When Marcianita holds her bazaar outside the church, the priest and people conveniently forget she was never baptized (even though she had been anathematized by the Church). When Marcianita is young, the people have already forgotten her origins and Father Tascón. Since Isaac Nessim is an unpopular and ostracized figure in Tuluá, his benevolent contributions (a rarity) have been forgotten. Nemesio forgets about Marcianita's German measles when she is pregnant with her second son. He also conveniently forgets the promise not to father any more children after the birth of the first idiot. With the exception of Marcianita, the people of Tuluá are manipulated and unable to distinguish between historical reality and reality as it is remembered; only the narrator's memory and organizing of historical reality have saved the story from being lost. The exact content of this narrator-historian's memory makes him a parody of the narrator-historian figure in novels with the historical pretensions of *El alférez real*.

The narrator's discourse approximates metalanguage in certain instances when he discusses this distortion of history. The very fact that he addresses himself overtly to the problem of distortion, and that distortion itself is the essence of Tuluá's story, places such discourse on the level of metalanguage. For example, the narrator comments on the exaggeration in an admonition against masturbation among the youth (Alvarez, 260). When the idiots rise to national fame, the narrator comments: "The magazine *Siete Días* didn't invent more lies because they really couldn't" (Alvarez, 228). The experience of the novel is to a certain extent a study of the phenomenon of exaggeration, including direct comments by the narrator himself. In this connection *El bazar de los idiotas* can be read as a parody of oral storytelling (with its exaggerated "heavy" characters) and of *Cien años de soledad*.

Alvarez Gardeazábal, like García Márquez, occasionally privileges orality over writing. In many instances premodern oral noetics are superior to writing culture's technology. In *El bazar de los idiotas* modern technology is totally ineffective: When Andrés is bitten, the local specialists and the Japanese experts fail to cure him; when Inesita is paralyzed, neither national doctors nor specialists from Boston can do anything for her. The irrationality of the idiots' methodology humorously underlines modern technology's failures. It is noteworthy that their first miracle is performed on a Swiss, a symbol of modern technological precision. Other irrational elements make up the experience of Tuluá, such as Marcianita's birthdate (October 31), the mysterious mare, and the magical effects of mare's milk on the idiots. The columnist Pangloss deprecates the idiots in his "rationalist column," but after the idiots burn the edition of the newspaper in which his explanation appears, he ceases to write for a month. Others oppose the idiots with "rationalist vigor" (Alvarez, 267).

A consideration of the expansion of the nuclear sentence "Two masturbating idiots become heroes in Tuluá" suggests that the basis for Alvarez Gardeazábal's inventive process lies in the development of the verb through incongruities, or what has also been noted as a certain lack of equilibrium in the narrative—in summary: incongruities, anomalies, and distortion. The incongruity of "masturbating idiots" in juxtaposition with "heroes" is the expression of this inventive process in its most basic form. From this basic expression the reader experiences a strong emphasis on the anecdote, which develops the basic anomaly of the nuclear verb on several levels of experience. The structure, or organization of the anecdotal material, creates an anomaly between short story, sequential tendencies in contrast with the work's overall precise and unified structure. In developing this structure the verb "becoming" is significant because of the incongruous elaboration of this "becoming." Thus, the narrator's pure invention may take precedence over developing the story line, as in the case of the spider episode. The methods of manipulating time made apparent by contrasting *histoire* and *récit* indicate that, besides disrupting pure chronology, the incongruity between historical time and *récit* time emphasizes invention over mimesis. In terms of the narrative situation, the narrator's focus on Tuluá creates humorous distortions through the use of language not totally congruent with its context—again, the detail of "to decide" within a much larger context—or by completely inverting the normal relationship between signifier and signified, as in the case of the commercial and ecclesiastical language. The position of the narrator in relation to the story indicates his role as organizer. The distance shared by the narrator and reader from the actions observed permits the dispassionate observation of the incongruities of social procedures, implying a denunciation of such relationships.

Like García Márquez, Alvarez Gardeazábal uses procedures intimately associated with oral storytelling. The narrator assumes the role of the writer who has access to anecdotes which the (oral-culture) citizenry of Tuluá has forgotten. This narrator's apparently total access to Tuluá's story includes both oral and written versions. Indeed, much of what he narrates has oral roots—what has been said (*dizque*) and perhaps repeated over the years. In addition, the narrator employs other procedures which emphasize orality, such as the use of colloquial language (*marica* rather than "homosexual"). The narrator's seemingly total access to orality and full exploitation of it constitute a successful exploitation of the Greater Cauca's cultural heterogeneity that had appeared in the background but was carefully avoided as "authentic" novelistic material in *María* and *El alférez real*.

Alvarez Gardeazábal, like Arnoldo Palacios, writes against the codes present in Greater Cauca fiction since *María*. Consequently, the most evident intertextual relationship between *El bazar de los idiotas* and *María* is the former's qualities as an anti-*María*. The characterization of the female figure as a Mary-figure from *María* forward in much fiction of the Greater Cauca is totally subverted by her iconoclastic characterization in *El bazar de los idiotas*. The Valle del Cauca represented as a paradise in *María* and as a classical paradise in *El alférez real* is a code which Alvarez Gardeazábal also undermines: This setting in the Valle del Cauca only promotes superstition, commercialism, irrational acts, and, in the end, ugly violence. The characterization of the male protagonists as eternal *niños* does correspond to the codes of characterization in *María* and *El alférez real*, but there are also radical differences in these codes: The idealistic activities of the two nineteenth-century protagonists are substituted by acts seen in society as fundamentally subversive and perverse. Like Arnoldo Palacios, this young author prefers crude physicality to lofty spirituality. Again, Alvarez Gardeazábal's incongruities point to the heterogeneity of the Greater Cauca's culminating regionalist text.

Conclusion

A review of novelistic production from the Greater Cauca, from the dominant codes established in *María* to the different intertextual relationships of the novels which follow, reveals it to be the most heterogeneous in novelistic production of the four regional tra-

ditions studied. This heterogeneity is representative of the Greater
Cauca's tri-ethnic and heterogeneous cultural traditions. Laurent
Jenny has offered the following conclusion with respect to inten-
tional intertextuality: "Whatever its avowed ideological underpinnings, the intertextual use of discourse always has a critical, playful,
and exploratory function. This makes it the most fitting instrument
of expression in times of cultural breakdown and renaissance."[63] For
the Greater Cauca Eustaquio Palacios initiated this critical enterprise, even though the final denouement of *El alférez real* represents
a nostalgic return to a Colonial status. *Las estrellas son negras* and
El bazar de los idiotas, however, serve the critical and exploratory
function to which Jenny alludes. In addition, *El bazar de los idiotas*
has a playful and iconoclastic relationship to texts such as *María*
and *Cien años de soledad*.

Using Rifaterre's concepts of intertextuality as synonym and antonym, we can conclude that novels such as *El alférez real*, *Julia*, and
La tierra nativa are synonyms with *María*, while *Las estrellas son
negras*, *Viento seco*, *Las memorias del odio*, and *El bazar de los idiotas*, among others, should be seen as antonyms to *María* and *El alférez real*. The two latter novels are spiritual journeys in the sense
that they tell the story of "souls" in suffering; *Las estrellas son
negras* and *El bazar de los idiotas* reject this spiritual conceptualization and emphasize, in different ways, crude physicality.

Isaacs and Eustaquio Palacios, as well as the authors who wrote
their intertextual synonyms, such as Scarpetta and Gamboa, effected projects of a traditional regionalism which did not function
with the confidence and technical expertise necessary to integrate
one of the most vital elements of its regional tri-ethnic culture—its
orality. Only the perspicacious reader will detect—implicitly, in the
background—the Greater Cauca's cultural heterogeneity, and then
only upon careful scrutiny of these novels. With Arnoldo Palacios
and Alvarez Gardeazábal, the Greater Cauca's narrative turns to its
vital cultural sources, including its orality.

Part Three

After Regionalism

Seven

The Modern and Postmodern Novel (1965–1987)

But if much of modernism appears hieratic, hypotactical, and formalist, postmodernism strikes us by contrast as playful, paratactical, and deconstructionist.

Ihab Hassan, The Postmodern Turn

By the mid-1960s it had become increasingly problematic to read the Colombian novel within a strictly regional or national context. Modern and postmodern novelists were fully immersed in the writing of international fiction, rather than the traditional, regional and oral cultures, with the exception of García Márquez and David Sánchez Juliao, whose early lives had been directly touched by the Costa's oral culture. And these two *costeños*, of course, were also as well versed in modern fiction as they were in the Costa's oral culture. Numerous factors had transformed Colombia and its novel. Most of the communication barriers of the previous century had been overcome by the 1950s, debilitating regional cultures and strengthening Colombia as one society and one culture. By the mid-1950s, television broadcasts began in all major cities, and during that same period Antonio Curcio Altamar published his now-classic study *Evolución de la novela en Colombia*, a book which assumed a national vision for the novel.[1] Similarly, the magazine *Mito*, rather than regional, was modern in conception and national and international in vision. It published writers from all regions, including the then young and relatively unknown *costeño* Gabriel García Márquez.[2]

The irreverent Nadaístas, primarily poets, successfully scandalized the still predominantly conservative and conventional cultural establishment. Whether or not the poetry and proclamations of

Gonzalo Arango and his Nadaísta cohorts will be judged of permanent value remains to be seen. Nevertheless, their rebellious textual and extratextual postures had a profound impact on literary tastes and paved the way for ongoing modern and postmodern literary activity in Colombia. The Nadaísta novel prize provided an outlet for the publication and distribution of the most experimental fiction of the time, even though the national concern for understanding and evaluating La Violencia meant that the novel of La Violencia was deemed much more important than novels of technical experimentation (see chapter 2).

The literary establishment also provided a heretofore unknown infrastructure for the creation and publication of a national novel of international impact. The magazine *Eco*, published in Bogotá from the early 1960s to the mid-1980s, was essentially European in content, with occasional contributions on Latin America and Colombia. The publishing house Tercer Mundo Editores, which began in the early 1960s, became the first truly national publisher to operate with professional criteria for the publication and national distribution of literature.[3] By the mid-1970s the Editorial Plaza y Janés, a multinational commercial operation based in Spain, was successfully publishing and distributing several Colombian novelists, including Gabriel García Márquez and Gustavo Alvarez Gardeazábal. In the 1980s a publishing boom in Colombia resulted in the publication of Colombia's novelists with Plaza y Janés, Tercer Mundo, Planeta, and other firms.

The novel of major impact during this period was García Márquez's *Cien años de soledad*, and the most resonant literary event of the 1960s was the international heralding of this novel. A second round of the García Márquez phenomenon took place in 1982, when he received the Nobel Prize. During the late 1960s and early 1970s aspiring writers in Colombia often spoke of the "shadow" that García Márquez cast upon them. The general crisis of literary modernism experienced in the West had a double edge in Colombia: García Márquez produced in 1967 one of the most celebrated texts of the supposedly exhausted modern tradition of the West; on the other hand, this modern product enjoyed such an enormous success that it made fiction writing afterward a formidable task in Colombia.[4] By the mid-1970s the shadow of García Márquez's Macondo proved less burdensome in Colombia as several writers, such as R. H. Moreno-Durán, Albalucía Angel, Gustavo Alvarez Gardeazábal, and Marco Tulio Aguilera Garramuño found new, non-Macondian directions for the Colombian novel. Previously marginal and repressed discourses surfaced in the 1970s and 1980s as part of a new, postmodern attitude. They were discourses not necessarily related to the novel of La Violencia or Macondo.

With the increased novelistic production of the 1970s and 1980s and other international factors in play, these directions for the Colombian novel were more heterogeneous than they had ever been before. In the broadest of terms, it is possible to identify an essentially modern novelistic tradition and another fundamentally postmodern tendency over the approximately two-decade period under consideration (1965 to 1987). The modern novel entered Colombia with the publication of three seminal works: García Márquez's *La hojarasca* (1955), Alvaro Cepeda Samudio's *La casa grande* (1962), and Héctor Rojas Herazo's *Respirando el verano* (1962). With respect to ideology, the modern texts tend to exhibit their social agenda more explicitly by portraying an identifiable Colombian empirical reality. The modern novel has been cultivated in Colombia by García Márquez, Fanny Buitrago, Rojas Herazo, Manuel Zapata Olivella, and others. A more innovative and experimental postmodern fiction, best understood within a context of theory and other literary forms, has been published by R. H. Moreno-Durán, Albalucía Angel, Marco Tulio Aguilera Garramuño, Darío Jaramillo Agudelo, Andrés Caicedo, Rodrigo Parra Sandoval, and Alberto Duque López. Two of the most salient products of the modern and postmodern novel during this period were, respectively, García Márquez's *El otoño del patriarca* and Moreno-Durán's *Los felinos del Canciller.*

Gabriel García Márquez and the Modern Impulse

García Márquez's may well be the most significant enterprise of modern fiction by a single author. Since the publication of *Cien años de soledad* in 1967, a pinnacle of the modern novel in Colombia and in Latin America, García Márquez has written three novels: *El otoño del patriarca* (1975), *Crónica de una muerte anunciada* (1981), and *El amor en los tiempos del cólera* (1985). After his initial experiments in his early stories with the techniques of modernism, learned primarily from Kafka and Faulkner, he attained his first truly mature and successful modern writing with *La hojarasca.* In his total fiction, García Márquez appropriated some of the narrative techniques of modernism (fragmentation, collage, multiple points of view, etc.) and used these techniques in what is an identifiable modernist project—the seeking of order and the expression of the ineffable in a world lacking order and waiting to be named. García Márquez, like certain other contemporary Latin American writers (e.g., Vargas Llosa and Fuentes), is rooted in the moderns, began as a modern, and basically remained a modern, but not consistently so. He has also read the postmoderns and in his later work participates in some of their subversive and self-conscious exercises. As scholars of contemporary culture have pointed out, the postmodern is not necessarily a temporal concept in the sense of "after the modern."[5]

In many ways, García Márquez's *El otoño del patriarca, Crónica de una muerte anunciada,* and *El amor en los tiempos del cólera* represent a rupture from the fiction of Macondo. *El otoño del patriarca* is located in an unidentified region of the Caribbean, and its subject is a dictator. Conceiving this work in an international rather than regional or national context, García Márquez published this dictator novel in conjunction with an international series of novels of this type, including Alejo Carpentier's *El recurso del método* (1974) and Augusto Roa Bastos's *Yo, el supremo* (1974). *El otoño del patriarca* functions as a literary synthesis of numerous Latin American historical dictators, above all of Juan Vicente Gómez.[6] One indicator of the change in García Márquez's fiction is the fact that he does not locate the novel in Colombia. The exact location of the dictator's realm remains impossible to establish, although it is a nation in the Caribbean area, with images from different Caribbean nations.[7]

The basic anecdote of *El otoña del patriarca* can be reduced to the nuclear sentence "A corpse is found." This simple anecdote functions as the point of departure and frame for the storytelling. Each chapter begins with this anecdote, describing the discovery of the general's corpse in the presidential palace. The total narrative content of the novel relates the general's entire life by transforming this anecdote of the framework into a more complete biographical revelation. This change is effected by a series of technical procedures typical of the modern novel.

The transformation of this anecdotal material to the actual story of this modern text can be described by considering the novel's six chapters as a system of progressive apertures.[8] That is, the narrator develops the first chapter on the basis of an aperture, the second on another aperture, and so on. The qualifier "progressive" underlines the fact that the apertures occur at successively earlier points in each of the six chapters. These apertures occur on four levels. In the novel's experience these levels occur simultaneously. The four levels of aperture are (1) the opening of the original situation, (2) the opening of the sentence length, (3) the opening of narrative focus, and (4) the opening of a "seen" reality. The structure of progressive apertures provides for the dynamic reading experience typical of reader-engaging modern fiction.

The first chapter establishes the basic circumstance involved with the discovery of the general's corpse, the original situation (first level) in the presidential palace. With this sign, the narrator notes, he and some of his accomplices dare to enter the premises. Upon their entrance, the narrator describes the physical surroundings—for the most part decaying objects in the palace. After an initial two-and-one-half-page description of the physical surroundings, the narrator provides the first description of the general's body, an image that recurs throughout the novel. At approximately this point the narration changes from exclusively a description of the immediate surroundings to the telling of the general's story. By noting here that none of those present had ever actually seen the general before his death, the narrator moves from a description of the physical surroundings to relating *past* circumstances. This is the point in the first chapter that may be identified as the "aperture" in the narrative—an opening of the original situation into a broader story. Each of the five remaining chapters establishes the original situation as described above and follows it with an aperture to narration of the general's past.

Both traditionalism and modernity are descriptive of the effect of this aperture on the first level. The manner in which physical space functions in this novel corresponds to the realist-naturalist tradition: The beginning of the novel focuses more precisely on the physical space; then, after the physical environment has been described at the outset of the novel, the narrator elaborates the anecdotal material. On the other hand, the reader does not experience place in exactly the same manner as in the traditional novel. García Márquez manipulates physical space to such a degree that the reader is progressively more limited in terms of physical space and background setting and at the same time progressively more involved in the elaboration of the general's life.

These apertures that function as points indicating change from the original situation to the general's story are supported technically by the use of a progressive opening of the length of the sentence.[9] This is the second level of aperture. The sentences lengthen at approximately the same point in each of the chapters as the noted point at which the transformation from the original situation to the general's story occurs. In each chapter the beginning sentences might be identified as normal length. The sentences then expand in length as the chapter continues, a dilation that corresponds to switching from situational description to the general's story. The progressive nature of this development is evidenced by the fact that each chapter has fewer sentences: Chapter 1 has thirty-one sentences; chapter 2, twenty-four; chapter 3, nineteen; chapter 4, eighteen; chapter 5, fifteen; and chapter 6 is a single sentence. All these chapters, nevertheless, are of approximately the same length.

The progressive manner of organizing the sentence length in correspondence with the opening of the original situation contributes to the narrative system García Márquez constructs in this novel. The precision and complexity of a structure are essential to the reader's experience and, along with other factors, make *El otoño del patriarca* the epitome of the modern novel. Although apparently lacking in punctuation (in the first reading), this novel, as a modern product, employs punctuation in a manner different from its traditional function in prose; the specific placement of the period corresponds to the poetic use of textual space.

The third level of aperture, also corresponding to the first two, is the opening of narrative focus. The narrative focus in which each chapter begins is relatively limited; then it opens to other points of view and in some cases to multiple points of view within the same sentence. This variation of the narrative focus, by use of the apertures described, has various effects. Power is presented from the first page as something intangible but perceived by all under the general's rule. According to an "exterior" and distanced view, the general is a deity figure. The inside view of the general and his power supports this God-like characterization and also interjects humor by showing the pettiness of his concept of power (in contrast to the grandiosity of the God figure) and his paranoia and puerility. This simple and innocent figure in reality is often characterized as an oral-culture person, similar in this sense to characters in *Cien años de soledad* (see chapter 4).

The fourth and final level of aperture in the structure of *El otoño del patriarca* is the opening to a "seen" reality; or one could say that this fourth level is an opening of the dimensions of reality experienced in the novel. Each chapter begins with defined limits of reality—that which can be seen. The reader experiences this manipulation of visible and invisible reality in conjunction with the three other levels of aperture.

In the first scene of the novel, vultures are entering the presidential palace, the first visual suggestion that the general is dead. From this sentence on, it becomes apparent that only that which is seen may possibly be believed: The general, the citizenry, and the reader learn to believe only what they can see.[10] This problem of visible and invisible reality is fundamental to the novel's central theme—the general's power—and to the reader's experience. After describing the

vultures, the visible sign of death, the narrator-discoverer emphasizes the importance of what can be *seen*. The first sentence in the
second chapter sets forth the actual theme, the problem of the visible
versus illusion, thus discussing the experience of living under the
general's power and the process elaborated by the novel's structure.
The beginnings of the following chapters also refer to the problem of
the visible, relating it consistently to illusion and to the general's
power. This fourth level of the structure is fundamental to the novel's
experiences, not only because this experience is based primarily on
the manipulation of the visible and the invisible, but also because
the general controls power as well as the image he projects by manipulating what is visible.

The four levels of the structure as described above function in the
elaboration of the text's themes and of the text as a modern novel.
The opening of the original situation into the general's story yields a
broad characterization of the general not limited by traditional subordination of the narration to the requirements of space and time.
The latter are subordinate, in this modern text, to the act of narrating itself. The opening sentence supports this first opening technically and is a specific device that provides for a progressively more
elaborate textual presentation of the story. The opening of the narrative focus creates a multiplicity of views of the general, and this is
significant not only in the complexity and completeness of his characterization but also in establishing the overall tone—the humor so
fundamental to the novel's experience. On the final level, the opening of a seen reality into a confluence of the visible and invisible, the
experience of the novel becomes similar to the principal theme it develops: the illusion of reality and power.

Crónica de una muerte anunciada and *El amor en los tiempos
del cólera*, far less complex in structure than *El otoño del patriarca*,
nevertheless represent a continuation of García Márquez's modern
project, even though the act of writing in itself is paramount, a characteristic both novels share with many postmodern texts. *Crónica
de una muerte anunciada* is comparable in some respects to the detective novel. The reader knows the outcome from the first line and
continues reading—with interests similar to those aroused in the
detective novel—to see the death consummated. The circumstances
surrounding the protagonist Santiago Nasar's death become increasingly more incredible: Everyone in his town knows he is going to die
except Santiago himself. Yet no one does anything. As in García
Márquez's earlier work, life is determined by seemingly inexplicable
forces and irrational acts (similar in this sense to how things would
be seen by a person in an oral culture; see chapter 4). The narrator

explains that attempts at rational explanation fall short, although the judge assigned to Nasar's case approached it with the intention of finding a rational interpretation. This novel turns upon itself without going beyond its own fixed ideological limits, that is, the limits of the town's mentality. The language and boundaries of this ideology are anchored on medieval tradition—a matter of honor. The bride is rejected; the murder is conceived and then allowed to be executed because of the entire town's tacit acceptance of a medieval concept of human relationships. The novel's structure (the development of the predetermined action) as well as the process in the town (the events that the town's citizenry witness) correspond to a world in which the development of events is determined by a hierarchical and static vision of reality.

El amor en los tiempos del cólera is a story of love and aging in an equally hierarchical and static society. Set in a Cartagena colored by some elements of other Caribbean cities (such as the Café de la Parroquia in Veracruz, Mexico), it tells of Florentino Ariza's wait of over fifty years for his beloved Fermina Daza, to whom he declares his love at the funeral of her husband, Dr. Juvenal Urbino. The novel is imbued with elements of late nineteenth- and early twentieth-century Colombia, elements notable in the context of this study for two reasons. On the one hand, this is the Colombia of the Regeneration as the Athens of South America. The narrator mentions Regeneration president Rafael Núñez and later president Marco Fidel Suárez, with Dr. Urbino as the Regeneration gentleman-scholar. On the other hand, García Márquez returns to the kind of incorporation of the Costa oral culture that formed part of *Cien años de soledad.* Whereas Dr. Urbino is the educated man of science, Florentino Ariza and Fermina Daza frequently see things as an oral-culture person would, even though they are literate. For Florentino Ariza one of the new hydro-planes "is like a flying coffin."[11] Fermina Daza, with rural roots, makes similar observations. Like *Cien años de soledad,* *El amor en los tiempos del cólera* is a novel of hyperbole and of prodigious people and events.

Several other writers have assimilated the stratagems of modern fiction, among them Fanny Buitrago, Manuel Zapata Olivella, and Héctor Rojas Herazo. In addition to her short fiction, Buitrago has published the novels *El hostigante verano de los dioses* (1963), *Cola de zorro* (1970), *Los pañamanes* (1979), and *Los amores de Afrodita* (1983). Much of her fiction emanates from *costeño* culture. Several voices narrate *El hostigante verano de los dioses,* the totality of which communicates the state of boredom endured by a spiritually exhausted generation of young people. *Cola de zorro* is Buitrago's most complex work and shares some of the generational attitudes found in her first novel: The characters lack clear direction and their existence tends to be boring. It deals with human relations within the context of a large, extended family. The novel's three parts, which take place in the Interior Highland and the Costa, tell the story of three generations. The characters' identities, a central theme, are in a constant state of fluidity but are defined primarily by family tradition. *Los pañamanes*, set on a Caribbean island, portrays the conflicts between, on the one hand, the legends and traditions in a disappearing oral culture on the island and, on the other hand, modernization and its "beautiful people" that are taking over. In *Los amores de Afrodita* Buitrago recurs to popular culture in a manner reminiscent of both Manuel Puig's fiction and of Mario Vargas Llosa's *La tía Julia y el escribidor*. In her novel she relates five love stories of different women. Using sources similar to Puig's and Vargas Llosa's, Buitrago cites in her epigraphs the popular women's magazine *Vanidades* and lines from the popular music of *boleros*.

Zapata Olivella has published six novels (see chapters 2 and 4), including two works during the period at hand, *Changó, el gran putas* (1983) and *El fusilamiento del diablo* (1986). His most ambitious novel, the massive (over five hundred pages) *Changó, el gran putas*, is broad in scope. The Changó in the title refers to the Yoruba deity of war, fecundity, and dance. The novel spans three continents and six centuries of African and Afro-American history. It begins in Africa and then moves to Colombia and other regions of the Americas, ending in the United States. Zapata Olivella incorporates cultural heroes such as Benkos Bioho, François Mackandal, and Nat Turner and ends with the death of Malcolm X. The author synthesizes a variety of voices and oral cultures in this saga of a people's striving for liberation, the latter a constant in his entire work.[12] In *El fusilamiento del diablo* Zapata Olivella re-elaborates the story of Manuel Saturion Valencia, which had been recounted by Rogerio Velásquez in *Las memorias del odio* (see chapter 6). In Zapata Olivella's version, numerous voices tell the story of this Afro-Colombian who was executed in Quibdó in 1907. The sum of these voices and the novel's numerous narrative segments elevate the protagonist to the level of myth.[13]

Héctor Rojas Herazo uses the narrative strategies of a Faulknerian modernity in his trilogy, *Respirando el verano* (1962), *En noviembre llega el arzobispo* (1967), and *Celia se pudre* (1986). These novels also evoke the premodern, oral world of Celia, the central character of this trilogy, and her family. *Respirando el verano* focuses on the aging matriarch and her grandson Anselmo (see chapter 4). Celia is a minor character in *En noviembre llega el arzobispo*, a denunciation of the local oligarchy's absolute domination of all sectors of society in the town of Cedrón. It carries with it, in addition, a consistent subtext of terror and violence. *En noviembre llega el arzobispo* characterizes a broader spectrum of society than did the first novel, its social critique being more strident than that of *Respirando el verano*. Just as *Cien años de soledad* synthesized García Márquez's Macondo, the massive (811 pages) *Celia se pudre* is the summa of the world of Cedrón. Although this hermetic work has multiple narrative voices, the decadence of Cedrón is filtered primarily through Celia's memory. As in *Respirando el verano*, the central image of *Celia se pudre* is the home—*la casa*—and the predominant tone accentuates the hatred that permeates Cedrón as well as Celia's life.

Younger writers who have produced a modern fiction since the appearance in 1967 of *Cien años de soledad* include Gustavo Alvarez Gardeazábal, Héctor Sánchez, Jorge Eliécer Pardo, Germán Espinosa, David Sánchez Juliao, Fernando Vallejo, and Oscar Collazos. In addition to *Cóndores no entierran todos los días* (see chapter 2) and *El bazar de los idiotas* (see chapter 6), Alvarez Gardeazábal's works include *Dabeiba* (1972), *El titiritero* (1977), *Los míos* (1981), *Pepe Botellas* (1984), *El divino* (1986), and *El último gamonal* (1987). Since *El titiritero*, the ideological function of Alvarez Gardeazábal's fiction has been unequivocal: It is dedicated primarily to questioning and denouncing the Greater Cauca's oligarchy. Héctor Sánchez published *Las maniobras* (1969), *Las causas supremas* (1969), *Los desheredados* (1974), *Sin nada entre las manos* (1976), *El tejemaneje* (1979), and *Entre ruinas* (1984). In its totality this fiction expresses the frustration over the seemingly useless life of its characters, who play out repetitive variations of their tedious daily activity. Jorge Eliécer Pardo's two novels, *El jardín de las Weismann* (1978) and *Irene* (1986), are examples of perhaps the most carefully conceived and structured modern fiction of the generation. *El jardín de las Weismann* (titled *El jardín de las Hartmann* in the first edition) deals with La Violencia in an abstract fashion, delineating parallels between the Colombian conflict and anti-Nazi resistance in Germany. Germán Espinosa published four novels of historical impulse, *Los cortejos del diablo* (1970), *El magnicidio* (1979), *La tejedora de coronas* (1982), and *El signo del pez* (1987). *Los cortejos del diablo*, set in Cartagena during the Colonial period, is an account of one of the major perpetrators of the Inquisition in Colombia and a denunciation of this Spanish institution. One of the most technically complex and engaging modern novels of the 1980s, *La tejedora de coronas* also takes place during the Colonial period. It consists of an interior monologue, a life story related by Genoveva Alcocer, a one hundred-year-old woman accused of witchcraft. David Sánchez Juliao, from the Costa, has explored the possibilities of secondary orality, writing a popular fiction using the technology of records and cassettes.[14] Sánchez Juliao embellishes *Pero sigo siendo el rey* (1983) with Mexican *rancheras* and other forms of popular music in order to narrate his melodramatic story of romance and conflict, an anecdote worthy of a soap opera.[15] Fernando Vallejo published the first Colombian novels to deal explicitly with homosexuality, *Los días azules* (1985) and *El fuego secreto* (1986). Oscar Collazos published a politically aggressive set of novels, testimonial in impulse, questioning the authority of the Colombian oligarchy and its values: *Crónica de tiempo muerto* (1975), *Los días de la paciencia* (1976), *Todo o nada* (1982), *Jóvenes, pobres amantes* (1983), and *Tal como el fuego fatuo* (1986). In its totality, Collazos's fiction could be seen as the testimony of a generation of intellectuals who experienced La Violencia in their childhood, the Cuban Revolution in their adolescence, and Colombia's National Front in their maturity. Other young writers who have pursued a fundamentally modern fiction are Roberto Burgos Cantor, Marvel Moreno, Eduardo García Aguilar, Fernando Cruz Kronfly, Umberto Valverde, Alonso Aristizábal, Luis Fayad, Tomás González, Amparo María Suárez, Julio Olaciregui, José Luis Garcés, José Stevenson, Darío Ruiz Gómez, Evelio Rosero Diago, Enrique Cabezas Rher, José Cardona López, Alvaro Pineda Botero, José Luis Díaz Granados, Juan José Hoyos, Alberto Esquivel, Humberto Tafur, Augusto Pinilla, Antonio Caballero, José Manuel Crespo, and Gustavo González Zafra.

Several writers born in the 1920s have published modern novels during the 1970s and 1980s, including Manuel Mejía Vallejo, Alvaro Mutis, Pedro Gómez Valderrama, Plinio Apuleyo Mendoza, and Mario Escobar Velásquez. After *El día señalado*, Mejía Vallejo wrote *Aire de tango* (1973), *Las muertes ajenas* (1979), *Tarde de verano* (1980), *Y el mundo sigue andando* (1984), and *La sombra de tu paso* (1987). In *Aire de tango* Mejía Vallejo mythifies the Argentine hero of the tango, Carlos Gardel. Mejía Vallejo's later novels are nostalgic evocations of rural Antioquia. Alvaro Mutis had published poetry and the novels *Diario de Lecumberri* (1960) and *La mansión de Araucaíma* (1973) before conceiving a trilogy on his lifetime obsession, the fictional character Maqroll el Gaviero—sailor, adventurer, and philosopher. The first book of this trilogy, *La nieve del Almirante* (1986), contains Gaviero's diary, followed by notes written by persons who knew him. These texts, composed of the protagonist's meditations and the thoughts of others about him, represent an examination of Gaviero's spiritual life.[16] Gómez Valderrama, Apuleyo Mendoza, and Escobar Velásquez also published novels of adventurers: *La otra raya del tigre* (1977) by Gómez Valderrama relates the nineteenth-century adventures of colonizer Geo von Lengerke in Colombia; Apuleyo Mendoza's *Años de fuga* (1979) is an account of the protagonist's experiences in Paris during the 1960s; *Cuando pase el ánima sola* (1979) and *Un hombre llamado Todero* (1980) by Mario Escobar Velásquez are rural adventure stories.

Women writers of this generation engaged in the creation of modern fiction include Flor Romero de Nohra, Rocío Vélez de Piedrahita, and María Helena Uribe de Estrada. This generation of women writers, who have not been engaged in the self-conscious and theoretically based feminist discourse of postmodern feminists such as Albalucía Angel, have been relatively conventional in their approach to storytelling. Romero de Nohra began with *3 kilates, 8 puntos,* a story of human relationships and conflicts associated with the emerald trade. *Mi capitán Fabián Sicachá* (1968) deals with the rural guerrilla movement of the 1960s, as does *Triquitraques de trópico* (1972), which is imbued with the language and magic of García Márquez's early Macondo fiction. *Los sueños del poder* (1978), a feminine version of the dictator novel, is an account of a female dictator in an unnamed Latin American country, described in great detail as the stereotypical tropical paradise. Vélez de Piedrahita's novels, traditional in narrative technique and supportive of conventional values, include *La tercera generación* (1962), *La cisterna* (1971), and *Terrateniente* (1986). Uribe de Estrada published *Reptil en el tiempo* (1986), more innovative in its language and narrative stratagems than the novels of Romero de Nohra or Vélez de Piedrahita.

R. H. Moreno-Durán and the Postmodern Gesture

García Márquez's accomplishments with his modern fiction project, his international critical acclaim, and his 1982 Nobel Prize in literature gained unprecedented visibility in the Colombia of the 1980s. On the other hand, R. H. Moreno-Durán's postmodern gesture, his public image as the writer's writer, and his hermetic fictional exercises gained him the attention of a smaller group of readers, writers, and critics interested in innovative fiction.[17] Solipsistic experiments do not usually become bestsellers, either in the original version or in translation. Nevertheless, Moreno-Durán and writers such as Albalucía Angel, Marco Tulio Aguilera Garramuño, Darío Jaramillo Agudelo, Andrés Caicedo, Rodrigo Parra Sandoval, and Alberto Duque López did pursue an innovative, fundamentally postmodern project during the 1970s and 1980s.[18] Cosmopolitan in interests, most of them have preferred to write abroad; Moreno-Durán and Angel have lived for most of their writing careers in Europe and have been as intellectually attuned to contemporary European writing and theory as to Colombia. Similarly, Duque López has been indelibly influenced by such diverse texts as Julio Cortázar's *Hopscotch* and American film. Aguilera Garramuño has postmodern texts in the sense that they present no privileged narrator upon whom the reader can rely, nor is there an authoritative discourse or figure to whom the reader can turn for something like an objective, final truth regarding its fiction.[19] Lucille Kerr has explained that reading difficulties with such postmodern texts are created by "this absence of an organizing, potentially omniscient mediator who could filter and interpret all the discursive performances in the text."[20] Having immersed themselves in writing culture's recent theory and having assimilated the fiction of the moderns, the postmoderns are the most removed from oral culture of any group of Colombian writers to date.

Moreno-Durán's *Los felinos del Canciller* (1985) lacks some of the hermetic qualities that Kerr observes in many typical postmodern texts; it represents a rupture from his more hermetic *Fémina Suite* trilogy. In this connection one might speak of an early postmodern attitude that produced hermetic and relatively inaccessible works (found in Moreno-Durán's trilogy, early Sarduy, and the Argentine Néstor Sánchez) and a later more accessible postmodern fiction (found in Latin American novels of the 1980s, among these *Los felinos del Canciller*). The difficulties and the inaccessibility of many postmodern texts are replaced in *Los felinos del Canciller* by wit: Rather than functioning as a hermetic barrier, Moreno-Durán's subtle manipulation of language is frequently the material of humor. A review of the plot suggests another family romance—the modern Latin American family story—as seen in García Márquez, Fuentes, or Carpentier.[21] *Los felinos del Canciller* chronicles three generations of the aristocratic Barahona's family of diplomats, from the patriarch Gonzalo Barahona to his son Santiago and his grandson Félix Barahona. Félix is the principal focalizer through whom the Barahona clan is remembered in New York in 1949. Historical referents allow the reader to follow the elegant diplomatic family's story from the Regeneration through the various *presidentes gramáticos* and the rise of the Liberal party in the 1930s and, finally, the swan song of the old-fashioned diplomatic life in the 1940s.

Only a superficial reading of *Los felinos del Canciller*, however, would emphasize the family history; the most important referents and the main subject of this novel are language and writing. The verb that essentializes the novel's action is "to manipulate." The superficial reading would thus render the nuclear sentence "The Barahona family manipulates others," underscoring three generations of political manipulation. Indeed, the art of diplomacy, as practiced by the Barahona family, is the art of manipulation. More significant to the experience of this novel, however, is the manipulation of language, for if diplomacy is Gonzalo's profession, philology is his passion. In this sense, a more accurate synthesis of the novel's action is "The Barahona family manipulates language." Gonzalo, Santiago, and Félix all control the art of manipulation and, above all, the manipulation of language.

The males of the family are always at least as obsessed with philology as with their respective careers. During the late nineteenth century, the years of the Regeneration, Gonzalo decides to study not medicine but philology and, as the ideal gentleman-scholar of the Regeneration, he finds access to politics and diplomacy by means of his philology. He first appears in the novel in this context: In the opening pages Félix remembers Gonzalo's philological tastes and consequently he mentions the Colombian term for the useless bureaucrat—*corbata*. At the end of this first chapter the narrator explains that the Barahona family, as philologists, "se limitaban a decir que el fulano era un kalos kagathos, expresión que a los más ignaros les sonaba a grosería" (they limited themselves to saying that the guy was a *kalos kagathos*, an expression that sounded like a vulgarity to the most ignorant ones).[22] This sentence, combining the Barahonas' knowledge of Greek and the narrator's colloquial language (*el fulano*, [the guy]), provides an entertaining introduction to the Barahonas' modus operandi. Félix Barahona studies Greek and tends to view the world within a philological context. For example, he enjoys observing his wife's interest in orchids, but the narrator explains that his smile, "like almost everything of his," was etymological (Moreno-Durán, 43). What the narrator identifies as Gonzalo's verbal and linguistic excesses (Moreno-Durán, 124) results in a situation in which everything becomes a matter of language manipulation: "Todo, pues, desde lo más grave a lo más cotidiano, se convertía de pronto, gracias al ejemplo renovador del viejo, en enfermedades de lenguaje" (Everything, from the most serious to the most common, suddenly turned into language sicknesses, thanks to the old man's example) (Moreno-Durán, 125). In a humorous anecdote, Gonzalo suffers impotency with a señora Montoya, failing with *altura filológica* (philological height) to perform. He explains that the event was a mere *contradictio in erectio* (Moreno-Durán, 126).

As a novel written against the Hispanic and Highland tradition (see chapter 3), *Los felinos del Canciller* contains numerous intertexts from Spanish and Colombian literature. Gonzalo is a grand connoisseur of this tradition, from Cervantes to the last of the *presidentes gramáticos*, Marco Fidel Suárez. Other texts are absorbed into this novel in an intertextual relationship that becomes the basis of Moreno-Durán's humorous writing against the Highland tradition.[23] When speaking of the *presidentes gramáticos*, the narrator refers to Luciano Mancipe satirically (Moreno-Durán, 85). This type of sentence is an exercise in intertextuality, for the name Luciano Mancipe evokes *Los sueños de Luciano Pulgar*, a book by Marco Fidel Suárez. The sentence also transforms the egalitarian language of Antioquia when it refers to the Artemidoro, who "había salido de la nada" (came from nowhere). The ideal of the independent, self-made man who evolves from *la nada* is precisely the language of Antioquian tradition (see chapter 5). The final part of the sentence, referring to "la democracia bien entendida" (well-understood democracy) incorporates the language of the early twentieth-century Conservative regimes.

Moreno-Durán uses a sign system to set forth an encounter between the old-style, Conservative gentleman-scholar and the new type of intellectuals who follow them. The narrator writes against certain monuments of the Highland literary tradition, questioning its dominant language. He uses a series of phrases evoking José Eustasio Rivera (without ever naming Rivera) in order to question the role of Colombia's major writers inside and outside their country, evoking Rivera's poems *Tierra de promisión* and *La vorágine*. More important than the allusion to literature is the frame of reference: Félix's vision as an intellectual of the Conservative, philological tradition is inscribed by the literary monuments of the Highland tradition. The Barahonas' thoughts and actions are founded on a Conservative literary and philological agenda and its relationship to the new language they are facing, from Rivera's to that of the Liberals of the 1930s and 1940s.

The narrative situation in *Los felinos del Canciller* consists, technically speaking, of an extradiegetic-heterodiegetic narrator who relates the Barahona story in a fundamentally omniscient fashion. Two prominent factors in this narrative situation are the temporal framework and the use of focalizers, both of which relate to Félix Barahona's role in the novel. The Barahona story is related by this narrator, but the constant point of departure is Félix in 1949: The family story is told as Félix remembers it in New York during 1949. This present of 1949 and Félix's role as focalizer are the two key intermediary elements to the extradiegetic narrator's relating of the story. The narrator appropriates the characters' language, which, when referring to the Barahonas, once again points back to a Conservative language of the Regeneration.

This narrator engages in the same word play that characterizes the Barahona family, employing feline images throughout the text when speaking of the Barahonas. His introduction to Félix and his credentials refer to papers that "convirtieron a Barahona tercero en un felix viator" (an untranslatable sentence which plays with double meanings in Spanish; Moreno-Durán, 13). In the first chapter the narrator plays with the words *victorianos* (Victorians) and *victor y anos* (Victor and anus) (Moreno-Durán, 28), as well as with *rabel/ Ravel/rabo* in an allusion to a character's homosexual interest in a boy's rear end (Moreno-Durán, 28). The narrator continues with this type of word play throughout the novel; consequently, the narrator functions as one more Barahona.

This novel employs an extradiegetic-heterodiegetic narrator in the most superficial sense. Both his position with respect to the story and his omniscience are subverted in the process of relating the Barahona story. The text initially seems to promise a potentially omniscient mediator, but the narrator's actual performance in the text suggests the kind of postmodern novel described by Kerr, with no omniscient mediator and no consistently authoritative discourse. Rather than defining an authoritative discourse, *Los felinos del Canciller* undermines and subverts the authority of language practices in Colombia during the early twentieth century.

Los felinos del Canciller parodies Colombian institutions, above all, the institutionalized concept of the Athens of South America.[24] Félix, after all, is characterized as "la máxima encarnación del kalos kagathos, el perfecto caballero ático, pues no en vano vivían en la Atenas sudamericana" (the maximum embodiment of the *kalos kagathos*, the perfect Attic gentleman, for they hadn't lived in the Athens of South America in vain) (Moreno-Durán, 50). The novel also questions the cultural superiority claimed by Colombian intellectuals who were rooted in this classical tradition. In order to carry out his parody of Bogotá as Athens, the narrator presents Colombia as a distant *ese país* (that country). On those rare occasions when the narrator admits identity with this nation, using the first-person plural ("our"), the vision is of a citizen abroad, observing this philological paradise with spatial and temporal distance.

The transgression of sexual norms is yet another level of parodic play in *Los felinos del Canciller*. As in *María* and *Cien años de soledad*, the sexual transgressions often consist of symbolic rather than

direct physical acts. Félix Barahona is depicted from the novel's first
paragraph as potentially incestuous. He feels that the day begins
with the odor of his daughter (Moreno-Durán, 11). Diplomacy, as
practiced by the Barahonas, is incestuous: International relations are
a function of a family—an incestuous grouping of inward-looking individuals—rather than an outward-looking group of international
mediators. Additional allusions to physical incest abound in the
text, frequently relating to Félix Barahona's desire for his sister
Angélica.

Significant parallels are drawn among several of the elements discussed above: The Barahona family, as diplomats, manipulate human beings and relationships; the Barahonas, as philologists, manipulate language; the narrator, as another Barahona, manipulates
both individuals (characters in the novel) and language. As has been
noted, moreover, the narrator engages in humorous and parodic language manipulation, quite similar in content and effect to the operations of the Barahonas. These parallels lead to an initial equation: In
Los felinos del Canciller diplomacy is equal to language. Similarly,
the narrator cultivates equivalencies between language and diplomacy. Key images for this equivalency are the use of diplomacy and
language as art and as protocol. Luisa, for example, appears as the
ideal diplomat's woman because she manipulates the "art of cour-
tesy" with such virtuosity (Moreno-Durán, 30). Diplomacy in general is often mentioned as "art," or the "art of diplomacy." As seen
by the Barahona family, diplomacy, like the study of Greek, is a matter of conjugating verbs; that is, a matter of technique. Similarly, in
the world of the Barahonas, the protocols of language have an importance equal to those of diplomacy. In a reference reminiscent of
Rama's proposition on the *ciudad letrada* in Colombia, the narrator
states: "Politics and philology were the same thing in this country:
In the beginning was the verb and the verb was made with power"
(Moreno-Durán, 85).

The equivalencies between language and diplomacy lead to entertaining consequences. The postmodernity of this text is signaled by
the fact that, in the end, not just diplomacy but everything becomes
the art of language and writing. That is, unique equivalencies are
created between language and sexuality, between language and politics, and, finally, between language and writing. The relationship
between language and sexuality has already been suggested in the
above-cited passage relating Gonzalo's exercise in impotency with
philological discourse. Other anecdotes from his life confuse his
philological and sexual activity, until the narrator even concludes
that Gonzalo "spoke the same way that he manipulated in the bed-

room" (Moreno-Durán, 151). The narrator, as just one more Barahona, uses the same type of equivalencies as do the Barahonas.

All activity (all acts of manipulating) in *Los felinos del Canciller* refers to language and writing or is a metaphor for them, both for the characters and for the narrator. When Gonzalo initiates his love affair with Lesley-Anne, the two of them convert the relationship into a writing affair, exchanging love letters. The narrator transforms this affair into a literary relationship by stating that their letters crossing in the mail became *soliloquios cruzados* (crossed soliloquies) (Moreno-Durán, 90). In one of the most intricate passages of the novel (Moreno-Durán, 123–124), Gonzalo, the patriarch of the Barahonas, elaborates a complex formula, using impersonal verbs, to reconcile "sus inquietudes filológicas, políticas y sentimentales" (his philological, political, and emotional concerns) (Moreno-Durán, 123). This complex formula (which takes a full page of the text to explain) equates verb conjugations with human relationships.

Published in 1987, at the very end of the period encompassed by the present study, *Los felinos del Canciller* is a significant expression of the postmodern. For both the reader and the narrator, it is a novel of surfaces: All actions are superficial in the sense that the very act of manipulation is always more significant than any content or product of this manipulation. Both language and diplomacy are void of content. In a narrative situation in which characters act as focalizers (mostly Félix), consequently sharing the revelation of the fictional world with the narrator, and in which this narrator ultimately only manipulates, the novel in the end possesses no final authority. Having language as its subject and only absences and indeterminacy as its constants, *Los felinos del Canciller* emerges as the postmodern text par excellence. Like the narrator and the Barahonas, all etymologists who seek truth in origins, Moreno-Durán investigates his own origins in the language of the Hispanic and Highland traditions, synthesized in the phrase "Athens of South America."

Moreno-Durán's postmodern writing is best understood by considering the three novels of his *Fémina Suite* as an integral part of his project. The trilogy explores several of his concerns observed in *Los felinos del Canciller*, beginning with his parody of Bogotá as the Athens of South America, a concept also ridiculed in *Juego de damas*. The ironic distance necessary for the humorous effects in *Los felinos del Canciller* as well as the pervasive and subversive wordplay are experienced throughout the fiction of *Fémina Suite*.

The roots of the *Fémina Suite* are not found in the empirical reality of Colombia but rather, as in the case of postmodern fiction, in modernist literature. Moreno-Durán has explained how poems by

T. S. Eliot and Paul Valéry generated the first novel of the trilogy, *Juego de damas.*[25] The reader's most immediate literary association with *Juego de damas* is the work which announced the postmodern project in Latin America, Cortázar's *Rayuela:* Both elements of the form (such as the split columns on a single page) and the content (such as youths listening to jazz) recall Cortázar's proposal for a new, open novel, as articulated in *Rayuela.*[26] *Juego de damas* deals with Colombian female intellectuals, beginning with their radicalized student life of the 1960s and passing through three stages of social climbing and power acquisition, stages in which the narrator identifies them as *Meninas* (young intellectuals), *Mandarinas* (middle-aged social climbers), and *Matriarcas* (aged women in power). As in *Los felinos del Canciller,* Moreno-Durán develops elaborate relationships between language and power: He employs a series of strategies, including parody and euphemism, to subvert language once again. This subversive activity is supported in the text by Monsalve, a character who serves as an author figure. The two main characters of *Toque de Diana,* Augusto Jota and Catalina Arévalo, are also intellectuals who engage in the linguistic and sexual exercises of power noted in *Los felinos del Canciller* and *Juego de damas.* Augusto is a military man who fails both in the military and in his sexual relationship with Catalina, for in the lovemaking of these two devotees of Latin, she "conjugated" while he literally "declined." In the third and most hermetic novel of the trilogy, *Finale capriccioso con Madonna,* Moreno-Durán exploits to the utmost both the eroticism of language and the language of eroticism. He poses the question, for example, of the relationship between "semantics" and "semen" and in the process creates a lengthy, playful, and dense passage of a *ménage à trois.* From the introduction to Laura, the main character, who finds herself caught between two men, this novel develops a series of triangular relationships. It is a playful novel of erotic and linguistic excesses with intertextual allusions ranging from Proust to the Mexican postmodern novelist Salvador Elizondo.[27] Several factors unify Moreno-Durán's trilogy as one postmodern project, but, above all, the role of language itself is the main subject of all three books.

Other postmodern novelists—Albalucía Angel, Marco Tulio Aguilera Garramuño, Darío Jaramillo, Alberto Duque López, Rodrigo Parra Sandoval, and Andrés Caicedo—are generally as demanding of their readers as Moreno-Durán. Albalucía Angel's recent fiction, particularly *Misiá Señora* (1982) and *Las andariegas* (1984), is part of a feminist project that emanates directly from feminist theory and fiction. She had already published two early experimental

novels, *Los girasoles en invierno* (1970) and *Dos veces Alicia* (1972),
in addition to one on La Violencia, *Estaba la pájara pinta sentada
en el verde limón* (1975). Since then Angel has become the most
prominent feminist writer among Colombian novelists. *Los girasoles en invierno* consists of brief narrative segments narrated by a
female voice who reacts to her surroundings in Paris and relates
memories of an immediate past while travelling around Europe. An
indication of Angel's experimentation is evident in her handling of
plot: There is no consistently developed plot and only a sketchy
story line tracing the narrator's relationship with a novice painter.
Dos veces Alicia, set in Great Britain, relates the female protagonist's relationship with a series of real and imagined friends.
The only consistent element in the novel's disperse associations is
the presence of the narrator. She openly invites the reader to imag-
ine with her, making *Dos veces Alicia* yet another product of that
postmodern novel proposed by Cortázar in which the reader takes an
active role in the creative process. *Estaba la pájara pinta sentada en
el verde limón* begins with a quotation from a politician who refers
to a labyrinth of facts, men, and opinions. This "labyrinth" indeed
serves as an appropriate description of the reader's experience. The
early sections of the novel communicate the images of La Violencia
perceived by an innocent young girl who later in the novel will experience La Violencia at the side of the revolutionary Lorenzo. Angel's
use of historical documents makes *Estaba la pájara pinta sentada
en el verde limón* a documentary novel as well.[28]

The two novels of Angel's self-conscious feminist discourse, *Misiá
Señora* and *Las andariegas*, are also her most hermetic. The protagonist of *Misiá Señora*, Mariana, is reared by a family of the landed
aristocracy in a coffee-growing region of Colombia. She eventually
finds herself caught between the expectations a traditional society
holds for young women—marriage and motherhood—and a less conventional but potentially more meaningful existence. The nontra-
ditional life-style is stimulated through her friendships with two
women. The structure of *Misiá Señora*, which is divided into three
parts, relates three chronological stages of Mariana's life. These
three parts are formally identified as *Imágenes*, the first of which is
entitled "I have a doll dressed in blue" and deals with Mariana's
childhood and adolescence. The second, "Ancient without shadow,"
tells of her courtship, her marriage, her two children's births, and her
degenerating psychological state. The third *Imagen* relates a series
of dramalike visions often concerning her mother and grandmother.
Gender differences are the paramount issues of *Misiá Señora:* Much
of the first *Imagen* deals with different aspects of female sexuality;

Mariana's childhood involves sexual harassment, initial experiences with *machismo,* and the gradual discovery of her own sexuality. Gender issues are also associated with class structure and Christian ideology. The fictional world of *Misiá Señora* creates a tenuous line between empirical reality and pure imagination. An important aspect of this richly imaginative experience is the creation of a new, feminist discourse as part of Angel's feminist project.

Las andariegas is Angel's most radical experiment in fiction. It can be read as a double search: on the one hand, a search for a female language; on the other, an evocation of a feminine identity. It begins with two epigraphs, followed by a statement by the author which proposes a feminist program, and then a third epigraph. The first epigraph is from *Les Guérrillères* by Monique Wittig, referring to females breaking the existing order and needing, above all, strength and courage. The second epigraph is from *Las nuevas cartas portuguesas* by María Isabel Barreno, María Terda Horta, and María Velho da Costa and refers to women as firm and committed warriors. The author, setting forth her feminist program, explains these two epigraphs in a page-long statement, the third prefatory section to appear before the narrative itself. Angel states that she once found Wiggit's *Les Guérrillères* illuminating, and consequently she decided to undertake this project with female warriors who advance "from nowhere toward history." She used as a guide images from stories from her childhood, transformed into fables and cryptic visions. The third epigraph is from the mythologies of the Kogui (a Colombian indigenous group) and emphasizes the role of the female figure in creation.

Rather than a traditional plot line, the sixty-two brief anecdotes of this novel present a vision of women who have been censored from history. These anecdotes are parables which previously had been denied a female voice; they now relate in an affirmative manner the experience of *viajeras* (female travellers).

As in the fiction of Moreno-Durán, language is the principal subject in *Las andariegas.* Much of the narrative consists of brief phrases with unconventional punctuation which often function on the basis of an image. The use of verbal imagery is supported by visual images—a set of twelve drawings of a female body in the novel. Angel also experiments with the physical space of language in the text, often in a manner similar to concrete poetry. The four pages of this type offer a variety of circular and semicircular arrangements with the names of famous women. The total effect of this visual imagery is to associate the body of the text with the female body. *Las andariegas* ends with a type of epilogue—another quotation from

Monique Wittig—consisting of four brief sentences calling precisely for the project that is the radical essence of these two novels: a new language, a new beginning, and a new history for women.

The postmodern projects of Moreno-Durán and Angel are distant from the modernity of García Márquez's cycle of Macondo. Marco Tulio Aguilera Garramuño, on the other hand, began his writing career with a self-conscious reaction to the Macondo fiction in his parodic *Breve historia de todas las cosas* (1975). The narrator, Mateo Albán, playfully narrates from prison the story of a small town in Costa Rica. In addition to the town's development (similar in many ways to Macondo), Mateo Albán describes the problems he confronts as creator and as narrator. The metafictional mode reaches its most extreme situation in the sixth chapter when Albán discusses his problems with his fictional readers. Like Moreno-Durán and Angel, Aguilera Garramuño playfully subverts some of Colombia's most sacred institutions: in this case, the Catholic Church, *machismo*, and the fiction of García Márquez. In *Paraísos hostiles* (1985), a dialogue on fiction and philosophy, Aguilera Garramuño moves away from the context of Colombia and García Márquez, but he continues in the metafictional mode. He creates a perverse and hellish fictional world located in a sordid hotel. Several of its economically impoverished but intellectually rich inhabitants write novels, and one of them proposes a novelistic aesthetic that is quite similar— though not coincidentally—to the reader's experience in *Paraísos hostiles*.

Darío Jaramillo Agudelo's only novel, *La muerte de Alec* (1983), is also a metafiction—in this case, a self-conscious meditation on the function of literature. It is an epistolary work directed to an unidentified "you" who is one of the characters implicated with Alec. This "you" and the letter writer are friends of Alec, who dies during an excursion. The characters are Colombian, but the novel is set in the United States; the letter writer is a novelist in the University of Iowa Writers' Program.[29] Jaramillo Agudelo inverts the commonly accepted relationship between empirical reality and fiction: According to the narrator, it is not literature but life that is artificial, baroque, and twisted. Similarly, the acts of storytelling (placing order to a story) and interpretation (giving meaning to a story) become the predominant forces, taking precedence over other forms of understanding reality. As in *Paraísos hostiles*, the novel also alludes to the very mechanisms used in telling the story.

Andrés Caicedo, Rodrigo Parra Sandoval, and Alberto Duque López conceived different kinds of postmodern projects. Caicedo's

¡Que viva la música! (1977), like the fiction of the *Onda* writers in Mexico, involves a fictional world of 1960s rock music and drugs. Beyond this superficial comparison, however, Caicedo has little in common with the young Mexican writers, for *¡Que viva la música!* is an experimental confrontation with a particular generation's cultural crisis in 1960s Colombia. Caicedo deals with this crisis with sobriety rather than with the humor and playfulness of the Mexican writers of the *Onda*. Rodrigo Parra Sandoval's *El álbum secreto del Sagrado Corazón* (1978) is a collage of texts—books, newspapers, letters, documents, voices—representing an assault on the novel as a genre. The implied author suggests that the genre suffers limitations similar to those experienced by the protagonist in a very limiting and repressive religious seminary. Colombia's cultural crisis, as seen in Caicedo, is depicted in Parra Sandoval's novel as a questioning of the nation's official, institutional images. *El álbum secreto del Sagrado Corazón* contains two main characters so ambiguously portrayed that they could well be the same person; Alberto Duque López proceeds similarly in *Mateo el flautista* (1968), which in two parts offers two different versions of the protagonist, Mateo. There is no authoritative voice in this narrative nor any authoritative version of Mateo's life. Consequently, *Mateo el flautista* is a quintessential postmodern text that clearly emanates from *Rayuela*, as indicated by the novel's dedication to one of its characters, Rocamadour.

The modern and postmodern novel published from 1965 to 1987 is a heterogeneous, multivoiced cultural product that far surpasses the ideological and aesthetic limits previously set for the genre in Colombia. The dominant elite had never been particularly interested in the novel, but until the 1960s it had controlled most aspects of its production, from publication to literary history and criticism. The García Márquez phenomenon in the late 1960s, in addition to factors such as the rise of international Latin Americanism and the expansion of multinational publishing houses, opened the Colombian novel to a heterogeneity of voices heretofore impossible in Colombia's regional, often provincial, and always well-controlled literary scene. It is important to recall that a spectrum of figures as broad as García Márquez, Moreno-Durán, Angel, and Alvarez Gardeazábal established their careers abroad (beyond the control of the local literary establishment) in the sense that all four published a substantive portion of their work abroad and that international Latin Americanism carried out the vast majority of the critical and scholarly activity on these four writers. Given the writers' new independence and the multiple directions found in the novel by the 1980s, it was no longer necessary or even appropriate to speak of a "shadow" of García Márquez.

The modern and postmodern tendencies of the Colombian novel are as ideological as in any text, but there are some general differences in these novelists' approaches to institutions. The moderns such as García Márquez, Rojas Herazo, and Alvarez Gardeazábal tend to be more overtly political in the sense that they fictionalize elements generally associated with Colombian and Latin American empirical reality. They criticize or denounce specific institutions and at times specific individuals. The postmoderns, such as Moreno-Durán, Angel, and Aguilera Garramuño, create novels more mediated by theory and other texts and more directed specifically to issues of language. All conventions, including those of the traditional and modern novel, are potentially questioned by these irreverent postmodern writers.

More specific comparisons between García Márquez's modern impulse and Moreno-Durán's postmodern gesture can help illuminate the differences between the modern and postmodern in Colombia. *El otoño del patriarca* functions on the basis of a structure of progressive apertures, whereas *Los felinos del Canciller* functions on the basis of language play. Both authors use humor for subversive ends, but García Márquez's is anecdotally based, while Moreno-Durán's depends more specifically on language to achieve his goals. Generally speaking, García Márquez, Buitrago, and Rojas Herazo create myths out of history and story; Moreno-Durán and Angel destroy myths by means of language and theory. García Márquez, Buitrago, and Rojas Herazo often employ a controlling, omniscient narrator, whereas the reader of Moreno-Durán, Angel, and Jaramillo Agudelo encounters no consistent authority figure in the text. Although writers such as García Márquez and Moreno-Durán do share some characteristics, as do many modern and postmodern novelists, their total projects also differ considerably.

Conclusion

The dynamics of orality and writing, in their literary manifestations, are most intense and probably most interesting in those cultures in transition between the two conditions. Plato's Greece, Europe during the Renaissance, and certain areas of the Third World in the nineteenth and twentieth centuries (among other regions) have experienced this transition in ways that have produced unique literary manifestations. In the case of Colombia, the interaction between oral and writing cultures becomes particularly intense in the novel from the late nineteenth to the mid-twentieth centuries—from Carrasquilla to García Márquez.

Oral culture has left its strongest mark on the fiction of Antioquia and the Costa. In Antioquia, Tomás Carrasquilla initiated the region's novel by incorporating elements of Antioquia's vital orality in *Frutos de mi tierra* and subsequent fiction. From Carrasquilla forward, with the advent of such writers as Bernardo Arias Trujillo, César Uribe Piedrahita, and Manuel Mejía Vallejo, the act of writing a novel in egalitarian Antioquia assumes that the writing-culture novelist will be attuned to the local oral culture. In the Costa, on the other hand, a more elitist position toward a strong oral culture resulted in its being virtually ignored by novelists until the 1950s. Manuel María Madiedo demonstrated some awareness of differences between orality and writing, but it was not until García Márquez that the Costa's oral culture played a vital role in that region's fiction. The narrators of Carrasquilla's *Frutos de mi tierra* and García Márquez's *Cien años de soledad* frequently assume roles of participants in an oral culture, and these fictionalized roles are essential to the experience of these two novels.

Orality has been less important to the fiction of the Interior Highland and Greater Cauca regions. Eugenio Díaz, a Highland writer with rural roots, was well aware of differences between orality and writing, as demonstrated in his characterization of literate and illiterate characters in *Manuela*. Eduardo Zalamea Borda also demonstrated a certain distanced interest in the Costa's oral culture in *Cuatro años a bordo de mí mismo*. Generally speaking, however, Highland writers have been so immersed in writing culture's literary traditions that they ignore the possibilities of incorporating orality into their frequently self-conscious literary texts. The Greater Cauca's elitist writers Jorge Isaacs and Eustaquio Palacios portray popular and oral cultures in the background of their work but do not actually incorporate them into their texts. In *El bazar de los idiotas*, Alvarez Gardeazábal, writing in response to the Greater Cauca's orality as well as against the fiction of García Márquez, uses a narrator who occasionally assumes the role of a participant in oral culture.

The complex interaction between orality and ideology was played out from the earliest novels, such as *Manuela*, and reached moments of crucial importance during periods of intense identity search, such as the Regeneration and the 1920s. The relationship between orality and the novel has taken numerous forms in Colombian fiction. During the Regeneration, the Athens of South America, which conceived literature as an elitist exercise centered in Bogotá, privileged writing over orality. Consequently, novels of the Regeneration demonstrated little or no interest in oral, popular, or folk culture. Texts resulting from a more egalitarian impulse, such as those of Carrasquilla, Arias, Trujillo, and Uribe Piedrahita, tend to incorporate orality. These novelists project the cultural values of the Antioquian region. The century-long search for a "national" literature, most intensely evident in the *criollista* novel of the 1920s and 1930s, has also been a search for an authentic orality in fiction. As is implied in the analyses of these novels, the most successful text in carrying out this national project was not *La vorágine* but rather *Toá* or *Risaralda*.

Once regional and oral-culture values were novelized by writers who appropriated the discourse of modernism, the Colombian novelist began to produce a fiction of interest beyond regional boundaries. This type of fiction in Latin America has been identified by some critics as *neoregionalism* or *transcendent regionalism*, but both terms—and others too—refer to writers who have used a regional base to fictionalize experiences considered "universal." This type of fiction, popularized by the novels of Faulkner in the Costa of Colombia (and in other regions of Latin America), has been cultivated in Colombia by Gabriel García Márquez, Alvaro Cepeda Samudio, Héctor Rojas Herazo, Manuel Mejía Vallejo, Arnoldo Palacios, Manuel Zapata Olivella, and Gustavo Alvarez Gardeazábal.

One of the most obvious manifestations of the rapport between ideology and the novel has been observed in the political dialogue of the novel. This function of the novel has been evident from the fictionalized political pamphlets of the 1840s to the critiques set forth by García Márquez and Zapata Olivella in their fiction. Postmodern novels, such as those written by Moreno-Durán and Angel, are equally "ideological" in their function, but their subversive activities are more subtly directed at fundamental institutions, especially language, than has been the case with García Márquez and Zapata Olivella.

Historical contingencies have played an essential role in determining which works have been considered "major" in Colombia. Indeed, several of these "major" novels, such as *María, Frutos de mi tierra, La vorágine, El buen salvaje,* and *Cien años de soledad,* have been accorded a central role in this study. In some cases—*María* and *La vorágine* are prime examples—it has been suggested that certain historical contingencies have played a significant role in the respective status of these works. Certainly aesthetic value has also been a significant factor in the survival of some of these works as part of the Colombian and Latin American canon. Such is the case, in particular, of *María* and *Cien años de soledad,* works that a broad consensus of readers have considered aesthetically superior during their respective periods. If "major" novels were exclusively the products of genius, however, one would need to include not only relatively unknown works, such as *Ingermina, Diana cazadora, Toá, Las estrellas son negras,* and *La casa grande,* but also representative fiction by Soledad Acosta de Samper, José María Vargas Vila, Héctor Rojas Herazo, Albalucía Angel, and others.

The regional approach and focus on orality in the study of a nation's literature evoke the inevitable speculation about the "applicability" of such an approach to other national literatures. It is important to recall the assumptions set forth in the preface and supporting arguments in the following chapters, particularly chapter 2, concerning Colombia's exceptional regionalism. Even though almost all of Latin America is still marked by regional differences, often within national boundaries, these differences have been less intense and less deeply rooted in history than they have been in Colombia. In the Colombian case, regionalism has been a significant factor in novelistic production. As a Latin Americanist, I am confident in speculating that the model presented in this study would be far less revealing—and, quite simply, of little viability—if applied to the national literatures of Mexico, Argentina, Uruguay, or Chile. (This statement, of course, does not preclude the possibility of analyzing the orality of individual works or groups of works in these countries.) The Caribbean area in general and Cuba in particular seem more promising because of their historically strong oral traditions, but the relative "success" of a study similar to this would depend, above all, on the extent to which novelists of any specific Caribbean nation have been aware of oral culture and interested in incorporating it in their fiction. Brazil, with a strong regionalism and oral tradition, might well lend itself to a study of its novel using the model for regionalism and orality proposed in the present study. A modified version of the regional approach could apply to some of the Andean nations, particularly since their indigenous populations have sustained strong oral cultures. Given the differences between the regional makeup and strong indigenous cultures in the Andean region and Colombia (where indigenous cultures today are relatively weaker), I assume the results of such a study would be quite different. In the cases of any of these regions and countries, the precise roles of the elites in literary culture as well as the role of literature in society would probably show some difference from that in Colombia. These complex factors, all affecting the interaction of orality and writing, of course, are the subject of further study.

Appendix

Chronologies of Colombian Novelists

Interior Highland Chronology

1844 José Joaquín Ortiz, *María Dolores*
1845 Juan Francisco Ortiz, *El Oidor*
       Eladio Vergara y Vergara, *El mudo*
1850 José Antonio Plaza, *El Oidor*
1851 José María Angel Gaitán, *El Doctor Temis*
1856 Juan Francisco Ortiz, *Carolina la bella*
       Felipe Pérez, *Atauallpa*
       Felipe Pérez, *Huayna Cápac*
1857 Felipe Pérez, *Los Pizarros*
1858 Raimundo Bernal Orjuela, *Viene por mí i carga con usted*
       Eugenio Díaz, *Manuela*
       Eugenio Díaz, *Una ronda de don Ventura Ahumada*
       Felipe Pérez, *El caballero de la barba negra*
1859 Bernardino Torres Torrente, *Sombras y misterios o los embozados*
1860 Eugenio Díaz, *María Tricince*
       Daniel Mantilla, *Una tarde de verano*
1861 Josefa Acevedo de Gómez, *Cuadros de la vida privada de algunos granadinos*
1863 Eugenio Díaz, *Pioquinta*
1864 Jesús Silvestre Rozo, *El último Rei de los Muiscas*
       José María Samper, *Los claveles de Julia*
       José María Samper, *Viajes y aventuras de dos cigarros*
1865 Temístocles Avella Mendoza, *Los tres Pedros*
       Temístocles Avella Mendoza, *Anacoana*
       Próspero Pereira Gamba, *Amores de estudiante*

1866 Nepomuceno J. Navarro, *El camarada*
José María Samper, *Martín Florez*

1867 José I. Neira Acevedo, *El sereno de Bogotá* (Greater Cauca: Jorge Isaacs, *María*)

1868 José María Vergara y Vergara, *Olivos y aceitunos todos son unos*

1869 Medardo Rivas, *Dolores*
Soledad Acosta de Samper, *El corazón de la mujer*

1871 José Joaquín Borda, *Kovalia; leyenda de los llanos del Orinoco*
Nepomuceno J. Navarro, *El gamonal*
Nepomuceno J. Navarro, *El zapatero*

1873 Eugenio Díaz, *Los aguinaldos en Chapinero*
Eugenio Díaz, *El rejo de enlazar*
Jesús Silvestre Rozo, *Las travesuras de un tunante*

1875 Felipe Pérez, *Los jigantes*
José María Samper, *Florencio Conde*

1876 Soledad Acosta de Samper, *Una holandesa en América*
Bernardino Torres Torrente, *El anjel del bosque*

1877 José David Guarín, *Las aventuras de un santo*

1878 Soledad Acosta de Samper, *Las dos reinas de Chipre*
Eugenio Díaz, *Bruna la carbonera*

1879 Soledad Acosta de Samper, *La juventud de Andrés*
José María Samper, *Clemencia*
José María Samper, *Coriolano*

1880 Soledad Acosta de Samper, *La familia de tío Andrés*
José María Samper, *El poeta soldado*

1881 Felipe Pérez, *Carlota Corday*

1882 Emilio A. Escobar, *La novia del Zipa*

1883 Felipe Pérez, *Sara*
Medardo Rivas, *Las dos hermanas*

1884 Soledad Acosta de Samper, *Una familia patriota*
Waldina Dávila de Ponce de León, *El trabajo*
Herminia Gómez Jaime de Abadía, *Dos religiones*
José David Guarín, *Las tres semanas*

1886 Soledad Acosta de Samper, *Los piratas en Cartagena*
Cándido Amézquita, *La mujer infiel*
José David Guarín, *Las bodas de un muerto*
Luis Segundo de Silvestre, *Tránsito*

1887 Soledad Acosta de Samper, *Episodios novelescos de la historia patria*
Felipe Pérez, *El caballero Rauzán*

1889   Luis Segundo de Silvestre, *¿Por qué no tengo patillas?*
        José María Vargas Vila, *Aura o las violetas*
1890   Constancio Franco V., *Policarpa*
1891   José Caicedo Rojas, *Don Alvaro*
        Constancio Franco V., *Galán el comunero*
1892   Waldina Dávila de Ponce de León, *La luz de la noche*
        Waldina Dávila de Ponce de León, *La muleta*
        Enrique Alvarez Bonilla, *El dios del siglo*
1894   José Caicedo Rojas, *Juana la bruja*
        Angel Cuervo, *Dick*
        Herminia Gómez Jaime de Abadía, *Del colegio al hogar*
1895   José María Vargas Vila, *Flor de fango*
1896   Marroquín, *Blas Gil*
        José Asunción Silva, *De sobremesa*
1897   José Manuel Marroquín, *Entre primos*
        José Manuel Marroquín, *El moro*
1898   Soledad Acosta de Samper, *Gil Bayle—Hidalgo de Zamora*
        José Manuel Marroquín, *Amores y leyes*
1899   José María Samper, *Lucas Vargas*
1900   José María Vargas Vila, *Ibis*
1901   Jacinto Albarracín, *Almíbar*
        José María Vargas Vila, *Alba roja*
        José María Vargas Vila, *Las rosas de la tarde*
1902   José María Rivas Groot, *Resurrección*
1905   José María Vargas Vila, *La simiente*
1906   Soledad Acosta de Samper, *Aventuras de un español entre
        los indios de las Antillas*
        José María Rivas Groot, *El triunfo de la vida*
        Clímaco Soto Borda, *Polvo y ceniza*
1907   Soledad Acosta de Samper, *Un hidalgo conquistador*
        Lorenzo Marroquín and José María Rivas Groot, *Pax*
        Jorge Wilson Price, *Emma Perry*
1908   Jacinto Albarracín, *Castidad*
        Luis Augusto Cuervo, *Venganza*
1909   Emilio Cuervo Márquez, *Phinées*
1911   Guillermo Forero Franco, *La parroquia*
1913   José María Vargas Vila, *La caída del Cóndor*
1915   Clímaco Soto Borda, *Diana cazadora*
        Luis Enrique Osorio, *Primer amor*
1916   José María Rivas Groot, *El triunfo de la vida*
1917   Luis Enrique Osorio, *Lo que brilla*
        José María Vargas Vila, *El huerto del silencio*

José María Vargas Vila, *María Magdalena*

1918   José María Vargas Vila, *Salomé*

1919   Jorge Wilson Price, *El diamante rojo*
       José María Vargas Vila, *Vuelo de cisnes*

1923   Daniel Arias Argáez, *Un pescador de perlas*

1924   Emilio Cuervo Márquez, *La selva oscura*
       Luis Gómez Corena, *Princesita criolla*
       José Eustasio Rivera, *La vorágine*
       Daniel Samper Ortega, *En el cerezal*

1926   Luis Enrique Osorio, *La cara de la miseria*
       Daniel Samper Ortega, *La obsesión*
       Luis Tablanca (Enrique Pardo Farelo), *Tierra encantada*

1928   Jorge Mateus, *El extranjero, novela americana*
       José María Vargas Vila, *La novena sinfonía*

1929   Alfredo Gómez Jaime, *Bajo la máscara*
       Isabel de Montserrate, *Hados*

1930   Antonio Alvarez Lleras, *Ayer, nada más*
       José Antonio Osorio Lizarazo, *La casa de vecindad*

1931   Daniel Samper Ortega, *Zoraya*

1932   Luis Alberto Castellanos, *Jenny*
       José Antonio Osorio Lizarazo, *Barranquilla 2.132*

1934   Manuelita Mallarino Isaacs, *Las memorias de Marcela*
       Roberto Pineda Castillo, *Panorama de cuatro días*
       Eduardo Zalamea Borda, *Cuatro años a bordo de mí mismo*

1935   José Antonio Osorio Lizarazo, *La cosecha*
       José Antonio Osorio Lizarazo, *El criminal*
       Luis Tablanca (Enrique Pardo Farelo), *Una derrota sin batalla*

1937   Tomás Vargas Osorio, *Vidas menores*

1938   Augusto Morales-Pino, *Los de en medio*
       José Antonio Osorio Lizarazo, *Hombres sin presente*

1939   Carlos Nossa Monroy, *Estampa rústica de la tierra*
       José Antonio Osorio Lizarazo, *Garabato*

1941   Rafael Gómez Picón, *45 relatos de un burócrata, con cuatro paréntesis*

1942   Ernesto Camargo Martínez, *De la vida de Iván el mayor*
       Roberto Pineda Castillo, *Muchedumbre*

1943   Jaime Ardila Casamitjana, *Babel*
       Eduardo Caballero Calderón, *El arte de vivir sin soñar*
       Jaime Ibáñez, *No volverá la aurora*

1944   Gonzalo Canal Ramírez, *Leonardo*
       Jaime Ibáñez, *Cada voz lleva su angustia*
       José Antonio Osorio Lizarazo, *El hombre bajo la tierra*

1945   Próspero Morales Pradilla, *Perucho*
1947   Jaime Ibáñez, *Donde moran los sueños*
        Ramón Manrique, *La venturosa*
        Augusto Morales-Pino, *El pequeño señor García*
1948   Clemente Airó, *Yugo de niebla*
        Próspero Morales Pradilla, *Más acá*
1949   Germán Arciniegas, *En medio del camino de la vida*
        Gonzalo Canal Ramírez, *Orú*
        Elisa Mújica, *Los dos tiempos*
1951   Clemente Airó, *Sombras al sol*
        Pedro Gómez Corena, *El 9 de abril*
        Ignacio Gómez Dávila, *El cuarto sello*
        Eduardo Santa, *La provincia perdida*
1952   Eduardo Caballero Calderón, *El cristo de espaldas*
        José Antonio Osorio Lizarazo, *El día del odio*
        José Antonio Osorio Lizarazo, *El pantano*
        Jorge Zalamea, *El gran Burundún Burundá ha muerto*
1953   Ignacio Gómez Dávila, *Viernes 9*
        Alfonso López Michelsen, *Los elegidos*
        Alfonso Hilarión Sánchez, *Las balas de la ley*
1954   Eduardo Caballero Calderón, *Siervo sin tierra*
        Eduardo Santa, *Sin tierra para morir*
        Roberto Velandia, *Guipas del Magdalena*
        Roberto Velandia, *Hijos de la calle*
1955   Eduardo Caballero Calderón, *La penúltima hora*
1956   Eduardo Santa, *El girasol*
1957   Augusto Morales-Pino, *Días en blanco*
1959   Luis Hernando Vargas Villamil, *La Gaitana*
1960   Manuel González Martínez, *Llanura, soledad y viento*
1961   Clemente Airó, *La ciudad y el viento*
        Augusto Morales-Pino, *La confesión*
1962   Eduardo Caballero Calderón, *Manuel Pacho*
        Fernando Soto Aparicio, *La rebelión de las ratas*
        Alirio Vélez Machado, *Sargento Machado*
1963   Gonzalo Canal Ramírez, *Eramos doce*
        Elisa Mújica, *Catalina*
1964   Eutiquio Leal, *Después de la noche*
        Augusto Morales-Pino, *Redoblan los tambores*
1965   José Antonio Osorio Lizarazo, *El camino en la sombra*
1966   Víctor Aragón, *Los ojos del buho*
        Eduardo Caballero Calderón, *El buen salvaje*
        Pablus Gallinazo (Gonzalo Navas), *La pequeña hermana*
        Germán Pinzón, *El terremoto*

Costa Chronology

1844   Juan José Nieto, *Ingermina*
1845   Juan José Nieto, *Los moriscos*
1850   Juan José Nieto, *Rosina*
1859   Manuel María Madiedo, *La maldición*
1867   (Greater Cauca: Jorge Isaacs, *María*)
1871   Candelario Obeso, *La familia Pygmalión*
       Candelario Obeso, *Las cosas del mundo*
1887   Arturo G. Ruiz, *Un mundo sin sol*
1897   Abraham Z. López-Penha, *Camila Sánchez*
1903   Abraham Z. López-Penha, *La desposada de una sombra*
1904   Pedro Sonderéguer, *Cóndor*
1921   Pedro Sonderéguer, *Todo el amor*
1922   Antonio García Llach, *Alma traidora*
1923   Fernando de Andreis, *Tula del Real*
       Gregorio Castañeda Aragón, *Zamora*
       Manuel García Herreros, *Asaltos*
       Francisco Gnecco Mozo, *Un beso lo hizo todo*
1924   (Highland: José Eustasio Rivera, *La vorágine*)
1926   Pedro Sonderéguer, *El fragmentario*
       Pedro Sondereguer, *El miedo de amar*
1927   José Félix Fuenmayor, *Cosme*
       Ramón Martínez Zaldúa, *Los asteroides*
1928   José Félix Fuenmayor, *Una triste aventura de 14 sabios*
       José Gnecco Mozo, *Sabiduría melancólica*
1929   Dionisio Arango Vélez, *El inocente*
       Ramón Martínez Zaldúa, *Tras el nuevo Dorado*
1931   Dionisio Arango Vélez, *Memorias de un tal Pastrana,
       mojiganga baladí*
       Aquileo Lanao Loaíza, *Leo Agil*
1934   Antolín Díaz, *Sinú, pasión y vida del trópico*
1936   Priscila Herrera de Núñez, *Un asilo en la Goajira*
       José Ramón Lanao Loaíza, *Las pampas escandalosas*
1940   Gilberto García González, *El clérigo y el hombre*
1941   Amira de la Rosa, *Marsolaire*
1942   Gabriel A. Pacheco, *Maldita sea la guerra*
1944   Gabriel A. Pacheco, *Juventud y vicio*
1946   Gabriel A. Pacheco, *Un mejicano en el frente*
       Rafael Carazo Fortich, *Los ilegítimos*
1947   Marzia de Lusignan, *A la sombra de las parábolas*
       Manuel Zapata Olivella, *Tierra mojada*
1948   Julio Quiñones, *En el corazón de la América*

1950   Daniel Lemaitre, *Mompós, tierra de Dios*
1953   Olga Salcedo de Medina, *Se han cerrado los caminos*
1955   Gabriel García Márquez, *La hojarasca*
1960   Manuel Zapata Olivella, *La calle 10*
1961   Carlos Delgado Nieto, *La frontera*
       Gabriel García Márquez, *El coronel no tiene quien le escriba*
1962   Alvaro Cepeda Samudio, *La casa grande*
       Gabriel García Márquez, *La mala hora*
       Héctor Rojas Herazo, *Respirando el verano*
1963   Fanny Buitrago, *El hostigante verano de los dioses*
       Manuel Zapata Olivella, *Detrás del rostro*
1964   Efraín Tovar Mozo, *Zig-Zag en las bananeras*
       Manuel Zapata Olivella, *En Chimá nace un santo*
1967   Gabriel García Márquez, *Cien años de soledad*
       Héctor Rojas Herazo, *En noviembre llega el arzobispo*

Greater Antioquia Chronology

1867   (Greater Cauca: Jorge Isaacs, *María*)
1868   Juan Clímaco Arbeláez, *Adelaida Hélver*
1896   Tomás Carrasquilla, *Frutos de mi tierra*
1897   Samuel Velásquez, *Madre*
       Eduardo Zuleta, *Tierra virgen*
1898   Pedro Nel Ospina, *En el silencio de las selvas*
       Samuel Velásquez, *Al pie del Ruiz*
1899   Camilo Botero Guerra, *De paso*
1900   Marco Antonio Jaramillo, *Mercedes*
1902   Francisco Posada, *La muerte del apestado*
1903   Tomás Carrasquilla, *Salve, Regina*
       Alfonso Castro, *Vibraciones*
1904   Francisco de Paula Rendón, *Inocencia*
       Samuel Velásquez, *Hija*
1905   Alfonso Castro, *Hija espiritual*
       Gabriel Latorre, *Kundry*
       Francisco Posada, *Contrastes*
1907   Francisco de Paula Rendón, *Lenguas y corazones*
1908   Jesús Arenas, *Inés*
       Samuel Velásquez, *Madre*
1909   Francisco de Paula Rendón, *Sol*
1910   Tomás Carrasquilla, *Grandeza*
       Alfonso Castro, *Los Humildes*
       Samuel Velásquez, *Al abismo*
1911   Roberto Botero Saldarriaga, *Sangre conquistadora*

Gaspar Chaverra, *Rara avis*
Ernesto Gómez V., *La hija de la montaña*
1912   Alfonso Javier Gómez, *Madre glotona*
Juvencio Jalla, *Amarguras del pasado*
1914   Manuel Baena, *Aventuras de un estudiante*
Alirio Días Guerra, *Lucas Guevara*
1916   Arturo Suárez, *Montañera*
1918   Arturo Suárez, *Rosalba*
1920   Jesús Arenas, *Luchas sociales*
Arturo Suárez, *El alma del pasado*
1922   Roberto Botero Saldarriaga, *Uno de los catorce mil*
Alfonso Castro, *Abismos sociales*
1923   Rómulo Cuesta, *Tomás*
Wenceslao Montoya, *Orgullo y amor*
1924   Bernardo Arias Trujillo, *Luz*
Bernardo Arias Trujillo, *Cuando cantan los cisnes*
Juan José Botero, *Lejos del nido*
(Highland: José Eustasio Rivera, *La Vorágine*)
1925   Tomás Carrasquilla, *El Zarco*
Romualdo Gallego, *La pródiga avaricia*
Wenceslao Montoya, *Del remolino*
1926   Tomás Carrasquilla, *Ligia Cruz*
Alfonso Mejía Robledo, *Rosas de Francia*
José Restrepo Jaramillo, *Ventarrón*
1927   Jesús Arenas, *Isabel*
Tomás Carrasquilla, *La marquesa de Yolombó*
Alfonso Castro, *El señor doctor*
Wenceslao Montoya, *La fiera*
1928   Romualdo Gallego, *El sabor de la vida*
Adel López Gómez, *Por los caminos de la tierra*
Luis López de Mesa, *La tragedia de Nilse*
Arturo Suárez, *Así somos las mujeres*
1929   Eduardo Arias Suárez, *Bajo la luna negra*
Manuel Baena, *Cómo se hace ingeniero un negro en
Colombia*
Luis López de Mesa, *La biografía de Gloria Etzel*
Julio Posada, *"El machete"*
1930   Alfonso Mejía Robledo, *La risa de la fuente*
1931   Luis Carrasquilla, *Abismos*
Alfonso Castro, *De mis libres montañas*
José Restrepo Jaramillo, *David, hijo de Palestina*
José Quijano (José A. Gaviria), *A Londres directamente*
Alejandro Vallejo, *Entre Dios y el diablo*

1932   Fernando González, *Don Mirócletes*
        Roberto Restrepo, *La guerra entre Candorra y Tontul*
1933   César Uribe Piedrahita, *Toá*
1934   Rafael Arango Villegas, *Asistencia y camas*
        Rafael Jaramillo Arango, *Barrancabermeja*
        Arturo Suárez, *El divino pecado*
1935   Bernardo Arias Trujillo, *Risaralda*
        Tomás Carrasquilla, *Hace tiempos*
        Romualdo Gallego, *Ricos vergonzantes*
        Fernando González, *El remordimiento*
        César Uribe Piedrahita, *Mancha de aceite*
1936   Gabriel Carreño, *Disloques*
        Fernando González, *Don Benjamín, jesuita predicador*
        Eduardo Posada, *El dorado*
        Alejandro Vallejo, *La casa de Berta Ramírez*
1937   Efe Gómez, *Mi gente*
        Bernardo Uribe Muñoz, *Psiqué*
1938   Jaime Buitrago, *Los pescadores del Magdalena*
        Simón Pérez y Soto, *De poetas a conspiradores*
1939   Antonio J. Arango, *Bajo Cero*
1940   Antonio J. Arango, *Quindío*
        Alfonso Castro, *Clínica y espíritu*
        Iván Cocherín, *Túnel*
1941   Luis Carlos Flórez, *Llamarada, novela obrera anti-
        imperialista*
        Adel López Gómez, *La noche de Satanás*
1942   Antonio J. Arango, *Oro y miseria*
        Arcesio Escobar, *La Gabriela*
        Adel López Gómez, *El niño que vivió su vida*
        Bernardo Uribe Muñoz, *El suicida moral*
1943   Jaime Buitrago, *Hombres trasplantados*
        Efe Gómez, *Almas rudas*
        Gonzalo Ríos Ocampo, *Más allá de la sombra*
        Arturo Suárez, *Adorada enemiga*
        Bernardo Toro, *Minas, mulas y mujeres*
1945   José Alvear Restrepo, *El hombre de la granja*
        Iván Cocherín (Jesús González), *Esclavos de la tierra*
        Efe Gómez, *Guayabo negro*
        Ricardo Jaramillo Arango, *Al roce de los años*
        Eduardo Londoño Villegas, *El rey de los cangrejos*
        Manuel Mejía Vallego, *La tierra éramos nosotros*
1946   Rafael Arango Jaramillo, *Cuaderno de notas de Gabriel
        Sandoval*

1947   Jesús Botero Restrepo, *Andágueda*
1948   Euclides Jaramillo Arango, *Las memorias de Simoncito*
       Magda Moreno, *El embrujo del micrófono*
       Wenceslao Montoya, *Abismo florecido*
       Jaime Sanín Echeverrí, *Una mujer de cuatro en conducta*
1950   Libardo Bedoya Céspedes, *Nieve maldita*
1951   Eduardo Acevedo Latorre, *Un poco de amor . . . y nada más*
       Fabiola Aguirre, *Dimensión de la angustia*
1954   Iván Cocherín, *El sol suda negro*
1955   Jaime Buitrago, *La tierra es del indio*
1958   Manuel Mejía Vallejo, *Al pie de la ciudad*
       Victoriano Vélez, *Del socavón al trapiche*
1959   Iván Cocherín, *Carapintada*
       Euclides Jaramillo Arango, *Un campesino sin regreso*
1960   Arturo Echeverri Mejía, *Marea de ratas*
       Jaime Sanín Echeverri, *¿Quién dijo miedo?*
1962   Fernando González, *La tragicomedia del padre Elías y Martina la Velera*
       Alfonso Mejía Robledo, *Un héroe sin ventura*
1963   Adel López Gómez, *El diablo anda por la aldea*
       Rocío Vélez de Piedrahita, *La tercera generación*
1964   Manuel Mejía Vallejo, *El día señalado*

Greater Cauca Chronology

1867   Jorge Isaacs, *María*
1870   Mercedes Hurtado de Alvarez, *Alfonso*
1871   Adriano Scarpetta, *Julia*
1873   Adriano Scarpetta, *Eva, novela caucana*
1886   Eustaquio Palacios, *El alférez real*
1888   Luciano Rivera y Garrido, *Dónde empieza y cómo acaba*
1889   Mercedes Gómez Victoria, *Misterios de la vida*
1894   José Rafael Sañudo, *La expiación de una madre*
1895   Florentino Paz, *La ciudad de Rutila*
1904   Isaías Gamboa, *La tierra nativa*
1917   Guillermo Franky, *Cepas de la aristocracia*
       Ramón Franky Galvis, *Mariana*
1920   Gregorio Sánchez Gómez, *La tierra desnuda*
       Octavio Valencia, *Marbella*
1924   Guillermo Franky, *Amelia*
       Nicolás Olano Borrero, *En pleno valle*
       Francisco María Renjifo, *Eufrosina de Alejandría; novela histórica del siglo V de la era cristiana*

(Highland: José Eustasio Rivera, *La vorágine*)
Gregorio Sánchez Gómez, *La envidia*
1925 Guillermo Franky, *Los misterios de Bogotá*
Gregorio Sánchez Gómez, *La derrota*
1927 Gregorio Sánchez Gómez, *Rosario Benavides*
1929 Guillermo Navia Carvajal, *El dolor hecho luz*
Gregorio Sánchez Gómez, *La casa de los del Pino*
Gregorio Sánchez Gómez, *La virgen pobre*
Mario Zamorano, *Dos almas fuertes*
1930 Guillermo Navia Carvajal, *El caballero rojo*
1931 Manuel Jesús Lucio, *Entre dos almas*
1933 Gregorio Sánchez Gómez, *El Gavilán*
1934 Gregorio Sánchez Gómez, *Casada y sin marido*
1936 Gregorio Sánchez Gómez, *Vida de un muerto*
1938 Gregorio Sánchez Gómez, *El burgo de don Sebastián*
1939 Alfonso Alexander, *Sima*
Antonio Gamboa, *Ruta negra*
1942 Diego Castrillón Arboleda, *José Tombé*
1943 Juan Alvarez Garzón, *Los clavijos*
1946 Guillermo Edmundo Chaves, *Chambú*
1947 Gregorio Sánchez Gómez, *La bruja de las minas*
1948 Enrique Arroyo Arboleda, *La ciudad perdida*
1949 Diego Castrillón Arboleda, *Sol en Tambalimbú*
Roberto José Falla, *Ichó, novela chocoana*
Arnoldo Palacios, *Las estrellas son negras*
1950 Aulo Zegrí, *Agarrando el vacío*
1952 Miguel A. Caicedo M., *La palizada*
Mario Zamorano, *Un solo pecado*
1953 Daniel Caicedo, *Viento seco*
Rogerio Velásquez, *Las memorias del odio*
1954 Daniel Caicedo, *Salto al vacío*
Alberto Dow, *Guandurú*
Alberto Montezuma Hurtado, *Ceniza común*
Fernán Muñoz Jiménez, *Horizontes cerrados*
1958 Arnoldo Palacios, *La selva y la lluvia*
Gregorio Sánchez Gómez, *La Amazona de cañas*
Gregorio Sánchez Gómez, *Magola*
1960 Raúl Silva Holguín, *Caucania*
1961 Nelly Domínguez Vásquez, *Manatí*
1962 Juan Alvarez Garzón, *Gritaba la noche*
1963 Alberto Dow, *Unos años, una noche*
1964 Alberto Montezuma Hurtado, *Piedras preciosas*

1966   Alberto Montezuma Hurtado, *El paraíso del diablo*
1967   (Costa: Gabriel García Márquez, *Cien años de soledad*)
1972   Gustavo Alvarez Gardeazábal, *Cóndores no entierran todos
        los días*
1973   Gustavo Alvarez Gardeazábal, *Dabeiba*
1974   Gustavo Alvarez Gardeazábal, *El bazar de los idiotas*
        Nelly Domínguez Vásquez, *Esa edad*

Modern and Postmodern Chronology, 1965–1987

1965   Pedro Acosta Borrero, *El cadáver del Cid*
        Augusto Morales-Pino, *Cielo y asfalto*
        José Antonio Osorio Lizarazo, *El camino en la sombra*
1966   Eduardo Caballero Calderón, *El buen salvaje*
        Pablus Gallinazo (Gonzalo Navas), *La pequeña hermana*
        Oscar Hernández Monsalve, *Al final de la calle*
        Alberto Montezuma Hurtado, *El paraíso del diablo*
        Humberto Navarro, *Los días más felices del año*
        Germán Pinzón, *El terremoto*
        Flor Romero de Nohra, *3 kilates 8 puntos*
        Fernando Soto Aparicio, *Mientras llueve*
1967   Mario Arrubla, *La infancia legendaria de Ramiro Cruz*
        Gabriel García Márquez, *Cien años de soledad*
        Manuel González Martínez, *La canija*
        Héctor Rojas Herazo, *En noviembre llega el arzobispo*
        Fernando Soto Aparicio, *El espejo sombrío*
1968   Alberto Duque López, *Mateo el flautista*
        Jaime Ibáñez, *Un hueco en el aire*
        Flor Romero de Nohra, *Mi capitán Fabián Sicachá*
1969   Javier Auqué Lara, *Los muertos tienen sed*
        Eduardo Caballero Calderón, *Caín*
        Héctor Sánchez, *Las causas supremas*
        Héctor Sánchez, *Las maniobras*
        Benhur Sánchez Suárez, *La solterona*
        José Stevenson, *Los años de la asfixia*
        Alvaro Valencia Tovar, *Uisheda*
1970   Clemente Airó, *El campo y el fuego*
        Albalucía Angel, *Los girasoles en invierno*
        Fanny Buitrago, *Cola de zorro*
        Germán Espinosa, *Los cortejos del diablo*
        Augusto Morales-Pino, *Requiem por un corazón*
        Fernando Soto Aparicio, *Después empezará la madrugada*
1971   Gustavo Alvarez Gardeazábal, *La tara del papa*
        Fernando Soto Aparicio, *Viaje a la claridad*

1972   Gustavo Alvarez Gardeazábal, *Cóndores no entierran todos
         los días*
         Albalucía Angel, *Dos veces Alicia*
         Flor Romero de Nohra, *Triquitraques del trópico*
         Benhur Sánchez Suárez, *La noche de tu piel*
         Jesús Zárate Moreno, *La cárcel*
1973   Gustavo Alvarez Gardeazábal, *Dabeiba*
         Manuel Mejía Vallejo, *Aire de tango*
         Héctor Sánchez, *Los desheredados*
         Fernando Soto Aparicio, *Mundo roto*
         Humberto Tafur Charry, *Tres puntos en la tierra*
         Jesús Zárate Moreno, *El cartero*
1974   Gustavo Alvarez Gardeazábal, *El bazar de los idiotas*
1975   Marco Tulio Aguilera Garramuño, *Breve historia de todas
         las cosas*
         Albalucía Angel, *Estaba la pájara pinta sentada en el verde
         limón*
         Oscar Collazos, *Crónica de tiempo muerto*
         Néstor Gustavo Díaz, *La loba maquillada*
         Gabriel García Márquez, *El otoño del patriarca*
         Augusto Morales-Pino, *La agonía de la abuela y el
         Chevrolet azul y blanco*
         Benhur Sánchez Suárez, *El cadáver*
1976   Oscar Collazos, *Los días de la paciencia*
         Carlos Perozzo, *Hasta el sol de los venados*
         Héctor Sánchez, *Sin nada entre las manos*
1977   Gustavo Alvarez Gardeazábal, *El titiritero*
         Eduardo Caballero Calderón, *Historia de dos hermanos*
         Andrés Caicedo, *¡Que viva la música!*
         Alberto Duque López, *Mi revólver es más largo que el tuyo*
         Pedro Gómez Valderrama, *La otra raya del tigre*
         R. H. Moreno-Durán, *Juego de damas*
         David Sánchez Juliao, *Cachaco, Palomo y Gato*
         José Stevenson, *Nostalgia Boom*
1978   Laureano Alba, *El barrio de las flores*
         Jorge Eliécer Pardo, *El jardín de las Weismann*
         Rodrigo Parra Sandoval, *El album secreto del Sagrado
         Corazón*
         Flor Romero de Nohra, *Los sueños del poder*
         Darío Ruiz Gómez, *Hojas en el patio*
1979   Plinio Apuleyo Mendoza, *Años de fuga*
         Carlos Bastidas Padilla, *Hasta que el odio nos separe*
         Fanny Buitrago, *Los pañamanes*

Fernando Cruz Kronfly, *Falleba*
Néstor Gustavo Díaz, *El valle sagrado de los hijos del sol*
Mario Escobar Velásquez, *Cuando pase el ánima sola*
Germán Espinosa, *El magnicidio*
Luis Fayad, *Los parientes de Ester*
Luis Fernando Macías, *Amada está lavando*
Manuel Mejía Vallejo, *Las muertes ajenas*
Augusto Pinilla, *La casa infinita*
Héctor Sánchez, *El tejemaneje*
Benhur Sánchez Suárez, *A ritmo de hombre*
Humberto Tafur, *La última noticia*

1980 Jaime Manrique Ardila, *El cadáver de papá*
Benjamín Baena Hoyos, *El río corre hacia atrás*
Alberto Dow, *El rey*
Mario Escobar Velásquez, *Un hombre llamado Todero*
Manuel Mejía Vallejo, *Tarde de verano*
Julio Mercado Benítez, *Los sagrados motivos*
Alvaro Rodríguez Lugo, *El guerrillero viejo*
Fernando Soto Aparicio, *Camino que anda*
Amparo María Suárez, *Santificar al diablo*

1981 Gustavo Alvarez Gardeazábal, *Los míos*
Enrique Cabezas Rher, *Miro tu lindo cielo y quedo aliviado*
Gabriel García Márquez, *Crónica de una muerte anunciada*
Manuel Giraldo-Magil, *Conciertos del desconcierto*
R. H. Moreno-Durán, *El toque de Diana*
Alvaro Pineda Botero, *El diálogo imposible*
Benhur Sánchez Suárez, *Venga le digo*
Umberto Valverde, *Celia Cruz*

1982 Clemente Airó, *Todo nunca es todo*
Albalucía Angel, *Misiá Señora*
Carlos Castro Saavedra, *Adán ceniza*
Oscar Collazos, *Todo o nada*
Germán Espinosa, *La tejedora de coronas*

1983 Fanny Buitrago, *Los amores de Afrodita*
Oscar Collazos, *Jóvenes, pobres amantes*
Tomás González, *Primero estaba el mar*
Darío Jaramillo Agudelo, *La muerte de Alec*
R. H. Moreno-Durán, *Finale capriccioso con Madonna*
Alvaro Pineda Botero, *Trasplante a Nueva York*
David Sánchez Juliao, *Pero sigo siendo el rey*
Manuel Zapata Olivella, *Changó, el gran putas*

1984 Arturo Alape, *Noche de pájaros*
Gustavo Alvarez Gardeazábal, *Pepe Botellas*

Albalucía Angel, *Las andariegas*
Roberto Burgos Cantor, *El patio de los vientos perdidos*
Antonio Caballero, *Sin remedio*
José Manuel Crespo, *La promesa y el reino*
Alberto Duque López, *El pez en el espejo*
José Luis Garcés, *Los extraños traen mala suerte*
Juan José Hoyos, *Tuyo es mi corazón*
Manuel Mejía Vallejo, *Y el mundo sigue andando*
Héctor Sánchez, *Entre ruinas*
Francisco Sánchez Jiménez, *Sala capitular*
Humberto Tafur Charry, *El séptimo hombre*
1985 Marco Tulio Aguilera Garramuño, *Paraísos hostiles*
Alonso Aristizábal, *Una y muchas guerras*
Carlos Barriga, *Demasiado tarde para despertar*
Fernando Cruz Kronfly, *La obra del sueño*
José Luis Díaz Granados, *Las puertas del infierno*
Alberto Esquivel, *Acelere*
José Luis Garcés, *Entre la soledad y los cuchillos*
Gabriel García Márquez, *El amor en los tiempos del cólera*
Gustavo González Zafra, *Los frutos del paraíso*
Alfonso Hilarión Sánchez, *Las embrujadas del Cinaruco*
Carlos Orlando Pardo, *Lolita golondrinas*
Carlos Orlando Pardo, *Los sueños inútiles*
Héctor Rojas Herazo, *Celia se pudre*
Fernando Vallejo, *El río del tiempo: los días azules*
1986 Gustavo Alvarez Gardeazábal, *El divino*
José Cardona López, *Sueños para una siesta*
Oscar Collazos, *Tal como el fuego fatuo*
Néstor Gustavo Díaz, *Se necesita mensajero ciego*
Eduardo García Aguilar, *Tierra de leones*
Próspero Morales Pradilla, *Los pecados de Inés de Hinojosa*
Alvaro Mutis, *La nieve del almirante*
Julio Olacirequi, *Los domingos de Charito*
Jorge Eliécer Pardo, *Irene*
Alvaro Pineda Botero, *Gallinazos en la baranda*
David Sánchez Juliao, *Mi sangre aunque plebeya*
Fernando Vallejo, *El fuego secreto*
Manuel Zapata Olivella, *El fusilamiento del diablo*
1987 Gustavo Alvarez Gardeazábal, *El último gamonal*
Roberto Burgos Cantor, *De gozos y desvelos*
José Manuel Crespo, *Largo ha sido este día*
Fernando Cruz Kronfly, *La ceniza del libertador*
Germán Espinosa, *El signo del pez*

Eduardo García Aguilar, *Bulevar de los héroes*
Tomás González, *Para antes del olvido*
Manuel Mejía Vallejo, *La sombra de tu paso*
Marvel Moreno, *En diciembre llegaban las brisas*
R. H. Moreno-Durán, *Los felinos del Canciller*
Evelio Rosero Diago, *Juliana los mira*

Notes

Preface

1. Ong, *Orality and Literacy*. "Noetics" refers here to the processes of cognition or intellectual apprehension. Ong's *Orality and Literacy* is a succinct and clear synthesis of work in orality and literacy by him and other scholars of orality, such as Jack Goody and Marshall McLuhan. The pioneer literary studies of Milman Parry, Albert Lord, and Eric A. Havelock are comparable to some of the readings offered in the present study, although my interests in ideology and narratology render my readings of Colombian novels considerably different too. Recent work on orality by Hispanists specializing in Hispanic balladry can be found in a special issue of *Oral Tradition* 2, nos. 2–3 (May–October 1987).

2. Genette, *Figures III*; Rimmon-Kenan, *Narrative Fiction*. Genette's *Figures III* appeared in English as *Narrative Discourse: An Essay in Method*. See also Bal, *Narratology*, and Prince, *Narratology*.

3. See Eagleton, *Marxism and Literary Criticism* and *Theory of Literature*.

4. Tompkins, *Sensational Designs*.

5. Identification of a novel as "regionalist" has often been a form of deprecation in contemporary literary criticism, in Colombia as well as in the United States. For example, Wendell Berry discusses the term *regional* as basically a slur in "The Regional Motive," in *A Continuous Harmony*, pp. 63–70. I use the terms *regional* and *regionalist* in this study without the derogatory connotations that often accompany these words.

6. Among the novels published before 1957 (when Antonio Curcio Altamar's book appeared in print), most of the seventeen novels selected for detailed analysis in this study were recognized by Curcio Altamar. Six of the ten novels which Seymour Menton identifies as *planetas* or major novels in his *La novela colombiana* are highlighted in the present study. In his prologue he mentions three novels which he laments not being able to in-

clude, and each of these three appear prominently in the present study: *El alférez real, Toá,* and *La casa grande.*

7. I use the concept of the institutionalization of literary value as set forth by Tompkins in chapter 7, "But Is It Any Good?" in *Sensational Designs.*

8. The typology of narrators proposed by Genette and Rimmon-Kenan results in the usage of four basic terms: *extradiegetic-heterodiegetic, extradiegetic-homodiegetic, intradiegetic-heterodiegetic,* and *intradiegetic-homodiegetic.* These terms refer to the narrative level to which the narrator belongs and the extent of his or her participation in the story. A narrator who is "above" or superior to the story narrated is extradiegetic (Genette, *Figures III,* pp. 255–256; Rimmon-Kenan, *Narrative Fiction,* p. 94). To this category belong the narrators of Fielding's *Tom Jones* (1749), Balzac's *Père Goriot* (1834), and García Márquez's *Cien años de soledad* (1967). If the narrator is also a character in the first narrative told by the extradiegetic narrator, then he or she is a second degree, or intradiegetic, narrator (ibid.). Examples are Marlow in Conrad's *Heart of Darkness* and the pardoner in *The Canterbury Tales.* Rimmon-Kenan explains that both extradiegetic and intradiegetic narrators can be either absent from or present in the story they narrate. A narrator who does not participate in the story is called heterodiegetic (Rimmon-Kenan, *Narrative Fiction,* p. 95), whereas the one who takes part in it, at least in some manifestation of his or her "self," is homodiegetic.

9. Eagleton, *Theory of Literature.*

1. Colombia, Its History and Its Regions

1. Arciniegas, *Biografía del Caribe,* p. 102.

2. Kline, *Colombia,* p. xiii.

3. Ibid.

4. Rama, *La ciudad letrada.*

5. The relationship between writing and power is an issue throughout Foucault's work. See particularly *The Order of Things, The Archaeology of Knowledge,* and *Language, Counter-Memory, Practice.*

6. Safford, *The Ideal of the Practical,* p. 4.

7. Delpar, *The Red against the Blue,* p. xii.

8. For an overview of the first part of this period, see Bushnell, *The Santander Regime in Gran Colombia.*

9. Safford, *The Ideal of the Practical,* p. 35.

10. McGreevey, *An Economic History of Colombia,* p. 31.

11. For a more precise analysis of the situation in Colombia at mid-century and immediately thereafter, see Helguera, "The Problem of Liberalism."

12. Safford, *The Ideal of the Practical,* p. 55. Walter Ong has pointed out that these two aspects are typical of oral cultures: They are fundamentally conservative, and instruction in reading and writing is irrelevant and even dangerous. See Ong, *Orality and Literacy,* pp. 41–42.

13. McGreevey, *An Economic History of Colombia*, p. 51.
14. Personal interview with Gabriel García Márquez, Mexico City, May 12, 1987.
15. McGreevey points out these two lines of argument in *An Economic History of Colombia*, p. 67.
16. Ibid., p. 76.
17. Bergquist, *Coffee and Conflict in Colombia*, p. 3.
18. Jaramillo Uribe, *El pensamiento colombiano*, p. 158.
19. Park, *Rafael Núñez and the Politics of Colombian Regionalism*, p. 265.
20. Safford, *The Ideal of the Practical*, p. 145.
21. Bergquist, *Coffee and Conflict in Colombia*, p. 195.
22. Ibid., p. 16.
23. Ibid., p. 21.
24. Levine, *Religion and Politics in Latin America*, p. 58.
25. The basis for these comments on Olaya Herrera is Davis, *Historical Dictionary of Colombia*, p. 162.
26. McGreevey, *An Economic History of Colombia*, p. 278.
27. Fluharty, *Dance of Millions*, p. 46.
28. Antonio Gómez Restrepo and Rafael Maya are among the most distinguished of numerous Conservative literary critics who predominated in Colombia during this period. See Gómez Restrepo, *Historia de la literatura colombiana*, and Maya, *Obra crítica*.
29. Fogelquist, *Revolutionary Theory and Practice in Colombia*.
30. Fals Borda, Guzmán Campos, and Umaña Luna, *La Violencia en Colombia*, p. 14.
31. Safford, *The Ideal of the Practical*, p. 240.
32. Bagley, "The National Front and Beyond," p. 6.
33. Ibid.
34. Zapata Olivella, *El hombre colombiano*.
35. A basic thesis of Margarita Jiménez and Sandro Sideri is that Colombia's regionalism has always been based on foreign economic ties abroad rather than on an interregional basis. See Jiménez and Sideri, *Historia del desarrollo regional en Colombia*.
36. McGreevey, *An Economic History of Colombia*, p. 253.
37. Ibid., p. 245.
38. Ibid., p. 228.
39. Fluharty, *Dance of Millions*, p. 25.
40. Safford, *The Ideal of the Practical*, p. 228.
41. Park, *Rafael Núñez and the Politics of Colombian Regionalism*, p. 20.
42. Rafael Núñez, *La federación* (Bogota, 1885), pp. 7–8, 13.
43. Park, *Rafael Núñez and the Politics of Colombian Regionalism*, p. 5.
44. Ibid., p. 105.
45. Ibid., p. 7. In addition, Joseph L. Love, in a study of Latin American regionalism, emphasizes the importance of Colombian regionalism: "The

problems of regional conflict—relationships of domination and subordination, the competition for scarce resources, and the tension between national integration and regional separatism—are of major importance in the history of Mexico, Brazil and Colombia." Love, "An Approach to Regionalism," p. 138.

46. For a lucid discussion of how political power and writing were associated in Latin America during the Colonial period, see Rama, *La ciudad letrada*.

47. Delpar, *The Red against the Blue*, p. 10.

48. Ibid., p. 190.

2. Ideology and the Novel in Nineteenth- and Twentieth-Century Colombia

1. Safford, *The Ideal of the Practical*, pp. 6–8.

2. Ibid., p. 4.

3. I use the concept of the institutionalization of literary value from Tomkins, *Sensational Designs*. See especially chapter 7, "But Is It Any Good?"

4. I use the term *Conservatives* here with the understanding that, in fact, in the 1830s the future Conservatives were designated *moderados*, in the late 1830s and 1840s they were called *ministeriales*, until the formation of the Conservative party in 1849.

5. Safford, *The Ideal of the Practical*, p. 31.

6. Ibid., p. 49.

7. Safford cites directly from the law of the Congress of Cúcuta. See ibid., p. 50.

8. Ibid., p. 73.

9. Terry Eagleton discusses the different concept of literature in eighteenth-century Great Britain in *Theory of Literature*. See especially chapter 1, "The Rise of English."

10. Eagleton has made the point that for Henry Fielding the concepts of "personal response" and "imaginative uniqueness" would not have made sense. See his *Theory of Literature*.

11. Felipe Pérez is cited here by Luis de Greiff Obregón in *Semblanzas y comentarios*, p. 239.

12. Felipe Pérez, *El caballero de la barba negra* (Bogotá: Imprenta de Ovalles y Compañía, 1858), p. 19.

13. Ibid.

14. James William Park cites this Conservative contemporary of Madiedo in *Rafael Núñez and the Politics of Colombian Regionalism*, p. 128.

15. Safford, *The Ideal of the Practical*, p. 193.

16. Duffey, *The Early Cuadro de Costumbres in Colombia*, p. 106.

17. José María Samper, *Martín Flores* (Bogotá: Imprenta de Gaitán, 1866), p. 9.

18. Ibid., p. 166.

19. Felipe Pérez, *Los jigantes* [sic] (Bogotá: Imprenta de Gaitán, 1875), p. 4.

20. Felipe Pérez, *Sara* (Bogotá: Imprenta Echeverría Hermanos, 1883), p. 6.

21. Inés de Hinojosa was novelized once again in the 1980s by Próspero Morales Pradilla in the novel *Los pecados de Inés Hinojosa.* See chapter 7.

22. Temístocles Avella Mendoza, *Anacaona* (Bogotá: Imprenta Constitucional, 1865), p. 5.

23. Maya, *Obra crítica,* vol. 1, p. 278.

24. Ibid., p. 285.

25. Duffey, *The Early Cuadro de Costumbres in Colombia,* p. 111.

26. Acosta de Samper, "La misión de la escritora en Hispanoamérica."

27. Ibid., p. 3.

28. Guerra Cunningham has observed how the females nurture males in "La modalidad hermética."

29. For a discussion of Soledad Acosta de Samper's other novels, see McGrady, *La novela histórica en Colombia.*

30. For an overview of the concept of the Athens of South America, see Palacios, "La Atenas Sudamericana," pp. 55–64.

31. Guillén Martínez, *La regeneración,* p. 34.

32. Gilberto Gómez Ocampo has analyzed the national song as parallel to the Constitution of 1886. See *Entre María y La vorágine,* pp. 17–61.

33. Soledad Acosta de Samper, *Gil Bayle* (Bogotá: Imprenta de la Luz, 1898), p. 3.

34. Soledad Acosta de Samper, *Los piratas en Cartagena* (Bogotá: Biblioteca Popular Colombiana, 1946), p. 21.

35. Duffey describes Marroquín as "always correct" and "probably the best of the Colombian *costumbristas*" in *The Early Cuadro de Costumbres,* p. 69.

36. Uribe Celis, *Los años veinte en Colombia,* p. 18.

37. Arrom, *Esquema generacional de las letras hispanoamericanas.*

38. Naranjo Villegas, *Generaciones colombianas.*

39. See Charry Lara, "Los poetas de 'Los Nuevos,'" pp. 633–681.

40. Uribe Celis, *Los años veinte en Colombia,* p. 37.

41. Ibid., p. 32.

42. See Castillo, "*La vorágine,*" p. 41.

43. See Luis Eduardo Nieto Caballero, "*La vorágine,*" in Ordóñez, *La vorágine,* pp. 29–34.

44. Manrique Terán, "*La vorágine,*" p. 39.

45. Gómez Restrepo, "*La vorágine,*" p. 47.

46. Gutiérrez Girardot, "La literatura colombiana en el siglo XX," pp. 470–471.

47. Carrasquilla, "Homilia No. 2," in *Obras completas,* vol. 2, p. 688. See also note 6 of chapter 5.

48. Carrasquilla speaks of "nuestro ambiente" in *Obras completas,* vol. 1, p. 259.

49. Romero, "La novela colombiana de entreguerras," p. 872.

50. Romero, *Las palabras están en situación,* p. 58.

51. Ibid., p. 46.
52. Ibid., p. 47.
53. Gilard, "Un eco temprano de la aparición de *Bestiario*, Barranquilla, 1951," pp. 32–35.
54. Osorio Lizarazo, *Novelas y crónicas*, p. 425.
55. Ibid., p. 82.
56. Wade, "An Introduction to the Colombian Novel," p. 480.
57. García Márquez, "La literatura colombiana, un fraude a la nación," pp. 787–793.
58. Wade, "An Introduction to the Colombian Novel," p. 467.
59. Escobar, "The Professionalization and Institutionalization of 'Development' in Colombia."
60. Kooreman, "Two Novelistic Views of the Bogotazo," p. 135.
61. For further discussion of heteroglossia in *La mala hora*, see Williams, *Gabriel García Márquez*, pp. 66–68.
62. Girard, *Violence and the Sacred*, p. 2.

3. The Interior Highland Tradition

1. Personal interview, Alfonso López Michelsen, August 20, 1987.
2. Rama, *La ciudad letrada*.
3. Isaacs also paid homage to Bogotá's cultural power by participating in activities of the group of *El Mosaico* during the 1860s.
4. Vergara y Vergara, *Historia de la literatura en Nueva Granada*.
5. For studies of the narrative of this period in Latin America, see Burgos, ed., *Prosa hispánica de vanguardia*; Pérez Firmat, *Idle Fictions*; and Brushwood, *The Spanish American Novel*, chapters 6–8.
6. Mikhail Bakhtin has done pioneer work on conflicting languages in literary texts. See especially "Discourse in the Novel," in *The Dialogic Imagination*, pp. 259–442. Bakhtin's concept of conflicting discourses informs much of the present study. Thomas K. Seung has also studied language and ideological conflict. See Seung, *Semiotics and Thematics in Hermeneutics*, pp. 202–203, and Souza's discussion of Seung in the context of Alejo Carpentier in *La historia en la novela hispanoamericana moderna*, pp. 47–48.
7. Gómez Ocampo has studied the counter-discourse of late nineteenth-century Colombian fiction in *Entre "María" y "La vorágine."*
8. *Biblioteca de señoritas*, March 20, 1858.
9. Article reproduced by José María Vergara y Vergara, *Obras escogidas*, vol. 3 (Bogotá: Editorial Minerva, 1944).
10. Camacho Roldán, *El Liberal Ilustrado* 896–899 (February 1914): 134.
11. See Julio Cejador y Frauca, as cited in Antonio Gómez Restrepo, *La literatura colombiana* (New York: Hispanic Institute in the U.S., 1963); see also Suárez-Murias, *La novela romántica en Hispanoamérica*; Curcio Altamar, *Evolución de la novela en Colombia*, pp. 117–131; Menton, *La novela colombiana*, pp. 53–107; Maya, "*La Manuela* y el Criollismo Colom-

biano," in *Obra crítica*, vol. 1, pp. 265–276; Gerardo Ramos, *De Manuela a Macondo*.

12. Jaramillo Uribe, *El pensamiento colombiano en el siglo XIX*, p. 158.

13. Ibid., p. 33.

14. Ibid., p. 195.

15. Bergquist, *Coffee and Conflict in Colombia*, p. 11.

16. For a complete overview of nineteenth-century Liberal ideas in Colombia, see Molina, *Las ideas liberales en Colombia*.

17. In *Coffee and Conflict in Colombia*, Bergquist explains: "Imbibing an integral world view which had become dominant in the industrializing nations of the West, Liberals ultimately sought to write into law a philosophy of man and society fundamentally at odds with the structure of the society they lived in—a society their conservative opponents cherished and fought to maintain" (p. 11).

18. For a more complete discussion of the *gólgotas*, see Molina, *Las ideas liberales en Colombia*, p. 62.

19. Both Antonio Curcio Altamar and José María Vergara y Vergara have described *Manuela* as a political novel. See Curcio Altamar's *Evolución de la novela en Colombia*, p. 125. He also cites Vergara y Vergara's statements with respect to Díaz's interest in Colombian politics (p. 125).

20. Another example of this procedure is chapter 24, which is titled "El San Juan" and begins as the typical *costumbrista* interlude, but after a brief descriptive passage the entire chapter is a discussion of the nascent republic's system of law and justice.

21. Eugenio Díaz, *Manuela* (Medellín: Editorial Bedout, 1978), p. 186. All subsequent quotations are from this edition.

22. In chapter 23, "El Angelito," Demóstenes offers written solutions to the young nation's problems and in the following chapter, "El San Juan," he proposes to resolve a matter "por la imprenta" (p. 342).

23. Walter Ong explains the homeostatic nature of oral cultures as follows: "By contrast with literate societies, oral societies can be characterized as homeostatic (Goody and Watt 1968, pp. 31–34). That is to say, oral societies live very much in the present which keeps itself in equilibrium or homeostasis by sloughing off memories which no longer have present relevance." See Ong, *Orality and Literacy*, p. 46. See also Goody and Watt, "The Consequences of Literacy," in Goody, ed., *Literacy in Traditional Societies*, pp. 27–84.

24. See González Echevarría, "*Cien años de soledad*," pp. 358–380. I will further pursue the issue of the novel as Archive, as set forth by González Echevarría, in chapter 4.

25. José María Samper is cited in Jaramillo Uribe, *El pensamiento colombiano en el siglo XIX*, p. 219.

26. Londoño V., "La nueva lira y su época," pp. 50–53.

27. Miguel Cané, *Notas de viaje* (Bogotá: 1903), p. 152.

28. Londoño V., "La nueva lira y su época," pp. 51–52.

29. Carrasquilla, "*Entre primos*," p. 486.

30. Restrepo, "Carta de Carlos E. Restrepo," p. 492. With respect to the role of weeping in *María*, see Brushwood's analysis of the preface to *María* in *Genteel Barbarism*, pp. 82–106.

31. Restrepo, "Carta de Carlos E. Restrepo," p. 492.

32. For a study of the pre-Raphaelite art in *De sobremesa*, see Picón Garfield, "*De sobremesa*." See also González, *La novela modernista hispanoamericana*; Zalamea, "Una novela de José Asunción Silva"; Gutiérrez Girardot, "*De sobremesa*," Orjuela, "J. K. Huysmans, María Bashkirtseff y Silva"; Schanzer, "Lo 'MOD' del modernismo"; Villanueva-Collado, "*De sobremesa* de José Asunción Silva."

33. Loveluck, "*De sobremesa*."

34. Orjuela, "*De sobremesa*" y otros estudios sobre José Asunción Silva.

35. Asunción Silva, *De sobremesa*, pp. 165–166.

36. *El Espectador* (Bogotá), "Espectador de Cien Años," no. 18, July 1, 1987.

37. Gómez Ocampo has analyzed *Polvo y ceniza* in *Entre "María" y "La vorágine*," pp. 149–171.

38. This reaction to *Diana cazadora* appeared immediately upon the publication of the novel in *El Espectador* (September 10, 1918), compiled later by Luis Eduardo Nieto Caballero in *Libros colombianos*. Four decades later Curcio Altamar confirmed the novel's merit: "A pesar de su dramático final, *Diana cazadora* es un mar de risa, porque su autor es uno de los mejores, el epígono quizás, de los novelistas de humor." Curcio Altamar, *Evolución de la novela en Colombia*, p. 165.

39. Clímaco Soto Borda, *Diana cazadora* (Medellín: Bedout: 1971), p. 31. All subsequent quotations are from this edition.

40. Genette sets forth the idea of a nuclear verb which essentializes a novel's action in *Narrative Discourse*, pp. 30–31.

41. Nieto Caballero, *Libros colombianos*.

42. For a volume of thirty-seven reviews and essays on *La vorágine*, originally published from the 1920s to the 1980s, see Ordóñez, ed., *La vorágine: textos críticos*.

43. See Anderson Imbert, *Historia de la literatura hispanoamericana*, vol. 2; Curcio Altamar, *Evolución de la novela en Colombia*, pp. 175–185; Green, "La estructura del narrador y el modo narrativo de *La vorágine*"; Loveluck, "Aproximación a *La vorágine*"; Menton, *La novela colombiana*, pp. 145–188; Olivera, "El romanticismo de José Eustasio Rivera," pp. 41–61; Porras Collantes, "Interpretación estructural de *La vorágine*"; Valente, "La naturaleza y el hombre en *La vorágine* de José Eustasio Rivera." A recent study in many ways similar to the analysis offered in this chapter is Unruh, "Arturo Cova y *La vorágine*."

44. See Pope, "*La vorágine*," and Magnarelli, "Women and Nature," pp. 38–58.

45. Schwartz, for example, affirms that Arturo Cova is the author. See *A New History of Spanish American Fiction*, vol. 1, p. 254.

46. Ibid., p. 259.

47. Brushwood, for example, finds Cova unbearable. See *The Spanish-American Novel*, pp. 42–45. For Carrasquilla's comments on Rivera, see Neale-Silva, *Horizonte humano.*

48. See Pope, "*La vorágine,*" and Magnarelli, *The Lost Rib*, p. 38.

49. Jean Franco and Otto Olivera, among others, have called Cova a "Romantic poet." See Franco, *The Modern Culture of Latin America*, and Olivera, "El romanticismo de José Eustasio Rivera."

50. Pope, "*La vorágine,*" pp. 256–267.

51. Magnarelli, *The Lost Rib*, p. 40, and Ford, "El marco narrativo de *La vorágine.*"

52. See, for example, Brushwood, *The Spanish American Novel*, pp. 53–55, and Bull, "Nature and Anthropomorphism in *La vorágine.*"

53. Magnarelli, *The Lost Rib*, p. 42.

54. Magnarelli has also discussed how the literary informs Cova's world vision: "and who cannot understand what he observes because he is an outsider, *totally influenced by literature* and by his preconceived notions of what he should find in his new land." See ibid.

55. Seymour Menton thoroughly demonstrates similarities between *The Aeneid* and *La vorágine* (and other classic models) in *La novela colombiana*, p. 148. Another study which relates this novel to the capacious literary structures of archetypal myths is Callan, "The Archetype of Psychic Renewal in *La vorágine,*" pp. 470–476.

56. For a history of the editions of *María*, see McGrady, *Jorge Isaacs.*

57. Neale-Silva, *El horizonte humano.* For an overview of *La vorágine*'s reception, see chapters 15 and 16.

58. In the original edition of Neale-Silva's study, a photo of Arturo Cova as it appeared in an edition of *La vorágine* is included. See Neale-Silva, *Horizonte humano*, p. 297.

59. Tittler, *Narrative Irony in the Contemporary Spanish American Novel*, p. 190.

60. Eduardo Zalamea Borda, *Cuatro años a bordo de mí mismo* (Medellín: Editorial Bedout, 1978), p. 210. All subsequent quotations are from this edition.

61. Eduardo Jaramillo Zuluaga has studied the narrator's perceptions and use of metaphors in "La poesía en *Cuatro años a bordo de mí mismo.*"

62. Caballero Calderón, *Brevario del Quijote*, p. 9.

63. See Ordóñez, "Elisa Mújica," and Araújo, "Dos novelas de dos mujeres."

64. See Armando Romero's introduction to the generation of *Mito* in chapter 5, "Mito," in *Las palabras están en situación*, pp. 107–138.

65. See Bedoya and Escobar, *Conozca a Eduardo Caballero Calderón*, pp. 26, 47.

66. For studies on Caballero Calderón's early novels, see Menton, "*Manuel Pacho: La vorágine* desvoraginada," in *La novela colombiana*, pp. 189–217; Brushwood, *The Spanish American Novel*, pp. 189–190; and Lyday and Herrera et al., "Trayectoria de un novelista."

67. Caballero Calderón, *Brevario del Quijote*, p. 86.

68. I use *scribbler* as Roland Barthes has used the term and José Miguel Oviedo has applied it to Pedro Camacho in his study of Mario Vargas Llosa's *La tía Julia y el escribidor*. See Oviedo, "*La tía Julia y el escribidor*," in Rossman and Friedman, eds., *Mario Vargas Llosa*.

69. Eduardo Caballero Calderón, *El buen salvaje* (Barcelona: Destino, 1967), p. 9. All subsequent quotations are from this edition.

70. See Brooks and Warren, *Understanding Fiction*. The first edition of this now classic manual on narrative was published in 1943.

71. See Bedoya and Escobar, *Conozca a Eduardo Caballero Calderón*, p. 143.

72. Ong, *Orality and Literacy*, pp. 56–57.

73. Ibid., p. 41.

74. Bloom, *The Anxiety of Influence*.

75. I use the term *intertextuality* here as originally set forth by Julia Kristeva, who refers to the transposition of one or more systems of signs into another. See Kristeva, *Desire in Language*. The issue of intertextuality is pursued in more detail and more consistently in chapter 6. See also Culler, *In Pursuit of Signs*, and Genette, *Palimpsests*.

76. See Barth, "The Literature of Exhaustion."

77. Alter, *Partial Magic*.

78. Pérez Firmat, "Apuntes para un modelo."

79. Spires, *Beyond the Metafictional Mode*, p. 15.

80. Seymour Menton has demonstrated self-conscious qualities of *Manuela* by delineating parallels between *Manuela* and *Don Quijote* and by showing how the protagonist Demóstenes is a self-conscious writer: "La unidad artística de la novela también se estrecha con el uso de ciertos motivos recurrentes además de los ya comentados; con los repasos de los acontecimientos que se van intensificando hacia el final de la novela; con la autoconciencia del proceso creativo, anticipando obras como *La vorágine* y otras que comentan el mismo proceso de escribir novelas" (*La novela colombiana*, p. 92).

81. Jonathan Tittler has identified irony as a fundamental element of the contemporary Spanish-American novel. See Tittler, *Narrative Irony in the Contemporary Spanish-American Novel*.

4. The Costa Tradition

1. Gabriel García Márquez once told President Belisario Betancur that "*Cien años de soledad* no es más que la tentativa de un vallenato de 450 páginas." This quotation is from Secretaría de Información y Prensa, *Un pueblo, un canto, un cantor*, p. 17.

2. Personal interview, Germán Vargas, August 5, 1987.

3. For background and history of the *vallenato*, see Posada, *Canción vallenata y tradición oral*, and Quiroz Otero, *Vallenato*.

4. Alvaro Cepeda Samudio made this statement in Secretaría de Información y Prensa, *Un pueblo, un canto, un cantor*, p. 74.

5. Ibid., p. 78.

6. For an introduction and overview of *costeño* fiction, see McCarty and Menton, "La novelística de la costa colombiana."

7. Roberto González Echevarría has proposed three basic characteristics of the novel as Archive: the presence of historic and the mediating documents through which the novel was narrated; the existence of an inner historian; the presence of an unfinished manuscript that the inner historian is trying to complete. See González Echevarría, "The Novel as Myth and Archive." See also González Echevarría, "Redescubrimiento del mundo perdido." He proposes in the latter article that two novels which are Archives are *Los pasos perdidos* by Alejo Carpentier and *Cien años de soledad* by Gabriel García Márquez.

8. I use the terms *tri-ethnic, popular culture,* and *oral tradition* here as Orlando Fals Borda describes the Caribbean Coast of Colombia in his incisive four-volume study of the region, *Historia doble de la costa.*

9. Fals Borda, *Historia doble de la costa,* vol. 1, p. 91B.

10. Fals Borda discusses the uneven development of the Costa in ibid., vol. 4, p. 112B.

11. The concept of oral residue or residual orality is from Ong, *Orality and Literacy,* chapters 3 and 4.

12. For a history of Cartagena, see Nichols, *Tres puertos.*

13. For a discussion of the relationship between the Spanish *romance* and the Costa's *vallenato,* see Posada, *Canción vallenata y tradición oral,* and Quiroz Otero, *Vallenato.* For an introduction to the *romance* in Colombia, see Beutler, *Estudios sobre el romancero español en Colombia.*

14. Gutiérrez Azopardo, *Historia del negro en Colombia,* p. 16.

15. African slaves were shipped to the inland towns of Popayán, Santa Fe de Antioquia, Honda, Anserma, Zaragoza, Cali, and others. See ibid.

16. Ong has described oral cultures close to the human lifeworld: "In the absence of elaborate analytic categories that depend on writing to structure knowledge at a distance from lived experience, oral cultures must conceptualize and verbalize all their knowledge with more or less close reference to the human lifeworld, assimilating the alien, objective world to the more immediate, familiar interaction of human beings." See *Orality and Literacy,* pp. 42–43. Fals Borda explains the presence of the *hombre-hicotea* in the Costa in *Historia doble de la costa,* vol. 3, pp. 34B–49B.

17. See note 23, chapter 3.

18. The titles of Fals Borda's four-volume study of the Costa, *Historia doble de la costa,* are *Mompox y Loba,* vol. 1; *El Presidente Nieto,* vol. 2; *Resistencia en el San Jorge,* vol. 3; *Retorno a la tierra,* vol. 4.

19. Friedemann and Patiño Rosselli, *Lengua y sociedad en el Palenque de San Basilio,* p. 21.

20. Ibid., p. 23.

21. See Bickerton and Escalante, *Palenquero.*

22. See Friedmann and Patiño Rosselli, *Lengua y sociedad en el Palenque de San Basilio;* Bickerton and Escalante, *Palenquero,* Megenney, *El palenquero.*

23. Orlando Fals Borda explains the uneven development (*desarrollo desigual*) of the Costa in *Historia doble de la costa*, vol. 4, pp. 112B–139B.

24. For an overview of the modernization of Barranquilla, Cartagena, and Santa Marta, see Nichols, *Tres puertos*.

25. For an overview of coffee production in the late nineteenth century, see Bergquist, *Coffee and Conflict in Colombia*, and Palacios, *El café en Colombia*.

26. See Vargas, "Revisión de *Voces*."

27. For an introduction to the Group of Barranquilla, see Brushwood, "José Félix Fuenmayor," and Gilard, "García Márquez, le groupe de Barranquilla, et Faulkner."

28. Charles Bergquist discusses this aspect of the Costa in an article still unpublished at the time of this writing: "Gabriel García Márquez: A Colombian Anomaly." This paper was presented at the Conference on Literature and History in Twentieth-Century Latin America, Washington University in St. Louis, April 13–15, 1983.

29. See Fals Borda, *Historia doble de la costa*, vol. 4 for a discussion of these foreign companies in the Sinú area and the Costa in general.

30. See ibid., pp. 140B–156B.

31. For an overview of the towns founded in the Department of Magdalena in the late eighteenth century, see ibid., vol. 1.

32. Ibid., vol. 2, p. 131A.

33. Orlando Fals Borda has explained Nieto's geography as follows: "El propio Nieto contestó a los incrédulos criticones de su tierra y de su época con una *Geografía histórica, estadística y local de la provincia de Cartagena* (Cartagena, 1839) que no sólo es la primera geografía regional que se escribió en el país, sino que contiene descripciones generales de costumbres, datos políticos y económicos que anticipan el tratamiento sociológico posterior." See ibid., vol. 2, p. 54B.

34. Orlando Fals Borda explains Nieto's background: "Nieto pertenecía a una familia triétnica de vecinos libres pobres que allí vivían de la pequeña agricultura y oficios varios." See ibid., p. 37B.

35. At the time of this writing, no full-length critical article or book chapter had been published on *Ingermina*. Antonio Curcio Altamar mentions *Ingermina* briefly in his *Evolución de la novela en Colombia*, p. 73.

36. In using the term *archival source* I am referring to the novel as Archive. See González Echevarría, "*Cien años de soledad*."

37. With respect to technology of writing, we note that Nieto published the first Colombian novel at a time when there were no publishing houses in Colombia, at least in the modern sense of a publisher who contracts, markets, and distributes a book.

38. Juan José Nieto, *Ingermina* (Kingston, Jamaica: Imprenta de Rafael J. de Cordova, 1844), p. iii. All subsequent quotations are from this edition.

39. Roberto González Echevarría has proposed that science was the mediating document for the nineteenth-century Latin American novelist. See "*Cien años de soledad*."

40. See ibid.

41. Roberto González Echevarría also refers to the Colonial chronicles in his description of the novel as Archive. See ibid.

42. I use the term *implied reader* from Iser, *The Implied Reader*.

43. Djelal Kadir cites Carlos Fuentes in *Questing Fictions*, p. 300.

44. Souza, *La historia en la novela hispanoamericana moderna*. See chapter 1, "Introducción: la historia en la imaginación literaria latinoamericana," pp. 11–32.

45. See González Echevarría, "*Cien años de soledad.*" See note 7 of this chapter for the basic characteristics of the novel as Archive.

46. Roberto González Echevarría sets forth these characteristics in ibid., esp. p. 371.

47. The three notes which are an expansion of the *récit* (expanding the story line) are notes 7, 8, and 13. Note 7 reads as follows: "Don Pedro de Heredia era natural de Madrid. Un lance de honor en que mató tres de sus adversarios, le obligó para libertarse del castigo a huir de la Península, y refugiarse en la Isla de Santo Domingo, donde tenía un hermano. De aquí, siguió su descubrimiento y conquista de la provincia de Santa Marta, haciendo de segundo de Pedro de Badillo, jefe de la expedición. Con el dinero que adquirió en ella, fue a España, salió triunfante de la causa, y solicitó el adelantamiento de Cartagena, que le fue concedido." See *Ingermina*, p. 1.

48. The eleven notes with historical content are 1, 2, 10, 12, 14, 17, 20, 21, 22, 23, 25.

49. The three notes of a "scientific" nature are 3, 4, and 15. (I place "scientific" in quotation marks as an indication of a nineteenth-century understanding of science.)

50. Two notes that would be classified as social science in content are 5 and 9.

51. The six notes which are identified only with the word "Histórico" are 6, 11, 16, 18, 19, 24.

52. Fals Borda discusses Nieto's class aspirations in *Historia doble de la costa*, vol. 2. See esp. pp. 32B–61B.

53. Juan José Nieto, *Los moriscos* (Kingston, Jamaica: Imprenta de Rafael J. de Cordova, 1845), p. 1.

54. Manuel María Madiedo, *El Mosaico*, November 5, 1859, p. 356.

55. For a study of Barranquilla's carnival as expression of popular culture, see Friedemann, *Carnaval en Barranquilla*.

56. Vargas, "Revisión de *Voces.*"

57. Ibid., p. 16.

58. Pedro Sonderéguer, *Quibdó* (Buenos Aires: Maucci Hermanos, 1927), pp. 3–4.

59. Germán Vargas, "José Félix Fuenmayor," in *Sobre literatura colombiana*, pp. 185–186.

60. Alvaro Cepeda Samudio is cited by Juan Gustavo Cobo Borda, "Prólogo," in José Félix Fuenmayor, *Cosme* (Bogotá: Carlos Valencia Editores, 1979), p. 13.

61. Ibid., p. 19. All subsequent quotations are from this edition.
62. The century-long debate in Colombia over practical and technical education is examined by Safford in *The Ideal of the Practical.*
63. I discuss García Márquez's early fiction and the creation of an "other reality" in *Gabriel García Márquez,* chapter 2.
64. For an overview of the personalities involved with the Group of Barranquilla, see Fuenmayor, *Crónicas sobre el Grupo de Barranquilla.*
65. In a personal interview with Germán Vargas (November 1987), he explained the meetings of the Group of Barranquilla in the Café Roma, including the presence of Rafael Escalona.
66. Jacques Gilard discusses this special attitude of the Group of Barranquilla in "Un Eco Temprano de la aparición de 'Bestiario': Barranquilla, 1951," in Varios, *Lo lúdico y lo fantástico en la obra de Julio Cortázar,* pp. 33–44.
67. Ibid.
68. Personal interview, Germán Vargas, Barranquilla, October 12, 1987.
69. Franz Stanzel distinguishes between a "narrating self" and an "experiencing self" in *Narrative Situations in the Novel.*
70. Héctor Rojas Herazo, *Respirando el verano* (Bogotá: Ediciones Faro, n.d.), p. 66. All subsequent quotations are from this edition.
71. Ong states that oral and writing noetics are so profoundly different that the way a writing-culture person thinks may seem ridiculous or senseless to an individual in an oral culture, and vice-versa. The fact that oral cultures use situational rather than abstract noetic processes can result in responses that seem irrational in writing culture. This manner of thinking is prevalent among characters in *Respirando el verano,* as irrational as it may seem to readers of a writing culture. See Ong, *Orality and Literacy,* p. 51.
72. For a discussion of the conceptualization of things close to the human lifeworld, see ibid., pp. 42–43, and note 16 of this chapter.
73. González Echevarría, *"Cien años de soledad,"* p. 374.
74. Seymour Menton, *"Respirando el verano,* fuente colombiana de *Cien años de soledad,"* in *La novela colombiana.* Originally published in *Revista Iberoamericana* 41, no. 91 (April–June 1975): 203–217.
75. Manuel Zapata Olivella, *En Chimá nace un santo* (Barcelona: Seix Barral, 1974). The epigraph reads as follows: "Los mitos son un producto necesario de la mentalidad infantil, al igual que la de los pueblos primitivos. Se originan como una evasión hacia el campo de lo mágico, como una explicación aparentemente aceptable, como una esperanza de salvación. Castiglioni, *El mundo mágico"* (p. 7).
76. Lewis, *Treading the Ebony Path,* p. 108. For a thorough overview of Zapata Olivella's complete fiction, see chapter 5 of this book, "From Oppression to Liberation: Manuel Zapata Olivella," pp. 85–119. See also Captain-Hidalgo, "El espacio del tiempo en *Changó, el gran putas."*
77. In "Big Mama's Funeral," García Márquez ridicules numerous Colombian institutions, including its famed beauty pageants. See "Big Mama's

Funeral," in *No One Writes to the Colonel and Other Stories by Gabriel García Márquez* (New York: Harper/Colophon Books, 1968), p. 168.

78. I have discussed this explicitly political era of García Márquez's fiction in chapter 3, "The Middle Years (1956–1962)," in *Gabriel García Márquez*, pp. 40–68.

79. I have discussed the multiple languages or heteroglossia of *In Evil Hour* in ibid., pp. 65–66.

80. Gabriel García Márquez, *One Hundred Years of Solitude* (New York: Avon Books, 1971), p. 11. All subsequent quotations are from this edition.

81. Wayne Fields has studied *Cien años de soledad* in the context of the United States' tall tale in "*One Hundred Years of Solitude* and New World Storytelling."

82. García Márquez reveals this discovery in a lengthy interview with Plinio Apuleyo Mendoza. See Apuleyo Mendoza, *El olor de la guayaba*, p. 77.

83. John S. Brushwood has noted the narrator's tone in *The Spanish American Novel*, p. 291.

84. Fields has noted similarities between *Cien años de soledad* and the United States' tall tale in "*One Hundred Years of Solitude* and New World Storytelling."

85. See Ong, *Orality and Literacy*, p. 29.

86. Ong has explained how oral cultures see writing noetics as irrelevant or ridiculous. See ibid., pp. 50–52, and note 72 of this chapter.

87. Ong has explained how individuals in oral cultures, like Ursula, are not interested in definitions: "Oral cultures of course have no dictionaries and few semantic discrepancies. The meaning of each word is controlled by what Goody and Watt call 'direct semantic ratification', that is, by the real-life situations in which the word is used here and now. The oral mind is uninterested in definitions." See ibid., p. 47.

88. Ong describes the oral mind as situational rather than abstract in ibid., p. 49.

89. For an analysis of the final pages of *Cien años de soledad*, see Rodríguez Monegal, "*One Hundred Years of Solitude*."

90. Ong explains the function of "heavy" characters as follows: "The heroic tradition of primary oral culture and of early literate culture, with its massive oral residue, relates to the agonistic lifestyle, but it is best and most radically explained in terms of the needs of oral noetic processes. Oral memory works effectively with 'heavy' characters, persons whose deeds are monumental, memorable and commonly public." See *Orality and Literacy*, p. 70.

91. Ong describes the relationship between oral cultures and closeness to the human lifeworld in ibid., pp. 42–43. See also note 16 of this chapter.

92. I am indebted to Walter Ong for this observation about *Cien años de soledad*. He mentioned this to me in a personal interview, St. Louis, April 1985.

93. Ong, "African Talking Drums and Oral Noetics," in *Interfaces of the Word*, pp. 114–117.

94. Studies on time and repetition in *Cien años de soledad* include

Ciplijauskaité, "Foreshadowing as a Technique and Theme in *One Hundred Years of Solitude*"; Pinard, "Time In and Out of Solitude in *One Hundred Years of Solitude*"; McMurray, *Gabriel García Márquez;* Vargas Llosa, *Gabriel García Márquez.*

95. Walter Ong has discussed the relationships between gender, literacy, and writing in *Fighting for Life: Contest, Sexuality, and Consciousness.*

96. González Echevarría, "*Cien años de soledad,*" p. 371.

97. Lucila Inés Mena provides the historical background to *One Hundred Years of Solitude,* including the banana workers' strike, in *La función de la historia en Cien años de soledad.*

98. González Echevarría, "*Cien años de soledad,*" p. 371.

99. Ibid., p. 377.

100. Ong maintains that oral cultures are conservative. See *Orality and Literacy,* pp. 41–42.

5. The Greater Antioquian Tradition

1. Antioquia's work ethic and tradition of individualism, among other stereotypes, have been the topic of a long-standing debate among social scientists. See especially Parsons, *Antioqueño Colonization in Western Colombia;* Hagen, *El cambio social en Colombia;* Twinam, *Miners, Merchants, and Farmers in Colonial Colombia.*

2. For a discussion of the administration of Oidor Juan Antonio Mon y Velarde, see Ann Twinam, "Comercio y comerciantes en Antioquia," in Ospina, ed., *Los estudios regionales en Colombia,* pp. 115–134. See also Twinam, *Miners, Merchants, and Farmers in Colonial Colombia.*

3. See López, "El desarrollo histórico de la industria en Antioquia; el período de consolidación," in Ospina, ed., *Los estudios regionales en Colombia,* p. 205.

4. Jaime Mejía Duque has discussed the desire of the dominating classes in Antioquia to maintain a paternalistic society that was disappearing with industrialization. See "Tomás Carrasquilla en *Hace tiempos,*" in *Nueve ensayos literarios,* pp. 163–196.

5. Jaramillo Londoño, *Testamento del paisa,* p. 9.

6. Carrasquilla, "Homilía No. 2," in *Obras completas,* vol. 2, p. 688.

7. Menton, *La novela colombiana,* p. 112.

8. Menton explains these plot details in ibid., p. 114.

9. For a discussion of technical education in Colombia at the turn of the century, see Safford, *The Ideal of the Practical.*

10. Tomás Carrasquilla, *Frutos de mi tierra* (Bogotá: El Ancora, 1987), p. 7. All subsequent quotations are from this edition.

11. Menton demonstrates parallels with this and other classical literature in *La novela colombiana,* pp. 111–144.

12. Walter Ong has set forth the idea of how a text fictionalizes a reader in "The Writer's Audience Is Always a Fiction," pp. 9–21.

13. See Escobar Calle, "Las revistas literarias en Antioquia," in *La his-*

toria de Antioquia, supplement to *El colombiano*, February 24, 1988, pp. 335–338.

14. Samuel Velásquez, *Al pie del Ruiz* (Medellín: Librería de Carlos A. Molina, 1898), p. 153.

15. Carrasquilla, "Carta a Max Grillo," in *Obras completas*, vol. 2, p. 2164.

16. Eduardo Zuleta, *Tierra virgen* (Medellín: Librería de Carlos A. Molina, 1897), p. 9.

17. Arango Ferrer, *Dos horas de literatura colombiana*, p. 60.

18. *El Montañés* 1, no 1 (September 1897).

19. Kurt Levy counts six short novels by Carrasquilla, but he includes the story "Dimitas Arias" as a short novel. See Levy, *Tomás Carrasquilla*, pp. 40–41.

20. Ibid., p. 88.

21. Kurt Levy has discussed the similarities between *Grandeza* and *Frutos de mi tierra*. See ibid., pp. 54–55.

22. Carrasquilla, *Obras completas*, vol. 1, p. 259.

23. Brushwood has explained this narrative situation in *The Spanish American Novel*, p. 64.

24. Seymour Menton mentions *Toá* as a work meritorious of study in the preface to his *La novela colombiana*. See also Brushwood, *The Spanish American Novel*, pp. 103–104; Curcio Altamar, *Evolución de la novela en Colombia*, pp. 202–203; Sohn, *La novela colombiana de protesta social*, pp. 19–36.

25. This border conflict is historical. Robert Davis has succinctly explained the dispute in his *Historical Dictionary of Colombia*, p. 137.

26. Housková, "Tipo de novela mundonovista," p. 69.

27. Brushwood, *The Spanish American Novel*, p. 96.

28. César Uribe Piedrahita, *Toá* (Bogotá: Instituto Colombiano de Cultura, 1979), p. 41. All subsequent quotations are from this edition.

29. Housková, "Tipo de novela mundonovista," p. 79.

30. Brushwood, *The Spanish American Novel*, p. 103.

31. Yolanda Forero Villegas has analyzed several oral-culture features of the *caucheros* in an unpublished work which has informed the present study, "*Toá* o el rechazo a la civilización dominante."

32. Seymour Menton has studied *La vorágine* in the context of classical myths and the descent into hell. See *La novela colombiana*, pp. 147–188.

33. Brushwood, *The Spanish American Novel*, p. 104.

34. Ibid.

35. José Camacho Carreño characterizes Arias Trujillo as such in "Arias Trujillo, o el criollismo," in Arias Trujillo, *Diccionario de emociones*, pp. 5–15.

36. Silvio Villegas characterizes Arias Trujillo as such in his preface to *Risaralda*, "Bernardo Arias Trujillo," in Bernardo Arias Trujillo, *Risaralda* (Medellín: Bedout, 1978), pp. 7–19.

37. Ibid., p. 229. All subsequent quotations are from this edition.
38. Arias Trujillo, like Carrasquilla, unfortunately reveals occasional stereotypical racist attitudes typical of his time. For example, he describes the blacks' expression of emotion as "savage passions" (p. 182) and uses similar stereotypes on pages 50, 73, and 86.
39. An unpublished study by Guillermo García demonstrates oral features of this text, "La función del narrador en *Risaralda:* la problemática de la identidad nacional."
40. Fals Borda, Guzman Campos, and Umaña Luna, *La violencia en Colombia,* vol. 1, p. 90.
41. See Levy, *"Marea de ratas,"* pp. 29–32.
42. Otto Morales Benítez has reviewed *Generación* in *Perfiles literarios de Antioquia,* pp. 11–64.
43. Montoya Candamil, *Manuel Mejía Vallejo,* p. 18.
44. Manuel Mejía Vallejo, *El día señalado* (Barcelona: Ediciones Destino, 1966), p. 23. All quotations are from this edition.
45. Seymour Menton has noted the inconsistencies of the two lines in *La novela colombiana,* pp. 217–246.
46. Manuel Mejía Vallejo has spoken for many years of his admiration for Carrasquilla. For example, see his essay "Don Tomás Carrasquilla y Kurt Levy," in *Hojas de papel,* pp. 41–54.
47. Brushwood has set forth the term *transcendent regionalism* to speak of these types of texts in *The Spanish American Novel,* pp. 334–335.
48. Franco, "Narrador, Autor, Superestrella," p. 130.

6. The Greater Cauca Tradition

1. Gutiérrez Azopardo, *Historia del negro en Colombia,* p. 41. With respect to Afro-Colombian history of Colombia, see also Zapata Olivella, ed., *El negro en la historia de Colombia.*
2. Gutiérrez Azopardo, *Historia del negro en Colombia,* p. 24.
3. Friedemann and Arocha, *Herederos del jaguar y la anaconda* contains a general history of the indigenous populations in each region of Colombia.
4. Ibid., p. 196.
5. Rojas G., *Sociedad y economía en el Valle del Cauca,* p. 14.
6. The exact years of economic stagnation in the Valle del Cauca were 1858 to 1890, except 1867 to 1875 and 1879 to 1883. For an explanation of the economic situation during this period, see Preston Hyland, *Sociedad y economía en el Valle del Cauca,* pp. 11–46.
7. Ibid., p. 29.
8. Pardo, *Literatura Oral Emberá.* The Indian cited here is Floresmino Dogiramá. It is interesting to note his oral-culture mentality. For example, in the introduction, Pardo cites Dogiramá making a typical statement of an oral-culture person: "Que los jóvenes no olviden, porque si olvidan es como si murieran." Ong has pointed out how memory is life in oral cultures. See also Vanin, ed., *El príncipe Tulicio.*
9. Sandra Garabano has studied the oral qualities of *emberá* stories in an

unpublished study, "La Literatura oral Emberá," which has informed my understanding of this culture.

10. Isaacs, *Canciones y coplas populares.*

11. For an overview of Jorge Isaacs's life, see McGrady, *Jorge Isaacs,* and Arciniegas, *Genio y figura de Jorge Isaacs.*

12. See Brown, "Chateaubriand and the Story of Feliciana in Jorge Isaacs' *María.*" For a study of the black presence in *María,* see Umberto Valverde, "La cultura negra en *María,*" in Mejía Vallejo et al., *María más allá del paraíso,* pp. 51–59.

13. See Embeita, "El tema del amor imposible en *María* de Jorge Isaacs"; López Michelsen, "Ensayo sobre la influencia semítica en *María*"; McGrady, "Las fuentes de *María* de Isaacs"; Naranjo M., "Alrededor de *María*"; Olivera, "*María,* tema predilecto de Isaacs"; Ramos, "Mujer, paisaje y ambiente en la novela *María*"; Sánchez Montenegro, "Jorge Isaacs y 'El Mosaico'"; Warshaw, "Jorge Isaacs' Library: New Light on Two *María* Problems." For more recent readings of the novel, see Magnarelli, "*María* and History," and Tittler, "Paisajes figurales en tres novelas colombianas."

14. See Anderson Imbert, "Prólogo," in *María,* by Jorge Isaacs.

15. See Menton, "La estructura dualística de *María.*"

16. John S. Brushwood's analysis is an experiment in the analysis employed by Roland Barthes in *S/Z, an Essay* (New York: Hill and Wang, 1974). Brushwood establishes five codes in *María:* (1) María-Milieu, (2) Separation, (3) Omen, (4) Test, and (5) Intensification. See "Codes of Character Definition: Jorge Isaacs's *María,*" in *Genteel Barbarism,* pp. 82–106.

17. Stanzel, *Narrative Situations in the Novel.*

18. Brushwood, *Genteel Barbarism,* p. 89.

19. Jorge Isaacs, *María* (Buenos Aires: Losada, 1969), p. 17. Subsequent quotations are from this edition.

20. Brushwood, *Genteel Barbarism,* pp. 102–103.

21. See Mejía Duque, *Isaacs y María,* p. 8.

22. Brushwood has made these two points in *Genteel Barbarism,* p. 85.

23. See Donald McGrady's discussion of the changes of personal pronouns in *Jorge Isaacs,* pp. 59–60.

24. Leo Bersani has explained as follows: "The exertion toward significant form in realist fiction serves the cause of significant, coherently structured characters. The revealing incident makes personality intelligible; real beginnings and definitive endings provide a temporal frame in which individuals don't merely exist, but move purposefully from one stage of being to another. . . . The richly detailed textures of characterization in realistic fiction seldom subvert the coherent wholeness of personality—or if they do, criticism has to deal with what we call 'interesting' esthetic values." See Bersani, *A Future for Astyanax,* pp. 55–56.

25. Bersani cites the work of Jacques Derrida in exposing this cultural assumption of a center. Bersani states: "*Les Chants de Maldoror* is one of literature's most daring enterprises of decentralization. It is a major document among modern efforts to break away from what Jacques Derrida has

been brilliantly anatomizing as the Western cultural habit of referring all experience to centers or beginnings, or origins of truth and being." See ibid., p. 196. See also Derrida, *De la grammatologie.*

26. Jaime Mejía Duque offers the following explanation of the language Efraín directs to his father: "En casa de Efraín los actos son solemnes y esta solemnidad aparece oficiada por el padre, a quien Efraín se refiere a menudo en lenguaje reverencial, adecuado a ese ambiente de culto patriarcado: 'La noble fisonomía de mi padre mostraba.'" See Mejía Duque, *Isaacs y María,* p. 107.

27. Ibid., p. 124.

28. I use the term *intertextuality* here and throughout this chapter not in the interest of discussing one writer's influence upon another nor in tracing "sources" but rather as originally proposed by Kristeva, and later developed by Culler, as a sign system. In this radical use of the term, as explained by Gerald Prince, it designates the relations between any text and the sum of knowledge, the potentially infinite network of codes and signifying practices that allows it to have meaning. In this chapter I am particularly interested in how codes established in *María* are absorbed, rewritten, or generally transformed in later texts from the Greater Cauca. See Kristeva, *Desire in Language: A Semiotic Approach to Literature and Art;* Culler, "Presuppositions and Intertextuality," in *The Pursuit of Signs;* Prince, *Dictionary of Narratology,* p. 46. In addition, see Genette, *Palimpsests;* Jenny, "The Strategy of Form," in Todorov, *French Literary Theory Today,* pp. 34–63; Pérez Firmat, "Apuntes para un modelo de la intertextualidad en literatura," pp. 1–14; Ricardou, *Pour une théorie du nouveau roman;* Riffaterre, *Semiotics of Poetry;* Riffaterre, *Text Production;* Sternberg, "Proteus in Quotation Land." I would like to express my appreciation to Harold Boudreau and Luis González-del-Valle for their thoughtful contributions to my understanding of intertextuality.

29. Adriano Scarpetta, *Julia* (Palmira: Imprenta de Teodoro Materón, 1871), p. 6.

30. Brushwood has set forth the idea of a "separation code" in *María* as follows: "Certain incidents and situations threaten the separation of the lovers or suggest the possibility of such a separation. This code might be referred to as 'suggestive.' Sometimes the sense of threatened separation derives from a logically expected sequence of events; in other instances, the suggestion of separation is metaphoric. Therefore, the subtlety of the suggestions varies greatly." See *Genteel Barbarism,* pp. 87–88.

31. Raúl Silva Holguín, *Eustaquio Palacios: de su vida y obra* (Cali: Impresora Feriva Ltda., 1977).

32. Critical studies on *El alférez real* are sparse. The main sources are the general histories, such as Curcio Altamar's. See also Martin, "*El Alférez Real,*" and Scarpetta, "*El Alférez Real.*"

33. Eustaquio Palacios, *El alférez real* (Bogotá: Ediciones Universales, 1985), p. 153. Subsequent quotations are from this edition.

34. Additional examples where the narrator of *El alférez real* mentions

specific dates in this seemingly obsessive fashion appear on pages 174, 177, 186, 198, 209, 218, 219, 230, 232, 233.

35. For an explanation of my use of the term *intertextuality*, see Kristeva, Culler, and Riffaterre, note 28.

36. See Brushwood, *Genteel Barbarism*, and Menton, "La estructura dualística de *María*."

37. Siemens, *Los juglares de Tuluá: Don Pedro Uribe*.

38. Luciano Rivera y Garrido in Silva Holguín, *Eustaquio Palacios*, p. 249.

39. Ibid., p. 253.

40. Ibid.

41. Porras Collantes, *Bibliografía de la novela en Colombia*, p. 308.

42. Isaías Gamboa, *La tierra nativa* (Medellín: Bedout, 1982), p. 52.

43. For studies on the modernity of Cali and the Greater Cauca region in general, see Webber and Ocampo Zamorano, comps., *Valores, desarrollo e historia*.

44. Guillermo Edmundo Chaves, *Chambú* (Medellín: Bedout, 1985), p. 253.

45. Diego Castrillón Arboleda, *José Tombé* (Bogotá: Editorial Antena, 1942), p. 143.

46. Diego Castrillón Arboleda, *Sol en Tambalimbú* (Bogotá: Editorial Kelly, 1949), p. 312.

47. Until the recent critical studies of Marvin A. Lewis, Arnoldo Palacios virtually had become a forgotten figure in Colombia. Nevertheless, Curcio Altamar dedicates a page to *Las estrellas son negras* in *Evolución de la novela en Colombia* (p. 210), and Arnoldo Palacios is mentioned briefly in Anderson Imbert, *Historia de la literatura hispanoamericana II*, and in López Tamés, *La narrativa actual de Colombia y su contexto social*. Richard L. Jackson dedicates a chapter to Palacios in *Black Writers in Latin America*.

48. See Lewis, *Treading the Ebony Path*. This book deals with these five writers.

49. Ibid., p. 16.

50. Arnoldo Palacios, *Las estrellas son negras* (Bogotá: Editorial La Revista, 1971), p. 33.

51. With respect to physicality and bodily functions in *Las estrellas son negras*, see Lewis, *Treading the Ebony Path*, pp. 19–21.

52. The idea I have set forth here of five conflicting discourses has its theoretical base, of course, in Bakhtin and his concepts of heteroglossia and dialogism. For Bakhtin, the heterogeneity found in fiction is a response to the basic condition governing the operation of meaning in any utterance—heteroglossia. Heteroglossia is in opposition to a concept of a static unitary language. Rather, it is language as a continuous flux of incorporated languages. Dialogism is the mode of a world dominated by heteroglossia. See Bakhtin, *The Dialogic Imagination*, p. 428.

53. These *figuras consagradas* represent the same official language sati-

rized by Gabriel García Márquez in "Los funerales de la mamá grande." For an analysis of this story's official language, see Williams, *Gabriel García Márquez*, pp. 41–57.

54. Lewis, *Treading the Ebony Path*, p. 21.

55. It could also be logically and successfully argued that the language of Christianity in this novel also represents a predominance of orality over writing. Even though the source of Christian language is writing (the Bible), this biblical language of originally oral sources is transmitted orally to the blacks of Chocó.

56. Lewis, *Treading the Ebony Path*, p. 25.

57. With respect to synonyms and antonyms, Riffaterre has stated the following: "An intertext is a corpus of texts, textual fragments, or textlike segments of the sociolect that shares a lexicon and, to a lesser extent, a syntax with the text we are reading (directly or indirectly) in the form of synonyms or, even conversely, in the form of antonyms. In addition, each member of this corpus is a structural homologue of the text: the depiction of a stormy night may serve as an intertext for a tableau of a peaceful day; crossing the trackless sands of the desert may be the intertext of furrowing the briny deep." See "Intertextual Representation," p. 142.

58. Lewis, *Treading the Ebony Path*, p. 26.

59. For a study on Carlos Arturo Truque, see Lewis, "The Literary Synthesizer," chapter 3 in ibid., pp. 38–62.

60. For additional analysis of *La tara del papa* and family tradition, see Williams, *Una década de la novela colombiana*, pp. 58–61.

61. Gustavo Alvarez Gardeazábal, *El bazar de los idiotas* (Bogotá: Plaza y Janés, 1974). Subsequent quotations are from this edition.

62. For more detailed analysis of chapters 6, 7, 10, 12, and 14, see Williams, "Structure and Transformation of Reality in Alvarez Gardeazábal."

63. Jenny, "The Strategy of Form," p. 61.

7. The Modern and Postmodern Novel (1965–1987)

1. In chapter 2, I review problems inherent in Curcio Altamar's vision of a "national" novel since the independence.

2. For an overview of the contributions of *Mito*, see Romero, "Los poetas de 'Mito.'"

3. Regional publishing operations had been flourishing in Colombia since the 1920s, as has been mentioned in previous chapters. Consequently, Tercer Mundo Editores had numerous predecessors, including Ediciones Espiral, which was active in the publication of Colombian novels during the 1950s. Nevertheless, it was not until the advent of Tercer Mundo Editores and the Editorial Plaza y Janés that truly professional criteria were applied for the selection, publication, and distribution of the Colombian novel.

4. For a discussion of the crisis of the modern and the advent of the postmodern, see Foster, "Postmodernism: A Preface," in *The Anti-Aesthetic*, pp. ix–xvi.

5. Kadir, in *Questing Fictions*, points out that Lyotard has discussed a postmodern that is not "after the modern." See Kadir, *Questing Fictions*, and Lyotard, *The Postmodern Condition*.

6. García Márquez has explained how *The Autumn of the Patriarch* evolved as a synthesis of numerous Latin American dictators in Plinio Apuleyo Mendoza, *El olor de la guayaba* (Bogotá: Oveja Negra, 1982), p. 86.

7. García Márquez has explained how *The Autumn of the Patriarch* contains images from different Caribbean nations. See ibid., p. 89.

8. I have delineated the structure of *The Autumn of the Patriarch* in much more detail in "The Dynamic Structure of García Márquez's *El otoño del patriarca.*"

9. José Miguel Oviedo has noted the progression in sentence length. See "García Márquez," p. 7.

10. Seymour Menton has suggested that even what is seen cannot be believed, yet only that which is seen offers the possibility of being believed. See *La novela colombiana*, pp. 281–322.

11. Gabriel García Márquez, *Love in the Time of Cholera* (New York: Alfred A. Knopf, 1988), p. 306.

12. For an overview of Zapata Olivella's fiction, see chapter 5, "From Oppression to Liberation," in Lewis, *Treading the Ebony Path*.

13. Marvin Lewis discusses myth in *Las memorias del odio* in "Violencia y resistencia," pp. 15–20.

14. Ong defines secondary orality as the orality of the new technology, such as cassettes and television. See *Orality and Literacy*, pp. 136–138.

15. *Pero sigo siendo el rey* was adapted as an ongoing commercial television program in Colombia, the equivalent of a short-run sitcom or soap opera in the United States. Other novelists, such as Mejía Vallejo and Alvarez Gardeazábal, had novels adapted to television programs in the 1980s.

16. Alvaro Mutis continues his trilogy with *Ilona llega con la lluvia* (1988) and *Un bel morir* (1989). These books are not mentioned in the body of this study because they appeared after 1987.

17. Studies that have informed my understanding of the controversial term *postmodern fiction* include Foster, ed., *The Anti-Aesthetic*; González Echevarría, *La ruta de Severo Sarduy*; Hassan, *The Postmodern Turn*; Hutcheon, *A Poetics of Postmodernism*; Kaplan, ed., *Postmodernism and Its Discontents*; McHale, *Postmodernist Fiction*; Newman, *The Post-Modern Aura*. I reiterate that my vision of the postmodern, as presented in this chapter, is as a thread of the modern. The differences between a modern impulse and a postmodern gesture are not of essence but of emphasis. Consequently, specific elements of individual "modern" or "postmodern" texts should not be considered necessarily exclusive to one particular thread of the modern or postmodern projects. My presentation of postmodern fiction in Colombia should not be interpreted as an attempt to provide an exhaustive or conclusive definition for the term *postmodern*. Rather, I intend to

explain how several contemporary Colombian novelists are creating fictions with tendencies similar to those some critics of North American, Latin American, and European culture are describing as postmodern.

18. Two critics who have described Sarduy and Cabrera Infante as postmoderns are Roberto González Echevarría and William H. Gass. See González Echevarría, "Sarduy, the Boom, and the Post-Boom," and Gass, "The First Seven Pages of the Boom."

19. See Kerr, *Suspended Fictions*, p. 24.

20. Ibid.

21. For a study of the Latin American novel as family romance, see Kadir, *Questing Fictions*.

22. R. H. Moreno-Durán, *Los felinos del Canciller* (Barcelona: Ediciones Destino, 1987), p. 28. All quotations are from this edition.

23. I use the term *intertextuality* as set forth by Kristeva, explored in the present study in chapter 6.

24. For a discussion of the institutionalized concept of the Athens of South America, see chapters 2 and 3.

25. See Moreno-Durán, "Fragmentos de *La Augusta Sílaba*," pp. 861–881.

26. Moreno-Durán has explained that Cortázar was of great importance to his literary formation. Personal interview, Boulder, Colorado, November 18, 1988.

27. For a study of intertextuality in this novel, see Fajardo, "Culminación de una trilogía," pp. 121–129.

28. For a study of this novel as a documentary work, see Gerdes, "*Estaba la pájara pinta sentada en el verde limón.*"

29. Darío Jaramillo Agudelo was in the University of Iowa Writer's Program in 1974–75.

Bibliography

Acosta de Samper, Soledad. "La misión de la escritora en Hispanoamérica." In *La mujer en la sociedad moderna*. Paris: Garnier Hermanos, 1895. Republished in *Revista de Estudios Colombianos* 5 (1988): 3–6.

Alonso, Carlos J. *The Spanish American Regional Novel: Modernity and Autochthony*. Cambridge: Cambridge University Press, 1990.

Alter, Robert. *Partial Magic: The Novel as a Self-Conscious Genre*. Berkeley: University of California Press, 1975.

Anderson Imbert, Enrique. *Historia de la literatura hispanoamericana*. Vol. 2. Mexico City: Fondo de Cultura Económica, 1954.

———. "Prólogo." In *María*, by Jorge Isaacs. Mexico City: Fondo de Cultura Económica, 1951.

Arango Ferrer, Javier. *Dos horas de literatura colombiana*. Bogotá: Instituto Colombiano de Cultura, 1978.

Araújo, Helena. *Signos y mensajes*. Bogotá: Instituto Colombiano de Cultura, 1976.

Arciniegas, Germán. *Biografía del Caribe*. Bogotá: Plaza y Janés, 1978.

———. *Genio y figura de Jorge Isaacs*. Buenos Aires: Editorial Universitaria de Buenos Aires, 1967.

Arias Trujillo, Bernardo. *Diario de emociones*. Medellín: Bedout, 1963.

Arrom, Juan José. *Esquema generacional de las letras hispanoamericanas*. Bogotá: Instituto Caro y Cuervo, 1963.

Ayala Poveda, Fernando. *Novelistas colombianos contemporáneos*. Bogotá: Universidad Central, 1983.

Bagley, Bruce. "The National Front and Beyond: Politics, Public Power and Public Policy in an Inclusionary Authoritarian Régime." Occasional Paper No. 4, Central American and Caribbean Program, School of Advanced International Studies, Johns Hopkins University, June 1984.

Bakhtin, Mikhail. *The Dialogic Imagination*. Austin: University of Texas Press, 1981.

Bal, Mieke. *Narratology: Introduction to the Theory of Narrative.* Toronto: University of Toronto Press, 1985.
Barth, John. "The Literature of Exhaustion." *Atlantic Monthly* (August 1967): 29–34.
Bedoya, Luis Iván, and Augusto Escobar, *Conozca a Eduardo Caballero Calderón.* Medellín: Editorial Lealón, 1984.
Bell Lemus, Gustavo. *El caribe colombiano: selección de textos históricos.* Barranquilla: Ediciones Uninorte, 1988.
Bergquist, Charles. *Coffee and Conflict in Colombia, 1886–1910.* Durham, N.C.: Duke University Press, 1978.
Berry, Wendell. "The Regional Motive." In *A Continuous Harmony: Essays in Cultural and Agricultural,* pp. 63–70. San Diego: Harcourt, Brace, Jovanovich, 1970.
Bersani, Leo. *A Future for Astyanax.* Boston: Little, Brown and Company, 1969.
Beutler, Gisela. *Estudios sobre el romancero español en Colombia en su tradición escrita y oral desde la época de la conquista hasta la actualidad.* Bogotá: Instituto Caro y Cuervo, 1977.
Bickerton, Derek, and Aquiles Escalante. *Palenquero: A Spanish-based Creole of North Carolina. Lingua 24.* Amsterdam: North Holland Publishing Company, 1970.
Bloom, Harold. *The Anxiety of Influence: A Theory of Poetry.* New York: Oxford University Press, 1973.
Brooks, Cleanth, and Robert Penn Warren. *Understanding Fiction.* New York: Appleton-Century-Crofts, 1959.
Brown, Donald F. "Chateaubriand and the Story of Feliciana in Jorge Isaacs' *María.*" *Modern Language Notes* 62 (1947): 326–329.
Brushwood, John S. *Genteel Barbarism.* Lincoln: University of Nebraska Press, 1981.
———. "José Félix Fuenmayor y el regionalismo de García Márquez." *Texto crítico* 7 (May–August 1978): 110–115.
———. *The Spanish-American Novel: A Twentieth Century Survey.* Austin: University of Texas Press, 1975.
Bull, William. "Nature and Anthropomorphism in *La vorágine.*" *Romanic Review* 39 (December 1948): 307–318.
Burgos, Fernando, ed. *Prosa hispánica de vanguardia.* Madrid: Discurso/Orígenes, 1986.
Bushnell, David. *The Santander Regime in Gran Colombia.* Newark: University of Delaware Press, 1954.
Caballero Calderón, Eduardo. *Brevario del Quijote.* Madrid: Aguilar, 1977.
Callan, Richard. "The Archetype of Psychic Renewal in *La vorágine.*" *Hispania* 54, no. 3 (September 1971): 470–476.
Camacho Carreño, José. "Arias Trujillo, o el criollismo." In *Diccionario de emociones,* ed. Bernardo Arias Trujillo, pp. 5–15. Medellín: Bedout, 1963.
Captain-Hidalgo, Yvonne. "El espacio del tiempo en *Changó, el gran putas.*" In *Ensayos de literatura colombiana,* ed. Raymond L. Williams, pp. 157–166. Bogotá: Plaza y Janés, 1985.

Carrasquilla, Rafael María. *"Entre primos."* In José Manuel Marroquín, *Entre primos*, ed. Cecilia de Mendoza, pp. 472–489. Bogotá: Instituto Caro y Cuervo, 1978.

Carrasquilla, Tomás. "Carta a Max Grillo." In *Obras completas*, vol. 2, pp. 752–761. Madrid: Ediciones y Publicaciones Españolas, 1952.

———. "Homilia No. 2." In *Obras completas*, vol. 2, pp. 673–689. Medellín: Bedout, 1964.

Castillo, Eduardo. *"La vorágine."* In *La vorágine: textos críticos*, ed. Montserrat Ordóñez, pp. 41–44. Bogotá: Alianza Editorial Colombiana, 1987.

Charry Lara, Fernando. *José Asunción Silva: vida y creación.* Bogotá: Procultura, 1985.

———. "Los poetas de 'Los Nuevos.'" *Revista Iberoamericana* 128–129 (July–December 1984): 633–681.

Ciplijauskaité, Birute. "Foreshadowing as a Technique and Theme in *One Hundred Years of Solitude.*" *Books Abroad* 47, no. 3 (1973): 479–484.

Culler, Jonathan. *In Pursuit of Signs: Semiotics, Literature, Deconstruction.* Ithaca: Cornell University Press, 1981.

Curcio Altamar, Antonio. *Evolución de la novela en Colombia.* Bogotá: Instituto Colombiano de Cultura, 1975.

Davis, Robert H. *Historical Dictionary of Colombia.* Metuchen, N.J.: Scarecrow Press, 1977.

De León Hazera, Lydia. *La novela de la selva hispanoamericana.* Bogotá: Instituto Caro y Cuervo, 1971.

Delpar, Helen. *The Red against the Blue: The Liberal Party in Colombian Politics, 1863–1899.* University: University of Alabama Press, 1981.

Derrida, Jacques. *De la grammatologie.* Paris: Minuit, 1967.

Duffey, Frank. *The Early Cuadro de Costumbres in Colombia.* University of North Carolina Studies in Romance Languages and Literatures, No. 26. Chapel Hill: University of North Carolina Press, 1956.

Eagleton, Terry. *Marxism and Literary Criticism.* Berkeley: University of California Press, 1976.

———. *Theory of Literature: An Introduction.* Minneapolis: University of Minnesota Press, 1983.

Embeita, María J. "El tema del amor imposible en *María* de Jorge Isaacs." *Revista Iberoamericana* 32, no. 61 (1966): 109–112.

Escobar, Arturo. "The Professionalization and Institutionalization of 'Development' in Colombia in the Early Post–World War II Period." *Occasional Papers in Latin American Studies,* Stanford/Berkeley Joint Center for Latin American Studies, No. 14, Spring 1988.

Escobar Calle, Miguel. "Las revistas literarias en Antioquia." In *La historia de Antioquia,* supplement to *El colombiano,* February 24, 1988, pp. 335–338.

Fajardo, Diógenes. "Culminación de una trilogía: *Finale capriccioso con Madonna.*" *Hispamérica* 48 (1987): 121–129.

Fals Borda, Orlando. *Historia doble de la costa.* 4 vols. Bogotá: Carlos Valencia Editores, 1979.

Fals Borda, Orlando, Germán Guzmán Campos, and Eduardo Umaña Luna.

La Violencia en Colombia. Bogotá: Carlos Valencia Editores, 1980.

Fields, Wayne. "*One Hundred Years of Solitude* and New World Storytelling." *Latin American Literary Review* 15, no. 29 (January–June 1987): 73–88.

Fluharty, Vernon Lee. *Dance of Millions: Military Rule and the Social Revolution in Colombia 1930–1956.* Pittsburgh: University of Pittsburgh Press, 1957.

Fogelquist, Alan F. *Revolutionary Theory and Practice in Colombia.* Buffalo, N.Y.: Council on International Studies, 1981.

Foster, Hal, ed. *The Anti-Aesthetic: Essays on Postmodern Culture.* Seattle, Wash.: Bay Press, 1983.

Foucault, Michel. *The Archaeology of Knowledge.* New York: Pantheon, 1972.

———. *Language, Counter-Memory, Practice.* Selected essays and interviews, ed. with an introduction by Donald F. Bouchard and trans. Donald F. Bouchard and Sherry Simon. Ithaca: Cornell University Press, 1977.

———. *The Order of Things.* New York: Random House, 1970.

Franco, Jean. *The Modern Culture of Latin America: Society and the Artist.* New York: F. A. Praeger, 1967.

———. "Narrador, Autor, Superestrella: la narrativa latinoamericana en la época de la cultura de masas." *Revista Iberoamericana* 47, nos. 114–115 (1981): 129–148.

Friedemann, Nina S. *Carnaval en Barranquilla.* Bogotá: Editorial La Rosa, 1985.

Friedemann, Nina S., and Jaime Arocha. *Herederos del jaguar y la anaconda.* Bogotá: Carlos Valencia Editores, 1985.

Friedemann, Nina S. de, and Carlos Patiño Rosselli, *Lengua y sociedad en el Palenque de San Basilio.* Bogotá: Publicaciones del Instituto Caro y Cuervo, 1983.

Fuenmayor, Alfonso. *Crónicas sobre el Grupo de Barranquilla.* Bogotá: Instituto Colombiano de Cultura/Gobernación del Atlántico, 1978.

García Márquez, Gabriel. "La literatura colombiana, un fraude a la nación." In Gabriel García Márquez, *Obra periodística,* vol. 4, compilation and prologue by Jacques Gilard, pp. 787–793. Barcelona: Bruguera, 1983.

Gass, William H. "The First Seven Pages of the Boom." *Latin American Literary Review* 15, no. 29 (January–June 1987): 33–56.

Genette, Gérard. *Figures III.* Paris: Editions du Seuil, 1972. (English edition: *Narrative Discourse: An Essay in Method.* Ithaca: Cornell University Press, 1980.)

———. *Palimpsests: La Littérature au second degré.* Paris: Seuil, 1982.

Gerdes, Dick. "*Estaba la pájara pinta en el verde limón:* novela testimonial/documental de 'la violencia' en Colombia." *Revista de Estudios Colombianos* 2 (1987): 21–26.

Gilard, Jacques. "García Márquez, le groupe de Barranquilla, et Faulkner." *Caravelle* 27 (1976): 159–170.

———. "Un eco temprano de la aparición de *Bestiario,* Barranquilla, 1951."

In *Lo lúdico y lo fantástico en la obra de Cortázar,* ed. Saúl Yurkiévich et al., pp. 33–44. Caracas: Editorial Fundamentos, 1986.

Girard, René. *Violence and the Sacred.* Baltimore: Johns Hopkins University Press, 1977.

Gómez Ocampo, Gilberto. *Entre "María" y "La vorágine": la literatura colombiana finisecular (1886–1903).* Bogotá: Ediciones Fondo Cultural Cafetero, 1988.

Gómez Restrepo, Antonio. *Historia de la literatura colombiana.* Bogotá: Imprenta Nacional, 1945.

———. *La literatura colombiana.* New York: Hispanic Institute, 1963.

———. *"La vorágine."* In *La vorágine: textos críticos,* ed. Montserrat Ordóñez, pp. 45–48.

González, Aníbal. *La novela modernista hispanoamericana.* Madrid: Gredos, Biblioteca Románica Hispánica, 1987.

González Echevarría, Roberto. *"Cien años de soledad:* Novel as Myth and Archive." *MLN* 99, no. 2 (March 1984): 358–380.

———. "Redescubrimiento del mundo perdido: el *Facundo* de Sarmiento." *Revista Iberoamericana* 143 (April–June 1988): 385–406.

———. *La ruta de Severo Sarduy.* Hanover, N.H.: Ediciones del Norte, 1987.

———. "Sarduy, the Boom, and the Post-Boom." *Latin American Literary Review* 15, no. 29 (January–June 1987): 57–72.

———. *The Voice of the Masters: Writing and Authority in Modern Latin American Literature.* Austin: University of Texas Press, 1985.

Goody, Jack, ed. *Literacy in Traditional Societies.* Cambridge: Cambridge University Press, 1968.

Green, Joan R. "La estructura del narrador y el modo narrativo de *La vorágine.*" *Cuadernos Hispanoamericanos* 205 (January 1967): 101–108.

Greiff Obregón, Luis de. *Semblanzas y comentarios.* Medellín: Ediciones Autores Antioqueños, 1985.

Guerra Cunningham, Lucía. "La modalidad de la subjetividad romántica en la narrativa de Soledad Acosta de Samper." In *Soledad Acosta de Samper: una nueva lectura,* ed. Montserrat Ordóñez, pp. 353–367. Bogotá: Ediciones Fondo Cultural Cafetero, 1988.

Guillén Martínez, Fernando. *La regeneración: primer frente nacional.* Bogotá: Carlos Valencia Editores, 1986.

Gutiérrez Azopardo, Ildefonso. *Historia del negro en Colombia.* Bogotá: Editorial Nueva América, 1986.

Gutiérrez Girardot. "La literatura colombiana en el siglo XX." In *Manual de historia de Colombia,* ed. Helena Araújo et al., pp. 447–536. Bogotá: Instituto Colombiano de Cultura, 1982.

———. *"De sobremesa:* el arte en la sociedad burguesa moderna." In *José Asunción Silva: vida y creación,* ed. Fernando Charry Lara, pp. 445–456.

Hagen, Everett E. *El cambio social en Colombia: el factor humano en el desarrollo económico.* Bogotá: Tercer Mundo, 1963.

Hassan, Ihab. *The Postmodern Turn: Essays in Postmodern Theory and Culture.* Columbus: Ohio State University Press, 1987.

Havelock, Eric A. *The Muse Learns to Write: Reflections on Orality and*

Literacy from Antiquity to the Present. New Haven and London: Yale University Press, 1986.

——. *Preface to Plato.* Cambridge, Mass.: Belknap Press of Harvard University Press, 1963.

Helguera, J. León. "The Problem of Liberalism versus Conservatism in Colombia: 1849–1885." In *Latin American History: Select Problems,* ed. Frederick B. Pike, pp. 224–258. New York: Harcourt, Brace and World, 1969.

Housková, Anna. "Tipo de novela mundonovista." *Revista de Crítica Literaria* 13, no. 26 (1987): 67–85.

Hutcheon, Linda. *A Poetics of Postmodernism: History, Theory, Fiction.* New York: Routledge, 1988.

Isaacs, Jorge. *Canciones y coplas populares.* Bogotá: Procultura, 1985.

Iser, Wolfgang. *The Implied Reader: Patterns of Communication in Prose Fiction from Bunyan to Beckett.* Baltimore: Johns Hopkins University Press, 1974.

Jackson, Richard L. *Black Writers in Latin America.* Albuquerque: University of New Mexico Press, 1979.

Jaramillo Londoño, Agustín. *Testamento del paisa.* Medellín: Ediciones Susaeta, 1981.

Jaramillo Uribe, Jaime. *El pensamiento colombiano.* Bogotá: Editorial Temis, 1982.

Jaramillo Zuluaga, Eduardo. "La poesía en *Cuatro años a bordo de mí mismo.*" *Revista Casa Silva* 1 (January 1988): 29–42.

Jenny, Laurent. "The Strategy of Form." In *French Literary Theory Today,* ed. Tzvetan Todorov. Cambridge: Cambridge University Press, 1982.

Jiménez, Margarita, and Sandro Sideri. *Historia del desarrollo regional en Colombia.* Bogotá: Fondo Editorial CEREC, 1985.

Kadir, Djelal. *Questing Fictions: Latin America's Family Romance.* Minneapolis: University of Minnesota Press, Theory of History of Literature, 1986.

Kerr, Lucille. *Suspended Fictions: Reading Novels by Manuel Puig.* Urbana: University of Illinois Press, 1987.

Kline, Harvey. *Colombia: A Portrait of Unity and Diversity.* Boulder, Colo.: Westview Press, 1983.

Kooreman, Thomas. "Two Novelistic Views of the Bogotazo." *Latin American Literary Review* 3, no. 5 (1974): 131–135.

Kristeva, Julia. *Desire in Language: A Semiotic Approach to Literature and Art.* New York: Columbia University Press, 1980.

Laverde Toscano, María Cristina, and Luz Helena Sánchez Gómez, eds. *Voces insurgentes.* Bogotá: Universidad Central, 1986.

Levine, Daniel H. *Religion and Politics in Latin America.* Princeton, N.J.: Princeton University Press, 1981.

Levy, Kurt. "*Marea de ratas:* testimonio de masa o dilema de individuo?" *Revista de estudios colombianos* 1 (1986): 29–32.

——. *Tomás Carrasquilla.* Medellín: Instituto de Integración Cultural, 1985.

Lewis, Marvin A. *Treading the Ebony Path: Ideology and Violence in Contemporary Afro-Colombian Prose Fiction*. Columbia: University of Missouri Press, 1987.

———. "Violencia y resistencia: una perspectiva literaria afrocolombiana." *Revista de Estudios Colombianos* 6 (1986): 15–20.

Londoño V., Santiago. "La nueva lira y su época." *Boletín Cultural y Bibliográfico* 23, no. 9 (1986): 50–53.

López Michelsen, Alfonso. "Ensayo sobre la influencia semítica en *María*." *Revista de las Indias* 20, no. 6 (1944): 5–10.

López Tamés, Román. *La narrativa actual de Colombia y su contexto social*. Valladolid: Universidad de Valladolid, 1975.

Lord, Albert. *The Singer of Tales*. Cambridge, Mass.: Harvard University Press, Harvard Studies in Comparative Literature, 1960.

Love, Joseph L. "An Approach to Regionalism." In *New Approaches to Latin American History*, ed. Richard Graham and Peter Smith, pp. 137–155. Austin: University of Texas Press, 1974.

Loveluck, Juan. "Aproximación a *La vorágine*." *Atenea* 39 (July–September 1962): 92–117.

———. "*De sobremesa*, novela desconocida del modernismo." *Revista Iberoamericana* 31, no. 59 (January–June 1965): 17–32.

Lyday, Leon, and Luis Carlos Herrera et al. "Trayectoria de un novelista: Eduardo Caballero Calderón." *Boletín Cultural y bibliográfico* 12, no. 2 (1969): 13–103.

Lyotard, Jean-François. *The Postmodern Condition: A Report on Knowledge*. Minneapolis: University of Minnesota Press, 1984.

Magnarelli, Sharon. *The Lost Rib: Female Characters in the Spanish-American Novel*. Lewisburg: Bucknell University Press, 1985.

———. "*María* and History." *Hispanic Review* 49 (1981): 209–217.

Manrique Terán, Guillermo. "*La vorágine*." In *La vorágine: textos críticos*, ed. Montserrat Ordóñez, pp. 335–354.

Martin, John L. "*El Alférez Real*: Another Novel of the Cauca Valley." *Hispania* 24 (1941): 193–196.

Maya, Rafael. *Obra crítica*. Vols. 1 and 2. Bogotá: Banco de la República, 1982.

McCarty, Nancy, and Seymour Menton. "La novelística de la costa colombiana: especulaciones históricas." *Revista de estudios colombianos* 3 (1987): 35–38.

McGrady, Donald. "Las fuentes de *María* de Isaacs." *Hispanófila* 24 (1966): 43–54.

———. *María*. Boston: G. H. Hall, 1972.

———. *La novela histórica en Colombia*. Bogotá: Editorial Kelly, n.d.

McGreevey, William Paul. *An Economic History of Colombia*. Cambridge: Cambridge University Press, 1971.

McHale, Brian. *Postmodernist Fiction*. New York: Methuen, 1987.

McLuhan, Marshall. *The Gutenberg Galaxy: The Making of Typographic Man*. Toronto: University of Toronto Press, 1962.

McMurray, George. *Gabriel García Márquez.* New York: Ungar Publishing Company, 1977.

Megenney, William W. *El palenquero: un lenguaje post-criollo de Colombia.* Bogotá: Instituto Caro y Cuervo, 1986.

Mejía Duque, Jaime. *Isaacs y María: el hombre y su novela.* Bogotá: La Carreta, 1979.

————. *Nueve ensayos literarios.* Bogotá: Instituto Colombiano de Cultura, 1986.

Mejía Vallejo, Manuel. *Hojas de papel.* Bogotá: Universidad Nacional de Colombia, 1985.

Mejía Vallejo, Manuel, et al. *María umár allá del paraíso.* Cali: Alonso Quijada Editores, 1984.

Mena, Lucila Inés. *La función de la historia en Cien años de soledad.* Barcelona: Plaza y Janés Editores, 1978.

Mendoza, Plinio Apuleyo. *El olor de la guayaba.* Bogotá: La Oveja Negra, 1982.

Menton, Seymour. "La estructura dualística de *María.*" *Thesaurus* 25 (1970): 1–27.

————. *La novela colombiana: planetas y satélites.* Bogotá: Plaza y Janés Editores, 1978.

Minta, Stephen. *García Márquez: Writer of Colombia.* New York: Harper and Row, 1987.

Molina, Gerardo. *Las ideas liberales en Colombia 1849–1940.* Bogotá: Universidad Nacional de Colombia, 1970.

Montoya Candamil, Jaime. *Manuel Mejía Vallejo: vida, obra y filosofía literaria.* Bogotá: Universidad Central, 1984.

Morales Benítez, Otto. *Conozca a Manuel Mejía Vallejo.* Medellín: Extensión Universidad de Antioquia, 1982.

————. *Perfiles literarios de Antioquia.* Bogotá: Universidad Nacional de Colombia, 1987.

Moreno Durán, R. H. *De la barbarie a la imaginación.* Barcelona: Tusquets Editores, 1976.

————. "Fragmentos de *La augusta sílaba.*" *Revista Iberoamericana* 128–129 (July–December 1984): 861–881.

Naranjo M., Enrique. "Alrededor de *María.*" *Revista Iberoamericana* 5, no. 9 (1942): 103–108.

Naranjo Villegas, Abel. *Generaciones colombianas.* Bogotá: Banco de la República, n.d.

Neale-Silva, Eduardo. *Horizonte humano. Vida de José Eustasio Rivera.* Madison: University of Wisconsin Press, 1960.

Newman, Charles. *The Post-Modern Aura: The Act of Fiction in an Age of Inflation.* Chicago: Northwestern University Press, 1985.

Nichols, Theodore E. *Tres puertos.* Bogotá: Biblioteca Banco Popular, 1973.

Nieto Caballero, Luis Eduardo. *Libros colombianos.* Bogotá: Editorial Minerva, 1928.

Olivera, Otto. "María, tema predilecto de Isaacs." *Symposium* 14 (1960): 7–25.

————. "El romanticismo de José Eustasio Rivera." *Revista Iberoamericana* 17 (December 1952): 41–61.

Ong, Walter. *Fighting for Life: Contest, Sexuality, and Consciousness.* Ithaca: Cornell University Press, 1981.

————. *Orality and Literacy: The Technologizing of the Word.* London and New York: Methuen, 1982.

————. "The Writer's Audience Is Always a Fiction." *PMLA* 90, no. 1 (January 1975): 9–21.

Ordóñez, Montserrat. "Elisa Mújica: el recuerdo de Catalina." In *Voces insurgentes,* ed. María Cristina Laverde Toscano and Luz Helena Sánchez Gómez, pp. 51–67. Bogotá: Universidad Central, 1986.

————, ed. *Soledad Acosta de Samper: una nueva lectura.* Bogotá: Ediciones Fondo Cultural Cafetero, 1988.

————, ed. *La vorágine: textos críticos.* Bogotá: Alianza Editorial Colombiana, 1987.

Orjuela, Héctor H. "J. K. Huysmans, María Bashkirtseff y Silva." In *José Asunción Silva: vida y creación,* ed. Fernando Charry Lara, pp. 471–484.

————. *"De sobremesa" y otros estudios sobre José Asunción Silva.* Bogotá: Instituto Caro y Cuervo, 1976.

Ortega, Julio, ed. *Gabriel García Márquez and the Powers of Fiction.* Austin: University of Texas Press, 1988.

————. *Poetics of Change: The New Spanish-American Narrative.* Austin: University of Texas Press, 1984.

————. "La risa de la tribu: los signos del intercambio en *Cien años de soledad." Nueva Revista de Filología Hispánica* 33, no. 2 (1984): 396–430.

Osorio Lizarazo, José Antonio. *Novelas y crónicas.* Bogotá: Instituto Colombiano de Cultura, 1978.

Ospina, Juan Manuel, ed. *Los estudios regionales en Colombia.* Medellín: Fondo Rotatorio de Publicaciones FAES, 1982.

Oviedo, José Miguel. "García Márquez: la novela como taumaturgia." *American Hispanist* 1, no. 2 (October 1975): 7–9.

Palacios, Marco. "La Atenas Sudamericana." *Boletín Cultural y Bibliográfico* 25 (1988): 55–64.

————. *El café en Colombia, 1850–1970.* Bogotá: El Colegio de México/El Ancora Editores, 1983.

Pardo, Mauricio. *Literatura Oral Emberá* [sic]. Bogotá: Centro Jorge Eliécer Gaitán, 1984.

Park, James W. *Rafael Núñez and the Politics of Colombian Regionalism.* Baton Rouge: Louisiana State University Press, 1985.

Parry, Milman. *L'Epithète traditionelle dans Homère.* Paris: Société Editrice Les Belles Lettres, 1928.

Parsons, James. *Antioqueño Colonization in Western Colombia.* Berkeley: University of California Press, 1968.

Peña Gutiérrez, Isaías. *La narrativa del frente nacional.* Bogotá: Universidad Central, 1982.

Pérez Firmat, Gustavo. "Apuntes para un modelo de la intertextualidad en literatura." *Romanic Review* 69 (1978): 1–14.

————. *Idle Fictions: The Hispanic Vanguard Novel, 1926–1934.* Durham, N.C.: Duke University Press, 1982.

Picón Garfield, Evelyn. "*De sobremesa:* José Asunción Silva: el diario íntimo y la mujer prerrafaelita." *Revista de Estudios Colombianos* 2 (1987): 3–12.

Pinard, Mary. "Time In and Out of Solitude in *One Hundred Years of Solitude.*" In *Critical Perspectives on Gabriel García Márquez,* ed. Bradley A. Shaw and Nora Vera-Godwin, pp. 65–72. Lincoln, Nebr.: Society of Spanish and Spanish-American Studies, 1986.

Piotrowski, Bogdan. *La realidad nacional colombiana en su narrativa contemporánea.* Bogotá: Instituto Caro y Cuervo, 1988.

Pope, Randolph. "*La vorágine:* la autobiografía de un intelectual." In *The Analysis of Literary Texts: Current Trends in Methodology,* ed. Randolph Pope, pp. 256–267. Ypsilanti, Mich.: Bilingual Press, 1980.

Porras Collantes, Ernesto. *Bibliografía de la novela en Colombia.* Bogotá: Instituto Caro y Cuervo, 1976.

Posada, Consuelo. *Canción vallenata y tradición oral.* Medellín: Universidad de Antioquia, 1986.

Preston Hyland, Richard. *Sociedad y economía en el Valle del Cauca, Tomo IV: el crédito y la economía.* Bogotá: Banco Popular, 1983.

Prince, Gerald. *Narratology: The Form and Functioning of Narrative.* Berlin: Mouton, 1982.

Quiroz Otero, Ciro. *Vallenato: hombre y canto.* Bogotá: Icaro Editores, 1982.

Rama, Angel. *La ciudad letrada.* Hanover, N.H.: Ediciones del Norte, 1984.

Ramos, Oscar Gerardo. *De Manuela a Macondo.* Bogotá: Instituto Colombiano de Cultura, 1972.

————. "Mujer, paisaje y ambiente en la novela *María.*" *Universidad de Antioquia* 171 (1968): 169–193.

Ricardou, Jean. *Pour une théorie du nouveau roman.* Paris: Seuil, 1971.

Riffaterre, Michael. "Intertextual Representation: On Mimesis As Interpretive Discourse." *Critical Inquiry* 11 (September 1984): 141–162.

————. *Semiotics of Poetry.* Bloomington: Indiana University Press, 1978.

————. *Text Production,* trans. Teres Lyons. New York: Columbia University Press, 1983.

Rimmon-Kenan, Shlomith. *Narrative Fiction.* New York: Methuen, 1983.

Rodríguez Monegal, Emir. "*One Hundred Years of Solitude:* The Last Three Pages." *Books Abroad* 47, no. 3 (1973): 485–489.

Rojas G., José María. *Sociedad y economía en el Valle del Cauca Tomo V: empresario y tecnología en la formación del sector azucarero en Colombia 1860–1980.* Bogotá: Banco Popular, 1983.

Romero, Armando. "La novela colombiana de entreguerras." *Revista Iberoamericana* 141 (October–December 1987): 861–885.

————. *Las palabras están en situación.* Bogotá: Procultura, 1985.

————. "Los poetas de 'Mito,'" *Revista Iberoamericana* 128–129 (July–December 1984): 689–755.

Ruiz Gómez, Darío. *Proceso de la cultura en Antioquia.* Medellín: Ediciones Autores Antioqueños, vol. 33, 1987.

Safford, Frank. *The Ideal of the Practical: Colombia's Struggle to Form a Technical Elite.* Austin: University of Texas Press, 1976.

Sánchez Montenegro, Víctor. "Jorge Isaacs y 'El Mosaico.'" *Bolívar* 19 (1953): 669–800.

Scarpetta, Oswaldo. "*El Alférez Real.*" *Boletín de la Academia de Historia del Valle del Cuenca* 28, no. 118 (1960): 627–633.

Schanzer, George O. "Lo 'MOD' del modernismo: *De sobremesa.*" In *José Asunción Silva: vida y creación,* ed. Fernando Charry Lara.

Schwartz, Kessel. *A New History of Spanish American Fiction.* Coral Gables: University of Miami Press, 1972.

Secretaría de Información y Prensa. *Un pueblo, un canto, y un cantor.* Bogotá: Secretaría de Información y Prensa, 1985.

Seung, Thomas K. *Semiotics and Thematics in Hermeneutics.* New York: Columbia University Press, 1982.

Shaw, Bradley, and Nora Vera-Godwin. *Critical Perspectives on Gabriel García Márquez.* Lincoln, Nebr.: Society of Spanish and Spanish-American Studies, 1986.

Siemens, William L. *Los juglares de Tuluá: Don Pedro Uribe.* Cali: Impresora Feriva Ltda., 1977.

Silva Holguín, Raúl. *Eustaquio Palacios: de su vida y obra.* Cali: Impresora Feriva Ltda., 1977.

Sohn, Guansu. *La novela colombiana de protesta social.* Bogotá: Ediciones UNINCCA, 1978.

Souza, Raymond D. *La historia en la novela hispanoamericana moderna.* Bogotá: Tercer Mundo Editores, 1988.

Spires, Robert C. *Beyond the Metafictional Mode: Directions in the Modern Spanish Novel.* Lexington: University of Kentucky Press, 1984.

Stanzel, Franz. *Narrative Situations in the Novel.* Bloomington: Indiana University Press, 1971.

Steinberg, Meir. "Proteus in Quotation Land." *Poetics Today* 3, no. 2 (Spring 1982): 107–156.

Suárez-Murias, Margarite. *La novela romántica en Hispanoamérica.* New York: Hispanic Institute in the United States, 1963.

Tittler, Jonathan. *Narrative Irony in the Contemporary Spanish American Novel.* Ithaca: Cornell University Press, 1984.

———. "Paisajes figurales en tres novelas colombianas." *El café literario* 38 (1984): 26–31.

Todorov, Tzvetan. *French Literary Theory Today.* Cambridge: Cambridge University Press, 1982.

Tompkins, Jane. *Sensational Designs: The Cultural Work of American Fiction.* New York: Oxford University Press, 1985.

Troncoso, Luis Marino. *Proceso creativo y visión del mundo en Manuel Mejía Vallejo.* Bogotá: Procultura, 1986.

Twinam, Ann. *Miners, Merchants, and Farmers in Colonial Colombia.* Austin: University of Texas Press, 1982.

Unruh, Vicky. "Arturo Cova y *La vorágine:* la crisis de un escritor." *Revista de Estudios Hispánicos* 21 (January 1987): 50–60.

Uribe Celis, Carlos. *Los años veinte en Colombia: ideología y cultura.* Bogotá: Ediciones Aurora, 1985.

Valente, José Angel. "La naturaleza y el hombre en *La vorágine* de José Eustacio Rivera." *Cuadernos Hispanoamericanos* 67 (July 1955): 102–108.

Vanin, Alfredo, ed. *El príncipe Tulicio: cinco relatos orales del literal pacífico.* Buenaventura: Centro de Publicaciones del Pacífico, 1986.

Vargas, Germán. "Revisión de *Voces.*" In *Voces, 1917–1920, selección de textos,* pp. 9–17. Bogotá: Instituto Colombiano de Cultura, 1977.

———. *Sobre literatura colombiana.* Bogotá: Fundación Simón y Lola Guberek, 1985.

Vargas Llosa, Mario. *Gabriel García Márquez: historia de un deicidio.* Caracas: Monte Avila, 1971.

Vergara y Vergara, José María. *Historia de la literatura en Nueva Granada.* Bogotá: Imprenta de Echeverría Hermanos, 1867.

———. *Obras escogidas,* vol. 3. Bogotá: Editorial Minerva, 1944.

Villanueva-Collado, Alfredo. "*De sobremesa* de José Asunción Silva y las doctrinas esotéricas en la Francia de fin de siglo." *Revista de Estudios Hispánicos* 11, no. 2 (May 1970): 9–22.

Villegas, Silvio. "Bernardo Arias Trujillo." In *Risaralda,* by Bernardo Arias Trujillo, pp. 7–19. Medellín: Bedout, 1978.

Volkening, Ernesto. *Ensayos I.* Bogotá: Instituto Colombiano de Cultura, 1975.

Wade, Gerald. "An Introduction to the Colombian Novel." *Hispania* 30, no. 4 (November 1947): 467–483.

Webber, Irving L., and Alfredo Ocampo Zamorano, eds. *Valores, desarrollo e historia: Popayán, Medellín, Cali y el Valle del Cauca.* Bogotá: Ediciones Tercer Mundo, 1975.

Williams, Raymond L. *Una década de la novela colombiana: la experiencia de los setenta.* Bogotá: Plaza y Janés, 1981.

———. "The Dynamic Structure of García Márquez's *El otoño del patriarca.*" *Symposium* 32, no. 1 (Spring 1978): 56–75.

———. ed. *Ensayos de literatura colombiana.* Bogotá: Plaza y Janés, 1985.

———. *Gabriel García Márquez.* Boston: G. K. Hall, 1984.

———. "Structure and Transformation of Reality in Alvarez Gardeazábal: *El bazar de los idiotas.*" *Kentucky Romance Quarterly* 27, no. 2 (1980): 245–261.

Zalamea, Jorge. "Una novela de José Asunción Silva." In *José Asunción Silva,* ed. Fernando Charry Lara, pp. 439–444. Bogotá: Procultura, 1985.

Zapata Olivella, Manuel. *El hombre colombiano.* Bogotá: Canal Ramírez Antanares, 1974.

———. *El negro en la historia de Colombia: fuentes escritas y orales.* Bogotá: Fondo Interamericano de Publicaciones de la Cultura Negra, 1985.

Index